John W. Hepburn, PhD, FRSC
Vice President Research & International

Indian Higher Education

Praise for the Author's Work*

It is first-rate...well written and organized..., it gives the empirical overview...yet also does so in nice int'l perspective, gives both a macro/aggregate vision and shows variation. In short this ranks in my judgment among the top of recent single-country higher education system reports.
—**Prof. Daniel C. Levy**, PROPHE Director and
Distinguished Professor, University of Albany, SUNY

...besides the ideas, arguments and suggestions contained, it is virtually a reservoir of precious data that will be immensely useful for everyone, who may be interested in understanding the state of higher education in India as well as the global trend.
—**Prof. V.C. Kulandaiswamy**, Former VC, IGNOU and two other universities

...comprehensive and solid work. Best overall discussion of higher education in India in some years.
—**Prof. Philip G. Altbach**, Director,
Center for International Higher Education, Boston College

...outstanding document.
—**Prof. P. Rama Rao**, Chairman, IIT Review Committee,
Formerly Secretary (DST) & VC (Hyderabad University)

...this will be a very valuable base on which to build a progressive and forward looking policy on higher education.
—**Prof. P. Balaram**, Director, Indian Institute of Science, Bangalore

...paper has come out at a very appropriate time, when policy makers, academics, students and their parents and the community at large are looking for solutions in a sector...useful base document for opening a fresh debate on HE policy.
—**Mr. B. S. Baswan**, Former Education Secretary, Government of India

...paper is well structured. It covers a large spectrum of issues relating to higher education. It contains valuable and relevant national and international data. .... presentation is lucid. .... paper will be a distinct contribution to stimulating further discussions and beneficial actions.
—**Prof. M. Anandakrishnan**, Chairperson,
Madras Institute of Development Studies

It is indeed an excellent, comprehensive paper with some thought provoking recommendations.
—**Dr. Shashi K. Shrivastava**, Senior Education Specialist
for the South Asia Region (World Bank)

Higher Education in India: The Need for Change, ICRIER Working Paper Number 180. The book is based on this working paper.

Indian Higher Education

Envisioning the Future

◆

Pawan Agarwal

SAGE www.sagepublications.com
Los Angeles • London • New Delhi • Singapore • Washington DC

First published in 2009 by

 SAGE Publications India Pvt Ltd
B1/I-1 Mohan Cooperative Industrial Area
Mathura Road, New Delhi 110044, India
www.sagepub.in

SAGE Publications Inc
2455 Teller Road
Thousand Oaks, California 91320, USA

SAGE Publications Ltd
1 Oliver's Yard, 55 City Road
London EC1Y 1SP, United Kingdom

SAGE Publications Asia-Pacific Pte Ltd
33 Pekin Street
#02-01 Far East Square
Singapore 048763

Published by Vivek Mehra for SAGE Publications India Pvt Ltd, typeset in 10.5/12.5 pt. Goudy Old Style by Star Compugraphics Private Limited, Delhi and printed at Chaman Enterprises, New Delhi.

Library of Congress Cataloging-in-Publication Data

Agarwal, Pawan.
Indian higher education: envisioning the future/by Pawan Agarwal.
   p. cm.
   Includes bibliographical references and index.
   1. Education, Higher—India. 2. Education and state—Indian. 3. Universities and colleges—India. 4. Educational change—India. 5. India—Social conditions. 6. India—Social policy. I. Title.

LA11 53.A635   378.54—dc22   2009   2009018479

ISBN: 978-81-7829-941-9 (HB)

The SAGE Team: Rekha Natarajan, Anupam Choudhury, Mathew P.J. and Trinankur Banerjee

Contents

List of Tables

List of Tables

List of Figures

List of Boxes

Foreword

PAWAN Agarwal has done a significant service to the international higher education community by writing an informative, up-to-date and analytical book about Indian higher education. Internationally, little is known about Indian higher education—and what is known is not particularly favourable. *Indian Higher Education: Envisioning the Future* will also be immensely useful for Indians—policymakers, the academic community and the public—because it provides an overview of the complexity of the academic system and analysis of the problems facing higher education.

It is surprising that India has no major higher education research centre and no group of researchers focusing on this key subject. Higher education as an academic subject is not taught in Indian universities, and the large cadre of administrators in India's sprawling higher education system have no training about how universities function, their role in society, or the finances or academe. This is in sharp contrast to China, which has an extensive network of higher education training programmes attached to universities, several excellent higher education research centres, and a general understanding that policy and management of higher education is a matter of considerable national importance.

Pawan Agarwal's book is important because it provides the beginning of a dialog about higher education that can inform policy discussions. It discusses most of the central issues facing India's higher education establishment—the immense challenge of funding the massive system in ways that can provide quality and access, regulation and quality assurance, workforce development, the role of research, and others.

The fact is that India's higher education system is well below the standard of the countries with which it is competing globally. India has no universities anywhere near the top in any of the international rankings. Only the IITs, which of course are not universities but are small technologically focused institutions, show up in the rankings. Only one or two of the universities are anywhere near the quality of competitors in China, Korea, Singapore and other rapidly developing countries. Some argue that while India graduates large numbers of engineers and other technologically oriented people, many do not have the skills needed for the global economy. Many bright Indians choose to study abroad in part because they cannot get the quality that they want at home—and a large majority does not return home.

India has several competitive advantages. The widespread use of English, some innovative high tech and other companies that can absorb well-trained graduates and a large population of bright and energetic students, all contribute to India's potential. Yet, without careful attention to improving the universities, providing more adequate funding, expanding the top-quality sector of the system, eliminating corruption and ensuring that students who get access to higher education can successfully complete their studies, India's academic potential, and eventually its economic success, will be put in jeopardy.

Philip G. Altbach
Monan University Professor
Director, Center for International Higher Education
Boston College

Preface

THIS book really began on 26 October 1998. After 13 years in the civil services in West Bengal, when I joined the Government of India, I was assigned the higher education bureau in the Ministry of Human Resource Development (HRD). I was a bit disappointed. Prized postings in the undivided department of education were in the elementary education and adult education bureaus. These bureaus had large and increasing budgets, interesting job content and the bureaucrats posted in these bureaus enjoyed occasional trips abroad. In contrast, higher education was then a low priority.

A year ago, a white paper on public subsidies had declared higher education as a non-merit service. The University Grants Commission (UGC) pay commission had put a huge burden on the state exchequer. Despite a decent bounty, academic community was aggrieved. Higher education budget was shrinking. New central institutions of higher education were a strict no-no. Government was suspicious of the private providers. After a fierce debate on the private universities bill initiated in 1995, it was almost written off. All foreign providers were seen as *fly-by-night operators* and the government had no clue what to do with them.

Thus, it was not the best of times when my association with the policy and practice of higher education in India began way back in 1998. Things were however set to change. Indian IT strategy: NASSCOM–Mckinsey Report released in December 1999 predicted that the IT sector would be the country's engine for economic growth. During the 1980s and 1990s, private engineering colleges and private IT training sector had grown large despite government ambivalence. Acknowledging the contribution made by them in feeding trained manpower to the IT sector, severe skill shortages in IT sector were projected. This gave a boost to further private expansion, but government apathy for higher education continued. A high-powered task force constituted to look at the IT manpower needs noted that while the numbers were sufficient, quality would be a bottleneck. Several initiatives were conceived, but no funds were provided. The general feeling was that private expansion would take care of the increased demand.

Meanwhile, with the economy continuing to grow at 9 per cent per annum, other sectors of economy began to face skill shortages. This was attributed to the inadequacy of higher education system. Tiny quality sector, low employability of graduates, declining interest in science and low base of enrolment in doctoral programmes were identified as concerns. The prime minister constituted the National Knowledge Commission (NKC) to look at the knowledge sectors, including higher education. In 2006, there was a nation-wide agitation, mainly against, but also in favour of, the numerical-based quotas in central higher education institutions, which paralysed the country for months. The crisis went out of control; it required the Supreme Court to intervene. While the crisis was unfortunate, it brought to focus higher education and its concerns.

At the same time, NKC came out with its report on higher education advocating massive expansion, significant increase in financial outlay and restructuring of regulatory arrangements. It was in this backdrop that the Eleventh Five Year Plan (2007–12) for the country was finalised. There is a nine-fold increase in outlay for higher education with proposals for many new central institutions. The prime minister has called the Eleventh Plan as the National Plan for Education with focus on higher education and skill development. As they say, there was an opportunity in the crisis. Fortunately, the opportunity was not missed. Though, many believe that mere increased outlay and new institutions would not help much. Further action is required on several fronts.

Nevertheless, higher education moved from government's peripheral interest to a key agenda. Higher education is now seen as critical to India's emergence as a major player in the global knowledge economy. Role of higher education in support of overall education is clearly seen as the country moves from the universalisation of basic education to the progressive massification of secondary education. It is now widely accepted that the country had found and created an advantage in skill-based activities on the strength of its large pool of qualified manpower. This is fed by its large and growing higher education system. Growing prosperity and rapid advances in communications and mass media have resulted in raising the aspirations of the people. Higher education enables upward social and economic mobility. Access to higher education is rightly seen as an effective means to meet raised aspirations. Thus, higher education today enjoys solid political support.

I have watched these developments closely over the years. From the higher education bureau, I had shifted to the technical education bureau in 1999 and continued there until 2003—responsible for premier institutions like the Indian Institutes of Technology and IT education, those were interesting times. All India Engineering Entrance Examination was established. Indian National Digital Library for Engineering, Science and Technology (INDEST) was set up. National Programme Technology Enhanced Learning (NPTEL) was initiated and exclusive education channels, Gyan Darshan and Eklavya were started.

During this period, the Regional Engineering Colleges were upgraded to National Institutes of Technology with greater academic autonomy and financial muscle. A policy framework for post-graduate education and research in engineering was put in place. Indian Institutes of Technology were funded liberally based on the newly devised performance matrix. There were several unfinished tasks, failures and controversies. Systematic collaboration between research labs and academic institutions and networking between IITs and NITs could not be operationalised. Public opinion was against the ministry's decision of routing of donations through Bharat Shiksha Kosh and regulating fees in the Indian Institutes of Management. Working of the ministry of HRD was seen as intrusive.

On completion of my tenure with the ministry of HRD, I shifted to the UGC as a financial adviser. I found the UGC financing very complex with glaring fallacies. Funds were grossly inadequate and skewed in favour of select universities and colleges. Input-based deficit financing was inefficient and promoted status quo. Apart from streamlining funding arrangements, the then Chairman, Professor Arun Nigavekar allowed me to work on several new initiatives. A national repository of theses and dissertations, national students data repository and development of higher education information system were planned. Disclosure standards to curb deceptive practices by institutions of higher education were drafted. Policy for protection and management of intellectual property rights in the university system was in put in place and a research handbook was published to nurture research culture. The UGC took initiatives to promote Indian higher education abroad. These were however uncertain times for the UGC. Amidst this uncertainty, several of these tasks could not be concluded.

In the year 2000, going beyond the traditional bilateral exchange format, Fulbright had established the New Century Scholars programme for multilateral engagement and multidisciplinary research collaboration in order to examine topics of global significance. Reflecting the importance of higher education as a global issue, the topic for the year 2005–06 was 'Higher Education in the 21st Century: Global Challenges and National Response'. Long association with the sector enabled me to successfully compete. I was chosen as one of the 31 New Century Scholars from 20 countries for collaborative research on the topic for the year 2005–06.

I was exhausted and confused with continued long association with policy and practice of higher education. I needed a break. I wanted to understand the manner in which higher education relates to the economy, society and polity and what could be the way forward. I needed to deepen my understanding of the challenges faced by countries around the world in higher education and the manner in which they respond to them. I decided to take a sabbatical during my Fulbright tenure. I had a chance meeting with Dr Rashmi Banga, a researcher at the Indian Council for International Economic Research (ICRIER), who introduced me to the then Director, Dr Arvind Virmani. Dr Virmani, now the Chief Economic Advisor to the Government of India, agreed to host me. I continued to get support from Dr Rajiv Kumar, who succeeded him a few months later. He has a deep personal interest in higher education.

On a high growth path, country's economy was the envy of the developing world. The ICRIER was in its sliver jubilee year. Dr Isher

Judge Ahluwalia as its Chairperson was keen that ICRIER seizes the opportunity to emerge as the country's top think-tank shaping her economic policies. There were numerous seminars and events and several important visitors. Interactions with highly qualified in-house researchers and important visitors from around the world were intellectually stimulating. Having collegial atmosphere with excellent research facilities, ICRIER provided the right setting to think through the issues with a clear mind. I had an obligation to write a research paper as a New Century Scholar. However, I was inadequately prepared. My engineering education and tight job schedule as a civil servant left me little time for social sciences and writing research papers. Dr Rashmi Banga, an accomplished researcher herself, taught me the intricacies of writing research papers and was a continuous source of inspiration and encouragement.

In 2006, ICRIER published my working paper, *Higher Education in India: The Need for Change* (WP No. 180). Despite some gaps in data and analysis, the paper was well received both in India and abroad. I got many helpful comments. Substantial comments were received from Mr B.S. Baswan, Senior Consultant in the Planning Commission and earlier Education Secretary, Government of India, Professor M. Anandakrishnan, Chairperson of the Madras Institute of Development Studies, Professor Philip G. Altbach, Director of the Centre for International Higher Education at Boston College, Professor Stephen Heyneman, formerly Lead Educator with the World Bank, Professor Daniel C. Levy, PROPHE Director and Distinguished Professor at the State University of New York at Albany, Professor V.C. Kulandaiswamy, former Vice Chancellor, IGNOU, Professor P. Rama Rao, Chairman, IIT Review Committee, and Dr Shashi K. Shrivastava from the World Bank. These comments led to some significant revisions.

Over the next two years, I conducted several studies, wrote many reports and published numerous articles. I participated in many seminars and conferences on higher education both in India and abroad. All this contributed significantly to my understanding of the higher education sector. An intense engagement with fellow New Century Scholars as a part of the Fulbright programme gave me a global perspective. I realised that countries around the world face similar challenges in higher education.

Now I needed to synthesise the material in the ICRIER working paper with various studies and reports that I did subsequently, insights and learning from interactions with many people. I decided to publish it as a book. SAGE enthusiastically agreed to publish it. This book was thus born. It has a comprehensive review of the Indian higher education, particularly developments over the past couple of years. Considering the country's outward orientation in the recent years, the review is done in a global context, factoring in the changes in economy, demography and society. The book breaks several myths, assesses the needs, identifies the gaps and provides several useful ideas. While, it does not provide a single vision for the future, but the analytical framework and data provided in the book would hopefully stimulate insights and new trains of thought to envision future of the country's higher education and enable informed policy debate.

Like complete disagreement among the blind men touching different and only one part of an elephant to learn what it is like, its various stakeholders, depending on their own perspectives, view higher education differently. I had the occasion to work at the policy level in higher education for many years, therefore, though I tried to write this book as a detached observer, it brings my own views on the subject, shaped by my experience. I need not apologise for this, but the readers are entitled to form their own opinion on the issues discussed in this book.

As the book goes for print, the country, like the rest of world, is passing through a major slow down. Rather than skill shortages, media is reporting job losses and weak placements even for the graduates from the Indian Institutes of Management. In these times of recession, many people are opting for post-graduation and research. With the pay hike in 2008, faculty is now paid more than group 'A' officers in the government at the entry-level and enjoy several perks. Several universities are reporting at least 25 per cent increase in applications for post-graduate programmes. Several new central institutions, including those with focus on science education and research, are also functional. Many others are proposed. Existing institutions are more liberally funded.

Preface

With increased demand for higher education, private providers are upbeat and are on an expansion spree. This appears to be a good time for Indian higher education. As the new national government with a decisive mandate takes up the task of nation building, this book would help it to create a new vision for the Indian higher education under the changed realities.

Acknowledgements

THIS book has evolved over many years. During the slow and often interrupted evolution of this book, I have accumulated many debts, only a few of which I have space to acknowledge here. During my years with the higher education sector in the government, many of my superiors and colleagues encouraged and supported me. I would like to specially mention the following: Education Secretaries Maharaj Krishen Kaw, Kumud Bansal, B.S. Baswan and R.P. Agrawal, and Joint Secretaries, Vijay Shankar Pandey and V.K. Pipersenia in the Ministry of HRD; Chairman, Professor Arun Nigavekar and Secretary, Professor Ved Prakash, Dr Pankaj Mittal, Dr Dev Swarup and Diksha Rajput at the UGC; and Chief Secretary, Amit Kiran Deb in the Government of West Bengal. I would like to express my sincere thanks to them.

Participation in the Fulbright New Century Scholars (NCS) Programme gave me an opportunity to understand higher education in a global perspective. It enabled me to work together with many experts, visit new places including some of the best universities in the world and attend very intense seminars on the future of higher education. In doing so, I appreciate the help I got from the Executive Director, United State-India Education Foundation, Professor Jane E. Schukoske and her colleagues, in particular Sarina Paranjape; the Director of the Center for International Exchange of Scholars, Patti McGill Paterson and her staff; and Director of the Center for International Higher Education at Boston College, Professor Philip G. Altbach and his staff, in particular Laura E. Rumbley. Fellow NCS scholars were a pleasure to work with and always very helpful. I thank them all for their support.

During my study visit to the United States, Professor Jagdish N. Sheth was my host at the India–China–America Institute in Atlanta and Professor Richard B. Freeman at the Labor and Work Life Programme at the Harvard University. They were excellent hosts and interactions

Acknowledgements

with them and their colleagues, particularly Professor Robert De Haan at the Emory University, Professor Elaine Bernard and Professor Jack Trumbour at the Harvard University were very invigorating and gave useful insights.

Mark Hutcheson at the India–China–America Institute coordinated my seminars and visits to Georgia State University, Kennesaw University and Georgia Tech. Professor Robert Kennedy and Ajay Sharma invited me for a seminar at the William Davidson Institute under the University of Michigan. Deepti M. Nijhawan coordinated my interactive meeting with researchers under the MIT-India Program. Professor Sugata Bose invited me for a seminar under the South Asia Initiative at the Harvard University. Professor Daniel C. Levy invited me for a seminar with his colleagues in the Program for Research on Private Higher Education at the State University of New York at Albany. Dr Shashi K. Shrivastava organised a seminar with the education team at the World Bank headquarters. All these visits, interactions and seminars were intellectually stimulating and gave new insights. I thank them all.

The sabbatical at ICRIER was fun and a great learning experience. The Chairperson, Dr Isher Judge Ahluwalia, Directors, Dr Arvind Virmani and Dr Rajiv Kumar and senior faculty Dr Shankar Acharya and Professor Nitin Desai were very supportive. Intense discussions with learned colleagues, Dr Rashmi Banga, Nisha Taneja, Dr Arpita Mukheree, Dr Danish Hashim, Dr Rajiv Ahuja, Dr Suparna Karmakar and Dr Surabhi Mittal were always useful in getting an alternate perspective. I am thankful to all of them.

Apart from the above, in the course of my work and while writing this book, I met many people whom I admire for their vision and understanding of higher education. I would like to mention a few of them: Sam Pitroda, Kiran Karnik, Rajendra Pawar, F.C. Kohli, Professor Arvind Panagariya, Professor Suman Bery, Professor Devesh Kapur, Arun Maira, Dr James Tooley, Sushma Berlia, Professor Govardhan Mehta, Professor A. Gnanam, Professor K.B. Powar, Professor Amrik Singh, Professor Yash Pal, Professor G.K. Chadha, Professor Pratap Bhanu Mehta, Professor Bibek Debroy, Professor D.P. Agrawal, Professor Deepak Pental, Professor K.K. Agarwal, Professor Subimal Sen, Professor Suranjan Das and Vivek Bharati. There were researchers from abroad like Professor Nicholas Barr, Dr Neil Kemp and Vivek Wadhwa. And then there are many others whom I never met, but whose work I read in course of writing this book. The list is long and their names are included in the endnotes and references, but here I would like to mention three: Gurcharan Das, Rafiq Dossani and Nandan Nilekarni. Their insights have added immeasurably to the content of this book. I wish to acknowledge their contribution and convey my gratitude to all of them.

Several professional acquaintances of these years are now personal friends. I shared my passion for higher education with them. I would like to specially mention Professor Sanjay G. Dhande, Dr Jagdish Arora, Professor Sudhir Jain, Professor Furqan Qamar, Professor Binod Khadria, Dr Kavita Sharma, Dr Meenakshi Gopinath, Professor Sudhanshu Bhushan, Professor Ashok Ranjan Thakur, Professor Rupa Chanda, Dr Usha Munshi, Dr Xavier Alphonse, Dr Asha Gupta, Dr Sheel Nuna, N.V. Sathyanarayana, K. Satyanarayan, Suren Rasaily, Dr Jaganath Patil, Dr Jamshed Siddiqui, Pervin Malhotra, Dr Veena Bhalla, Dr M.D. Tiwari, Dr Yamini Gupt, Dr Vijaya Khandavilli, Dr Yaj Medury, Rajesh Jain, Ajay Mohan Goel, Sanchita Chatterjee, S. Shekhar Singh, Nitu Jain, Ajay Bohora and Shobha Mishra. They all assisted me one way or another, especially in challenging me with alternative views. I am indebted to all of them.

My wife Monika, daughter Ayushi and son Arnav were very patient with my late nights. Monika, herself a teacher, read through the manuscript, served as a willing sounding board and voice of moderation for her book-obsessed spouse. I love them for their faithful support. Dr Sugata Ghosh, Rekha Natarajan, Anupam Choudhury, and their colleagues at SAGE Publications were uncomplaining when I missed my deadlines in the course of production of this book. They worked diligently to see that this book finally got published.

Professor Philip G. Altbach is highly respected for the study of higher education globally. My association with him began as the New Century Scholar under the Fulbright programme, which he ably led as its Distinguished Scholar Leader. It continued beyond that. He was a Fulbright professor in India way back in 1968 and has a continuing interest in the Indian higher education. Over time, he became my guide

Acknowledgements

and mentor. He continually pushed me to conclude this book that he jovially referred to as a *magnum opus* on Indian higher education. When I requested him to write the foreword for this book, he readily agreed. I am deeply indebted to him for guidance, support and encouragement.

Writing of this book has been truly a joint enterprise and a collaborative exercise. Apart from names mentioned, there are many others who contributed. I could not give all the names for want of space. They have contributed to my understanding of the complexities of Indian higher education. I appreciate their help and thank them for their support.

Introduction

Education is an ornament in prosperity and a refuge in adversity.
— Aristotle

INDIA has seen a consistently high rate of economic growth in the recent years. It has now become a major player in the global knowledge economy. Skill-based activities have made significant contribution to this growth. Such activities depend on the large pool of qualified manpower that is fed by its large higher education system. It is now widely accepted that higher education has been critical to India's emergence in the global knowledge economy. Yet, it is believed that a crisis is plaguing the Indian higher education system. While, the National Knowledge Commission (NKC) set up by the Prime Minister calls it a 'quiet crisis', the Human Resource Minister calls higher education 'a sick child'. Industries routinely point towards huge skill shortages and are of the opinion that growth momentum may not be sustained unless the problem of skill shortages is addressed.

There appear to be endless problems with the Indian higher education system. The higher education system produces graduates that are unemployable, though there are mounting skill shortages in a number of sectors. The standards of academic research are low and declining. An unwieldy affiliating system, inflexible academic structure, uneven capacity across subjects, eroding autonomy of academic institutions, low level of public funding, archaic and dysfunctional regulatory environment are some of its many problems. Finally, it is widely held that it suffers from several systemic deficiencies and is driven by populism, and in the absence of reliable data, there is little informed public debate.

More than 35 years ago, Nobel laureate Amartya Sen, while analysing the crisis in Indian education, rather than attributing the crisis in Indian education to administrative neglect or to thoughtless action, pointed out that the 'grave failures in policy-making in the field of education require the analysis of the characteristics of the economic and social forces operating in India, and response of public policy to these forces' (Amartya Sen, 'The Crisis in Indian education', Lal Bahadur Shastri Memorial Lectures, 10–11 March 1970). He emphasised that 'due to the government's tendency to formulate educational policies based on public pressure, often wrong policies are pursued.' Unfortunately, it is believed that policy-making suffers from similar failure even today. Rather than pragmatism, it is populism, ideology and vested interests that drive policy. It seeks to achieve arbitrarily set goals that are often elusive and, more than that, pursued half-heartedly.

Worldwide higher education reforms

The emergence of a global economy due to increased trade, investment and mobility of people and, more recently, work across borders has forced nation states to adapt their systems of higher education to the changed global realities. Rather than continuing with their inward looking policies, several countries are reshaping their systems of higher education for making them globally competitive. Pragmatism rather than ideology is driving this change. The United States of America has major plans for investment in higher education. The United Kingdom has injected new dynamism in the higher education sector through competition and incentives. China has undertaken a package of comprehensive reforms in higher education for over the past two decades. The government in China has declared education, science and technology to be the strategic driving forces of sustainable economic growth. Pakistan has embarked upon wide-ranging systemic reforms.

Despite the fact that the United States has the finest system of higher education in the world, it had set up a commission to examine the future of higher education in September 2005, with a mandate to ensure that America remains the world's leader in higher education and innovation.[1] While the report of the commission has been received and is being processed for implementation, the US government has already committed to invest USD134 billion in higher education over the next 10 years. In the United Kingdom, where higher education is primarily in the public sector, faced with problems of deteriorating standards due to inadequate funding and failing accountability, several innovations in financing, such as performance-based funding for teaching and research and portable students' aid, and so on, were introduced over the past decade. This helped the UK higher education system to become one of the best systems of higher education in the world again. In a highly sensitive and bold decision, the UK government has now allowed the universities to compete for students and charge variable fees, bringing an end to the regulated fee regime in the UK (DfES, 2003).

Higher education reforms in China were initiated along with wider economic reforms to become a market economy in the year 1978. Prior to that, higher education was in the public sector. There was no tuition fee. The government even took care of living expenses of the students. Since then, the system of higher education has radically changed. The concept of cost-sharing and cost recovery was introduced in the early years of reforms. Tuition fees have now been made compulsory. The higher education institutions in China were expected to diversify their revenue sources and, therefore, allowed to have affiliated enterprises (Sanyal and Martin, 2006).

Apart from increased support from alternative sources, higher education received increased financial allocations from the government. Thus, in spite of massive expansion in enrolment, average funding per student did not go down. Through a national legislation in 2002, China proactively involved the private sector to contribute and invest in higher education. This accelerated the growth. To nurture excellence, a selective approach in funding was adopted. In 1993, special financial allocations were provided for China's top 100 institutions to upgrade them to international standards. In the year 1998, an even higher-level funding was provided to nine top universities to make them world class.

Australia initiated comprehensive reforms in higher education in 2003. Government funding was significantly enhanced along with increased provision for subsidised loans and scholarships for students. The reform package included areas as diverse as teaching, workplace productivity, governance, student financing, research, cross-sectoral collaboration and quality (Commonwealth of Australia, 2003). Apart from the advanced countries, many developing countries took up ambitious programmes to reform their higher education sector. It was realised that though primary and secondary education is important, it is the quality and size of the higher education system that will differentiate a dynamic economy from a marginalised one in the global knowledge-based economy.

Based on the recommendation of the Task Force for Improvement of Higher Education, neighbouring Pakistan replaced its University Grants Commission (found ineffective) by a proactive Higher Education Commission that initiated wide-ranging systemic reforms in 2002. Public funding for higher education was increased significantly from Rs 3.8 billion in 2002 to Rs 33.7 billion in 2007. To bring in a degree of transparency and accountability, recurrent funds were allocated amongst universities on the basis of a funding formula. To address faculty related issues, changes in the salary structure of academics under the tenure track system were made. Salaries of active research scholars were increased significantly. Stringent requirements for the appointment and promotion of faculty members and strict quality control of PhD programmes were put in place. The reform programmes also addressed the issue of access to quality teaching, learning and research resources (Agarwal, 2008b).

Changing Policy on Higher Education in India

From the early 20th century, there have been several high level com-missions set up to provide policy orientation to the development of higher education in India. On the basis of the report of the Sadler Commission (1917–19), also referred to as the Calcutta University Commission, the Central Advisory Board of Education (CABE) was set up to define the general aims of educational policy and coordinate the work of various provinces and universities by guarding against needless duplication and overlapping in the provision of the more costly forms of education. The University Education Commission, presided over by Dr S. Radhakrishnan, in its report in 1949 recommended that university education should be placed in the Concurrent List so that there is a national guarantee of minimum standards of university education. The constituent assembly did not agree to it. It was much later, in 1976, that education was made a concurrent subject with the 42nd Amendment of the Constitution.

The Kothari Commission (1964–66) examined various aspects of education at all levels and gave a very comprehensive report full of insight and wisdom. This report became the basis of the National Policy on Education, 1968. With this, a common structure of education (10+2+3) was introduced and implemented by most states over a period of time. In the school curricula, in addition to laying down a common scheme of studies for boys and girls, science and mathematics were incorporated as compulsory subjects and work experience assigned a place of importance. A beginning was also made in restructuring of courses at the undergraduate level. Centres of advanced studies were set up for post-graduate education and research. Detailed estimates were made to meet requirements of educated manpower in the country.

In 1985, a comprehensive appraisal of the existing educational scene was made. This was followed by a countrywide debate. It was noted that while the achievements were impressive in themselves, the general formulations incorporated in the 1968 policy did not, however, get translated into a detailed strategy of implementation, accompanied by the assignment of specific responsibilities and financial and organisational support. It was further noted that problems of access, quality, quantity, utility and financial outlay, accumulated over the years, had assumed such massive proportions that these required to be tackled with the utmost urgency.

In the background explicated previously, the National Policy on Education (NPE), 1986 was put in place. It was noted in the preamble to the policy that education in India stood at the crossroads, and neither normal linear expansion nor the existing pace and nature of improvement of the situation would help. It was also noted that education has an acculturating role. It refines sensitivities and perceptions that contribute to national cohesion, a scientific temper and independence of mind and spirit—thus furthering the goals of socialism, secularism and democracy enshrined in our Constitution. Education develops manpower for different levels of the economy. It is also the substrate on which research and development flourish, being the ultimate guarantee of national self-reliance. Accepting the fact that education is a unique investment in the present and the future, a very comprehensive policy document was approved in 1986. This was supplemented with a Programme of Action (PoA) in 1992.

On review now, one sees that many of the recommendations of the NPE, 1986 read with PoA, 1992 have been only partly fulfilled. Moreover, there has been no effort to modify the previous policy prescriptions or to develop a new one. After the economic reforms were undertaken in the early 1990s, their influence on development of higher education has been ignored. With the economic reforms of the 1990s, the private sector has come to occupy a central role in the economic development of the nation. There is a need for a holistic review of the instruments currently available for managing the higher education system such as the University Grants Commission (UGC) Act, the All India Council of Technical Education (AICTE) Act, and so on, which have become outdated in the present context. In this context, it is important to develop a new national policy framework for higher education in the current and emerging contexts. Such a policy framework should not be developed by political processes, but by an independent, high-powered commission.

Recent Developments in Indian Higher Education

Higher education has received a lot of attention in India over the past few years. There are four reasons for this recent focus. First, country's weak higher education system is being blamed for skill shortages in several sectors of economy. Second, reservation quotas in higher education institutions, particularly the more reputed ones that provide access to high status and best-paid jobs became a highly divisive issue, central to the policy of inclusive growth and distributive justice, and hence politically very important. Third, in the backdrop of the first two developments, it began to be argued that the country would not be able to sustain its growth momentum and maintain competitiveness unless problems with higher education are fixed. Last, demand for higher education continues to outpace the supply due to growing population of young people, gains in school education, the growing middle class and their rising aspirations.

It is widely believed that technological advances and a shift in demographic provide India with a window of opportunity to productively engage its huge pool of human resources, and become a leader in both the rapidly expanding sectors of services and highly skilled manufacturing. This would, however, require revamping the higher education sector. Hence many steps have been taken to augment supply, improve quality and fix many of the problems faced by higher education. The National Knowledge Commission (NKC) that was set up to examine the higher education sector (amongst other things) made several useful and important recommendations. The Government of India has increased funding significantly during the Eleventh Five Year Plan. Many new institutions have been planned and some of them are already operational. There are many good ideas in the plan document. All these efforts, however, appear to be somewhat disconnected. Some even appear to be at cross-purposes with each other. Several suggestions appear to be merely impressionistic views of individuals, rather than being supported by data and research. Overall, these efforts do not give a sense of an integrated reform agenda for Indian higher education. And in absence of credible data and good analysis, the media continues to perpetuate and exacerbate certain fallacies and inconsistencies.

With ambiguity in defining its purpose and vagueness about its quality, debate on higher education is usually full of rhetoric. As pointed out by Kapur and Crowley, for the higher education 'sector whose main purpose is to train people with strong analytical skills, it is ironical that its own self-analysis is replete with homilies and platitudes, rather than strong evidence' (Kapur and Crowley, 2008). Institutions of higher education today are an integral organ of the state and economy. They are embedded in the history and culture of a nation and are shaped by its contemporary realities, ideologies and vested interests. India's large size, long history and diverse culture and the complicated nature of Indian polity and policy process make Indian higher education a very complex enterprise.

This book unravels this complexity by taking up a comprehensive review of the Indian higher education system, assesses its needs, identifies gaps and provides perspectives for the future. In doing so, it takes into account several measures planned or taken and provides a glimpse of a vibrant emerging private sector. Evolving an integrated reform agenda for higher education in India (or, for that matter, anywhere in the world because of the various sensitive issues involved) with a long-term perspective is both complex and difficult, but by looking at the big picture that the book presents, one could think strategically about it.

The Plan of this Book

To intervene in complex systems like ecologies, economies, societies and nations, it is necessary to first understand how the system is put together. Thus, the first chapter of the book maps the size, structure and growth of higher education in India, both in terms of enrolment and institutions. In doing so, the book also examines trends about Indians enrolled overseas and international students in India. While analysing overall growth trends, the book notes the transition from elite to mass higher education and compares the enrolment pattern with countries around the world, and discusses the emergence of new providers and new forms of delivery.

Issues of access and equity are central to higher education in most countries around the world, particularly in democratic societies. Chapter 2 examines these issues. The chapter also examines the impact of growth in private finance on access and equity.

Higher education in the private sector has grown fast over the past two decades. This has not only increased capacity and enhanced students' choices, but also affected the dynamics of regulation. Its impact on financing arrangements has been very significant. With this in view, Chapter 3 has its focus on the growing and vibrant private sector in higher education, its growth and prospects.

Chapter 4 deals with the financing issues. It analyses the funding of higher education from both public and private resources. It also examines overall funding patterns and trends, issue of institutional funding and student financing (student aid and loans). Keeping the trends in mind, it offers suggestions on sustainable funding arrangements, with a particular focus on student financial aid. There is an organic link between financing and management of higher education, and thus the chapter also discusses issues relating to institutional management in the context of new public management philosophy.

Chapter 5 analyses the role of higher education in the development of workforce, to meet the domestic as well as the global demand for qualified manpower. It specifically addresses the issue of transition from education to work and the disjunction between them, which calls for specific action and the problem of skill shortages. The chapter also provides a brief outline of the vocational education and training sector. The two complement each other in skill development, and therefore a holistic treatment of the subject makes it necessary to cover this sector as well.

Chapter 6 benchmarks Indian research performance globally and then evaluates the critical role of academic research in fostering innovation. On review of its weaknesses, the chapter suggests action on several fronts.

Chapter 7 discusses the regulatory environment for higher education as it exists in India today. It identifies specific areas of concern, taking into consideration the emerging market structure for higher education and the peculiar nature of competition in higher education. The chapter proposes a new regulatory environment to address minimum regulatory concerns, taking care of information failure and facilitating coordination.

Chapter 8 analyses the progress made on accreditation in India and points out that accreditation, as it exists today, serves little purpose. Specific suggestions for changes in accreditation system have been made.

Chapter 9 examines the conclusions reached in the context of changing socio-economic and political realities and growing optimism. It analyses three conceptual issues—purpose, diversity and competition, and examines the status and prospects of Indian higher education in terms of three key cross-cutting themes—access and expansion, equity and inclusion, and quality and excellence. Finally, this chapter looks at the changing nature of policy support and the imperatives for systemic governance in the changed scenario.

The focus on data in this book is deliberate, in order to sieve reality from myth. Perceptions, ideology, vested interests and policy debate have not been missed either. The evolution of economic purposes of higher education has been the single most important development in the education sector in the 20th century, and it resulted in enormous expansion of higher education in countries around the world, including India. It shaped debates over equity and access, social and economic mobility, curriculum and courses, innovation and competitiveness. The emphasis in this book on the economic role of higher education reflects this contemporary reality, though civic, moral and intellectual purposes of higher education are important and will continue to be so.

1

Size, Structure and Growth

The more complex the problem, the less one needs
to learn in order to have an opinion.
— A. Dubi

HIGHER education is rooted in the country's history and culture. Its growth depends upon the changing socio-economic environment of the country. Thus, though the modern higher education in India is largely based on the British model, it inherited the oriental culture, where learning takes place for its own sake, without reference to economic or other external factors. It remained a small system until independence in 1947, and then saw an isomorphic growth of institutions before being influenced by the higher education system in the United States, which was recognised as a powerful centre of learning. To a large extent, the academic system and the fundamental ethos (core principles, administrative organisations, the professoriate, personal affairs, research organisations, curriculum, teaching methods, examination systems, and so on) is still akin to the old universities in Britain. According to Altbach (1982), the model of higher education growth in India is based on a centre–periphery or dominance–subordination relationship, due to a long colonial relationship with Britain. This is to be distinguished from higher education growth in East Asia, where the focus is on its linkages with economic development.

Today, the Indian higher education system is a loose configuration of various types of institutions, based largely on the British model, but also in part on the American model of higher education. In the federal arrangement, most institutions of higher education are under the provincial governments, but several reputed institutions are directly under the national government. The new private sector has not only accelerated the growth, but also added a new dimension to the higher education landscape. The Indian higher education system is now a large and complex body. This chapter maps the institutional structures, enrolment patterns and trends of higher education growth in the country.

Institutional Structure

Higher education institutions in India include universities, colleges and other institutions. While universities award their own degrees, the colleges award their degree through the university to which they are affiliated. The affiliating system is unique to South Asia, where colleges conduct teaching and learning under the academic supervision of the university to which they are affiliated (detailed discussion on the affiliating system is in Chapter 7). All universities are not of the affiliating type; a majority of them are unitary bodies, having a single campus, while some even have multiple campuses. A few universities and colleges use the word 'institute' in their titles. This does not make them different from other universities and colleges. Table 1.1 lists various types of institutions by degree-granting power, legislative origin and funding.

TABLE 1.1 Types of institutions

By	Types
Degree-granting powers	University—unitary or affiliating; college
Legislative origin	Central; state or deemed-to-be university
Funding	Public (government/aided) institutions; private (unaided) institutions *not-for-profit (or de facto for-profit)*

Source Author.

2

Size, Structure and Growth

Universities and colleges vary in terms of their academic, administrative and financial arrangements. The Parliament or the state legislatures can establish universities. Those established by an act of Parliament are the central universities, and the ones set up by the state legislatures are state universities. Some institutions of higher education are granted 'deemed-to-be university' status by the central government, and will be referred to hereafter as deemed universities. A few institutions are established by the Parliament—and even state legislatures—as institutions of national importance. Universities, including deemed universities, and institutions of national importance are all degree-awarding institutions (DAIs). Table 1.2 gives the numbers and break up of DAIs in the country and their recent growth.

TABLE 1.2 Number of DAIs

University level institutions	As on 31.3.2002	As on 31.3.2006	As on 2.7.2007
State Universities	178	217	232
Deemed Universities	52	102	114
Central Universities	18	20	24
Private Universities	0	10	11
Subtotal	248	349	381
Institutes of National Importance	12	13	13
Institutions set up by State Legislature	5	5	5
Subtotal	17	18	18
Total	265	367	399

Source Background papers of the University Grants Commission for the Eleventh Five Year Plan: 2007.

Though there is no clear demarcation, the colleges usually focus on undergraduate education while the universities impart post-graduate education and conduct research. In addition, there are many institutions like the Indian Institutes of Management (IIMs) that award diplomas. These diplomas are considered equal to degrees granted by the universities. Most universities and colleges offer multidisciplinary programmes. There are also some universities that are discipline-specific, such as agriculture, law, technology, language, medicine, and so on.

In addition, there are open universities that offer distance education programmes. While earlier most of the institutions of higher education were established and run by the government, now many of them are established and/or run by private trusts and societies. The distinction between a government or public and a private institution is somewhat hazy, and is discussed in Chapter 3.

All of the different types of institutions above comprise the formal system of higher education. Besides, there is a large and growing training sector that caters to the demand for short-duration job-oriented training. Several training providers enter into partnerships with the institutions of higher education in the formal sector. As a result, the distinction between the formal higher education and the training sector is now blurred.

Universities and Colleges

The Indian higher education system is a large system. While it has the third largest enrolments in the world—after China and the United States, with nearly 18,500 institutions, the country has the distinction of having the highest number of institutions for higher education in the world—almost four times that in the US and Europe and more than seven times the number of institutions in China. The average size is, however, small.

Average enrolment per institution in India is about 550, though this has little meaning since there are a few institutions with more than 10,000 students, while some have less than a hundred. It is not necessarily true that the universities are big while the colleges are small. There are some colleges that have a large number of students, while there are a few universities that have less than a few hundred students enrolled. There are a couple of hundred universities and colleges, mainly in the metropolitan cities, that have more than 5,000 students enrolled. There are another 1,000 institutions with enrolment ranging from 1,500 to 2,500. The remaining colleges have a few hundred students only; such small colleges are usually in small towns and rural areas. A large majority of them are non-viable, understaffed and ill equipped;

two-thirds do not even satisfy the minimum norms of the University Grants Commission (UGC), the apex body for regulation of higher education in the country. Thus, the size of an institution is highly variable, and the system extremely fragmented.

Out of nearly 18,500 institutions, only 381 are universities and the remaining are colleges. In July 2007, there were 24 central universities, 232 state universities, 114 deemed universities, 18 institutions of national importance, and 11 private universities. While 131 (including five womens' universities) are multidisciplinary universities, 39 are agriculture, veterinary and fishery universities, 14 are technological universities, 11 language universities, nine medical universities and six law universities. A large majority (245 out of 380) of the universities are unitary, 120 universities are of the affiliating type and just 14 are open universities. Private and deemed universities and institutions of national importance are usually discipline-specific. With the exception of agriculture and medical universities, which fall under the purview of the Ministry of Agriculture and the Ministry of Health respectively, all others come within the purview of the UGC. Many colleges established in rural areas are non-viable, under-enrolled and have extremely poor infrastructure and facilities, with just a few teachers.

As of 31 March 2006, there were 18,064 colleges affiliated to six central and 114 state universities. Out of this, about four-fifth (14,000 colleges)—mostly arts, commerce and science (ACS) colleges—are under the purview of the UGC, though only 6,109 colleges are so far recognised by the UGC. Even lesser number (5,525) of colleges are eligible to receive development grants from the UGC, and only 2,780 colleges are accredited by the National Accreditation and Assessment Council (NAAC). The relevance and impact of UGC recognition, eligibility for UGC grants and accreditation are discussed in subsequent chapters.

Overall, the number of institutions in India is large, with the obvious result that the average enrolment is very small; just about 500 students per institution. As a result, the higher education landscape is dotted with a large number of tiny non-viable institutions. Though this ensures a good geographical spread, the colleges, particularly in rural areas, are of poor quality, small size and are non-viable in nature. Thus, the system is highly fragmented and organised sub-optimally. According to Professor D. Bruce Johnstone at the University of New York at Buffalo:

> India cannot be served well by its very large number of low quality institutions; the solution probably lies in the creation of better alternatives that will give rise to the natural process of either closures or mergers (which really means closures) by the force of the market rather than via governmental dictate. (Johnstone, personal communication, January 2007)

Academic Structure

Higher education in India covers all post-secondary education beyond class 12 in different subject areas, including professional streams such as engineering and technology, medicine, agriculture, and so on. It comprises three levels of qualifications—bachelor's or undergraduate degree programmes, master's or post graduate degree programmes and the pre-doctoral (Master of Philosophy, MPhil) and doctoral programmes (Doctor of Philosophy, PhD). Normally, a bachelor's programme requires three years of education after 12 years of school education. In some places, honours and special courses are also available. These are not necessarily longer in duration but indicate a greater depth of study. The bachelor's degree in professional fields of study, such as agriculture, dentistry, engineering, pharmacy, technology and veterinary medicine generally takes four years, while for architecture and medicine, a bachelor's degree takes five and five and a half years respectively. Bachelor's degrees in education, journalism and librarianship are treated as second degrees. A bachelor's degree in law can either be taken as a part of an integrated degree programme lasting five years or a three-year programme as a second degree.

The master's degree is normally of two-year duration. It could be based on course work without a thesis, or on research with a thesis. The MPhil degree is a pre-doctoral programme taken after the completion of the master's degree. This can be either completely research based or can include course work. A PhD degree is awarded two years after the MPhil degree, or three years after the Master's degree. The students are expected to write a substantial thesis based on original research for the award of a PhD degree.

The academic structure of the Indian higher education system is broadly based on the pattern of 3–2–3 year cycle of academic qualifications adopted by Europe under the Bologna process. However, a majority of institutions do not have a credit system. There is a fixed curriculum and limited options available in each area of study. Recent efforts to introduce choice-based credit system have met with limited success.

The higher education system requires greater flexibility to ensure horizontal and vertical mobility, in order to enhance student choice. Integrated programmes and the recent decision to allow three-year bachelor's degree holders in science admission in the third year of four-year engineering degree programmes are initiatives in this direction. Similarly, restructuring of master's and graduate degrees by introducing a four-year, flexible and modular Bachelor of Science (BS) programme and other integrated programmes are positive steps that will enhance student choice. The significance of such academic restructuring as important planks in higher education reforms is not fully understood.

Enrolments

There are ambiguities and gaps in data on enrolment in the Indian higher education system. A discussion on enrolment and its growth would depend on the source of the data used. Enrolment data is available to us from four sources. First, the annual report published by the UGC has data on trends in higher education enrolment. The UGC Annual Report 2005–06 provides provisional enrolment data up to 2002–03 and estimated data for subsequent years until 2005–06.

Next, the Statistics Division of the Department of Higher Education under the Ministry of Human Resource Development, Government of India publishes *Selected Educational Statistics* (SES). Usually there is a time lag of 2–3 years. SES 2004–05 has been published in 2007. It has enrolment data as on 30 September 2004. SES includes enrolment in open and distance education programmes. The SES 2004–05 data includes distance education enrolment in 11 (out of 30) major states.

Another source of enrolment data is the sample surveys done by the National Sample Survey Organization (NSSO). The 61st (and the last) round of the National Sample Survey (NSS) was done in the year 2003–04 and its data is now available. Finally, enrolment data is available on the basis of actual headcount and house to house enumeration done every 10 years, under the decennial census operations. The last census was conducted in 2001. Based on these four different sources, higher education enrolment—actual or projected for alternate years since 1999–2000—is given in Figure 1.1.

FIGURE 1.1   Higher education enrolment—various sources

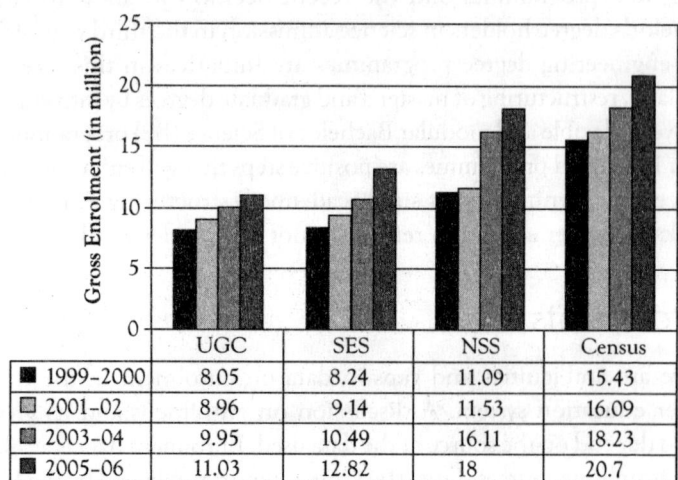

	UGC	SES	NSS	Census
■ 1999–2000	8.05	8.24	11.09	15.43
▢ 2001–02	8.96	9.14	11.53	16.09
■ 2003–04	9.95	10.49	16.11	18.23
■ 2005–06	11.03	12.82	18	20.7

Source Compiled from various sources by the author.

It is seen that enrolment estimates vary widely, from 11.03 million to 20.7 million. While some of it is due to problems in measurement, the main cause for divergence is due to the different definitions of higher education used in the process of measurement. While, as noted above, SES data includes distance education enrolment, NSS and Census data include non-formal, private, and diploma and certificate courses as well. University Grants Commission collects data directly from the universities and colleges. The response rate is usually poor, resulting in large gaps where estimates are used. Therefore, UGC data provides lower bound figures. Census data based on headcount is most accurate. However, it includes a significant amount of enrolment data in the non-university sector, and thus the census figures are upper bound estimates.

The SES data is collected by the central government through the state governments, and is in-between. Since the SES data also does not include the non-university sector, an enrolment of 11.77 million for 2004–05 (as on 30 September 2005) is perhaps the most accurate. The projected figure for 2005–06 is 12.82 million. The UNESCO Institute of Statistics also uses the SES data, and therefore, for international comparison, I will use the SES data. However, disaggregated data from SES source is not available. Hence, depending on the nature of analysis, I have used disaggregated data from other sources as available and indicated the source of the data.

Subject and Level-wise Enrolment

The UGC Annual Report 2005–06 provides level and subject wise enrolment data for the year 2005–06. It is seen that a majority of student enrolment is at the undergraduate level with 88.91 per cent (9,804,977) of total students enrolled in undergraduate programmes, and only 9.42 per cent (1,038,810) in the post-graduate programmes and a mere 0.64 per cent (70,716) in doctoral programmes. The remaining 1.03 per cent (113,517) students were enrolled in various types of diploma and certificate programmes in the formal system of higher education. Overall 87 per cent student enrolment is in affiliated colleges. On the basis of enrolment by level, while a bulk (90.3 per cent) of the undergraduate students and two-thirds (66.6 per cent) of the post-graduate students attend colleges, a majority (90.7 per cent) of doctoral students are enrolled in the universities.

In absolute terms, post-graduate enrolment is low and has proportionately decreased over the years from 13 per cent in 1980 to about 9 per cent in 2003. Similarly, proportion of doctoral students to overall enrolment was merely 0.58 per cent in 2003–04, while it was 0.88 per cent in 1980–81. The overall provision of doctoral education itself is very small. With just 65,525 students pursuing PhD programmes in 2005–06 and 17,898 PhD degrees awarded in 2004–05, doctoral education is the weak link in the higher education system. It has implications on academic research and the quality of the teaching faculty. These issues are discussed in subsequent chapters.

Distribution of capacity across subject areas is highly uneven and shows a bias towards general education. Of the total enrolment, 45.13 per cent (4,976,946) students are in arts, followed by 20.45 per cent (2,255,230) in science and 18 per cent (1,986,146) are in commerce and management. Thus, 83.59 per cent students are enrolled in ACS. Only the remaining 16.41 per cent are in professional programmes with a majority in engineering and technology, followed by medicine. Enrolment in agriculture is 0.58 per cent and in veterinary science merely 0.15 per cent. This skewed distribution has implication on labour market outcome of graduates, which will be discussed in Chapter 5.

Gross Enrolment Ratio

Gross enrolment ratio (GER) measures the level of access, by taking the ratio of persons of all ages enrolled in higher education with respect to the total population in the eligible age group, that is 18–23 years for higher education. The National Knowledge Commission, in its note on higher education, had stated the higher education GER at 7 per cent. This is a gross underestimation. The gross enrolment was 11.77 million in 2004–05 as per the latest SES report. An enrolment of 12.8 million has been projected for 2006–07 with a GER of 9.7 per cent, and the corresponding GER as per projected census and NSS figures are 15.6 per cent and 15.02 per cent (Srivastava, 2007).

The Global Education Digest 2007 of the UNESCO Institute of Statistics indicates a GER of 11 per cent with an enrolment of 11.77 million for the year 2004–05. Therefore, like the gross enrolment, GER data is also different depending upon its source. Currently, there are 112 million people in the age group of 18–23 years. With the current enrolment at 12.8 million, the GER works out to be 11.4 per cent. Given this data, taking 11 per cent GER would be most appropriate. This is low, considering that high income countries have an average

GER of 67 per cent and that the world average is 24 per cent. However, considering that India is still in the category of low income countries following the per capita income criteria of the World Bank, GER at 11 per cent appears to be reasonable at this stage of country's development. This issue will be discussed in detail later in this chapter.

Diversity in Student Population at Institution Level

Despite a large diversity in the overall student body, there is little diversity on the university campuses, especially the state universities. It is seen that except a small number of select institutions, most institutions cater to students in their close vicinity. A survey of 116 universities in 2004 revealed that on average about 69 per cent students are from within the state, about 18 per cent are from the neighbouring states, about 22 per cent are from the other states and about 1 per cent are foreign students.[1] A closer analysis reveals little or no student diversity in the non-professional institutions. The regional professional institutions were also seen to possess little student diversity, but the national professional institutions that conducted a national-level entrance exam showed a fair degree of student diversity. The number of foreign students in all institutions was negligible.

It is strongly felt that university campuses must have student diversity as a desired goal especially in a country like India with its variety of languages, customs, traditions, religions, music, dance, and other ways of life. Multicultural and diverse campuses are more dynamic and vibrant than the more homogenous ones. Diversity of student population in Indian universities reflecting the different regions can be an effective way of developing inter-regional understanding among young people. Their interpersonal skills would be improved and their horizons widened, making them more cosmopolitan and less parochial and rigid.

International Students Enrolment

Apart from domestic students, international students from over 145 countries study in India. During the academic year 2004–05, 13,627 international students[2] studied in Indian universities and institutions

11

and their number has increased since then (AIU, 2007). More than 90 per cent of the international students were from the developing countries of Asia (67 per cent) and Africa (25 per cent). Only 8 per cent of students were from Europe, Australia and the Americas. In terms of regional distribution, South and Central Asia were leaders, with more than 30 per cent coming from this region. Around 20 per cent of students were from North Africa and the Middle East. The majority of international students studying in Indian universities come from Nepal. Other countries with significant number of students in Indian Universities are Bangladesh, Malaysia, and Kenya (Agarwal, 2008a).

More than three-fourth of all the international students were enrolled in general programmes in arts (28.5 per cent), sciences (25.8 per cent) and commerce. While there were about 72.53 per cent students in undergraduate programmes, 17.8 per cent students were enrolled in post-graduate programmes. Only 28 per cent of all international students were girls (Agarwal, 2008a).

International students from advanced countries come to India primarily for short-term study abroad programmes that equip them with cross-cultural experience, enabling them to compete in the global economy. With its newfound position in the global knowledge economy, India is a popular destination for such programmes, evident from a sharp increase in the number of American students coming to India from 703 in 2002–03 to 1,767 in 2004–05 (Open Doors, 2005–06). Unfortunately, most Indian universities and colleges are not geared to host international students. The absence of semester based credit system makes it less attractive for international students.

Of late, India has attempted to revitalise its international student recruitment strategy, and the new private sector, led by Manipal University—which hosted the highest number of international students (2,031 in 2003–04)—is taking initiative in this regard. Yet, these efforts are nowhere close to aggressive posturing by several other countries (other than traditional host countries from the developed world) that are emerging as global magnates attracting large numbers of international students. These countries have set ambitious recruitment targets: Malaysia seeks to attract 100,000 international students by 2010 (up from 45,000 in 2005); Jordan announced plans to increase the number of international students to 100,000 by 2020; Singapore set a target of attracting 150,000 foreign students by 2015; China seeks to host 300,000 by 2020; and Japan has reportedly set the ambitious goal of hosting 1 million foreign students by 2025 (up from the current 120,000) (Obst, 2008).

With a large unmet domestic demand, there is a dilemma over whether it is actually desirable to adopt an aggressive international student recruitment drive. Current income from inward mobility is estimated at nearly USD 70 million each year. This is less than half a per cent of total annual expenditure on higher education. Through adopting the right approach, the number can easily go up from less than 20,000 at present to around 35,000 by the year 2010 (Agarwal, 2008), but its overall contribution to higher education finance would still be small. Thus, international student recruitment in Indian context needs to be seen as a strategy to promote the quality of its own system, as a means of creating multicultural ambience on Indian campuses that promotes diversity and international goodwill. By attracting bright students for post-graduate and research programmes, the country could fuel innovation and enterprise in the higher education system, as experienced by several advanced countries, particularly the United States.

Overseas Enrolments

Students not only move from one state to another for higher education, but a large and growing number of Indian students now study abroad. After China, India sends the largest number of students to other countries for higher education. There were over 160,000 Indian students studying abroad in 2005–06 with nearly half of them in the United States alone. Besides this, now the countries, such as the United Kingdom, Australia, New Zealand, Canada, and Ireland seek to woo Indian students. Though the main destination continues to be the English speaking countries, but now non-English speaking countries like Germany, France, and Holland run programmes in English to attract Indian students. Top hotel management schools in Switzerland; medical institutes in China, Russia, Eastern Europe and the Commonwealth of Independent States (CIS) attract students from India.

While most students go to the Universities in the West, Indians now find universities in Singapore and Malaysia equally good, less expensive and closer home. As a result, the number of Indian students in these countries has increased fast over the past couple of years. While, the United States and Germany mainly attract the post-graduate students, other countries are now admitting larger number of students in the undergraduate, and in some cases, even non-degree programmes. A majority of Indian students are fee-paying. Many countries provide opportunities to take up part-time work and most Indians are able to earn to pay at least a part of their expenses. Post-graduate and doctoral students are also able to find teaching or research assistantship in order to take care of their expenses while gaining useful experience in teaching and research. Figure 1.2 lays down the number of Indian students in the main destination countries from 1999–2000 to 2005–06. The number has more than tripled from 53,417 in 1999–2000 to nearly 160,000 in 2005–06.

Is It Brain Drain or Revenue Loss?

There are several push and pull factors responsible for student mobility across national borders. In a recent study on changing dynamics in international student circulation, De Wit (2007) laid down an extensive framework that identifies educational, political, social, cultural, and economic factors. These have been summarised in four categories: mutual understanding (political, social, and cultural factors), revenue earning (economic factors), skill migration (economic factors) and capacity building (educational factors). In different contexts, one of these approaches is found to be dominant. Large outward mobility from India is often seen as loss of revenue or brain drain.

There is concern that the country is losing revenue and valuable foreign exchange due to large exodus of students. It is estimated that India imported higher education worth USD 3,151 million in the year 2004. This is around 0.46 per cent of the Gross Domestic Product (GDP) (Bashir, 2007). The figure is comparable to the total public expenditure on higher education. Thus, the concern is genuine. However, it is seen that most of the students who go abroad finance their own study. It is

FIGURE 1.2   Indian students studying overseas

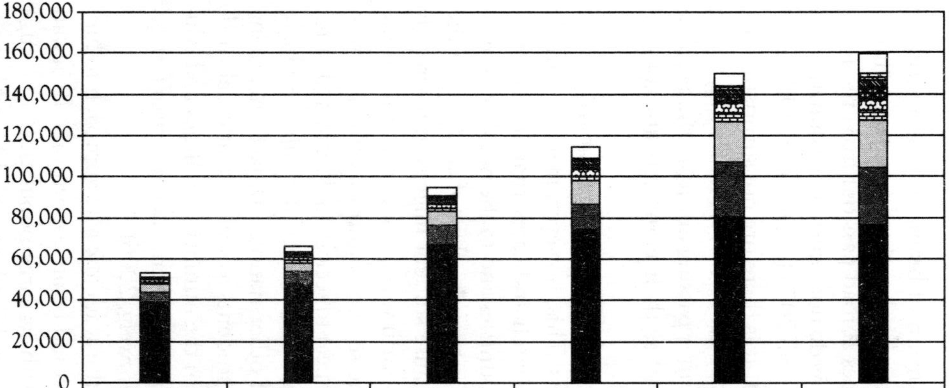

	1999–2000	2000–01	2001–02	2002–03	2004–05	2005–06
Other countries	2,500	3,200	4,000	5,000	6,000	10,000
France	185	239	309	625	1,200	1,500
Malaysia	91	714	497	1,000	1,500	1,800
New Zealand	201	355	952	1,800	3,000	3,300
Canada	867	1,200	1,800	2,200	3,000	6,000
Germany	1,282	1,412	2,196	3,429	4,500	4,700
Singapore	800	1,100	1,500	2,200	4,000	4,800
United Kingdom	3,829	4,649	6,817	11,707	20,000	23,515
Australia	4,578	6,195	9,539	12,462	26,548	27,661
United States	39,084	47,411	66,836	74,603	80,446	76,503
Total	53,417	66,475	94,446	109,577	150,194	159,779

Source Compiled by the author based on country level data from various sources/ OECD-UNESCO Institute of Statistics and EUROSTAT Database/Data for 2004–05 is from other sources and estimates by the author.

therefore private expenditure and not public money. Further, it is clear that these students or their families would have spent the money here if the students had stayed back. It is not known whether their motivation behind studying abroad is purely educational or to gain entry into the host country's labour market.

Besides, there is also an apprehension of brain drain as a result of outward student mobility. A significant proportion of students who go for post-graduate and doctoral studies abroad pass out from the more reputed institutions at home and many do not return. It is estimated that nearly one fourth of all IIT graduates till 2003 (31,900 out of 133,245) were staying abroad (MHRD, 2004). It is therefore not surprising that the Parliament's Standing Committee on HRD recommended taxing students who take up overseas jobs after passing out from the premier higher education institutions, as well as their employers abroad (*The Times of India*, 20 August 2007b).

It is argued that building domestic higher education capacity would enable the country to retain students. This, however, may not entirely be true. A recent econometric research indicates that increases in educational capacity in the source countries and in the number of institutions and teachers are likely to increase the flow of students to the United States. This is primarily because student migration is strongly affected by the promise of wage opportunities, not constraints in the domestic educational capacity of the source countries. Students from today's low wage, source countries appear to seek schooling in high-wage countries as a means of 'augmenting their chances of obtaining a high-wage job' in the United States and other nations. In fact, increasing educational capacity prepares more students to seek education abroad. The research finds that an increase in the number of colleges and educational capacity in source countries actually increases the flow of foreign students to the United States (Rosenzweig, 2006).

A number of countries now use the academic gate approach to lure talent. In the context of India, this could be an opportunity. Bhagwati (2004) points out that for India, with its large population and huge capacity to generate skilled professionals at home and by education abroad, out-migration of professionals is an opportunity and not a threat. Freeman (2005) observes that a country like India, with its large population and sizeable pool of scientists and engineers, could threaten the North's monopoly in the hi-tech sectors by producing innovative products and services. He refers to this as human resource leapfrogging that countries like India could possibly create. Thus, concerns about revenue loss and brain drain appear to be misplaced.

Finally, India would perhaps not like to behave like Belarus, a small landlocked country with state-controlled economy known for its antidemocratic policies. According to the Belarusian leader, Alexander Lukashenka, study abroad 'poisons the mind', and thus the Belarus government does not issue exit visas to students wanting to study abroad (*The Economist*, 2005a).

Higher Education Growth

Higher education has seen an impressive growth since India's independence in 1947. Overall, the number of universities has increased from 25 in 1950 to 371 in 2006, the number of colleges has increased from 700 to 18,064 and the enrolment has increased from a tiny base of 0.1 million to a whopping 11.2 million. The extent of capacity expansion can be seen in Table 1.3.

TABLE 1.3 Capacity expansion

	1950–51	1990–91	2003–04	2006–07
University Level Institutions	25	177	320	371
Colleges	700	7,346	16,885	18,064
Teachers (in thousand)	15	272	457	488
Students Enrolled (in million)	0.1	4.9	9.95	11.2

Source Author (compiled from various reports of the University Grants Commission).

Out of the total number of universities, six central and 114 state universities have affiliating powers. Together these universities have affiliated more than 18,000 colleges in the country. Accounting for nearly 90 per cent of the total enrolment, colleges constitute the bulk of the Indian higher education. Figure 1.3 gives the trends in the growth of institutions and enrolment since independence.

FIGURE 1.3   Growth of institutions and enrolment in higher education

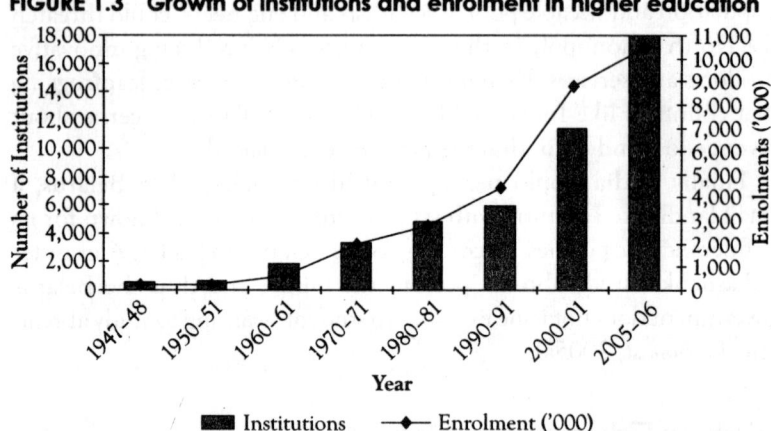

Source Author (compiled from various reports of the University Grants Commission).

In post-independence India, higher education growth occurred in two distinct phases. In phase 1, from 1947 to 1980, there was steady growth. Large number of colleges were started and affiliated to the new and the existing universities. The government set up universities and colleges at places not having higher education facilities. Courses in new and under-represented subject areas were started. This resulted in geographical dispersal of higher education facilities and broadened the base of higher education. From 1980 onwards expansion has been largely driven by private initiatives. After 2000, there has been a consolidation of private initiatives, particularly in the area of professional higher education. Despite, explosive growth of private professional education, majority of the universities and colleges still impart education at the undergraduate level in arts, science and social sciences. Post-graduate and doctoral education continues to be small. Growth in three phases is discussed next.

Growth in Pre-independence India

Education in ancient India was highly advanced, as evident from the centres of learning that existed in the Buddhist monasteries of the

7th century BC and the 3rd century AD Nalanda. In these centres, gathering of scholars used to engage in intellectual debates in residential campuses. A few of these centres were large and had several faculties. Historians speculate that these centres had a remarkable resemblance to the medieval European universities that came up much later. The ancient education system in India was slowly extinguished following invasions and disorder in the country (Perkin, 2006).

Till the 18th century, India had three distinct traditions of advanced scholarship in the Hindu *gurukulas*, the Buddhist *viharas*, and the Quranic *madarsas*, before the British set up a network of schools to impart western education in English medium. British colonial regime laid the foundation of modern higher education in the mid-19th century. The colonial government favoured an 'anglicist' orientation for higher education. The (in)famous 'minute' penned by Macaulay on 2 February 1835 and Wood's Dispatch of 19 July 1854 bear testimony to this.

The first college to impart western education was founded in 1818 at Serampore near Calcutta. Over the next 40 years, many such colleges were established in different parts of the country at Agra, Bombay, Madras, Nagpur, Patna, Calcutta, and Nagapattinam. The first three universities were established at Bombay (now Mumbai), Calcutta (now Kolkata) and Madras (now Chennai) in 1857. Modelled on the University of London (established in 1836), these universities were largely affiliating and examining bodies with very little intellectual life of their own (Jayaram, 2006). Later, more universities were established.

The higher education system in the country saw an isomorphic pattern of growth thereafter. Higher education was conceived of as serving the economic, political and administrative interests of the British and, in particular, consolidating and maintaining their dominance in the country. Its courses were biased in favour of languages and the humanities, rather than science and technology. Thus, the Indian higher education system inherited what could be referred to as an 'anaemic, distorted and dysfunctional' situation (Raza et al., 1985). At the time of independence in 1947, there were 25 universities and several hundred affiliated colleges. Post-Independence growth of higher education in the country has been in two distinct phases, one before 1980, and one following 1980.

Pre-1980 Growth

As a lasting imprint of the British legacy, the growth of higher education in India until about 1980 was largely confined to courses in languages and the humanities, apart from a few institutions set up for professional education. Noticeable amongst these are the Indian Institutes of Technology (IITs) and Regional Engineering Colleges (later renamed as National Institutes of Technology) for engineering education and the Indian Institutes of Management (IIMs) for management education. The establishment of these high-quality institutions—particularly the IITs—is often considered as a masterstroke by many people. The IITs were set up with a package of foreign assistance (from the USA, the UK, the then USSR and the Federal Republic of Germany), which not only included funding for equipment but also foreign guest faculty and the training of Indian faculty abroad on a large scale. In the early 1960s, two IIMs were set up on the same pattern in collaboration with the Sloan School of Management (Massachusetts Institute of Technology) and the Harvard Business School. The role of guest faculty in these institutions helped in introducing not only new curriculum but a whole new academic culture in Indian higher education.

Unfortunately, that academic culture remained confined to this select group of institutions and did not spread to the rest of the system. Although the number of IITs has now increased from five to seven and IIMs from two to six, in terms of overall enrolment, they continue to be small players in the Indian higher education system. Alumni of IITs and IIMs have done well both in India and abroad. Entry to these institutions is very competitive. These are some of the most selective higher education institutions in the world and are ranked highly by peers in their respective fields. Although a small number of students get the opportunity to study at these elite institutions, several hundred thousand students undertake intense preparations in an attempt to gain admission into them. This has, in itself, given rise to a huge coaching industry but the end result is improved learning outcomes for a large section of the population.

Although higher education in India expanded steadily over the years and now has a large base, the number of quality institutions has remained small. In the rest of the system the standards are extremely heterogeneous, with a large number of sub-standard and non-viable institutions.

Yet another development during this phase has been the rapid growth in the number of private aided colleges. During the 1960s and 1970s, the government, in its enthusiasm to be seen as a welfare state, not only supported higher education by setting up universities and colleges, but also took over the financial responsibility of running the private institutions. These came to be known as grant-in-aid (GIA) institutions or private aided institutions. Their numbers increased very rapidly until the 1980s. By 1980, there were 132 universities and 4,738 colleges in the country, enrolling around 5 per cent of the eligible age group in higher education. Almost one-third of all colleges were private aided colleges.

Post-1980 Phase

Several developments took place in the post-1980 phase. There was an unprecedented demand for quality higher education relevant to the needs of business and industry. The growing middle class, which could afford higher fees, made non-subsidised education possible. A large number of private institutions at the elementary and secondary education had come up as viable enterprises all over the country. Due to financial constraints, the government found it difficult to set up new universities and colleges. According to some observers, this marked the withdrawal of the government from taking over additional responsibility for higher education (Tilak, 2005).

Thus, this period saw the emergence of new types of providers. Private institutions proliferated, distance education programmes gained wider acceptance, public universities and colleges started self-financing programmes, and foreign institutions started offering programmes either by themselves or in partnership with Indian institutions and the non-university sector grew rapidly. As result the entire higher education landscape got transformed over the past 25 years.

Growth of Private Institutions

Growth of financially independent private institutions has been the most significant development over the past few decades. Private trusts and societies started to set up higher education institutions and run them in large numbers. Such institutions proliferated all over the country over the years. Faced with financial constraints, the government had no option but to reluctantly allow their entry.

Until the late 1990s, the main mode of growth of private institutions was through establishing colleges affiliated to the existing universities or new universities carved out from the existing ones. By the late 1990s, many private promoters were getting uneasy of the regulatory controls. They felt that the affiliating university and the state governments were holding back their growth—they were not allowed to fully exploit their market potential. They explored possibilities to wriggle out of their control. While many institutions took the deemed university route to get degree-granting powers, a few private promoters were able to persuade the state governments to enact separate laws to set up private universities.

Private institutions grew in the country in a diverse manner and their impact on provision for higher education has been most significant—so much so that private higher education now occupies the centrestage in the debate on higher education. Thus, the next chapter deals exclusively with the emerging private higher education sector and the policy debates surrounding it. Two points that need to be mentioned at this stage are, first, that the new breed of private institutions are primarily *de facto* for-profit, and second, that a majority of them offer programmes in professional areas.

Until 1980, the growth of higher education was essentially 'more of the same'. A majority of students are enroled in ACS programmes and are euphemistically called as 'ordinary graduates' with hardly any employable skills. Private institutions that were the main venue for growth in enrolment in the post-1980 era offered courses in professional areas that had market demand, such as engineering and technology, medicine, teacher education at the undergraduate level, computer applications and management at the post-graduate level.

Private institutions now contribute as much as 80 per cent enrolments in professional programmes. Thus, the emergence of private higher education brought in a much desired occupational focus to the growth in higher education and brought in dynamism to the hitherto moribund higher education system.

Growth of Open and Distance Education

While the private higher education sector was growing, distance education also saw a major expansion. Distance education has its origin in the correspondence education. Unlike the West, where the private providers initially dominated the correspondence education industry, in India it was the conventional universities in the public sector that started correspondence education. It started with the University of Delhi offering bachelor's degree programmes in arts, sciences and social sciences in the year 1962. This soon became an economic and quick way of increasing enrolment and generating revenues in higher education. As seen in Table 1.4, from an enrolment of a few thousand in 1960s, enrolment in distance education grew fast, and reached a 2 million mark in 2002–03 and constituted 22 per cent of the total enrolment. In 2006–07, there were over 2.8 million students with nearly 1.3 million students registering each year in the distance education programmes. There are 14 open universities including the Indira Gandhi National Open University (IGNOU). Besides, there are 106 conventional universities that offer distance education programmes in addition to their on-campus programmes.

TABLE 1.4 Student enrolment in distance and conventional mode

Year	Conventional mode	Distance mode	As % of total enrolment
1967–68	1,370,261	8,577	0.62
1980–81	2,752,437	1,66,428	6.0
1990–91	4,990,000	560,000	11.2
1999–2000	7,730,000	1,580,000	20.4
2002–03	9,200,000	2,000,000	22.0

Source Author (compiled from various reports of UGC and DEC).

Often distance education programmes generate huge surpluses with fee levels usually higher than fees in similar regular programmes. Most open universities are able to generate all their operating expenses through their fee revenues; some of them even have surpluses. Conventional universities usually generate huge surpluses through distance education. For some of them, this is the main source of revenue. Some deemed universities also have large distance education programmes and earn huge sums of money. There are also few private providers outside the formal system that offer distance education programme. Overall, there are different types of providers offering a variety of distance education programmes.

The growth of open and distance education in the country has been haphazard and the quality is both unsatisfactory and uneven (NIEPA, 2006). Unlike the UK's Open University, which ranks fifth out of 100 British universities for the quality of its teaching programmes; neither the open universities nor the distance education programmes of the conventional universities are rated high in India, though some programmes of IGNOU and its self-learning materials are well regarded.

With new technologies, it is now possible to provide real classroom learning experience without compromising on quality—as a result, the boundaries between distance education and on-campus education are now blurred. Several universities like the Punjab Technical University run hundreds of learning centres across the country, where classes are regularly held, like their on-campus programmes. Such learning centres are run by the private sector under some kind of a franchise arrangement, offering high-demand programmes in management or IT. Blended learning, where the provision of on-campus learning is integrated with online and distance education holds great promise in future. Thus, the future of distance education will be marked with growing interrelations between different modes of teaching–learning. There will be both increasing competition and rising cooperation amongst various types of providers in the years to come.

Self-financing Courses in Public Institutions

While financial constraints had put a brake on the expansion of the government-funded universities and colleges, even the existing ones faced financial difficulties. Due to increased student demand they had no option but to start self-financing courses. The students were charged tuition fees not only to cover the operating costs, but also to generate surplus for other operations of the institution. The courses were obviously offered in subjects having a demand in the market, such as engineering and technology, medicine, teacher education at the undergraduate level, computer applications and management at the post-graduate level. The fee structure in conventional courses in public institutions continues to be low. The revenue from fees is often adjusted from government grants. As a result, the revenues from self-financing courses along with distance education courses form the main source of revenue for most public universities and colleges. In recent years, fee income from self-financing courses and distance education programmes are the main sources of revenue for many public universities and colleges in India.

Growth of Non-university Sector

The post-1980s also saw growth of the non-university sector. This grew to meet the immediate demand of skills from a growing economy. In the formal training sector, hundreds of Industrial Training Institutes (ITIs) and polytechnics were established. Together, these institutions provide more than a million places for training. Though large in absolute terms, it is grossly inadequate.

Besides this, a large private for-profit training sector emerged to meet the growing demand for usable training. This is financed by students and their parents and responds in more direct, and usually more effective ways, to the needs of industry and the labour market. With the gap between training and education getting narrower, this marks the erosion of the traditional monopoly that universities have enjoyed in providing training and granting credentials with good currency for jobs in the jobs markets. A detailed discussion on this is in Chapter 5.

Trends in Growth Pattern

There are several global trends in growth pattern of higher education. Most significant are: (i) the transition from elite to mass and then to universal higher education; *(ii)* the emergence of the private sector provision, mainly the *de facto* for-profit type; and *(iii)* the convergence of different technologies that opens new avenues to distribute knowledge and to engage larger student audience. These trends, along with shifting demographics, are resulting in internationalisation of higher education. This is changing the relationship between the institutions, the government and its regulatory arms.

Under the changed circumstances, the three near certainties about higher education: one, that it is supplied on a national basis to the local students; two, it is government regulated; and three, competition and profit are unknown concepts in higher education, are no longer true (*The Economist*, 2005a). With growing student mobility and the increasing demand in the global labour market for the highly skilled, higher education has now gone international. With the entry of a large number of private and foreign providers, there is intense competition in higher education. Providers are numerous and more diverse. Students and academics now have the choice to opt for the best deal.

While the discussion here suggests that the higher education landscape has significantly changed over the years, yet it must be understood that some of the basic issues have remained the same. It is amusing to note that at the 1924 conference of Indian universities, Lord Reading referred to the 'phenomenal increase in the number of universities' (the number had doubled in a decade) and the right road to 'educational efficiency' (Powar, 1999). Later, in the first meeting of the Inter University Board (IUB)[3] in 1925, the items that came up for discussion were 'equivalence of examinations' and 'traffic in bogus degrees' (Powar, 1999). Surprisingly, according to Powar (1999), in a century characterised by rapid changes, some of the basic problems of higher education have not only persisted but have increased in magnitude.

Thus, while some basic issues have remained the same, the system is now huge. Its implications are seen in financing, management and other aspects of higher education. Subsequent chapters discuss these aspects in detail. The cause and effect of transition to mass higher education, the impact of the new providers and lack of differentiation in the Indian system of higher education are discussed here. Despite limitations of analysis in international comparative perspective, a review is done by comparing trends elsewhere to develop a holistic view.

Transition to Mass Higher Education

Economist Martin Trow classified higher education systems worldwide according to their enrolments. He defined the 'elite', 'mass' and 'universal' states when the GER ratio is 'less than 15 per cent; between 15 and 50 per cent; and more than equal to 50 per cent respectively' (Trow, 1973).

Building upon Trow's work, Brennan summarised the characteristics of the elite, mass and universal higher education systems in 2004. According to him, whereas elite higher education shapes the mind and character of the ruling class and prepares students for broad elite roles in government and society; mass higher education undertakes the transmission of knowledge and prepares students for broad technical and economic elite roles. Universal higher education is concerned with adaptation of whole population to rapid social and technological changes (Brennan, 2004).

As seen in Table 1.5, all high income countries now have enrolments exceeding 50 per cent. Thus, higher education systems in these countries seek to adapt the entire population to rapid social and technological changes that are sweeping these countries. Upper-middle income and lower-middle income countries all have mass higher education systems. While the upper income countries have an average GER of 43 per cent, the lower-middle income countries have it at 22 per cent.

In these countries, higher education provides people with skills and competence required to discharge a wide range of technical and economic roles. Such roles would obviously depend on the nature of country's economy and the use of technology in it. It is obvious that economies that have a large share of their labour force in the agriculture sector tend to have less participation in higher education. Lower-middle income countries—China, Brazil, Philippines, and Indonesia—all have a large share of their labour in agriculture sector and thus less higher education enrolment. Usually countries with higher skilled labour force tend to have more enrolment. Across a range of countries, GERs are seen to be roughly twice the share of skilled labour in the total labour force.

TABLE 1.5   Higher education enrolment

Country	Enrolment (in million) 2005	1990	% Increase between 1990–2005	GER 2005%
High Income (Average GER—67%)				
USA	17.27	13.71	26	83
Japan	4.04	2.90	39	55
Korea	3.21	1.85	73	91
UK	2.29	1.26	81	60
France	2.19	1.70	29	56
Italy	2.01	1.45	38	66
Canada	1.33	0.84	58	56
Australia	1.01	0.49	106	72
Upper-middle Income (Average GER—43%)				
Russia	9.02	5.10	77	71
Malaysia	0.73	0.12	508	32
Lower-middle Income (Average GER—22%)				
China	21.34	3.82	459	20
Brazil	4.28	1.54	178	24
Indonesia	3.64	1.59	129	17
Philippines	2.40	1.71	40	28
Low Income (Average GER—9%)				
India	11.78	4.95	138	11

Source Enrolment and GER 2005 based on data from UNESCO; Classification of economies and average GER for them based World Development Indicators 2007.

India, with an enrolment ratio of about 11 per cent, is still an elite higher education system as per Trow's classification. The structure of the Indian economy, with a large population in the unorganised and the agriculture sectors that do not require higher education qualifications at this stage, pushes down the enrolment ratio to this low level. There is a wide variation between rural and urban areas and across the states. Whereas in urban metropolitan areas, enrolment mirrors that in the advanced developing nations, in the rural hinterland, enrolment continues to be very low. However, overall, in absolute terms it is huge—the third largest in the world. Access to higher education is no more restricted to the elite, but expansion over the years has democratised higher education. Thus, in many ways, the country already has a mass higher education system.

This massive expansion of higher education has been chaotic and unplanned. In an effort to meet rising aspirations and to make higher education socially inclusive, there has been a sudden and dramatic increase in number of institutions without a proportionate increase in material and intellectual resources. As a result, according to Béteille (2005), academic standards have been jeopardised. Several problems that the system faces include: inadequate infrastructure and facilities, large vacancies in faculty positions and poor faculty, outmoded teaching methods, declining research standards, unmotivated students, overcrowded classrooms and widespread geographic, income, gender, and ethnic imbalances. But, this is not unique to India. Most systems of higher education in the world have expanded fast over the past few decades and are in quasi-crisis and need reform.

Apart from differences in GERs, it is interesting to note that whereas in the high income countries enrolments are growing slowly, for middle and low income countries enrolments are rising rapidly. The most significant increase has been in China and Malaysia. Enrolment in India has also more than doubled in the 15-year period from 1990 to 2005. The global pattern of changing higher education enrolments show that most of the increase will happen in the developing world. While enrolment will expand modestly in the advanced (OECD) countries, rising from 46 million at present to 51 million in 2025, in the non-OECD countries, the enrolments will rise from 69 million to 255 million during the same period.

In India, despite a steady enrolment growth, barely 11 per cent of the 18–23 year age group is currently enrolled in higher education. There is a concern that India may not be able to reach a level of enrolment comparable to that of the advanced countries. With India playing a key role in the global knowledge economy, there is also a clamour for increasing the enrolment rate to at least 20 per cent. On purchase point parity basis, India is already in the lower-middle income category and on the verge of shifting to this category even on the nominal per capita income basis in coming years. Thus, it would be reasonable to target a GER of 20 per cent, closer to the global average of 24 per cent and category average of 22 per cent.

While due to demographic changes enrolments in higher education have either stagnated or are falling in the advanced nations, in India it is increasing rapidly. For instance, Russian universities and colleges are expecting a 30 per cent slump in applications for the next year, and in some regions students may be accepted virtually without entrance examinations. The Ministry of Education and Science's statistics show that 1.05 million young people will leave school this summer, compared to 1.32 million in 2005. There are about 1 million places in first-year courses in institutions of higher education, so for this year's school leavers only a small element of competition remains. But in 2009, the number of school leavers will fall to 930,000 and the year after to a mere 808,000.

Considering these developments, expansion of higher education in countries around the world, particularly those that earlier had low participation in higher education, is therefore a universal phenomenon. Globally, between 1991 and 2004, enrolment in higher education increased from 68 million to 132 million. Though the two advanced regions of the world—North America and Western Europe, and East Asia and the Pacific—continue to account for more than half of the enrolment; the greatest growth in enrolment occurred in South and West Asia, and the Latin America and the Caribbean, which saw enrolment growing from 6 and 7 million respectively to 15 million each (UNESCO, 2006: 21).

The government has set a target of 15 per cent by the year 2011, the terminal year of the Eleventh Five Year Plan. In international comparative perspective this is a reasonable expectation. If one takes GER on the basis of Census or NSS data, this may have already been achieved. However, if we take SES data; an additional enrolment capacity of 22.5 million students would be required by 2011.[4] This would mean 15 per cent compounded annual growth rate against 5–6 per cent being achieved over the years.

The expansion of enrolment needs to happen, but it is important to note that while more higher education is usually a policy objective, there is no magic figure of 15, 20 or even 50 per cent that a country could aspire to achieve. The demand for higher education is often driven by aspirations. This often results in creating overcapacities. Both the developed and emerging nations face this problem. According to Clausen (2006), there is huge overcapacity in American higher education. Jobs held by college graduates in sales, transportation, services, and even in computer industry can easily be performed by the people with little or no higher education. Going to college has become a 'defensive strategy—you do it because everyone is doing it' Clausen (2006).

In China, unanticipated expansion of higher education has resulted in skyrocketing unemployment rate. The number of university students has doubled since 2000, to 23 million in 2006. While the GER was merely 3 per cent in 1992, it has now jumped to over 20 per cent. Many universities have set up suburban campuses in just six months. In 2006, 4.13 million students graduated, compared to 1.15 million in 2001. Many college graduates work as security guards, maids and nannies. In a widely publicised survey released by the China Youth Daily, 35 per cent of the youth said that they regretted their university experience and did not consider it worth the time and money invested; more than half said that they had nothing of use (Melvin, 2006). Five hundred new graduates applied for six traditionally taboo positions working with the dead at a Beijing funeral home. Instances of several thousands of graduates and even post-graduates applying for a position of peon or driver in the public sector in India are common. Thus, enrolment expansion cannot be the sole objective.

Though higher education is only loosely connected to the country's economic performance, and has wider functions in the society than the simply economic one, yet higher education enrolment needs to be in sync with the absorptive capacity of the economy. While some oversupply of qualified people would help the economy on higher productivity growth path, a large mismatch could result in an acute problem of unemployment and underemployment. Since enrolment would depend upon the occupational structure of its economy, service economies of the developed countries have greater demand for higher education compared to a largely agrarian economy like that of India.

Considering the above realities, fixing enrolment targets in a manner done in India is an exercise in futility. Expansion of higher education has to keep rhythm with the developments in society and economy. Fixing an enrolment target is meaningless for yet another reason. Experience over the past two decades suggests that private institutions have been the main venue of growth of higher education; public investment has added very little new capacity. Private higher education in any case would expand if there is an unmet demand. Rather than numbers, quality is often the issue here. Thus, correctly regulating the private sector holds the key to higher education expansion in India.

The current GER at around 11 per cent, though low in comparison with developing countries, matches the current occupational pattern of the country. In India, the GER is twice the percentage of skilled people in the total workforce as in developing and developed countries alike. With services-led growth in India requiring a larger proportion of people having higher educational qualifications, and the possibility of the country supplying qualified manpower to countries having to face with declining number of people in the working age group, there is scope for further expanding enrolment in higher education. This issue has been discussed in details in Chapter 5.

Structure of enrolment in India differs from that in advanced nations with mature systems of higher education in several ways. One, enrolment of women at about 40 per cent in India is still less than that of men, while generally, more women than men are enrolled in higher education in the advanced countries. Two, enrolment of part-time students or mature students is still low even at the post-graduate level in India. Part-time students form a significant proportion of the enrolment in developed countries. In the UK, more than 40 per cent students are enrolled as part-time students; at the post-graduate level, their numbers are almost twice that of full-time students. Three, in India, most students who enrol complete their degrees. Large drop-out rate is a major concern in advanced countries. Four, India has ever-increasing application-to-acceptance ratios, particularly for more reputed institutions. In most developed nations, due to reducing number of young people, application-to-acceptance ratio has remained stagnant or decreased due to declining numbers of young people seeking higher education. And, finally, as seen from the diversity of students at the institutional level, most students are from the same region. Due to cultural differences, students travel large distances for higher education in many advanced countries where the parents' involvement in the lives of adolescent children is minimal. In India, enrolment of women is growing fast, and part-time studies and enrolment of mature students are appearing on the scene. On other fronts, differences continue to exist.

New Providers

Several other forces at play (apart from expansion) are transforming the higher education system. These are: shifting demographics, new technologies, entry of the private (mostly for-profit) providers, the changing relationship between the institutions, the government and its regulatory arms, and the move from an industrial to an information society (Hanna, 1998). The convergence of different technologies opens new avenues to distribute knowledge and to engage a larger audience. As a result, higher education providers are becoming numerous and more diverse. The traditional universities continue to be vertically integrated in their production function, and teaching and research go together. This, however, is under threat from the new providers. Now that teaching alone is considered profitable, private and new providers are interested only in teaching. Higher education itself is becoming more individualised, with the focus shifting from teaching to learning. Thus, the traditional functions of higher education could become un-bundled in future.

With the changing landscape of higher education in India, other than the traditional universities and colleges, two other types of providers, namely, private universities and colleges, and distance education providers have emerged in India. Their basic philosophy, mission, funding arrangement, curricula focus and instructional methodology is so different from the traditional universities and colleges that the government, the regulatory bodies, the higher education institutions themselves and finally, the students and their parents have not been able to come to terms with the changed realties. To understand and appreciate these differences, Table 1.6 illustrates how in the Indian context, the new providers differ from traditional providers of higher education.

TABLE 1.6 Different types of providers of higher education

Elements	Traditional universities and colleges	Private universities and colleges	Distance education providers
Philosophy	Students come to the campus	Both campus and non-campus philosophy	Campus goes to the students
Mission	Mission defined by level of instruction	Externally focused, degree completion and workforce development	Externally focused, degree completion and workforce development
Funding	Institution-based grants on deficit financing basis	More self-sustaining and market driven	Reduce cost of access to higher education
Curricula	Relatively stable and comprehensive curricula	More flexible curriculum content for workforce competence and development	More flexible curriculum content for workforce competence and development
Instruction	Most courses are lecture based	Greater variety of methods though still mostly lecture based	Mostly correspondence–print and readings based with increasing use of technology for interaction
Faculty	Primarily full-time faculty; academic preparation and credentials	Small full-time faculty with greater use of adjuncts with professional experience	Use of part-time faculty for contact programmes on periodic basis
Library	Volumes in library	Access to specific document and resources appropriate to programme	Extremely limited facility

Students	Selectivity in admissions depending on quality of institution	Selectivity in admissions depending on quality of institution and also capacity to pay, in most cases	Open admissions except for a few programmes
Learning Technology	Little use of technology to enhance learning	Some use of technology to enhance learning	Increasing use of one or two technologies supplemented by online instructional references and resources
Physical facilities	Old dilapidated, but extensive physical facilities	New but limited physical facilities	Almost no physical facilities—students are geographically separated from each other and the instructor
Governance	Governing board with nominees of government and funding bodies	Governing board with members from a family	Varies widely
Recognition and Accreditation	Large number of recognised and accredited institutions	Good number of recognised, but a small number of accredited institutions	Quite a confusion on recognition and accreditation mechanism

Source Adapted from Model by Donald E. Hanna (1998).

Growth trends in India show that the higher education sector was controlled by the government till about 1980. After that there has been a clear trend towards privatisation of higher education. Private higher education has grown fast over the past two decades. This not only increased capacity and enhanced students' choices but also affected the dynamics of regulation. Its impact on financing arrangements has been very significant. Taking this in view, next chapter is focused on the emerging private sector.

Conclusion

The size, structure and growth of the Indian higher education system are riddled with many contradictions. It is both large and small. In terms of absolute enrolment (about 12.8 million students), it is the third largest education system in the world, but in terms of gross enrolment ratio, it is small—just around 11 per cent. Universities and colleges together, there are more than 20,000 institutions. This is more than the rest of world taken together. Yet, the number of degree-granting institutions is just about 400. The number of institutions is large, with very small average enrolment, resulting in a higher education landscape dotted with a large number of tiny non-viable institutions.

Institutional and academic structures in India have an imprint of the old British universities, yet recent universities and colleges have adopted the organisational models of the universities in the United States. While there appears to be a large institutional diversity, careful analysis shows that such diversity is in terms of origin of these institutions, but not in terms of offerings or differences in mission. The system is often driven to achieve uniformity, disregarding the country's social diversity and increasingly complex division of labour in the Indian economy today. Thus, there is very little choice for the student.

The higher education system is highly fragmented and organised sub-optimally. Due to the affiliating university system, there are a large number of small and non-viable colleges. Poorly resourced, such colleges are at best tutorial classes, where learning takes place on the basis of a fixed curriculum for the purpose of cracking exams. Many experts suggest that India should do away with affiliated college system altogether. This, however, would not be feasible. Rather than totally dismantling the affiliating system, there is need to creatively deal with this in order to achieve geographical dispersal, using a blend of conventional and distance mode to address the quality issue. There is a need for consolidation by merging and clustering of universities and colleges to achieve critical mass for effective intellectual exchange, benefit from synergy and sharing of infrastructure and facilities. And each such merged entity should be given full academic autonomy in order to experiment and innovate. The concept of cluster of colleges and the National Knowledge Commission's recommendation to have 1,500 universities should be viewed in this context. It has been suggested that undergraduate affiliated colleges could be restructured to create smaller universities that are responsive to change and easier to manage.

Enrolment pattern is skewed in favour of arts and humanities. There is small enrolment at the post-graduate and doctoral levels. Rather than more of the same, the focus has to be on proper mix of streams in the expansion plan. More vocationally oriented programmes need to be given priority. To ensure holistic education, liberal arts education should be integrated with vocational programmes through curricular reforms. Further discussion on this issue is in Chapter 5.

Post-Independence, there were two distinct phases of growth of Indian higher education. Until 1980, growth was mainly in ACS colleges affiliated to public universities. After 1980, growth was primarily in private professional colleges. This is still continuing. After 2000, several private universities have come up. Overall, the number of universities and other degree-granting institutions is small and their numbers have grown slowly. In the recent years, the number of universities has begun to grow fast, but since the base was small, their numbers are still small. During the 1960s, several institutions of national importance, namely the IITs and the IIMs were set up. These institutes have different culture and status in the Indian system and their numbers continue to be small. Below this tiny top, quality falls rapidly, and the bulk of the institutions are of very low quality.

The government plans to expand enrolment to reach 15 per cent GER by 2012. This would require additional capacity for 7.5 million students. For this growth momentum has to be sustained and further accelerated over the next few years. Recently, the Indian government has decided to set up several IITs, IIMs and other premier institutions for higher professional education. Sixteen new central universities and 14 world-class universities have also been proposed. This would be the largest ever expansion. Yet, its impact on increasing enrolment numbers would be only marginal, since most of the growth in higher education now takes place in the private sector. With private and new providers and new forms of delivery, higher education landscape is seeing a lot of activity in recent years. Now, there is little distinction between the formal higher education and the training sector.

A significant enrolment in higher education is in institutions abroad. Earlier, it was not considered particularly significant. There was concern about the country losing revenue and valuable foreign exchange due to large exodus of students. Besides, there was also the apprehension of brain drain as a result of outward student mobility. Now, in a global economy, it is realised that concerns about revenue loss and brain drain were misplaced. Overall, the Indian higher education system is very complex. There are varying perceptions about it. Empirical mapping of size, structure and growth of higher education in the country would help in an informed debate.

◆

2

Access and Equity

Next to life and liberty, we consider education the greatest
blessing bestowed upon mankind.
— Anonymous[1]

ISSUES of access and equity are central to the higher education debates in countries around the world. The expansion of higher education and growing private share, as noted in the previous chapter, had obvious impact upon access and equity. As the socio-economic and political realities changed and enrolments grew, the purpose of higher education, which is only ambiguously defined, kept changing. For the Indian higher education system in transition, access and equity became two of its most intriguing aspects. These are very complex issues, intertwined with political, economic, demographic and international dimensions. This chapter connects the previous chapter with the next two on private higher education and financing by examining access and equity issues, keeping in mind the country's changing socio-political realities and evolving economic policy.

In this chapter, first we examine the expanding enrolment and its consequences and limitations on access when higher education is entirely provided by the public sector. With access spurned in public higher education, private higher education grew rapidly (to be discussed in Chapter 3). Thus, we discuss in this chapter the changing attitudes towards private higher education when the role of private sector was on rise in other sectors. We examine the issue of equity in terms of regional imbalances, differential participation of different groups and the policy of affirmative action for inclusive growth of higher education.

Expanding Access

The Indian higher education system has expanded manifold over the past six decades. The number of universities has increased from 20 in 1947 to over 400, colleges from less than 500 in 1947 to over 20,000 now. Enrolment has gone up from about 100,000 in 1950 to over 11 million now and enrolment ratio from less than 1 per cent in 1950 to about 10 per cent in 2007. Massive expansion has obviously enhanced access to higher education. In spite of large growth, however, India's GER, in relative terms, compares quite poorly with the advanced nations and many developing countries as well.

Interestingly, though access has been a key theme in the debates on higher education, the expansion of higher education until recently occurred primarily as a result of 'unplanned proliferation of institutions of higher learning' (MHRD, 1992). The main focus has been on consolidation and expansion of facilities in the existing institutions. Neither the National Policy on Education, 1986 (or the Programme of Action, 1992) nor the successive plans provided any explicit targets for enrolment expansion. In the Sixth Plan (1980–85), low priority was given to the expansion of educational facilities by way of new universities, centres for post-graduate studies, new departments and construction of buildings involving brick and mortar. In the Seventh Plan (1985–90), there was focus on making optimum use of the existing facilities in the universities/colleges, especially physical facilities. In the Eighth Plan (1992–97), emphasis continued on strengthening existing institutions, with a provision to support new departments and courses in developing universities if the need was justified.

The Ninth Plan (1997–2002) paid attention to higher education institutions in backward areas, hill areas and border areas to remove regional imbalances. There was also a thrust towards addressing the higher education needs of underrepresented social groups, namely SC/ST candidates, women, the disabled and minority candidates. This thrust continued in the Tenth Plan (2002–07) as well. Thus, the issue of access in the Ninth and the Tenth Plan was on equity in access. Adequate resources were not provided. New universities and colleges and departments were established to accommodate the hitherto underrepresented classes and communities in somewhat reckless manner, without due consideration to the resources available for their successful functioning. As the system expanded in this manner, there was democratisation of higher education. According to Béteille (2005), this was not a smooth and orderly process, and its consequences, at least in the short run, were not always beneficial. Academic standards were relaxed, sometimes abruptly and even arbitrarily, in the name of equality and justice.

The Indian experience of deteriorating standards with the universities becoming socially more inclusive is contrary to the experience in Europe. Between the middle of the 19th century and the middle of the 20th century, as the European universities became socially inclusive, they also gained academically, at least in the long run. In India, the drive to make the universities socially inclusive led to a sudden and dramatic increase in numbers without a proportionate increase in material and intellectual resources. Thus, academic standards were unsettled and placed in jeopardy until very recently.

With economic growth slowing down and public investment at very low levels, the decade of the 1970s saw large scale unemployment of graduates. There is a general view that primary, and to some extent secondary education are more effective instruments for promoting economic and social development. As a result, even within the education sector, higher education got lower priority in budget allocation. This has been the dominant view of the economists and policy makers alike at least until recently. In the context of higher education expansion in India, in 1970, Nobel Laureate Amartya Sen remarked, 'Right to higher education is the right of the educationally privileged to study further at the expense of the society irrespective of one's academic ability, and it is the right that is exercised by throwing children out of school' (Sen, 1970: 259).

Over the past couple of decades, the notion that the knowledge revolution (or the information society) is changing the nature of work requiring higher order skills has become increasingly insistent. For India, which followed a non-traditional pattern of development, availability of skilled manpower both for its growing services sector and its skill-intensive manufacturing sector is considered important. Thus, recent emphasis on higher education is primarily for economic reasons, while political and social factors were important in the past. Recent economic rationale has added a new impetus to higher education expansion.

It is for the first time that the Eleventh Plan (2007–12) document mentions explicit targets for enrolment in higher education, and public funding for higher education has also been increased significantly (see Box 2.1). The fact that there is reference to China illustrates a new confidence. Its need to meet both the growing needs of the economy and rising aspirations of young people suggests that the plan recognises the importance of higher education, both for social and economic development. A massive expansion of institutions of higher education has been planned to achieve this.

New Public Institutions

This proposed expansion includes setting up of 373 new colleges in districts with low enrolment ratio, setting up of 30 new central universities, setting up of eight IITs, seven IIMs and 37 other technical institutions (five IISERs, two SPAs, 10 NITs, 20 IIITs), and establishing

BOX 2.1 Higher education in the Eleventh Plan

The Eleventh Plan must also focus on the pressing need to expand capacity in our institutions of higher education and technical and professional education (engineering, medicine, law, etc.). The Gross Enrolment Ratio for higher education (percentage of the 18–23 age group enrolled in a higher education institution) currently is around 10 per cent whereas it is 25 per cent for many other developing countries. China has increased its GER in higher education from 10 per cent in 1998 to 21 per cent in 2005. We must aim at increasing the GER to 15 per cent by the end of the Plan and reaching 21 per cent by the end of Twelfth Plan. This is necessary not only to meet the needs of a growing economy, but also to meet the aspirations of younger people who see education as an essential requirement for advancement.

Source Planning Commission, 2007.

Access and Equity

50 centres for training and research in frontier areas. Of the 30 new central universities, 16 will come up in states that do not have a central university and 14 in states that provide land free of cost at attractive locations. The proposed universities are believed to have been modelled as unitary, non-affiliating universities on the pattern of the Jawaharlal Nehru and Hyderabad universities. This would be the biggest higher education expansion plan ever, much bigger than expansion in the 1960s when IITs and IIMs were set up. Ever since the announcement of these central institutions, there has been hectic political lobbying regarding the location of these institutions. While some of these institutions would ensure proper geographical spread and address issue of regional imbalances, there are apprehensions that several of these institutions may be set up at places that would suffer from location disadvantages and thus may never flourish. Nevertheless, as seen in Table 2.1, the location of most of these institutions has been finalised through a

TABLE 2.1 New institutions, locations and outlays

Number and type of institutions	Location	Eleventh Plan outlay	2008–09 outlay
16 New Central Universities	Jharkhand, Bihar, Orissa, Punjab, Haryana, Himachal Pradesh, Uttarakhand, J&K, Karnataka, Kerala, Tamil Nadu, Gujarat, Rajasthan, Goa#, MP$, Chhattisgarh$	2000 cr.	50 cr.
14 World-Class Central Universities	West Bengal (Kolkata), Assam (Guwahati), Orissa, Bihar, Maharashtra, Tamil Nadu, Karnataka, Andhra Pradesh, Gujarat, Rajasthan, Madhya Pradesh, Kerala, Punjab, UP	2800 cr.	60 cr.
8 New IITs & IT (BHU) to be Upgraded to IIT Status	Orissa (Bhubaneswar)*, Bihar (Patna)*, Gujarat (Gandhinagar)*, Punjab*, Andhra Pradesh (Hyderabad)*, Rajasthan*, Himachal Pradesh, Madhya Pradesh (Indore)	2000 cr.	50 cr.
7 New IIMs	Meghalya (Shillong)*, Jharkhand, Tamil Nadu, J&K, Chhattisgarh, Uttarakhand, Haryana	660 cr.	10 cr.

Source Compiled by author from media reports.

Notes *to start admissions in 2008–09 session; $existing universities to be taken over.
#state government declined for upgrading the state university to central university states.

tortuous political exercise reportedly steered by the Prime Minister himself. Though the Eleventh Plan outlays are substantial, only a small token provision has been made in the 2008–09 outlay for these institutions.

In any case, initial capacities in new institutions are usually small and they take several decades to mature and blossom, thus the expectation that these institutions would widen the base of quality higher education in the country anytime soon would be unreal. It is, however, expected that student intake in all these institutions will go up. For instance, it is proposed to be increased to 2,500 in each of the new IITs over time. There are, however, fears that these institutions might exacerbate the problem of faculty shortages that the existing institutions currently face. Thus, though an overall positive development, a lot will depend on how the entire plan of expansion unfolds over time.

In addition, several other government institutions have been or are being established by other ministries. Three Indian Institutes of Public Health are being set up at Hyderabad, Delhi and Gandhinagar through the Public Health Foundation of India, under the Ministry of Health and Family Welfare. Four new National Institute of Pharmaceutical Education and Research (NIPER) are being established at Ahmedabad, Hajipur, Hyderabad and Kolkata in addition to existing one at Mohali. The National Institute of Science Education and Research (NISER) has been set up at Bhubaneswar (Orissa) by the Department of Atomic Energy, and an Indian Institute of Space Science has come up near Thiruvananthapuram in Kerela under the Indian Space Research Organization. A Maritime University has been proposed at Chennai. Four more centres of the National Institute of Fashion Technology (NIFT) at Bhopal, Patna, Shillong and Kannur have been planned. Two Indian Institutes of Handloom Technology have been set up at Varanasi and Salem under the Ministry of Textiles. The Ministry of Information and Broadcasting plans a specialised School for Animation and Gaming at Pune. Six AIIMS-like hospitals are being set up at Patna, Raipur, Bhopal, Bhubaneswar, Jodhpur and Rishikesh.

Expansion by the national government, taking over the responsibility of state universities and setting up of new institutions by the various ministries is in sharp contrast to developments in China. China has been abandoning its Soviet-style system in favour of the Western model of multi-disciplinary universities. The numbers of major universities and colleges have been reduced from 387 to 212 to increase efficiency and boost competitiveness. Public universities overseen by the other ministries were merged with the ones under the Ministry of Education, and the Ministry has itself delegated its authority to the provinces, retaining direct supervision of just 70 first-tier universities.

New institutions are not coming up only under the government sector—hundreds of new private professional institutions are approved every year by the respective regulatory agencies. As seen in Table 2.2, during 2004-05, 627 new institutions were approved in engineering and technology, pharmacy, architecture, hotel management and catering technology, MBA and MCA. This growth may have slowed down marginally—with only about 456 new institutions approved in the year 2007-08, providing an additional intake capacity of 96,551 students (AICTE, 2007)—yet growth is still very significant and much rapid than that projected for government institutions by the government, and the number of private institutions continues to grow.

TABLE 2.2 New AICTE approvals during 2004–05

Discipline	PG	UG	Diploma	Total
Engineering & Technology	108	90	33	231
Pharmacy	33	129	54	216
Architecture	2	7	0	9
Hotel Management and Catering Technology	0	13	14	27
Master of Business Administration (MBA)	100	0	0	100
Master of Applications	44	0	0	44
Total	**287**	**239**	**101**	**627**

Source AICTE Annual Report, 2004-05.

Private Growth

It is realised that access to higher education is severely constrained when higher education is primarily public funded. As noted earlier in this chapter, there are significant private benefits accruing from higher education. Thus, there is a strong case for higher education to be funded by students and their families, at least partially. Despite this, Indian higher education is seen to be primarily publicly funded. The role of private financing—which has grown rapidly over the past two decades and shall continue to be so in the future (as noted in the next chapter)—in expanding access is often overlooked. Though private higher education enhances access, it is often viewed with suspicion and seen to compromise equity in access. Thus, private higher education has both positive and negative connotations and the two are closely intertwined.

In countries around the world, while overall trend has been growth in public financing of higher education at least in absolute terms, according to Hahn (2007), private finance has increased its role in the past two decades, particularly in the past decade. Though reliable data on the increasing role of private finance is not available, yet analysis of available data shows clearly that the rise in private financing of higher education is not an anomalous phenomenon but a global trend encompassing a majority of the world's population.

The single most important driver behind the rise of private finance is the explosion of private demand for higher education. This is due to two factors: demographics and economics. Demographic trends and improvements at lower levels of education have resulted in more people completing secondary education. Economic trends have brought about an increase in private returns to higher education, increasing the number of individuals who are willing to invest.

According to Levy (2008b), 'private higher education provides stark solutions to the dilemma of how to keep expanding access while not expanding public budgets.' While improving access, its impact on equity and quality are debatable. Thus, regulation becomes a central policy issue for determining the private higher education sector's role in the expansion of access. Even if the general disposition is that 'more is better', it does not follow that more is always better, depending on one's views on how and where the extra access is provided. It is therefore not surprising that public attitudes to private higher education kept changing along with socio-economic realities and economic policy. While the next chapter deals exclusively with private higher education, changing attitudes towards it are discussed next.

Access and Equity

Changing Attitudes towards Private Growth

In India, public policy has traditionally focused on public financing and the activities of the public higher education institutions. In 1985, while the private institutions were emerging in parts of the country, the government discussion document, *Challenges of Education: A Policy Perspective*, for the first time acknowledged the fact that a large number of private technical institutions had come up in the country. The document warned that private institutions were charging high fees for admission (called 'capitation fees') and were providing access to education on the basis of the ability to pay rather than on the basis of merit.

Whilst the National Policy on Education (NPE), 1986 made no direct reference to these developments, the two committees that reviewed the policy realised that while public spending on higher education was grossly inadequate, self-financing programmes might provide a solution by expanding capacity without increasing the government's financial contribution.[2] This gave legitimacy to full cost recovery from the students and made private self-financing institutions viable, particularly in fields of study for which students or their parents were willing to pay.

Whilst private institutions were emerging in different parts of the country, the government was coming around to the view that rapidly growing demand cannot be solely met by the public sector. There was direct reference to private higher education in policy discourse during the 1990s. The first indication of this paradigm shift became evident from the recommendations made in the government's Eighth Plan (1992–97) document. While discouraging opening of new conventional universities and colleges, the plan recommended the involvement of voluntary agencies and the private sector in higher education, with proper provisions for maintaining standards. The idea was to make higher education self-financing as far as possible.

Over the last decade there have been several policy statements that accept the role of private education. In 1998, the Prime Minister's Special Action Plan for Education recognised the role of the private sector in providing quality and cost effective education. It called for a comprehensive review of any laws and procedures that might hinder private participation in all segments of education. While addressing the Joint Session of the Parliament in 1999, the President of India categorically stated that the government would actively pursue private investment in higher and technical education.

In the same year, the Tenth Five Year Plan went a step further by defining the nature and scope for regulation of private higher education. According to it:

> Laws, rules and procedures for private, co-operative and NPO (not-for-profit organizations) supply of education must be modernized and simplified so that honest and sincere individuals and organizations can set up universities, colleges and schools. Oppressive controls on fees, teacher salaries, and infrastructure and staff strength must be eliminated. The regulatory system must be modernised based on economics of information and global best practices. Given the weak criminal justice system in our country; the regulatory system must also put greatest emphasis on fraud detection and punishment, while letting normal individuals to function normally. (Approach Paper for the Tenth Five Year Plan, 1999)

The controversial Birla–Ambani Report of 2000 suggested that a private universities bill should be passed and the user-pay principle should be enforced in higher education (Govt. of India, 2000). This issue was hotly debated at the meeting of the State Ministers for higher education, organised by the government at Bangalore on 11 January 2005. Though perceptions on the role of private initiative differed, there was a general consensus that there should be greater role of private sector in higher education, particularly in order to expand opportunities in the face of increasing pressure on public finances. However, there were differences in matters of details, and apprehensions about quality control and gross commercialisation if the private sector was allowed to operate unhindered. Later the same year, 64 eminent Indian educationists of the country deliberated on the issue in a National Seminar at New Delhi.[3] They favoured private investment in higher education, but wanted privatisation to be restricted to a 'minimum desirable level'.

Privatisation in general, and privatisation of higher education in particular is opposed by ideologues and teachers and student unions. For instance, the Left-wing Economist Professor Prabhat Patnaik warns that 'substantial privatization of higher education would create "organic intellectuals for the global job market", rather than creating "organic intellectuals of the people for individual thinking."'[4] Teachers and student unions fear that privatisation will commercialise education. They would instead like the government to spend more money on higher education.

The Planning Commission and the National Knowledge Commission (NKC) seem to favour private higher education on purely pragmatic grounds. In his letter dated 29 November 2006 to the Prime Minister, the Chairman of the NKC suggested that 'it is essential to stimulate private investment' in education as a means of extending educational opportunities (NKC, 2006b). It may be possible to leverage public resources, especially in the form of land grants, to attract more (not-for-profit) private investment. The plan panel desires to 'evolve an appropriate policy framework for facilitating greater inflow of private investments in education' (*The Economic Times*, 2007). It has suggested that there 'should be sufficient flexibility for centre-state and private sector participation under various PPP models.'

From reports appearing in newspapers, the nodal ministry for higher education, that is, the ministry of Human Resource Development (HRD) appears to think otherwise. The ministry is opposed to the suggestion of the plan panel on the grounds that facilitating private investments will 'provide new impetus to commercialising education' (*The Economic Times*, 2007). The Ministry fears this will 'go against national education policy, judgment of Supreme Court and even the national common minimum programme that promises to provide equality of opportunity to all areas such as education.'

There appears to be continuing confusion between means (ways of increasing supply of higher education so every one has access) and ends (ensuring enough supply for all). By focusing on ensuring 'equality' and 'non-commercialisation' of the means, we are losing track of the fact that we are moving further and further away from achieving the end. Though public policy has grown out of this thinking in approach to other important objectives like providing food, clothing, shelter and health care for all, it is still mired in it in the area of higher education. This thinking is reflected in many government reports, even in recent times.

The Central Advisory Board of Education Committee on Financing of Higher and Technical Education in its report in 2005 observed,

> Growth of self-financing courses in higher education institutions and private higher education should be regulated to avoid vulgar forms of commercialization. While stating that philanthropy in education should be encouraged by the government through appropriate fiscal incentives, the committee noted that the 'overall role of private sector in education cannot but be limited' (CABE, 2005a).

Thus, there continues to be a lack of clarity in attitude towards private higher education. It is viewed with suspicion. There is a notion that all private activities are motivated by considerations of profit and greed. It is also argued that encouraging private provision would amount to dilution of the State's constitutional responsibility. This marks the ambivalence in public policy on the issue. As a result private higher education has continued to grow in a policy vacuum. For clearing these several ambiguities, judicial interventions have become order of the day. More details on the current regulatory regime for the private sector are in Chapter 7.

This position needs to be understood in the context of Indian polity. Seen as anti-poor, political parties are usually cautious in their support for private higher education. It is only in recent times that there is growing acceptance of the private sector's role. Reminding his party colleagues about the merit of intelligent intervention on crucial policy issues, Rahul Gandhi, the Congress general secretary, recently firmly articulated the need for private investment in education (*The Indian Express*, 2007d).[5] He pointed out that decades of social control have restricted higher education to dreadful state universities and some shady private initiatives, and warned that the skill shortages that are driving up the salaries could become a binding constraint for growth soon. Later, in March 2008, even the HRD minister who has been usually wary of private participation in education welcomed private partnership in the sphere of education, saying that the available resources were not in keeping with the expansion in the area (*The Hindu*, 2008).[6]

Recently, the Planning Commission's High Level Group on Services Sector has found that it is necessary to involve the private and corporate sector fully for expanding facilities for higher education. The group goes on to suggest that for this purpose the private sector needs to be given freedom in respect of fees and even 'for-profit' entities be allowed in higher education. The group recommends that to begin with only technical education be opened up to for-profit enterprises. The private sector institutions should of course be subject to regulation, but only on matters related to curriculum and standards of staffing and physical infrastructure, not for fees and salaries (Government of India, 2008).

Overall, there is now growing realisation that the private higher education sector is inevitably destined to grow. Thus, there is need to build safeguards to prevent dilution of quality and ensure that private participation does not lead to exclusion.

Promoting Equity

Equity, the quality of being fair and impartial in higher education is viewed as the ability of the brightest students to study in the best universities, regardless of their socio-economic backgrounds. However, family backgrounds and places of residence do have influence over access to higher education opportunities. There is a large variation in availability of universities and colleges across states and rural and urban areas. Disparities in enrolment amongst various socio-economic and ethnic groups exist. Despite significant improvements, enrolment of women continues to be less. In a recent conference of vice chancellors of universities, it was noted that there would be a focus in the Eleventh Plan on the inclusiveness in higher education, with schemes that focus on regions and groups with lower enrolment ratio (UGC, 2007). Regions or groups identified for the purpose and strategy in each case would be as follows:

1. Rural and urban disparities—enhance access to rural population;
2. Inter-state variation—focus on states that have lower GER than the national average;
3. Gender disparities—special attention to higher education of women;

4. Inter-religious group disparities—special focus on promoting higher education amongst Muslims;
5. Social groups within religion—special focus on farmers, agricultural labourers, manual workers and lower castes within Muslims and Christians;
6. Disparities across income groups—support to poor and marginalised to access higher education;
7. Disparities across occupation group—special attention to agricultural labourers, other labourers and the self-employed in rural areas, and casual labourers in the urban areas;
8. Inter-caste disparities in GER—special attention for promotion of higher education among the SCs, ST and OBC.

The following section looks at regional imbalances in educational facilities, various types of disparities in enrolments and policy of correction in the form of affirmative action to promote equity in access to higher education.

Regional Imbalances

The spatial distribution of universities and colleges is skewed. There is huge variation in size, both in terms of population and area of the 35 states and union territories in the country. Even if this is factored in, spatial distribution of university level institutions is highly uneven across states. While five states—though the smaller ones—have just one university each, there are five other states that have in excess of 20 university level institutions. Sixteen states do not have a single central university, while two states, namely Uttar Pradesh and Delhi have four each. Deemed universities, whose numbers increased rapidly in recent years are concentrated in Maharashtra and Tamil Nadu.

Colleges are also not spread uniformly across the states. It is seen that while some states have less than five colleges per block,[7] many have from five to 10 colleges per block and few states have more than 10 colleges per block. Such imbalances are even more glaring with respect to the professional colleges that are mainly concentrated in a few states, though there is increasing dispersal now.

Though regional imbalances are a matter of concern, yet this imbalance is seen to be a worldwide phenomenon, with clustering of higher education institutions in some states or regions. With greater student mobility at higher education level, students from states or regions with poor facilities tend to migrate to cities with better facilities. This is evident from the fact that students in large numbers from all over the country, particularly from the North-Eastern states and Bihar, flock to universities and colleges in Delhi. In case of professional education, student mobility is even greater. With most institutions for professional education having hostel facilities, regional balance is a lesser concern.

Regional imbalances in higher education facilities arise due to natural clustering of institutions of higher education in and around metropolitan and urban areas. Such clustering is a global phenomenon. For instance, there are more than two hundred university level institutions in the Boston area in the United States. While new and large public institutions could foster economic development in the region where they are located, yet at times attempts to set up such institutions in remote and far-flung areas could backfire. There are cases of several public institutions that could not flourish due to their locational disadvantage. Thus, policies for geographical spread of institutions have to be carefully crafted.

Disparities in Enrolment

Disparities in GER as seen between male and female, Muslims, Hindus and others, poor and non-poor from rural and urban areas, Scheduled Castes (SC), Scheduled Tribes (ST), Other Backward Classes (OBC) and others are evident from Figure 2.1. Enrolment of women has seen a consistent upward trend from less than 10 per cent of the total enrolment in 1950–51 to about 40 per cent now. A similar growth trend is observed for students from the disadvantaged sections of the society. Expansion of higher education over the years has democratised higher education. Despite this, there are significant inequities in participation. To varying degrees, gender disparity, inter-religious group disparity, disparity across income groups, inter-caste disparity and rural–urban disparity all exist. The disparity is most glaring for the poor (particularly from the rural areas) and the STs. While the overall GER as per NSS (2003)

FIGURE 2.1   Disparities in enrolment

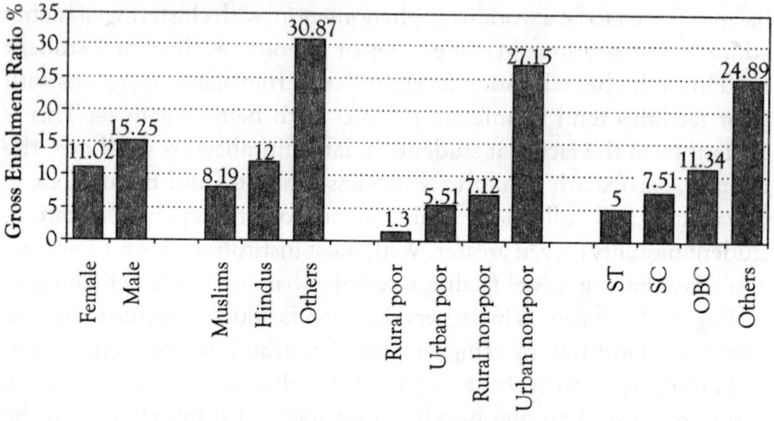

Source Author (compiled from various reports of UGC).

was 13.22, it was merely 1.3 for the rural poor and 5.51 for the urban poor. While positive discrimination is practiced for the SCs and the STs for many years and has helped address the problem of inter-caste disparity to some extent, positive discrimination to address income disparity and rural–urban disparity is needed.

SES data for 2004–05 that provides programme-wise disaggregated enrolment data is laid down in Table 2.3. It is seen that though participation of women students and students from the SCs and the STs has risen significantly, participation of girls, SCs and STs in professional, science and commerce programmes is proportionately less.

Further, it is seen that though the enrolment in higher education for the country as a whole is increasing over the years, it varies widely across different states. On analysis of these differences, it is seen to be linked to the variation in government expenditure on higher education, per capita income, percentage of people below poverty line (BPL) and the extent of urbanisation in different states. Besides, states with a higher enrolment in universities and colleges are those with higher ratio of urban population and a lower percentage of population BPL (Anandakrishnan, 2004).

Access and Equity

TABLE 2.3   Programme-wise enrolment (2004–05 as on 30.9.2004)

Programme	Total	% Girls	% SC	% ST
PhD/D.Sc./D.Phil	55,352	41.2	5.8	2.4
MA	469,291	46.6	16.2	4.9
M.Sc	198,719	45.7	10.4	2.8
M.Com	122,257	34.0	9.2	3.0
Post-graduate–sub total	790,267	44.4	13.6	4.1
B.A./B.A. Hons	3,772,216	43.9	14.9	5.2
B.Sc./B.Sc. (Hons.)	1,490,785	38.9	11.3	3.3
B.Com/B.Com. (Hons.)	1,465,028	36.6	8.5	3.3
B.E./B.Arch	696,609	23.7	8.5	3.1
Undergraduate–sub total	7,424,638	39.6	12.3	4.3
Medicine, Dentistry, Nursing, Pharmacy, Ayurvedic, Unani and Homeopathy	256,748	34.7	11.5	3.7
B. Ed./B.T	155,192	43.8	12.4	5.8
Others*	3,095,099	37.9	6.0	2.1
Total enrolment	11,777,296	39.4	10.7	3.7

Source Selected Educational Statistics (2004–05), MHRD, Govt. of India, 2007.
Note *Includes data of open and distance education in respect of 11 (out of 30) states.

Viewed in terms of income of the states, most states that show above-average enrolment are also the ones with per capita income above the national average as shown in Table 2.4. The coefficient of correlation between them is 0.5663. This suggests that the two are positively correlated, though the direction of this relationship cannot be established. It is difficult to say whether higher State Domestic Product (SDP) per capita leads to greater participation in higher education or alternatively, if the higher GER would result in greater prosperity measured in terms of higher SDP per capita. Despite the difficulty, this is often the rationale provided to push for expansion of higher education.

Analysis of GER on the basis of enrolment capacity within the state, however, does not take care of students from the state who move to other states for higher education. Considering high mobility in case of higher education, particularly professional education, problem of regional

TABLE 2.4   GER in higher education and per capita net SDP

State/Union Territory	Net SDP at current prices (2002–03) in Rs per Capita	GER in 2002–03 %
Andhra Pradesh	18,661	9.51
Assam	11,755	8.67
Bihar	6,015	7.3
Jharkhand	9,955	7.27
Gujarat	22,047	9.65
Haryana	26,632	10.56
Himachal Pradesh	22,576	12.76
Karnataka	18,521	8.12
Kerala	21,853	9.92
Madhya Pradesh	11,438	7.66
Chhattisgarh	11,893	7.77
Maharashtra	26,386	12.3
Orissa	10,340	8.71
Punjab	25,855	8.53
Rajasthan	12,753	8.77
Sikkim	20,456	6.29
Tamil Nadu	21,433	10.91
Uttar Pradesh	10,289	7.03
West Bengal	18,756	8.21
Delhi	47,477	10.94

Source Economic Survey 2004–05 and CABE Committee on Higher Education Financing (2005).

Notes Data for major states for the year 2002–03; GER: Gross Enrolment Ratio; SDP: State Domestic Product.

imbalances may be less severe in terms of education opportunities, except in case of programmes that have state domicile requirement for admission.

Affirmative Action

In higher education, affirmative action has been the most obvious and controversial policy of correction to achieve the equity objective. This recognises the fact that *equality* (the state of being equal) might not be *equity* (the quality of being fair and impartial). Removal of all barriers to access and differences in public resources might not eliminate the effects of family background and private resources. In societies where inequalities are large and take many different forms, there is almost an infinite list of inequities that affect the ability to take advantage of educational opportunities. Thus, relaxation of admission standards is often resorted to achieve equity objective. Such policies are stridently opposed by those who stand to lose. When it involves access to the highest-status and best-paid employment, such battles become ferocious (Grubb and Lazerson, 2004: 229–30).

Earlier parents were more directly responsible for the success of their children, either by continuing them in their family business or trade, or by finding appropriate apprenticeships or marriages. Rich children got higher levels of education than the children from poor households, but the occupational relevance of education—both in terms of occupational curricula, and in the sense of finding relevant employment was distinctly limited. Now the parents work for their children's success largely by gaining them access to the type of education that leads them to high status jobs. Thus, entry to most prestigious educational institutions, such as the IITs and the IIMs, by default provides access to the highest-status and best-paid employment. Families can go to any length to ensure that.

Because of the importance of caste identity in the Indian polity (as noted earlier in this chapter), caste has been the basis of preferential treatment for admission in institutions of higher education since independence. This is ostensibly done to correct historic wrongs and injustices. Numerical quotas have been in vogue for the SCs (15 per cent) and the STs (7.5 per cent) at the national level since independence. Later, some states also introduced quota-based reservation for the OBCs—a 27 per cent quota. There have been costs (in terms of loss of efficiency) and benefits (in serving equity objectives) of this policy. However, the equity–efficiency tradeoff has rarely been empirically studied.

Though not intended to be in place for perpetuity, the possibility of rollback of quota-based reservation, once started, is rare. With high stakes involved, particularly for admission into the more selective institutions, this privilege over a period of time becomes an entitlement, and no political party would like to isolate the important constituencies that benefit from reservations. Numerical quotas in institutions of higher education, particularly the more reputed institutions that provide access to high status and best-paid jobs have been an inflammatory issue and contested consistently. It remains and will continue to be a divisive and an emotive issue in India unless all political parties decide not to use caste, creed and religion in electoral politics.

While state-owned institutions had this policy of reservation for decades, some states were extending it to private unaided institutions that now outnumber the state institutions. This policy was, however, struck down by the Supreme Court judgement on 12 August 2005 in *PA Inamdar and Others versus States of Maharashtra and Others*. The court observed that '.... neither the policy of reservation can be enforced by the state nor any quota of percentage of admissions can be carved out to be appropriated by the state in private unaided institutions....' According to the ruling, any affirmative action on behalf of the disadvantaged castes would be unconstitutional if applied to private unaided institutions. Unwilling to accept this situation, the Parliament amended the Constitution through the 93rd Amendment Act, inserting Article 15(5) in the Constitution. This enabled the state to make any special provision, by law, for the advancement of socially and educationally backward classes of citizens or for the SCs and the STs in connection to their admission to educational institutions, including private educational institutions, whether aided or unaided by the state, except minority educational institutions.

With this constitutional amendment, governments could enact laws for caste-based reservation in private unaided institutions within their jurisdiction. For its part, the central government is to implement this reservation policy in the centrally funded institutions and deemed universities. For this purpose, the central government enacted the Central Educational Institutions (Reservation in Admission) Act, 2006 to provide for reservation in admission to certain central government–run educational institutions (including the IITs and the IIMs) for students belonging to the SC, ST and OBC categories. As expected, issue of reservations in central institutions, particularly in the reputed IITs and IIMs raised a storm of protest not seen in recent years. Both the

93rd Amendment Act and the Central Act of 2006 were challenged in the Supreme Court and heard by a five-judge Constitution bench over several months.

Meanwhile, in response to nationwide protest against the new reservation policy, the government declared its intentions to increase the number of seats in the affected central institutions proportionately (54 per cent) so that seats available to general category students remained the same. An oversight committee was also appointed to estimate additional financial resources required for the purpose. Though there were several reservations about the pressure on infrastructure and facilities and further exacerbating faculty shortages due to this increase, the government had made it clear that all these would be addressed and the rollout would be done in a phased manner. The Eleventh Plan outlay made financial provisions to accommodate this expansion.[8]

Finally, the much-awaited long and very complicated judgement of the Supreme Court in *Ashoka Kumar Thakur versus Union of India* case was read out on 10 April 2008. The judgement clarified that the 93rd Constitution Amendment Act does not violate the basic structure of the Constitution as it relates to aided educational institutions. The central act of 2006 has also been declared valid, subject to exclusion of the creamy layer. The quantum of 27 per cent reservation for the OBCs has also been declared legal with a proviso that the inclusion of specific groups in the OBC category be reviewed every five years. By excluding the creamy layer, the Supreme Court has made it clear that constitutional provisions bar discrimination based only on caste; compensatory discrimination has to take into account other factors such as social and economic advancement as well. Such exclusion was made mandatory in the context of reservations for the OBCs in central services as well.

While the recent judgement appears to have settled the issue and reservation for the OBCs in central institutions would be rolled out from the academic year 2008–09 after almost two years of uncertainty, several issues remain unsettled. On the creamy layer issue, the court has given a great deal of discretion to the government. According to the Political Scientist Pratap Bhanu Mehta, 'This will potentially be a great area of uncertainty in the future' (Mehta, 2008). The Supreme Court has refused to pronounce its judgement on the issue of whether private unaided institutions will come under the purview of reservations. Thus regulatory uncertainty on this issue is likely to continue for a long time. The Court has also upheld special status for minority institutions and exempted them from the purview of reservations. On closer scrutiny of the judgement, Mehta observes that the court observes that the 'current scheme of reservation remains at best very blunt in targeting' (Mehta, 2008).

During the fiery debate on the issue of reservations over the past two years, there were never any doubts on the need for affirmative action. The issue has always been about targeting. It is a fact that students from poor and weaker sections of the society tend to lose out in brutal competition for entry to educational institutions, due to the lack of access to quality education at lower levels and supplementary tutoring due to family circumstances. Considering that education, particularly higher education, is an effective instrument for social mobility, this deprivation creates undesirable inequities in the society. Given this reality, there is a case for an affirmative action policy to safeguard their interests.

Affirmative action policy, however, is to be based on certain principles. The first principle is that higher education should be equally accessible to all on the basis of merit as per Article 26 of the Universal Declaration of Human Rights. Any compromise on the principle of merit creates a sense of injustice in the minds of the youth that have grown up in a society where caste does not matter at all. They fail to understand the logic of caste-based reservation in this time and age. Thus, any relaxation in admission standards has to be relative so that the principle of merit is not completely ignored. Second, the principle of equality of opportunity and non-discrimination on grounds of religion, caste etc., are basic fundamental rights under the Constitution of India. Therefore, a composite index of deprivation rather than merely caste would be useful. Finally, in the changed global scenario, competitiveness of nations comes from the talent of its citizens. The signal that goes out when half of the people with top qualifications in India are not on the basis of their merit but for other considerations will result in India losing its long-term competitiveness.

Based on the principles laid down above, an affirmative action policy could be crafted to safeguard the interests of all those who are being deprived of quality higher education opportunities. Such policy could be based on a provision of deprivation bonus for all students coming from lower socio-economic backgrounds and backward regions in competition for entry to educational institutions, to compensate for the actual deprivation suffered by them. Deprivation bonus should be on the basis of transparent criteria such as students from families in the below poverty line (BPL) lists, students from educational institutions in rural and backward regions, physically disabled students, etc. Such bonus should not result in lowering the bar on merit for admission by more than 10 per cent on an average.

There is empirical evidence to suggest that a mix of students of varying merit could be a socially optimal strategy, yet if the proportion of the less meritorious and/or the extent of shortfall in their merit is high, the teaching–learning process suffers and the academic standard of the whole class goes down. Within this broad framework, institutions could have their scheme of affirmative action depending on the programme of study. Further, the issues relating to socio-economic backwardness vary from state to state—the states therefore could have their own policies for affirmative action for state level institutions. While devising affirmative action policy in India, there is the possibility of taking lessons from experience of other countries as noted in Box 2.2.

Back home, there are good practices of affirmative action that have potential of being replicated. Initiated in the 1990s, Jawaharlal Nehru University at New Delhi uses a system of awarding deprivation points to students hailing from backward districts. Other Backward Caste students, whose parents pay income tax, are excluded. Female OBC students get more points than their male counterparts. The maximum number of points is limited to 10, so that the sanctity of the entrance tests is maintained. While such a system has helped in getting more OBC students, it does not compromise on quality (*The Indian Express*, 23 April 2007). Such creative approach to affirmative action is needed.

BOX 2.2   International experience in affirmative action

In the United States, most educational institutions have affirmative action policies based on gender and colour (these are visible and biological differences, rather than differences created by the society or polity). These policies are essentially to have a diversity of student population in their enlightened self-interest. There is no pre-determined quota system. Students from Afro-American communities (blacks) and women are given some advantage in competition for entry to higher education institutions. This is completely decentralised, with the institutions enjoying great autonomy in the practice and the manner in which their affirmative action policies are designed and implemented.

In the United Kingdom, students coming from disadvantaged schools are given points to compete with students that have access to better schools with a view to provide opportunities to students who are otherwise meritorious but are not able to compete due to lack of opportunities at school level.

Source *The Economist* (various issues).

Affirmative action policies are more effective at lower levels of education. Therefore, these could be graded by the level of education. This would enable the deprived students to build capacities at lower levels to compete at higher levels. Facilities could be created for supplementary tutoring at different levels to enable deprived students to compete. The number of Navodaya Vidyalayas started with the objective of nurturing talent from rural areas could be increased or doubled. Despite affirmative action, the students from poor families will continue to be deprived of educational opportunities due to the rising cost of education at all levels. Therefore, the issue of affordability should be addressed simultaneously.

Affirmative action policy in the country should be based on providing equality of opportunity for higher education to all based on merit and work towards a non-divisive casteless society. It should be guided by Nehru's vision:

I have referred (above) to efficiency and to our getting out of traditional ruts. This necessitates our getting out of the old habit of reservations and particular privileges being given to this caste or that group.... I dislike any kind of reservation, more particularly in services. I react strongly against anything which leads to inefficiency and second-rate standards...if we go in for reservation on communal and caste basis. (Nehru, 1989: 456–57)

Thus, concern for efficiency and standards are crucial while designing an effective policy of correction.

Crafting an appropriate policy would require a trade-off between excellence and equity. The objective should be to mine raw talent that might remain deprived and hidden due to academic competition. The existing admission processes give undue advantage to the rich. An effort to push one section of society ahead of other for any other reason would create divisions in society and hurt the country's competitiveness in human resources. Though quota-based reservation policy has been preferred in India since it was found most workable, but considering the overall implications of such a policy, there is a case for better policy design in affirmative action. This policy should actually be able to eliminate sources of deprivation of the disadvantaged people. It should be flexible and be able to cater to the diversity of needs of such people by allowing different types of institutions to address their concerns in different manners.

It is widely believed that quota-based reservations in the present form raise issues of fairness and the constitutional requirement of equal treatment and efficiency. They also fragment the society. With the creamy layer excluded, defining such a layer is difficult. The NKC, two members of which resigned in the wake of the controversy surrounding reservations in central institutions, advocates a comprehensive frame-work that accounts for multidimensionality of differences in educational opportunities available to the students, and the usage deprivation index as a tool for positive affirmative action policies in the country (NKC, 2006).

Kirit Parikh, a member of the Planning Commission suggests a scheme that does not compromise on fairness and merit:

> Admission could be based on merit list adjusted in a transparent manner for differences in nurture to reflect true potential. While one way is to award deprivation points based on different attributes of deprivation, but in such cases awarding points is subjective and open to question. A more objective way would be to use performance in say school leaving examination for different sub groups and calculate handicap points based on differences between the average score of a subgroup and the highest average sub group. After adjusting this handicap, the admission

should be strictly on merit basis. Handicap points may be updated every three years. Such a system will not destroy the incentive for the people from disadvantaged groups from working hard. The creamy layer would automatically move to another subgroup with a lower handicap value. Over time, handicaps would disappear. (Parikh, 2007)

In sum, higher education is viewed as the most potent tool to address the problem of inequity in society, but it is almost impossible to completely do away with the influence of family background. This provides the underpinning to the policy of affirmative action in higher education. Thus, providing access to the less privileged in institutions of higher education while simultaneously maintaining quality will continue to be a major policy concern.

Conclusion

This chapter examines two critical issues concerning higher education: access and equity. While economic rationale and the skills agenda take a central place in the discourse on higher education, the issue of expanding access has been intimately associated with the rising aspirations in the recent years. A young population and improvements in school education have put pressure on the higher education system to expand. Over the past 60 years, it is the unplanned proliferation of universities and colleges, rather than proactive, intelligent interventions that have expanded access to higher education. With the recent focus on inclusive growth, there is now a clear direction to the expansion of access.

The issue of access is related to the size and nature of public funding for higher education. Due to financial limitations, there are constraints to the enhancement of access. Thus, access has improved largely due to expansion of private higher education in recent years. The impact of such expansion on equity and quality are debatable. As the socio-economic realities change and there is a gradual shift towards pro-market economic policies, public attitudes to private higher education have changed. Currently, almost 60 per cent school pass outs go on for higher education. Hence, there could be pipeline constraint in further expansion of higher education.

Access and Equity

Though with increased enrolment various disparities are less stark now, yet these persist. Gender disparity is decreasing, but at 4 to 6 per cent, it is still significant. Inter-caste disparities—with the enrolment of ST candidates being the lowest, the enrolment of SC candidates lower and that of OBC slightly lower than the general castes—are still high. Inter-religious disparities are stark, particularly lower participation of Muslims in comparison to others. With enrolment in rural areas being the one-third or one-fourth of that in urban areas, rural–urban divide is large. There is a wide inter-state variation in enrolment. The North-Eastern States, Bihar, West Bengal and even Karnataka have much lower enrolment in higher education than the national average.

With changes in the Indian polity, inclusive growth is central to the development agenda. Opportunities for higher education are viewed as the most potent tool to address the problem of such inequalities. The reform process over the past decade or so has created interpersonal, inter-state and rural–urban inequalities. There is an impression that the country's boom has mainly benefited the upper Hindu castes, the cities and certain regions of the country. Such people get access to the highest-status, best-paid jobs by ensuring that their children are admitted to high-quality institutions, which are very few in the country. Since family background operates in many ways to give an edge to the children of privileged parents for entry in these elite institutions, a policy of correction becomes necessary. Such policies are stridently opposed by those who stand to lose and seen to be compromising on excellence.

Thus, as the country adopts pro-market policies with outward orientation in several economic sectors, access policy is not necessarily in conformation to the pro-market policies. The issue of inclusive growth and equity in access dominates the discourse on higher education in the country. These developments have to be viewed in the context of the changes in the Indian society and the Indian polity and their influences on the policy process.

◆ ◆ ◆

3

Private Higher Education

It is unfortunate that in the present age of trade and commerce, money has entered the field of education as well. In these times, it may be impossible to divorce education from money and materialism.

Dr Rajendra Prasad[1]

THE private sector is the fastest growing segment in higher education in many countries around the world. During the past few years, more private institutions than public ones have been established in most developing countries and emerging economies of the world. About USD 400 billion is spent on private higher education annually. This is about 17 per cent of the global spending on higher education (Spencer, 2008).

While there has been a long tradition of private education in India, prior to independence it was primarily philanthropic. After Independence, when the demand for educational opportunities arose, the public education system expanded to meet this demand. When this demand outpaced the supply, private institutions emerged on the scene. Initially, private institutions were confined to the school sector. By 1980, private schools had a significant presence and continued to grow steadily and by 2004, almost one-third of all institutions for Class 10 and Class 12 were in the private sector.

As noted in Chapter 1, private institutions in the higher education sector are a post-1980 phenomenon. Until recently, all universities were public universities, but the colleges were allowed to be established on self-financing basis after 1980. Prior to 1980, private colleges were brought under government financing in a move that could be termed 'publicisation' of Indian higher education. Recurrent costs, particularly teachers' salaries were paid through government grant. These were referred to as private aided institutions or government-dependent private institutions. In recent years, private universities on self-financing basis have been allowed to be set up. Thus, there have been three phases in the growth of private higher education in the country and the distinction between the public and private sector is somewhat blurred.

This chapter maps the growth of private higher education in India. First, a distinction has been attempted on what could possibly be referred to as private institution in the Indian context. Then, the growth of private aided institutions has been examined before discussing private colleges and private universities. Prior to private universities being allowed in the country, degree-granting mandate was given to private institutions by declaring them as deemed universities. Thus, the growth trend of deemed universities, particularly the private deemed universities has been discussed next. Independent foreign providers are rare and most of the foreign provision is through partnership, mainly with private providers. This is discussed in the subsequent section. Private expansion has gone hand in hand with the expansion of professional education. Growth of professional education has been analysed in the section that follows. Afterwards, the growth in private share of institutions and enrolment is tracked. Institutional diversity, particularly in terms of new types of providers is then examined. The Indian experience with private growth has been analysed in a comparative perspective in the global context. And finally, prospects of private growth are analysed in this chapter before drawing conclusions on private higher education in the country.

Public–Private Distinction

Difference between a public and a private institution is usually seen along two dimensions–ownership and financing. Figure 3.1 shows four possible types of public and private institutions along the ownership

FIGURE 3.1 Typology of public and private institutions

		Ownership	
		Public	Private
Financing	**Public**	Government institutions	Government dependent private (or private aided) institutions
	Private	Government independent institutions	Private institutions

and financing dimensions. If the government promotes and sets up an institution, it is referred to as a public institution. On the other hand, an institution promoted and set up by a private promoter is referred to as a private institution. The word 'private' is used interchangeably with 'non-government', and the word 'public' with 'government'. The institutions in the other two quadrants, those that are set by the government and are now able to generate resources to meet all their recurrent costs and those that were set up by private promoters but now depend on government for recurrent grants are also usually referred to as government institutions. Thus, private institutions are only those set up by the private sector and also run by it. Such institutions alone shall be the subject matter of this chapter, though some discussion on private aided institutions in the following section would be in order.

In terms of financing, it is essential to distinguish between the initial capital cost for setting up of an institution and the obligation to meet the recurrent costs. Since, promoters—public or private—make the initial investment; therefore distinction in terms of financing is essentially about the source of recurrent expenses. There are private institutions in India that get operating funds from the government. Such institutions are referred to as private aided institutions. The unaided private institutions are known as private institutions. These are financially independent institutions, and are also referred to as self-financing institutions. Many government institutions (for example, the IIMs at Ahmedabad, Bengaluru and Kolkata) are able to generate their operating expenses internally and can be referred to as government unaided institutions. Though small currently, their numbers are increasing.

There is yet another dimension along which higher education institutions can be viewed: control. Control has to be seen from an academic as well as an administrative angle. Administrative control is usually linked with financing. Therefore, financially independent institutions have little administrative control, while the funded institutions are under the administrative control of their respective funding agencies. Funding of the central universities, a few deemed universities and some colleges—mainly Delhi-based—is done through the UGC. The UGC also provides development grants to state institutions. The IITs, the IIMs, the NITs and some technical institutions are funded directly by the central government. Remaining universities and colleges are either funded by the respective state governments or do not receive any public funds at all.

The academic control over the institution depends on the degree-granting power and programme of study. University level institutions have degree-granting powers, while colleges do not and are therefore subject to strong academic control of the respective affiliating universities. Universities have academic autonomy subject to some, usually very weak oversight of the UGC. In addition to its role as a buffer body for the funding of higher education, the UGC is responsible for determination and coordination of (academic) standards in universities and colleges in the country. The affiliating universities are all government universities. Therefore, all colleges are subject to indirect control of the government. Some programmes of study culminate in the award of professional degrees that are subject to regulation of the respective professional councils. These councils regulate the practice in those particular professions and therefore exercise strong controls over institutions that award professional degrees.

Table 3.1 summarises higher education institutions according to the nature of their ownership and financing, and the extent of academic and administrative control over them. The few foreign institutions that exist in the country are outside the existing regulatory framework and are not subjected to academic or administrative control except perhaps of their parent institution abroad.

From the above discussion, it is clear that various categories of institutions are subject to different levels of control. Their behaviour

TABLE 3.1   Ownership and financing of institutions

Type of institution	Ownership	Financing	Control Academic	Control Administrative
University	Public	Public	Weak	Strong
Private University	Private	Private	Weak	Weak
Govt. Deemed University	Public	Public	Weak	Moderate
Private Deemed University	Private	Private	Weak	Weak
Government College	Public	Public	Strong	Strong
Private aided College	Private	Public	Strong	Moderate
Private College	Private	Private	Strong	Weak
Foreign Institutions	Private	Private	No	No

Source Compiled by the author.

has also been subject to change over time. Public institutions now behave more like private enterprises, while private institutions are engaged in philanthropy. In the public institutions, there is a rise in self-financing programmes, projects are earned on competitive basis, private donations are solicited and the institutions are engaged in a variety of commercial activities. On the other hand, private institutions seek research funding and student aid from public sources. Thus, public and private institutions could be seen as one continuum rather than two distinct sectors.

Rather than making a distinction between a public and a private institution, Bray (1998) describe this as privatisation process. According to him, this is a process of moving away from public ownership, financing and/or control to more private ownership, financing and/or control. A change in one of them does not necessarily demand a change in the other two. There could even be simultaneous movements in opposite directions. A discussion on private higher education is therefore a review of the process of privatisation.

Another distinction is often made on whether or not an institution is for-profit or not-for-profit. Though all institutions in the formal system of higher education are not-for-profit institutions by law, yet many of the institutions, particularly private institutions, exhibit characteristics of for-profit entities. This will be evident from the discussion in the subsequent section that tracks the growth of private colleges in the

1980s. Public–private partnerships are common in the Indian system. Private colleges affiliated to public universities are public–private partnership, where the strengths of each sector are harnessed. Despite the blurring of boundaries between the public and private sector, this chapter is primarily concerned with institutions that are set up by the private promoters and also run by them. These are also financially independent. Before the discussion on private institutions, a brief discussion on private aided institutions follows in the next section.

Private Aided Institutions

Of the 500 colleges that existed at the time of independence in 1947 in India, many were private colleges. Such colleges continued to come up even after Independence. However, in its eagerness to spread higher education, the government took much of the financial responsibilities of these colleges through a Grant-in-aid (GIA) system during the 1960s and 1970s.

Under the GIA system—a form of supply-side financing—while the upfront cost is borne by the private sector, the government provides money to meet recurrent costs and sometimes capital costs. The GIA is often linked to teachers' salaries, which were placed at par with teachers in government institutions as in Kerala in the 1960s. This model was soon adopted in other states and continues to be the dominant form of financing education at all levels. The GIA model was responsible for major expansion of the education system till about 1980. The main push for expansion of the private aided sector was to safeguard the interest of teachers and staff who were paid poorly by the private managements.

While taking over the financing of private institutions, the government extended its control over their functioning as well. This was inevitable, and conforms to international experience that public financing brings in regulations that undermine autonomy of institutions. Student fees in private aided colleges were brought down to the level of fees in government colleges; though they continued to enjoy some freedom in levying other charges such as admissions fees, library fees, college development fees, and so on. The government regulated recruitment and admissions in these institutions to ensure quality and equity. Salary discrimination between government college teachers and private college teachers was no longer allowed. With price controls and cost underwriting, such private aided colleges became complacent. Efficiency gains expected from private management were lost and quality also deteriorated. Private colleges that were legally private but publicly financed dominated the higher education landscape until 1980. As a result, the earlier state-supervised system changed to a state-controlled system of higher education, bringing with it the demerits of a state-controlled system.

In effect, this led to the *de facto* 'publicisation' of private higher education. With government regulation and government zeal to protect teachers' interests, standards of many private institutions that had set high academic standards over the years deteriorated. It is also seen as a serious blow to the community-led private initiatives in higher education, as evident from experience in Bihar (noted in Box 3.1). Bihar could have been an extreme case, but most states followed a similar pattern of growth of the private aided sector.

More than one-third of the total enrolment was in private aided institutions in 2000–01 in the higher education sector for the country as a whole. This share is significantly higher in states with a larger

BOX 3.1   Private aided institutions in Bihar

In the 1970s, setting up of private colleges was a gainful business in Bihar. Given the large unmet demand for higher education, colleges were set up without proper infrastructure and facilities in the hope that the government would soon take over the responsibility of running them. Between 1975 and 1978, the state government took over the responsibility of running 286 private colleges, whereas in the thirty years prior to that only 17 private colleges were taken over by the state government.

Teaching in such colleges became a much sought after source of employment for mediocre housewives and indolent heirs of the powerful elite. Given the fact that such teachers got permanent tenures and government pay scales once the government took over, this mode of employment as teachers became available for a price. This proved to be a de-motivating factor for the deserving ones who consciously opted for teaching as a career. Parasitism, patronage and sycophancy became accepted practice in the academic world. This killed private initiatives and led to the retreat of a community from an area which rightly belonged to them.

Source From an article by Manoje Nath in *The Times of India*, New Delhi (Nath, 2005).

number of institutions. Most of the big states spent a significant amount of their money through the GIA institutions. In the 1990s, with the squeeze in public funds (with the exception of West Bengal) there has been a significant reduction in funding through GIA institutions. As a result, not only no new posts were created, even those that fell vacant could not be filled up. New GIA institutions that usually had very little infrastructure and facilities and skeleton staff, and teachers in rural areas were affected the worst.

There is no systematic study about the quality of the GIA institutions. However, a World Bank study (2003: 23) has drawn a few tentative conclusions, which are as follows:

> Where private managements are interested in providing the educational service (for whatever reason–political, cultural or religious), and where general demand for education is high, the quality and performance of private aided institutions on an average tends to be higher than that of government institutions. In this case, greater management control over teachers enables greater accountability and management also invests their own resources in improving quality. On the other hand where, the purpose of establishing aided institutions is not primarily educational but motivated by capturing public subsidies through employment of teachers, private management-control actually seemed to lower accountability and there is insignificant investment by the private management.

In all, private aided institutions are a key player in the Indian higher education system. Many of the reputed universities and colleges are in this category.

The rest of this chapter deals with private institutions that were established by private promoters and are run by them. As seen in the previous discussion, government-aided private higher education is a significant part of overall higher education. This could be referred to as the 'old' private sector in the Indian education landscape, with its distinct characteristics that are common to the public sector.

Private Colleges

Even after Independence, most of the expansion in higher education occurred through private initiatives. Till about 1980, the government could easily take over responsibility for providing recurrent grants to such institutions once they were in place. During the 1980s, it became increasingly difficult for the government to take additional financial responsibility for private institutions. Many of the new private colleges had to be run without government support. With economic prosperity, more and more people could afford higher fees. They were ready to pay higher fees for professional courses where the capacity was extremely limited. This led to the emergence of private unaided colleges, and many of them started offering professional degrees in the early 1980s.

The first few private colleges for professional education came up in Karnataka. Karnataka had put in place a liberal policy for the setting up of private professional colleges. Maharashtra, Andhra Pradesh and Tamil Nadu quickly followed suit. With the Supreme Court granting legitimacy to self-financing institutions in 1993, many states started encouraging self-financing institutions. The northern states were slow in allowing self-financing institutions. They did so only after they realised that many of their students were going to other states for professional education, often after paying high fees at the time of admission. The states of Kerala and West Bengal were initially reluctant to allow private institutions to come up. But even these states soon understood that the demand for admission to professional colleges far outstripped the available number of seats in their few government colleges, and that the fund-starved governments were no longer capable of providing quality educational facilities on their own. They needed support from the private sector. And therefore, finally, even these states allowed private institutions. In spite of this growth being spread almost throughout the country, there are still significant regional imbalances.

Private interests were largely confined to subject areas that are market friendly with low entry barriers, low initial investment (as courses in IT/computer science) and a liberal regulatory regime. A large number of private colleges were set up in engineering, management, hotel management, computer applications, pharmacy, medicine and other professional disciplines. To facilitate the setting up of such private professional colleges, many states established new affiliating universities exclusively for technical and/or medical disciplines.

Private Higher Education

While private colleges were confined to the professional education sector in most states, however, in some states it was found that there was an increased demand for general arts and science colleges. Because of either quality deficit or excess demand, it was possible to establish and run self-financing colleges even in arts and science subjects. For instance, in Tamil Nadu, as seen in Table 3.2, the number of private arts and science colleges increased from six in 1984–85 to 297 in 2006–07—a fifty-fold increase, while the number of government and private aided colleges increased only by six (from 187 to 193) in the same period. During the same period, the number of private engineering colleges increased from none in 1984–85 to 254 in 2006–07.

TABLE 3.2 Growth of arts and science, and engineering colleges in Tamil Nadu

	Government		Private aided		Private (unaided)		Total	
	AS	E	AS	E	AS	E	AS	E
1984–85	53	7	134	3	6	0	193	10
2002–03	60	7	134	3	247	212	441	222
2006–07	60	8	133	3	297	254	490	265

Source Higher Education Department, the Government of Tamil Nadu. Available online at http://www.tn.gov.in/policynotes/OLD_Files/higher_education_3.htm (accessed on 12 March 2008).

Notes AS: arts and science; E: engineering.

Tamil Nadu, along with Karnataka, Andhra Pradesh and Maharashtra, may be an extreme case of privatisation of higher education, but similar trends are seen in other states. Even in West Bengal, where only government or government-aided institutions were allowed to offer courses in traditional subjects, there is now a policy shift. Even private colleges are being allowed to offer degree courses in traditional subjects, while earlier, it was restricted to professional subjects or innovative courses only. Practical considerations rather than ideology have been behind this move. The government noted that frustrated with dearth of quality institutions, bright students were leaving the state for Delhi and Mumbai. Students were not willing to join the colleges set up by the government since these do not have proper infrastructure (*The Telegraph*, 2007). Thus, expansion of private colleges is a nationwide phenomenon. Though somewhat skewed in terms of subject areas and geographical spread, it is clear that the centre of gravity of higher education is shifting from the public to the private sector.

All private colleges are affiliated to universities that are directly under the government, in most cases the state governments. Therefore, the state governments are able to regulate fees and admissions in such institutions. Till the late 1990s, the expansion of higher education largely took place through this route. As the private sector expanded, the private promoters found the regulatory control of the affiliating university and state governments cumbersome; they could not fully exploit their full market potential. In the name of granting them autonomy—essentially to wriggle out of the control of state governments and affiliating universities—they sought university status. Thus, several private deemed universities and private universities were established. A discussion on them follows in the subsequent sections.

Deemed Universities

A university that awards an academic degree in India can only be setup by an Act of Parliament or State Legislature. However, the central government, on the recommendation of the UGC can grant status 'deemed-to-be university' to higher education institutions by an executive order. Earlier this provision was used sparingly, usually to declare premier institutions offering programmes at advanced level in a particular field or specialisation as a deemed university in order to enable it to award degrees. The Indian Institute of Science at Bengaluru and the Indian Agricultural Research Institute at Delhi were the first two institutions to be declared as deemed-to-be universities in 1958, for education and research at advanced level in the field of basic sciences and agriculture respectively. This number increased to 29 in 1990–91 and rose to 38 in 1998.

In the initial years, this privilege was restricted to the government and government-aided institutions. The Manipal Academy for Higher Education (MAHE), a pioneer in private higher education, became the first financially independent institution to be declared as a deemed university in 1976. To give boost to educational opportunities in emerging areas, the provision to grant deemed university status to new institutions was introduced in 1998. Monitored on a year-to-year basis, such institutions were granted full recognition only at the end of five years on achieving satisfactory progress. Over the past few years, many private institutions running programmes in traditional disciplines like engineering, medicine and management managed to get deemed university status without a wait period of five years using the *de novo* provision. As a result, there has been a sudden spurt in the growth of private deemed universities in recent years.

Granting deemed university status liberally, particularly using the *de novo* provisions, raised many issues. It was temporarily suspended in 2002 and efforts were made to frame stringent guidelines. The central government did not approve the revised guidelines. Efforts were also made to bring transparency to the system by introducing a system of screening in 2005. Due to the discomfort of the political establishment this was also abandoned. The process of grant of deemed university status remains somewhat non-transparent and arbitrary. A key capability required to get deemed university status is the ability to politically manoeuvre the system. Meanwhile, the numbers of private deemed universities continue to increase.

By early 2008, there were as many as 114 deemed universities. This number does not include the 17 Regional Engineering Colleges that were earlier given the status of deemed university and renamed as National Institutes of Technology (NITs), and later given the status of institutions of national importance by an act of Parliament. Of the 60 institutions declared deemed universities after 2000, the number of government and aided institutions is insignificant. Several hundred proposals are pending. A majority of them are from the private institutions. The geographical spread of deemed universities is uneven. A large proportion of them are from Tamil Nadu and Maharashtra. These two states also have the highest proportion of private colleges. There is a history of political patronage to private initiatives in these states.

Though deemed universities have no affiliating powers, yet many of them have several campuses spread throughout the country. Most private deemed universities run undergraduate programmes in professional disciplines and have very little research activity. Under the pretext of need for greater autonomy, such institutions exploit lacunae in the lax oversight of the UGC over them. They enjoy freedom in matters of fees and admissions. High tuition fees, large non-refundable deposits are a norm for getting admission into these institutions.

Private deemed universities are mostly family-run institutions. These are either families that play important role in politics themselves or earn political patronage by dispensing favours like out-of-turn admissions. It is therefore not surprising that they wield great influence in the shaping of policy on private higher education. Such policies would obviously be aimed at consolidating their own operations. Recently, deemed universities have got many concessions from the UGC and the central government. Such institutions can now use the term 'university' in their title. They can initiate teaching programmes at undergraduate as well as post-graduate levels in disciplines of their choice. This brings them at par with the universities established through legislation. The UGC has also been authorised to grant exemptions to sponsoring bodies from the creation of a separate trust or society for the establishment of a deemed-to-be university. A mere 'legal undertaking' for the use of assets to run educational activities would suffice. This has made deemed universities even more attractive.

According to experts who have watched them evolve closely over the years, such institutions have mastered the art of window dressing as regards the facilities. They undertake great public relations exercise to always remain in the limelight. The management of these universities is always retained with the family members and many of them appoint vice-chancellors from among the members of the family. While they are innovative, entrepreneurial, highly visible and exercise largest influence over policy, not all of them are of high quality. In many private deemed universities, quality is the first casualty. They make several compromises in infrastructure and in the employment of teachers. Thus, private deemed universities are nothing but private universities through an indirect route.

Private Universities

A proposal to permit the establishment of private universities has been around for more than a decade, first introduced in 1995 in Parliament as the Private Universities (Establishment and Regulation) Bill. The bill included specific provisions to maintain academic standards and prevent commercialisation and mismanagement. Teachers' and students' organisations, academics, and some political parties opposed the bill on the grounds that despite safeguards, such universities could compromise academic standards and could lead to gross commercialisation. The private sector, in contrast, found the proposed legislation too restrictive. An attempt to build consensus through consultation with the state governments added further confusion. As a result, a national legislation on private universities is still pending. Granting deemed university status to private institutions is an interim measure that has eased pressure on the government, yet the issue of a national legislation for private universities continues to haunt the government time and again.

Meanwhile, the state governments have begun to realise that as per the constitutional arrangement (education, including higher education, being on the concurrent list), they are able to establish private universities through state legislation. The first private university—the Sikkim Manipal University of Health, Medical and Technological Sciences—was established in Sikkim by the Manipal Group in partnership with the State Government of Sikkim in 1995, and started operations in April 1997. A small operation, but now known for the nationwide spread of its distance education programmes, this could be considered as the first private university in the country. Actual spurt in establishing purely private universities in the state sector came in the post-2000 period.

Several state governments went ahead and set up private universities on their own. While some states—Uttaranchal, Gujarat, Himachal Pradesh and Uttar Pradesh—did so on case-to-case basis through separate legislations, the state of Chhattisgarh went into an overdrive and created a crisis by allowing hundreds of sub-standard universities to come up all over the country through umbrella legislation. The state government of Chhattisgarh went overboard and passed an omnibus act that enabled it to set up any number of private universities by executive orders. The state government received 134 applications within a week of this enactment and went on to approve 97 of them. The resulting problem serves as a warning: many of these universities set up off-campus centres and study centres outside the state without any operations in Chhattisgarh and indulged in all kinds of malpractices, creating a chaotic situation.

The UGC was forced to respond, issuing regulations for private universities governing their establishment and standards in 2003.[2] The regulations required a private university to be set up only by a separate act, not an omnibus bill as in Chhattisgarh, and restricted their operations to within the state enacting such legislation. Many private universities however opposed the UGC regulations, claiming that as they received no funding from the UGC, they were not subject to UGC oversight. They also argued that the regulations were discriminatory, imposing regulations on private universities and not on public ones. A parliamentary committee[3] concluded that although these universities were established under state rather than national laws, they were nevertheless obliged to comply with the guidelines laid down by the national regulatory bodies, including the UGC. Despite this, the central government took an ambivalent stand on the proliferation of the private universities.

Meanwhile, responding to the chaos its omnibus legislation had created, the Chhattisgarh state government had revoked its approval of all but 37 of the new universities by the end of 2004. The UGC started inspecting the private universities as per its new regulations, approving only seven nationally, but the others continued to operate nonetheless before the Supreme Court[4] struck down the Private Universities Act of Chhattisgarh and upheld the validity of the UGC Regulations in February 2005. The observations of the Supreme Court in Box 3.2 illustrate the untenable situation in Chhattisgarh prevailing in 2004.

While a national legislation for establishing private universities is still pending, developments over the past few years have brought about some clarity on establishment and operation of private universities in the state sector. Currently, there are 11 private universities in the state sector recognised by the UGC in five states. Another seven new private universities are proposed. Attitudes towards private universities vary

Private Higher Education

BOX 3.2   Chhattisgarh private universities

The Supreme Court, while striking down the Private Universities Act of Chhattisgarh, observed that the State Government had simply issued notifications in a stereotyped manner in the Gazette, establishing universities (to conduct the syllabus and to grant degrees diplomas) in an indiscriminate and mechanical manner without having the slightest regard to the availability of any infrastructure, teaching facility or financial resources. All types of degrees were awarded by these universities. They were running professional courses without taking prior permission of the regulatory bodies. The legislation was enacted in a manner that had completely done away with any kind of control of the UGC. It was noted that many of these universities were functioning from small premises which are some times small single rooms in a commercial complex or a small tenement on the first or second floor of a building or an ordinary flat. These universities were issuing advertisements for opening up study centres in different parts of the country for award of any number of degrees or diplomas. They were alluring people all over the country to open study centres for which they were charging huge amounts, and also befooling students into applying for admission to unknown and unheard of courses that were not recognised by any statutory body.

Source   The Supreme Court's judgement in the writ petition number 19 of 2004.

from state to state. While some states have initiated action to establish private universities, many others are still not open to this idea. The Assam Government has enacted the Assam Private Universities Act, 2007 and invited proposals from private promoters for setting up private universities in Assam, with campus and study centres within the State (*The Indian Express*, New Delhi, 14 September 2007).[5] In contrast, the minister of education of Kerala has categorically ruled out the question of permitting private universities in the state (*The Hindu*, 19 September 2007).

Foreign Providers

Foreign institutions have operated in India for many years now. Initially, they merely recruited students for their home campuses abroad, but gradually they started offering programmes in India itself. The programmes were mostly offered with Indian partners, operating outside the national regulatory system. There are various modes of delivery of higher education by foreign providers. Table 3.3 describes these modes. While double degree or joint degree, twinning and franchise arrangements and validated programmes necessarily require local partners, branch campus and distance/open learning could be handled entirely by the foreign provider. Since there is no system even to register such operations, the information on the size and scope of foreign providers is patchy, with many discrepancies and information gaps.

TABLE 3.3 Different modes of delivery by foreign providers

Mode	Definition
Branch Campuses	Foreign institution establishes a subsidiary, either on its own or jointly with a local provider, and delivery is entirely by the foreign university, leading to a degree from the latter.
Double/Joint Degree	Students pursue a programme jointly offered by institutions in two countries. The qualification(s) can be either a degree that is jointly awarded or two separate degrees awarded by each partner institution.
Twinning	Students pursue part of the programme at the domestic institution and part in the partner foreign institution. The degree is awarded by the foreign institution.
Franchised Programme	Learning programmes designed by the foreign provider (franchiser) and delivered in the domestic institution (franchisee). The student receives the qualification of the franchiser institution. Variation range from 'full' to 'part' franchise.
Validated Programme	A programme established in a local higher education institution that has been 'approved' by a foreign institution as equivalent to its own, leading to the award of a qualification from the latter.
Distance/Open Learning (e-learning)	Course is through distance learning whether traditional or online and could be with a local partner or entirely foreign. 'Open Learning' also signifies that the programme does not have the normal academic entry requirements.

Source Definitions from Knight (2005) and Bashir (2007).

A study by India's National Institute of Educational Planning and Administration (NIEPA), and another by Powar and Bhalla give some idea about the foreign education providers in India. The NIEPA study identified 131 foreign education providers, enrolling several thousand students in India. The study did not record any branch campuses and only two franchise operations of foreign providers; the remainder were collaborative programmes or twinning arrangements. Most of these partnerships were with US universities (66 partnerships) and UK universities (59 partnerships) (Bhushan, 2006). The study further noted that out of the total sample of 131 institutions in India, 107 were providing professional programmes, 19 technical programmes, and only five general education programmes. Business management and hotel management constituted approximately 80 per cent of the total. Geographical distribution of these programmes was uneven: Maharashtra had most programmes in hotel management, whilst Delhi had the most in business management (Bhushan, 2006).

The study considered 50 of these operations in details. Of these, 60 per cent (30) offered a triple benefit—while foreign institutions are able to attract students to their home campus, part of the programme is completed within India, benefiting both the Indian institutions and the Indian students, who pay less than they would in studying abroad for the entire duration of a degree programme. The remaining 40 per cent (20) were collaborative programmes with joint-degree provisions. In such cases, the Indian partners design programmes with inputs from the foreign institutions and get the brand name of the foreign university.

Based on their scrutiny of advertisements published in national newspapers and of institutional websites in 2000, 2004 and 2006, Powar and Bhalla have put together information on foreign education providers in India. They found that while the number of institutions recruiting students for study on their home campuses has increased steadily, there has been a marginal reduction in the number of articulation arrangements. The number of institutions having their presence through franchise operations has decreased substantially. Ten foreign distance education providers have also been recorded in the survey. Further, it was found that almost all foreign providers were recognised higher education institutions, but their Indian partners were largely private commercial institutions. The United Kingdom is most active in Indian market, followed by Australia, the United States and Canada (Powar and Bhalla, 2006).

The media sometimes reports that universities from the West are planning to establish their branch campus in India, but only one—the Western International University of the United States—has actually opened its branch near New Delhi. The experience of Sylvan Universities International, which closed down its Indian operations in 2004 citing obstruction from the UGC, has been bad (OBHE, 2004). Recently, the US-based Georgia Institute of Technology has decided to open its campus near Hyderabad (OBHE, 2007). The state government of Andhra Pradesh is facilitating this and even made the land available for its campus (see Box 3.3). As of this date, there are no other firm plans of any of the super league universities to set up their campus in South Asia. The Harvard University and the Oxford University have both set up their research centres in India with a view to provide students enrolled in their home campuses exposure to the developments in India.

BOX 3.3   Georgia Tech in India

Georgia Tech University has signed a memorandum of understanding with the Andhra Pradesh Government to set up its international campus in the state. Initially on a 20 acre land near Hyderabad, it will shift to 70 acre land near Vizag. The land is being given by the State Govt. It plans to produce 20 per cent of Ph.D.s in technology. Georgia Tech has been scouting for a campus from 2004. First academic courses will begin in 2009. In initial years, Georgia Tech faculty would take care of the teaching requirements; later 80 per cent faculty will be from India. It will focus on systems engineering and research.

Source From an article in the *Business Standard*, 6 June 2007.

Recently, the author collected data from the British Council at New Delhi on UK universities offering programmes in India either by themselves or in partnership with an Indian institution. From the data, it is seen that 12 UK-based universities are offering, or are in the process of offering joint programmes with Indian partner institutions in India. Two of the programmes will be at the undergraduate level and 10 at the post-graduate level. While many of the programmes are in the hospitality sector, there are some in business administration, computing, nursing, and fashion design. In all, these programmes will enrol about 5,000 students.

Private Higher Education

According to Marginson (2007), in the changing landscape of higher education, a two-tier structure is emerging in the global market for higher education. While there are a small number of global universities that are in the super league, much larger numbers of lesser reputed institutions export higher education as businesses. Global universities do not expand to meet potential demand or establish franchises across the world like other businesses. Their prestige depends on their continued scarcity. They compete with each other for the best researchers and doctoral students as well as national and global leadership. On the other hand, the second-tier institutions include both the for-profit sector and the non-profit sector that provide foreign education commercially. While the super league universities were always global demand magnets, it is the second-tier institutions that are more active now.

In all, it is estimated that only about 10–15,000 students are enrolled in programmes offered by foreign providers, either by themselves or with Indian partners, mostly private. Foreign providers are thus peripheral and adjunct to the growing private sector. Independent campuses of foreign universities are rare, but partnerships are common. Prestigious universities are cautious, and content with setting up their research centres in India to provide their home students an exposure to the rapid changes taking place in the country. A plethora of the partnerships are with second-tier foreign universities that are trying aggressively to tap the huge potential here. A closer look reveals that at times the foreign academic association is 'hollow' and private institutions merely use it to lure gullible students desiring foreign education.

Foreign provision in partnership with domestic providers (mostly private) merely represents additional private access. Though most of the foreign partners are public universities, they function abroad like private entities. According to Levy (2008b), there is mutual attraction between the foreign university and its local partner. Through partnership, the foreign institution expands its reach geographically and often socio-economically, and garners tuition. The local private partner gains a legitimising link, a curriculum and the ability to offer a diploma or degree that may lack state recognition but can have job market or international value. While in India these partnerships have emerged on the fringes of legislation, Malaysia has pro-actively encouraged such arrangements (Lee, 2003). Not surprisingly, charges of imperialism greet some such attempts.

Though there is a trend of increasing presence of foreign institutions, foreign education providers will continue to be small. Compared to the total enrolment in higher education, this is insignificant. Despite its small size, the necessity to regulate foreign providers due to serious concerns about its indifferent quality have attracted public attention for over a decade now. A detailed discussion on regulating foreign providers is in Chapter 7.

Growth of Professional Education

Most private universities and colleges in India, like elsewhere in the world, primarily impart professional education. Thus, professional education expanded along with growth of the private education sector. It grew slowly before independence: the number of engineering colleges and polytechnics (including pharmacy and architecture institutions) at the time of independence in 1947 was merely 38 and 53, with an intake capacity of 2,940 and 3,960 respectively. The pace of growth increased after Independence, but it was in the 1980s, when private colleges affiliated to public universities were allowed on self-financing basis, that there was an accelerated growth of professional education.

Before 1980, the expansion of higher education was mainly confined to undergraduate programmes in arts, science and commerce. In these subject areas, private institutions could be set up with very little investment, and they fit in with India's tradition of liberal education, based on the view that learning should take place without reference to the economic or other external factors. Institutions were set up and run for a few years on a self-financing basis. Then they were brought under the government grant system. However, the changing structure of the Indian economy saw a need for the development of more professional programmes, leading to the rise of financially independent private professional colleges to answer this unmet demand. The rise of professional higher education in India follows trends seen elsewhere in the world, with a shift from liberal education towards professional programmes. This issue is discussed in detail in Chapter 5. Here it would suffice to say that people were willing to pay for professional education provided in the private institutions. Thus, financially independent private professional institutions became feasible.

Realising this, some of the state governments, especially the governments of Karnataka, Maharashtra, Tamil Nadu and Andhra Pradesh took a bold decision to permit private registered societies and trusts to establish and run professional institutions on a self-financing basis. As a result, a large number of private unaided colleges came up in early 1980s. Initially they offered degree programmes in engineering. Programmes in architecture, pharmacy, management, hotel management, computer applications, medicine, nursing, dentistry, physiotherapy and teacher education followed this trend. This spread to the other states over time. It is seen that states with the highest concentration of professional institutions are also the ones that have larger number of private institutions. There are large regional imbalances, since the growth of private initiatives did not occur in a uniform manner across all states and regions of the country.

Table 3.4 shows that professional education has grown rapidly over the past 6-7 years across a range of disciplines. In case of engineering, pharmacy, dentistry and physiotherapy, growth has been high and private share is as much as 90 per cent in terms of number of institutions. Few programmes like computer applications, management and teacher education grew in the public as well as the private sector. In the public sector, these were started as self-financing programmes. In disciplines like architecture and hotel management, growth has been moderate. In medicine and dentistry, where entry barriers are high in terms of large investment requirements and the need for an attached hospital, growth has been rather slow and private share is 50-60 per cent.

The growth of professional programmes in public universities and colleges on self-financing basis can be seen as the 'privatisation' of public institutions. From the early 1990s, faced with paucity of funds, public institutions have expanded primarily through self-financing programmes. In many cases, universities did not bother to get prior approval of the professional councils like the AICTE for starting these programmes.[6] Existing infrastructure and facilities were used for such programmes. Fee levels were often the same as private institutions.

TABLE 3.4 Professional higher education institutions: Growth and private share

Name of the course	1999–2000	July 2007 & (2006–07)	Percentage increase	Private share (%)
Engineering	669	1,617	142	91
Pharmacy	204	736	261	95
Hotel Management	41	80	95	94
Architecture	78	116	49	67
Computer Applications (MCA)	780	999	28	62
Management (MBA/PGDM)	682	1,150	69	64
Teacher Education (B.Ed.)	1,050	(5,190)	395	68
Medicine (MBBS)	174	(233)	32	50
Dentistry (BDS)	45	(189)	420	59
Physiotherapy	52	(205)	294	92
Total	3,775	10,515	178	80

Source Compiled by the author from AICTE and other professional council data.

Thus, they could generate huge resources without much additional costs. While no data on the extent of self-financing programmes in the public universities is available, most universities are believed to have started some self-financing programmes over the past couple of decades. In several institutions, such programmes outnumber regular programmes.

Professional education, falling under the regulatory control of the AICTE and referred to as technical education, saw the biggest expansion. The intake capacity of technical education increased manifold over the years. As on 31 July 2007, the total intake capacity was to the tune of 627,082 students in the 1,617 undergraduate degree level engineering institutions and 333,296 students in the 1,403 diploma-level institutions, 104,084 students in the 1,150 management institutions, 56,004 students in the 999 MCA institutions, 5,229 students in the 80 hotel management degree-level institutions, 44,476 students in the 736 pharmacy degree-level institutions, 4,707 students in the 116 architecture institutions and 650 students in the nine fine arts institutions making a grand total of 842,068 intake in 4,707 technical institutions. These numbers continue to increase rapidly. For the academic year 2007–08, about

Private Higher Education

456 new institutions have been approved providing additional intake capacity of about 96,551 students (AICTE, 2008).

While growth has been across a range of disciplines, it has been the fastest in engineering, that too in IT and related disciplines (see Table 3.5 for growth of degree-level engineering institutions). Rapid exponential growth of private engineering colleges is to be contrasted with stagnating number of government/aided engineering colleges.

TABLE 3.5 Growth of engineering colleges in India

Type	1947	1960	1970	1980	1990	2000	2006	2007
Govt. & Aided	42	111	135	142	164	202	212	215
Un-Aided	2	3	4	15	145	467	1,299	1,402
Total	44	114	139	157	309	669	1,511	1,617

Sources Compiled by the author from various AICTE reports.

While private engineering colleges continue to grow, in some states which saw an early expansion, saturation seems to be setting in. Several thousands of seats remain unfilled in private engineering colleges in many of these states (Box 3.4).

BOX 3.4 Engineering seats go a-begging in Tamil Nadu

Out of the 43,346 government quota seats available at the bachelor's level for engineering education, 11,059 (25.5%) seats—all in self-financing colleges remained vacant in Tamil Nadu in the year 2005. The situation was however better than previous year when nearly 20,000 seats had gone a-begging. Though 6,529 candidates applied, 29,242 (47.5%) either did not turn up or take a seat that was on offer. In about a dozen colleges, less than 10 students joined, in 14 others, the number of students that joined was in double digits and in one college only one student turned up. Whereas some joined their preferred courses and colleges under management quota, others preferred for arts and science courses. In many cases, high tuition fee of Rs. 75,000 per annum put them off.

Source New Indian Express, Bangalore, 29 August 2005.

While some colleges do not get adequate students, there are others that are able to charge premium for admissions. Due to a large number of seats remaining vacant, viability of several engineering colleges is at stake.

Many of them are on sale and are being acquired by more reputed and established institutions. Fierce competition has set in many disciplines and private colleges realise that in order to survive they need to provide better infrastructure, ensure that the quality of education is good, and charge reasonable fees. Due to the proliferation of engineering colleges there is a sharp decrease in the number of students seeking admission to polytechnics, which are facing survival problems. Some polytechnics are now converting to engineering colleges. Overall, private professional education is the most dynamic segment of Indian higher education with many interesting developments taking place.

Growing Private Share

Private higher education in India is large and diverse. There are several types of private institutions. While most of them are colleges, some are deemed universities, and a few are private universities established by state legislatures. There are institutions that are set up by various religious and linguistic minorities which enjoy certain privileges under law. Private institutions are usually established and operated under provisions of charitable societies or trusts, though only a very small number may be genuinely not-for-profit institutions. Old private institutions are now substantially funded by the government. There are some non-profit institutions that are financially independent and supported by the income of the charitable and religious trusts. Large numbers of private institutions meet all their expenses from tuition revenue. A significant number of them are family owned and *de facto* run as business enterprises (Altbach, 2005). There are also private training centres that are legally for-profit entities.

The new breed of private institutions are mostly *de facto* for-profit. Now private higher education is seen more as a business. Entrepreneurs, businessmen and politicians have set up institutions by floating family trusts or societies. Their earnings come mostly from the tuition fees. They are often costlier than the government institutions. Table 3.6 shows the growth of various types of institutions over the past five years. It is seen that while number of institutions as well as enrolment

Private Higher Education

TABLE 3.6   Higher education institutions and enrolment (by type of management)

Type	Higher education institutions (Universities + Colleges)				Enrolment (in thousand)	
	2000–01		2005–06		2000–01	2005–06
Government	4,342	(245+4,097)	4,493	(268+4,225)	3,443	3,752
Private aided	5,507	(10+4,997)	5,760	(10+5,750)	3,134	3,510
Private (unaided)	3,223	(21+3,202)	7,720	(70+7,650)	1,822	3,219
Total	13,072	(276+12,296)	17,973	(348+17,625)	8,399	10,481

Source Estimates by author (Agarwal, 2006).

has stagnated in government and private aided institutions, the private unaided sector has grown rapidly and this growth is of recent origin. Currently, 43 per cent of the number of institutions and 30 per cent of enrolment is in the private unaided institutions. A large proportion of these institutions offer programmes in the professional streams.

There is a great deal of confusion about private share in Indian higher education. The Eleventh Plan, while welcoming the increase in private share, has noted that private unaided institutions increased from 42.6 per cent in 2001 to 63.21 per cent in 2006. Their share of enrolments also increased from 32.89 per cent to 51.53 per cent in the same period. The plan expects that about half of incremental enrolment targeted for higher education will come from private providers. Though the emergence of the private sector has helped expand capacity, it is characterised by some imbalances. Private institutions have improved access in a few selected areas like engineering, management, medicine, IT, and so on, where students are willing to pay substantial fees. However, the distribution across country is uneven, with some states receiving most of the growth in private institutions (Planning Commission, 2007).

In addition to the private unaided sector, many public institutions also offer self-financing programmes. The past two decades saw a surge in private higher education. It has moved from the periphery to the centre stage now. There has been a shift in funding from the public resources to households. Though private initiatives have added dynamism to the higher education sector, it has posed new challenges on the regulatory front.

Institutional Diversity

Not only has private share increased over the years, its complexion is very different now. Initially, private colleges in narrow specialisations affiliated to public universities dominated the private higher education landscape. These were not very different from their public counterparts except for finance and administration. Now, there is a large variety of private institutions. It does not entirely comprises small affiliated colleges now; there are many big players with large operations and massive expansion plans. Many of them are making huge investments in modern and expensive infrastructure and facilities. Some of these institutions have fully air-conditioned buildings, wi-fi enabled campuses, and classrooms with smart-boards.

There are varying perceptions about private higher education. Some who consider it the panacea for higher education, would not want any regulation or interference in the establishment and operation of private institutions and would let the market forces determine their survival. There are others who consider private institutions as the fountain of malpractices, exploitation and poor quality, which are manipulated politically or financially. Though both perceptions are of course generalisations, both are based on actual experiences. It would be unfair to characterise all private institutions as indulging in undesirable practices.

There are certainly many private institutions, such as the Birla Institute of Technology, Thapar University, Nirma University, and so on, which are committed to educational excellence. They are conscious of their responsibility to their students and are known for transparency and academic commitment. An analysis of such institutions reveals that their governing bodies consist of eminent persons, known for their integrity and knowledge of educational systems. Such bodies are not controlled or manipulated by private individuals or family members. These are established as public trusts or societies true to the spirit that education is a charitable and non-commercial venture. They allow considerable autonomy to the head of the institution and the faculty and treat them with dignity so that competent teachers are attracted to such institutions.

The excess incomes generated by such institutions are generally not hidden or misappropriated but utilised for further growth and development of the institution. They are keen to offer post-graduate and research programmes and establish good reputation and academic image. In such institutions, the curriculum, recruitment procedures, admission requirements, various fees, details of faculty, results etc., are made transparent through their publications and websites. It is estimated that nearly 25 per cent of private institutions will fit this characterisation (Anandakrishnan, 2006). Other than private standalone institutions, there is a trend towards emergence of a chain of private institutions under the common brand name, institutions backed by the big corporate sector, for-profit institutions and private tuition and coaching centres. While the last two are not part of the private higher education sector, yet they form part of the overall education and training sector in the country.

Chain of Institutions

An interesting development in the country's new private higher education sector is the emergence of institutions tied together in a chain with common for-profit ownership (though often legally cloaked as non-profits). Their operations are put together under one brand name. According to Levy (2008b), this is not just a marketing ploy, but also a strategy that declares their product is working and can now be offered, through institutional cloning, to populations that cannot reach the initial places. Though the multiple sites may have some autonomy, but only some, as the core idea is a rather standard package for curriculum, pedagogy, hiring, and admissions. Due to economies of scale and growing demand, they are able to generate huge surpluses from their operations, most of which is ploughed back in expansion and consolidation. Tax laws bind the non-profits to reinvest rather share their surplus amongst the promoters.

While some of them are new and taking off, others have been around for decades and are now onto major expansion spree (*The Economic Times*, 6 April 2008).[7] The Birla Institute of Technology and Science (BITS), Pilani started in early 1900s as a small school and blossomed into a set of colleges for higher education, ranging from the humanities to engineering until 1964, when all these colleges were amalgamated into a reputed private deemed university. By setting up campuses at Goa and Hyderabad in India and at Dubai abroad, BITS, Pilani is now a multi-campus university with about 8,000 students and 12,000 students enrolled in off-campus work-integrated programmes. In recent years it has even set up a virtual university. Its main source of funding—both to meet recurrent costs and capital costs for expansion—come largely from the tuition and fees that are not steep and yet 22 per cent students at BITS receive scholarships.

The Manipal University, which started with a medical college in 1953 now has 24 colleges with an enrolment of over 80,000, in a range of disciplines at all levels. Manipal, a small town in coastal Karnataka, has now become an education hub that attracts students from across the country, and even overseas. From its initial narrow focus on engineering and medical programmes, programmes in humanities and social sciences are on offer now. The university is spending Rs 400 crore to upgrade its Manipal facilities. Other than India, it has presence in Nepal, Malaysia, Dubai and the Caribbean. It has massive expansion plans, both in India and abroad. Four more campuses with an initial investment of around Rs 100–130 crore for each campus are planned in India. Overseas expansion plans are to enter Oman, Indonesia and Vietnam.

The Institute of Chartered Financial Analysts of India (ICFAI), established in 1984 to impart training in finance and management to students, working executives and professionals, and the CFA Program (popular abroad) in 1985, now has seven private universities in Uttarakhand, Tripura, Sikkim, Meghalaya, Mizoram, Nagaland, and Jharkhand under its fold and another three in Rajasthan, Chhattisgarh and Punjab are planned. Each university is a separate and independent legal entity. Two of them at Dehradun (Uttarakhand) and Agartala (Tripura) are also recognised by the UGC. They offer a wide range of programmes in management, finance, banking, insurance, accounting, law, information technology, arts, commerce, education and science and technology at bachelor's and master's levels on full-time campus and flexible learning formats. Examinations are conducted at over 168 test centres all over India, four times a year. The universities have no study centres outside the authorised jurisdictions. Thus, the ICFAI universities are the biggest chain of universities with pan-India presence, enrolling several hundred thousand students.

The Amity University, which started just a decade ago, has two universities and 700 institutions that cater to 50,000 students in 130 different courses, from sciences to humanities to media. It has spent around Rs 1,000 crore so far and plans to invest around Rs 2,000 crore in the next two to three years and increase the student intake to 500,000 in the next five years. It claims it has been consistently growing at 50 per cent for the last five years and plans to accelerate its growth to 100 per cent in terms of student intake and revenues, which the university management is confident to achieve in the current Indian scenario.

The Pune-based Symbiosis, started in 1971, has 33 institutions in nine campuses enroling 45,000 students on campus and 100,000 students in distance learning programmes. It was granted deemed university status in 2002, and in recognition of the fact that it enrolls students from over 60 countries, renamed itself as the Symbiosis International University in 2006. The Coimbatore-based PSG Group, which has 10 colleges with an enrolment of 16,992 students, expects to become a deemed university soon. The Bengaluru-based Jain Group has 21 education institutions with an aggregate enrolment of 16,400 students and 1,750 employees, and plans 100 colleges within the next 10 years. The Apeejay Education Society, which started with schools about 40 years ago and later expanded into higher education, has 13 institutions of higher education enrolling 32,000 students in 80 courses across the country. In each state or region, new chains of institutions are emerging.

Even the states that were laggard in private professional education have embraced private growth for pragmatic reasons. West Bengal has the Techno-India Group, with 14 professional institutions including institutions at Mumbai, Delhi and Bengaluru under its fold. The case of the Lovely Professional University, spread over 325 acre at Phagwara in Punjab, is most spectacular.[8] This university, set up by the Jalandhar-based Lovely Group in late 2005, received UGC recognition in 2006.

Within a spell of a couple of years, it had 16,000 students on its rolls in a large variety of programmes and expects this number to go up to 40,000 in the next few years.

While a majority of them are family-owned initiatives, there are some that have trusts and societies with broad representation of a community or a religious group. The Mumbai-based Hyderabad (Sind) National Collegiate Board (HSNCB) comprises 24 higher education institutions with an aggregate enrolment of 45,000 students. They are expanding and plan a college in Dubai. The Kerala Catholic Bishops Council for Education manages 2,196 institutions, including medical, engineering and nursing colleges, secondary and primary schools, with a massive aggregate enrolment of 928,000 students. Most of the professional institutions in the state have been financed by donations from parishioners. These self-financing professional institutions run by the church are not elitist, nor are they meant only for members of the Christian community. In fact, the majority of students studying in these Christian institutions profess other religions.

New Institutions Backed by Big Business

Even among the family-owned initiatives, there has been a revival of the tradition of private philanthropy. From the early years of the 20th century until independence, big business houses like the Tatas, Birlas and Thapars generously donated for setting up institutions for higher learning. The Indian Institute of Science (earlier Tata Institute) at Bengaluru, Tata Institute of Social Sciences and the Tata Institute of Fundamental Research at Mumbai were established by the Tatas. The Birlas established BITS (Pilani) and the Thapar group set up Thapar University at Patiala in Punjab. These private institutions were unique in the sense that they promoted the concept of a private institution with a public purpose, and the notion of philanthropy and corporate social responsibility. A private university with a public purpose is a rare phenomenon outside the United States, except in universities with a religious lineage.

In recent years, the big corporate sector has again evinced interest in higher education. The big business house of the Ambanis set up

Private Higher Education

Dhirubhai Ambani Institute of Information Technology at Gandhinagar. Reliance Industries (Mukesh Ambani group) is setting up a Reliance School of Life Sciences near Mumbai. The steel magnate L.N. Mittal has set up a technical university at Jaipur. The most ambitious of these new initiatives is by Anil Agarwal of the Vedanta Group—setting up of a mega university, the Vedanta University in Orissa. Mahindra and Mahindra, the automobile major, is setting up a chain of five engineering colleges in collaboration with premier foreign institutions at Chandigarh, Goa and Pune (and two other locations that are yet to be finalised).

Of these, the Vedanta University, assisted by the State Government of Orissa, is the most ambitious initiative in the private sector so far in India, and possibly the world. The Vedanta group plans a foray into education with an investment of USD 1 billion, to set up a world-class fully residential university with 7–8 colleges spread over 6,000 acres. With the first batch starting from 2009–10, its ultimate capacity will be 100,000 students. While most people are unable to comprehend the size, those like Altbach (2007) are not very optimistic about Vedanta's chances for success. The size of world-class universities is much smaller, their locations close to fast growing cities and centres of emerging technologies and funding is not far more liberal than the announced but is usually supplemented with public money.

Despite these doubts, the Vedanta University project has made progress, and while it may not be as big or as prestigious as it claims to be, it will nonetheless be the biggest campus of private education in India so far. The current biggest private university campus, the 1,000 acre SRM University near Chennai, will look tiny in its comparison. Mukesh Ambani's Reliance School of Life Sciences that will come up near Navi Mumbai and starting with about 300 students will have 3,000 students by 2012 in 42 programmes in the biosciences and related areas at the post-graduate and doctoral level. With deemed university status and international collaboration, this could emerge as a world-class research university in the years to come. Both the Vedanta and the Reliance initiatives have the potential to be exemplars for private higher education institutions of the future.

Recognising the role of the private sector, several initiatives have been taken by the state governments to facilitate and encourage private institutions. The Chandigarh administration has earmarked 100 acres of prime land near the city for Education City and has invited offers from reputed higher education institutions to set up their campuses there. Several Special Economic Zones that are planned in the country have earmarked areas for higher education institutions; most of those would be private. A sizeable area of the recently opened Lavasa Knowledge Village near Pune has been taken by private higher education institutions.

For-profit Institutions

There are large numbers of for-profit private training institutions that operate at the periphery of formal higher education sector. While it all began with IT training, it has now spread to other vocational streams. These are mainly seen to offer short, non-formal, non-standard courses, focusing on a few types of skills and occupations, typically associated with information technology. Many of them are essentially a chain of training centres, bound together in franchisee networks. Most prominent of them is the NIIT that started its operations with three IT education centres in Mumbai, Delhi and Madras in 1982. It was the first to introduce franchising in IT education and training in India, and it has transitioned from an IT training company to a global talent development company. Today, NIIT offers comprehensive learning solutions for individuals, enterprises and institutions across 5,000 locations in 32 countries.

Based on a World Bank survey conducted in 2003, it was estimated that around 0.8–1.0 million students are enrolled in such institutions. Though some of them are accredited by a government agency (like the DOEACC Society), a majority of them are unaccredited. A bulk of these institutions offer training in IT-related and non-engineering trades, such as travel and tourism, hospitality, media and journalism, animation, aviation, event management, fitness consultancy, fashion designing and even clinical research.

Private Tuitions and Coaching Institutions

A large and growing non-formal sector comprising private tuition and coaching centres have spawned on the fringes of the formal system of higher education in recent years. Traditionally, poorly paid teachers used to supplement their meagre stipends by teaching a gathering of 10–15 students in makeshift classrooms after school hours. Essentially private tuition was given to weak students for remedial purposes.

However, high stake entrance tests to reputed institutions such as the IIMs, IITs and a plethora of competitive exams for entry into government and public sector companies have changed this. Today full-fledged 'coaching centres' boasting prime commercial addresses, with spacious classrooms capable of accommodating hundreds of students have mushroomed across the country. Their classrooms are air conditioned and equipped with modern teaching aids and comfortable furniture. Customised education packages, glossy brochures and complete marketing strategies for promotion are de rigueur. Big coaching schools such as FIITJEE, IMS, Career Launcher, and Career Point have become household names and run nationwide franchise operations with some of them even offering private tuitions over the Internet to students overseas. Some of them are so successful that they plan to start a chain of institutions for professional education and enter the formal higher education space.

While many coaching centres are exploitative, charging heavy fees, and prey on the anxieties of parents, there are others that are well-organised, employ specialised tutors, use self-learning instructional materials, and provide customised study programmes of high quality.[9] Little wonder that from being a somewhat guilty *sub rosa* activity centred around examinations, private tutoring is now a year-round phenomenon. A few cities, such as Kota and Hyderabad have become famous for such coaching centres.[10] Students, often with parents, shift to those cities. The students attend the coaching centres on a full-time basis and private schools operate a dummy to provide attendance and conduct board exams. Many private schools now have strategic arrangements with reputed coaching centres for supplementary tutoring after school hours on the school campuses itself.

Private tuitions and coaching is now a significant part of household expenditure. The expenditure on organised coaching in India is estimated at Rs 7,000 crore per year—nearly one-third of what the government spends on higher education annually. Despite attempts to curtail this activity, it is only on the rise.

In all, there is a frantic activity in the private higher education space in the country. A large variety of institutions have come up. With annual rush for admission into mid-price institutions with a reputation for delivering quality and relevant education, there is unstoppable edupreneur-led boom. Several heavyweights have emerged and they are positioning themselves to take a great leap forward. Many private operations have the potential to become global conglomerates in the higher education sector. The pace of this growth is so fast and its extent so deep and wide that it would transform Indian higher education significantly in the years to come.

Global Experience

There is rich and varied global experience with private higher education. Among the 78 countries of which information has been gathered by the Programme for Research in Higher Education (PROPHE), India's level of private enrolment exceeds 55 cases and trails behind just 22. If the private sector is loosely defined to include private aided institutions, then private share in India is one of the highest in the world. Table 3.7 provides private share of enrolment and number of institutions for 20 major countries. It is seen that while countries in East Asia and Latin America have high private share, even countries from the erstwhile Communist block have significant private share. The emerging economies such as South Korea, Taiwan and Malaysia have rapidly increased enrolment in higher education through private participation. Only the countries in Europe, such as Germany, United Kingdom, and France have low private share. The small Nordic countries like Finland have no private higher education at all. Higher share in terms of number of institutions than enrolment share for all countries suggest that size of private institutions is usually small.

Interestingly, private share in India exceeds that in the United States. In the United States, 77 per cent of the US students receive education at public institutions and 92 of the 100 largest universities are public or 'state-supported' (that is, supported by one of the 50 individual states, not the federal government). In India, a majority of large universities and colleges are public. These include some supported by the national

Private Higher Education

TABLE 3.7 Private enrolment and private institutions (various years)

Country	Private enrolment (%)	Year	Private institutions (%)	Year
South Korea	78.3	1994	87.0	2002
Japan	77.1	2000	86.3	2000
Philippines	75.0	1999	81.0	1999
Chile	73.3	2005	93.3	2000
Brazil	73.2	2005	89.3	2005
Taiwan	71.9	2004	65.8	2004
Indonesia	71.4	2001	96	2001
Malaysia	39.1	2000	92.2	2000
Mexico	31.8	2005	69.1	2002
India	30.7	2005-06	42.9	2005-06
Poland	30.3	2004	70.5	2004
Romania	23.2	2003-4	54.9	2003-4
USA	23.2	2000	59.4	2000
Pakistan	23.1	2003-04	48.6	2005-06
Argentina	16.5	2005	42.9	2000
Russia	14.9	2004	38.2	2004
Bangladesh	14.4	2003-04	48.6	2005-06
Vietnam	10.4	2005	12.6	2005
China	8.9	2002	39.1	2002
Germany	3.7	2003	29.5	2003

Source Adapted from PROPHE (available online at www.albany.edu/dept/eaps/
prophe/data/international.html, downloaded on 9 October 2007).

government, but most by individual states. Major private universities
occupy all but three or four of the top 25 slots in most rankings in the
United States. Thus, the private research university appears to be held
in especially high regard in the United States and around the world, a
phenomenon hardly seen anywhere else in the world. In India, no private
university so far has the profile of a world-class research university, even
though a few new ones aspire to achieve that status.

The South Korean experience with private higher education is
noteworthy. South Korea attained universal higher education access in
just three decades, an achievement that took many advanced countries
more than half a century. Its rapid transition to universal higher
education occurred immediately after, or simultaneously with the swift

transition to universal secondary education with private sector playing a major role in this unprecedented consecutive transition. Eighty three per cent of the national budget for higher education comes from the households, a phenomenon unseen even in America, where the private sector institutions are important. Around 80 per cent of the students are currently at private universities and colleges in Korea.

In most countries around the world, private growth occurred outside government planning, even catching the government and the others by surprise (Levy, 2006). But it is increasingly common for the governments today in Asia, Eastern Europe and now even Africa and Middle East to articulate a rationale for private access. India's ambivalence and continued dithering on private participation is in sharp contrast to a number of Asian countries including China where the national government has allowed considerable leeway to the provinces to set variable, more liberal policies to encourage the growth of private institutions in order to promote access to higher education.

Analysis of Growth Pattern

An analysis of the growth trends and evolving policy environment shows two distinct trends. On the one hand, there has been a continuous shift in funding of higher education from taxpayers to the students/parents. On the other hand, the expansion in higher education is marked by a shift in sectoral balance with the number of enrolments in public institutions growing rather slowly compared to the private sector where it has grown rapidly. This shift has implications on access, equity and quality. It opens avenues for a variety of partnerships. There are concerns about exploitative tendencies of the private sector and persistent discomfort about its growth. Despite this, prospects for private higher education look good and it will reshape Indian higher education in a significant manner. These issues and concerns are analysed below.

Access, Equity and Quality

While the positive role of private higher education in expanding access is fairly straightforward, its impact on equity and quality is debatable.

Private Higher Education

Private institutions enrol students who would not be otherwise in higher education and would not be covered through public funds. By bringing in additional revenue into the higher education system, private finance supplements public funds. As seen in Table 3.8, there is a different paradigm on fundraising in private higher education.

TABLE 3.8 Different paradigms on fundraising

Pure public funding	Recourse to private finance
No money, no plan	No vision, no money
Budget cut, activity reduction	Great vision, big money
Look for small money	Look for big money
Ask for money when poor	Ask for money when strong
Funding is the limit	Sky is the limit
Doing what we did	Scaling new heights
Advancement	Steady progress
Appropriation	Partnership

Source Author.

Private institutions are believed to expand access in yet another way. Private higher education operates at much lower costs per student, while public universities and colleges are often rightly criticised for being highly inefficient. It is often argued that private institutions operate with low quality. They have fewer staff with most teaching staff on part-time basis. Costly fields of study and other undertakings, such as conventional academic research, are usually bypassed. While some private institutions usually cut out frills and provide essential infrastructure and facilities that are in many cases superior to those available in the public counterparts, there are many that do not provide even bare minimum infrastructure and facilities and cut corners in everything, compromising the overall quality of higher education. Any generalisation of this nature, however, would be inappropriate. But overall, private higher education is viewed as efficient, though it may cut corners compromising quality.

Another important aspect is that through example and competition, private provision spurs reform in finance and management in public system. Encouraged by the experience of private institutions, many public universities in India started self-financing programmes (discussed in Chapter 1) in subjects with high demand, helping improve overall access. However, it is often argued that private institutions 'skim off' lucrative fields (Levy, 2008). Thus, apart from increased access, its positive outcome is enhanced relevance.

Private growth in India, at least until recently, was through private college-public university arrangement. Private colleges affiliated to public universities accommodated demand without terribly watering down academic standards and reaching out to more students than otherwise, even in remote geographic areas and often catering to students from modest family backgrounds. In India, private institutions constitute neither the topmost layer nor the lowermost rung of the academic sphere. Most of them focus on narrow specialisations relating to commercial fields of study, such as business administration, engineering, information technology, hotel management, pharmacy, and so on. Through institutional proliferation, these now outnumber public institutions. There is also evidence of subsequent institutional broadening with several private institutions starting a number of programmes, even in liberal arts areas, as they grow. A similar development is seen in China, where the narrow institutions are growing using revenues generated from their lead commercial fields, in order to finance the opening of new fields or new campuses.

According to Levy (2008b), private institutions in India provide access as a second choice for those who are academically unable to gain entry to the limited public sector, particularly in professional disciplines. Students from poor backgrounds are deprived of access to highly selective public higher education, due to poor quality of their schooling or their inability to perform well in very competitive entry tests. In such cases, private institutions often provide access for those who can win places at middle or lower rung public institutions even while they cannot gain access to the leading public universities. Not only in India, this is true of Japan, Korea, South Africa, and, far behind but increasingly, China. Thus private higher education in these countries seems to promote equity.

There is a growing acceptance of its increasing role even amongst the academic community. A Planning Commission-sponsored study in 2002 revealed that more than two-thirds of the vice-chancellors, teachers, researchers and educational administrators contacted felt that privatisation would bring improvement in efficiency and effectiveness, though about half of them felt that it would also add to excellence. Almost all of them (98 per cent) favoured participation of the industry in financing and management of higher education. Sixty six per cent wanted the government to enact a private universities bill, while some stressed that instead of fresh legislation, changes can be made in the present framework to facilitate private participation. A large majority (88 per cent) favoured self-financing courses. Though the study was conducted on a small sample—size not sufficient enough to make generalisations—but one could undoubtedly see a strong positive faith in privatisation of higher education (Azad and Chandra, 2002).

Partnerships

While, some private institutions (both for-profits and non-profits) come up and grow as free-standing institutions, most of the private growth is through a variety of partnerships. Three kinds of partnerships, namely private college–public university partnership (most common and very extensive), institutions tied together in a chain (new and emerging), and private institution–foreign university partnership (popular for many years) have been discussed elsewhere in this chapter.

Direct partnerships between businesses either as businesses running their own corporate universities, or working out agreements to pay for the students' education in exchange for work commitments are not seen in India. Several IT companies though have set up huge training infrastructure for induction and continuing training of their workforce. A chain of 20 Indian Institutes of Information Technology are planned in partnership with major IT companies, including multinationals like the IBM and Google. Industry response has however been lukewarm, particularly after the global recessionary trends. In addition, there have been several unconventional partnerships. New institutions for legal education that were set up with the initiative of the Bar Council of India (in some cases the State Bar Councils) fall in this category (see Box 3.5).

BOX 3.5 National Law School of India—a model for public–private partnership

In 1986, the Bar Council of India established a model law school in the joint sector to act as a pacesetter for legal education reforms. A self-financing, privately managed Law University, independent of government control, the first of its kind in the country was established in Bengaluru under the name of National Law School of India University. Today there are ten such Law Universities in different states of the country. This has changed the course of higher education in law, making it internationally competitive and socially relevant attracting the attention of industry, government and the public in the legal sector. It assiduously maintains its autonomy in academic and governance matters. Some of them are tying up with foreign universities on their own terms. National Law School accommodates access with quality and autonomy with accountability. It has influenced curriculum development even outside the National Law Schools and compelled the private unaided institutions to improve.

Source Madhava Menon (2006).

Compared to other modes of increasing access, partnership brings the private and public together. While in most cases such partnerships prioritise cooperation over competition, they do so in ways that tend to make mutual use of private–public distinctiveness rather than to minimise it.

Advertising and Branding

There has always been a strong brand orientation amongst higher education institutions. But with the emergence of private higher education, advertising and branding have become very important. Many private institutions spend heavily on advertisement to attract prospective students and build their brand (see Box 3.6).

Sensing a unique opportunity, the print media has been fast with its response. The print media launched special vehicles to capture this expenditure on advertisements and combined this with relevant editorial inputs. Today, most English language dailies have supplements and some vernacular newspapers have also jumped on to the bandwagon. This sudden rush to advertise is due to the growing competition and the increasing number of options for the students, such as course content, location and even costs.

BOX 3.6   Spending on advertisements by educational institutions

According to AdEx India estimates, among various categories, educational institutions were at the number one slot (up from sixth position in 2003) in print media expenditure in 2004 in India. They spent Rs 2.1 billion in 2004. This worked out to 3.9 per cent of the total print ad spend. This category is seeing double-digit growth over the last few years. Further analysis showed that this growth comprises advertising by thousands of institutions spending a small amount each on advertising, with the total volume turning out to be a substantial amount. Educational advertising is seasonal and happens more in the period from April to August, which is the typical season for admissions. The preference of educational institutions for advertising in print media (constituting more than 90 per cent of advertisement expenditure) rather than television is not surprising. While television is a big draw, particularly for lifestyle, the print media suits the livelihood and life issues.

Source   AdEx India (Research Division of TAM Media) Estimates.

The entry of foreign universities through education consultants and franchisees is another development. Students can truly choose between India, England, Australia, the US, China, Europe, and so on because of the free availability of foreign exchange, as well as the availability of loan on easy terms. The need to announce the arrival of training institutes for entirely new career options like airlines, travel, clinical research and animation has added to the advertising boom.

Most of the educational advertisements are 'notice' type today. However, this is likely to change in the next few years. With increasing competition, educational institutions will apply all the marketing principles. Advertising will be more focused on addressing the needs of the students. A shift is already evident. A few institutions like IIPM, ISB, Amity International, Rai University, Wellingkars, Wigan & Leigh, and so on, are using image-building elements to differentiate themselves from the rest of the crowd. It seems this sector will present some interesting challenges for the advertising industry in building brands that endure.

Since there is still a huge demand for quality higher education and the competitive forces are still weak but for a few old institutions, efforts towards branding and advertising are only confined to new institutions, sometimes with questionable credentials. With a weak regulatory system, such institutions are using the power of advertising to misrepresent and misinform prospective students. By creating an aura of high reputation, such institutions are attempting to create a perception of high quality. Sometimes this borders on cheating. This has raised serious concerns to the extent of some people suggesting that advertisements in higher education should be banned.

In the final analysis, the emerging trend for branding and advertising in higher education has to be seen both as an opportunity and a threat. There could be a serious problem of information asymmetries, contributing to market failure in higher education. Branding and advertising can address this problem or make it worse, depending on the way it is used.

India has an opportunity to build up strong global brands in higher education and attract bright students, star faculty and research funding from all over the world. India has the potential to seize a huge global opportunity by positioning itself as a hub for quality and affordable higher education.

All higher education institutions should be encouraged to disseminate credible information and build authentic brands by creating public information about their profile and achievements. This would help the students and parents in making informed choices. A strong brand orientation would promote good conduct of higher education institutions, since they would have a reputation to lose.

In order to curb deceptive practices, there is a need for a guide on advertising, promotion and marketing.[11] This guide could clearly state what constitutes misrepresentation of facts, misinformation and deceptive practices. This would be helpful to the various prosecuting agencies and consumer courts in addressing this problem and ensuring fair play.

Malpractices and Corruption

There is a common concern that a large majority of the private institutions provide access via fraud. They are often accused of collecting exorbitant capitation fees and other institutional fees not brought into regular accounts, manipulation of entrance results and admission processes to maximise illicit payments, and disregarding admission norms in favour of those willing to pay more. Private deemed universities and the new private universities are often the biggest offenders. Unlike colleges that come under the oversight of the affiliating universities, these universities are independent. Oversight of the UGC on their functioning is weak. Wielding large political influence, they have managed to get a free hand in admissions and on fee-related issues using the plea of autonomy.

Even when the fee is regulated, there are large variations. The norms are unclear and the fee levels vary considerably among the states and within the states for various courses. For instance, it varies from Rs 20,000 per annum for an undergraduate course in engineering in Chhattisgarh to Rs 72,000 in same course in Chandigarh. The system of high fees charged for management seats continues unabated. Capitation fees range from Rs 200 to 800,000 per annum for some of the courses, while this may go up to Rs 1-4 million per annum for medical courses (Anandakrishnan, 2006). Despite fee caps, its implementation is lax. Complaints about private institutions indulging in various fee-related malpractices are rampant. During the 2007 Directorate of Technical Education, Tamil Nadu conducted surprise checks in 142 colleges and found evidence of at least 14 colleges violating the prescribed fee structure.

Many private institutions admit students long before the actual start of the academic session, collect full fees and retain original certificates. Sometimes, they also advance joining time to pre-empt students from joining institutions of their choice and confiscate the entire fee collected.[12] Some of them are offering technical programmes in distance mode without approval of the statutory council and the Distance Education Council.[13]

According to the AICTE Act, 1987, no technical institution can be started without AICTE sanction, and even approved institutions need to apply while starting a new course or taking up foreign collaborations. In March 2007, AICTE published a list of 169 institutions that were offering unapproved courses; 104 of them were collaborating with foreign institutions without seeking prior sanction.

Many private institutions treat their faculty somewhat like bonded labour in matters of salary and service conditions. While private investment in higher education has become inevitable in the current environment, the nature of private participation is so poorly or ambiguously spelled out that pseudo-educational ventures have come to dominate the Indian educational system. Whereas legitimate return on private investment is justifiable, there is no effective mechanism to check the greed of private providers that results in exploitation of gullible masses. As a result, overall private higher education suffers from a poor image.

Public policy fails to recognise several peculiarities about private higher education delivered in market environment. Unlike other services, competition between private providers fails to set prices in higher education. Each provider could exhibit monopolistic behaviour and work towards maximising its own profit. Interventions by the courts for over a decade and the government's ambivalence have not helped to check the errant behaviour of unscrupulous private providers. As a result, even credible private providers are tempted to make money by exploiting loopholes in the existing regulatory environment. Principle of Gresham's Law—bad providers driving out good—seems to apply. Thus, regulation (discussed in Chapter 7) becomes the central policy issue for the private higher education.

Concerns from Foreign Providers

As noted earlier in this chapter, the number of foreign education providers in India has grown as an adjunct to the domestic private sector. It is still small, but functions in a largely unregulated manner. This is similar to trends elsewhere in the world. According to Altbach (2008), marketplace for international higher education is 'large, growing and basically unregulated.'

> [While there are some] prestigious universities hoping to build links overseas, recruit top students to their home campuses and strengthen their brand abroad. But many more are sub-prime institutions: sleazy recruiters, degree packagers, low-end private institutions seeking to stave

off bankruptcy through the export market and even a few respectable universities forced by government funding cutbacks to raise cash elsewhere (Altbach, 2008).

Comparing it with sub-prime mortgages in the housing sector in the United States, Altbach points out that today international higher education stands 'somewhere between exuberance and a bubble.' It is now time to examine which actions are sustainable, which policies will serve the interests of students and the academy, and which actions constitute mistaken policy or greed. He observes that the open door policy advocated by some would leave the academic world subject to irrational exuberance and bubble mentality now evident in the mortgage market in the United States. He calls for clear regulation, probably by government authority to ensure that national interests are served and students do not receive shoddy service from unscrupulous providers. He suggests that transparency would be the key step for building a healthy environment.

Prospects

Trends over the past two and a half decades show that while public higher education will move with a glacial speed to create new capacities, private higher education will grow rapidly (see Table 3.9 for future growth trends of various types of institutions in the country).

In most professional fields, higher education would be dominated by private providers. Within the public university system, self-financing courses would grow rapidly. Distance education would also expand fast. The growth of private providers would make higher education expensive and exacerbate problem of equity.

While some private providers would establish themselves as quality institutions, bulk of the private higher education providers would continue to suffer from a bad image. Private higher education would flourish and gain respectability only if the providers could organise themselves around ethical practices and earn the trust of the general public. This has the potential to make government regulation irrelevant over a period of time.

TABLE 3.9   Current status and growth prospects by type of institution

Type	Ownership	Financing	Number of institutions	Students enrolled	Growth trends
Govt. Universities	Public	Public	250	1,100,000	Not growing
Government Colleges	Public	Public	4,250	2,800,000	Not growing
Private aided Colleges	Private	Public	5,800	3,550,000	Not growing
Private Universities	Private	Private	10	60,000	Emerging on the scene
Govt. Deemed Universities	Public	Public	38	40,000	Growing slowly
Private Universities	Private	Private	63	60,000	Growing rapidly
Private Deemed Universities	Private	Private	72	250,000	Growing rapidly
Private Colleges	Private	Private	7,860	3,350,000	Growing rapidly
Foreign Institutions	Private	Private	150	12,000	Emerging on the scene
Total			18,493	11,222,000	

Source Estimates by the Author based on primary data for 2006–07.

Conclusion

The demand for higher education has grown far more rapidly than what public institutions can accommodate, and the government is not able to provide finances to meet the growing demand. Thus, the future of Indian higher education would largely depend upon the growing private sector. Primarily 'demand absorbing' due to supply constraints—both overall and job-oriented—but also in part a result of general dissatisfaction due to deteriorating standards, private institutions have grown rapidly over the past two decades and from the trends, it seems, that it is destined to grow further. Thus, private higher education has a positive role in expanding access. This fact is now beginning to be appreciated and understood. It is considered as more efficient than its public counterpart, though its impact on quality and equity is debatable.

Private higher education has flourished in low-risk high profit segments of higher education. Most private institutions are commercially-oriented (though they may claim to be otherwise) and prepare graduates for job markets. This private boom in India has been in secular institutions that absorb the demand that the public sector could not or would not accommodate. There are several concerns about the private sector. While there are fears of low quality and inequitable access, the main concern is that the private institutions sometimes use deception in their pursuit of profit. There are tendencies in the private providers to be exploitative, and thus regulation becomes the central policy issue for the private higher education.

In India, private higher education has grown in a policy vacuum, unlike many other countries such as Malaysia (even China) where the government took measures to enable, promote, or even steer the private growth. Unexpected growth left the government trying to catch up with this subsequently in their regulatory and funding policies. Despite the emergence of some quality private institutions, poor image overall plagues private provision, and hence it is often berated and dismissed. Notwithstanding this, private higher education continues to be the main venue for increasing access to higher education.

Growth of private higher education would leave large gaps. Public higher education would be required to fill in these gaps. The public higher education sector would have to step in the areas of post-graduate education and research and for education in liberal arts, humanities and languages. Public funding has to take care of those who cannot afford higher education. The challenges from foreign providers that have come up in recent years are similar to challenges from the domestic private provision. There is now time to face realities and correct the systemic anomalies and wrong notions about private higher education—both domestic and foreign. While private education would enhance access, foreign providers could energise local providers through both by example and competition.

In conclusion, private higher education has come to stay and is destined to grow. It will bring in competitive merit and force periodical changes in curriculum, pedagogy, examination and governance across the entire educational sector. However, the State will have to negotiate equality and equity through a fair, transparent, participatory regulatory system that will be driven more by consumer interests. A coherent policy framework that recognises the complementarities of public and private higher education and ensures the healthy growth of both is required. A sound regulatory framework that keeps the interest of the students at the centre for domestic as well as foreign providers is needed.

4

Financing and Management

We don't have the money. Therefore we have to think.
— E. Rutherford

HIGHER education has been primarily public funded so far. Now it is being funded from a variety of sources. While private financing is important and growing rapidly, higher education institutions now look for a diversity of alternative sources to expand, meet the rising costs and enhance quality in an increasingly competitive environment. With an explosive growth of the private sector and the growth of self-financing programmes in public institutions (discussed in the previous chapters), private financing is a significant part of overall financing of Indian higher education. Alternative sources of funding are emerging on the scene as well.

In framing policies for funding and regulation of higher education, it is realised that increased funding would not automatically result in better higher education. Thus, while the government support decreases noticeably (at least in relative, if not absolute terms), performance and accountability expectations have increased. The mechanisms for public funding contain important incentives to achieve higher education's three main goals, that is, quality, efficiency and equity. The public institutions are striving to maintain and enhance competitiveness.

Funding policies are designed to enforce accountability. An important element of financing reform is to efficiently manage the resources at the institutional level.

In view of the above developments, this chapter looks at issues of financing and management of Indian higher education. The chapter begins with the conceptual debate on resource flows to higher education and examines how this debate shapes funding policy. Patterns of public funding, private funding primarily through tuitions and fees and third stream funding is then analysed in the context of global patterns and trends. Funding arrangements are also discussed. To enhance efficiency in the use of resources, fund allocation mechanism and institutional management are important. These are examined. With focus on inclusive growth and achieving equity objective, students' financial aid is now critical. Schemes of grants and loans, particularly emerging trend towards income-contingent loans are therefore discussed. Finally, the core elements of sustainable funding in the Indian context are discussed. Though in large part teaching and research in the country are jointly funded, yet the focus of this chapter is primarily on funding of teaching. Issues relating to research funding are discussed in Chapter 6.

Resource Flows: Public and Private Sources

Resources flow to higher education institutions from a variety of sources. As seen in Figure 4.1, they receive funds from three main sources: governments (as grants), students and households (as tuitions and fees) and other private entities (as payment for services and donations). Higher education institutions also provide funds to students (as scholarships) and other private entities (towards services). Governments provide grants and loans to students and receive repayments from them. Other private entities provide financial assistance to households and students.

Financing higher education is often described in terms of three streams of funding. The first stream comprises the grants from the government. The second stream is the tuition and fees from students, and the third stream includes all other receipts including donations, royalty and consultancy income. First stream is public funding, which

FIGURE 4.1   Resource flows to and from a tertiary education institution

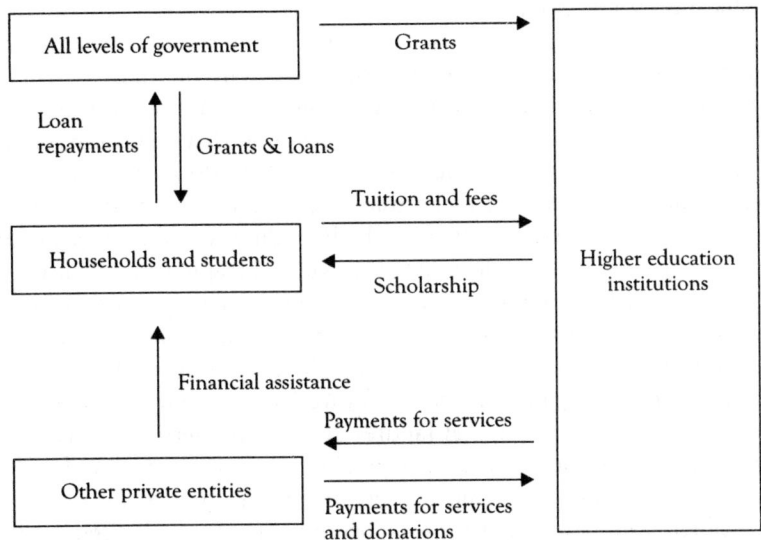

Source Jongbloed, 2004.

can also take the form of grants and loans directly to students and households. Second and third streams are primarily private funding, though third stream may also include funding from public sources. While the cost structures of public and private institutions are similar, the difference is primarily in terms of who pays. Private institutions have high reliance on private funds/gifts and tuition paying students. In the public institutions, there is a presumption of state subsidy, even though state funding levels have declined over the years.

There has been a long and unsettled debate on whether funding for higher education should be from public or private sources. This is rooted in the assertion that access to higher education is a 'right'. As a result, some people argue that higher education must be free, but they fail to appreciate that this does not automatically follow. While all agree that food is a basic right, its competitive supply at market prices is not disputed. The equity objective is fulfilled not in a 'free' higher education system, but a system in which no bright person—even if he or she comes from a disadvantaged background—is denied access to higher education (Barr, 2004).

At the conceptual level, the financing debate revolves around two questions: whether higher education is a public or a private good, and if social or private returns from higher education are higher. Government funding is justified on the ground that education, being a public good or at least a quasi-public good produces many positive externalities. This would mean that since the society at large—rather than the individual—benefits from higher education, the government should finance higher education. It is widely accepted that education helps in social mobility—therefore it is an effective instrument for promoting equity. Justifications given for public subsidisation of higher education include imperfections in capital markets that inhibit students from borrowing against uncertain future returns from investment in higher education and market failures due to asymmetric information. Finally, the production process in higher education is believed to be subject to economies of scale or decreasing returns to scale. Hence it is considered more efficient for the government to provide higher education (Tilak, 2005).

Several arguments against public subsidisation of higher education are also put forth. The social rates of returns of higher education are found to be lower than private returns. It is argued that subsidies in higher education mainly accrue to the rich, particularly in countries like India where the enrolment ratio is still low. This is regressive and increases income inequalities by transferring resources from the poor to the rich. It is contended that with public subsidisation by the state, educational institutions become vulnerable to government control, which is not desirable in higher education institutions. It is argued that since higher education has very low price elasticity, the cost recovery measures in higher education would not lead to any significant fall in enrolments. In fact, additional resources available for higher education would improve access. This would also lead to improvement in quality. Private provision of higher education is also considered more efficient and, therefore, desirable.

Despite differences in opinion, there is now a consensus on three issues. Principally, there is no opposition to public subsidisation of higher education *per se*, but higher education in its entirety cannot be funded through tax revenues due to competing—and politically more popular—claims for public funds from other sectors of the economy. Hence, there is a 'limited' scope for increased public spending in most countries around the world. Private financing thus becomes an important venue for funding higher education. Two, while higher education need not be free, there is a strong case for making higher education *free at the point of use*. Three, it is just not the level of funding but also the basis and criteria according to which public funds are made available that can improve the quality and accessibility of higher education.

Public Funding

With the expansion of higher education, there has been growing public funding for higher education. Numerous public benefits of higher education justify substantial government support. Public spending on education demonstrates political will to redistribute income and allocate investment in different sectors. Government spending on social sector and education is significant in India. More than one-fourth (27.19 per cent) of the total expenditure of the central and the state governments combined was on the social sector in 2006-07. Almost half of it (47.6 per cent) was on education alone. Education receives much higher priority than health in public spending, and the money allocated to education is more than twice the expenditure on health. Education is the primary responsibility of the state governments, thus funded mainly by them. As seen in Table 4.1, more than three-fourth of the education expenditure is met by the state governments and a major part of that is recurrent expenditure. Interestingly, a large part of expenditure on education (including training both formal and non-formal) is made by departments other than education departments. More than one-third expenses on education are made by other departments at the national level.

The central government gives high priority to education, as evident from Table 4.2. It is seen that expenditure on education by the central government has increased from 2.2 per cent in 2002-03 to 5 per cent proposed in 2008-09. Though defence continues to get high priority in public spending by the central government, increased outlay for the social sector, particularly education is a positive development. As much

TABLE 4.1 Education expenditure by departments and plan/non-plan (2005–06 BE)

	Per cent share	Total amount Rs billion	Education department	Other departments	Per cent share Plan	Non-plan
Central Government	24.0	289.29	63.4	36.6	81.1	18.9
State Governments	76.0	914.18	86.6	13.4	15.4	84.6
Total	100.0	1203.47	81.0	19.0	31.4	68.6

Sources Selected Educational Statistics, MHRD, Govt. of India, 2005–06.
Notes BE: Budget Estimate.

TABLE 4.2 Central government–priorities in spending

Year	Education amount in Rs billion	Per cent share Education	Health	Defence	Internal security
2002–03	90.69	2.2	1.6	16.1	2.8
2003–04	101.45	2.2	1.5	15.2	2.7
2004–05	130.98	2.6	1.6	18.0	2.9
2005–06	178.10	3.5	1.9	18.8	3.3
2006–07	238.10	4.0	2.0	18.0	3.0
2007–08	242.49	4.0	2.0	17.0	3.0
2008–09	387.03	5.0	2.0	16.0	3.0

Source Ministry of Finance, Govt. of India, various years.

as Rs 380 billion is budgeted for education during 2008–09, an increase of nearly 60 per cent over 2007–08.

Within the education sector, as seen in Table 4.3, elementary education receives high priority. Though elementary education is the responsibility of the state governments, the central government has begun to provide substantial support in recent years. The central government's support for secondary education has been around Rs 16 billion and rose to Rs 18.38 billion during 2007–08. This is being raised to Rs 51.40 billion in 2008–09 for taking up universalisation of secondary education during the Eleventh Five Year Plan period

Financing and Management

under a new Scheme for Universal Access and Quality at the Secondary Stage (SUCCESS).

There has been significant increase in the central government's support for higher and technical education. This support is mainly towards institutions run and maintained by the central government. Support for higher technical education has increased from less than 20 per cent in 2005–06 to 27.5 per cent in 2008–09. Plan share has increased suggesting that a large part is for new institutions that are in the process of being set up by the central government. The data in Table 4.3 does not include medical and agriculture education, but there has been a significant increase in funding for medical and agriculture education as well.

TABLE 4.3 Central government expenditure by level of education (2005–06 and 2008–09)

Sector	2005–06 (BE)			2008–09 (BE))		
	Amount (Rs billion)	Plan share %	Share by level %	Amount (Rs billion)	Plan share %	Share by level %
Elementary Education	112.20	99.8	62.0	197.77	100	50.1
Secondary Education	15.92	49.5	8.8	51.40	79.7	13.0
Higher and Technical Education	37.08	41.1	19.4	100.96	63.0	27.5
Adult Education	2.63	99.2	1.6	4.08	99.4	1.1
North East and Sikkim	13.15	100	7.2	32.77	100	8.3
Total	180.98	83.1	100.0	386.98	81.0	100.0

Source Demands for Grants, Ministry of Finance, Govt. of India. Available online at http://finmin.nic.in/the_ministry/dept_expenditure/index.html (downloaded on 10 May 2008).

Higher (including technical, medical and agriculture education) is the primary responsibility of the state governments. As per the analysis of the budgeted expenditure on education by the government for the year 2005–06, all taken together budget estimate for higher education was Rs 244.57 billion (as seen in Table 4.4). Two-third of this comes from the state governments, and that is mainly to meet recurrent expenditure. An analysis of funding patterns shows that the role of the central government is limited and spread unevenly.

TABLE 4.4   Higher education expenditure (2005–06 BE in Rs billion)

	General higher education	Technical education	Agriculture, medical and others	Total
Central government				
Plan	7.90	7.33	27.20	42.43
Non-plan	13.18	8.67	15.30	37.15
Subtotal	21.08	16.00	42.50	79.58
State governments				
Plan	5.57	7.78	9.50	22.85
Non-plan	80.23	13.41	48.50	142.14
Subtotal	85.80	21.19	58.00	164.99
Total	106.88	37.20	100.50	244.57

Source MHRD (2006b).

There is a very significant increase in funding for higher and technical education during the Eleventh Five Year Plan. Allocation for higher and technical education during the Eleventh Plan has been raised to Rs 849.43 billion from Rs 96 billion in the Tenth Plan period. Rs 306.82 billion has been allotted for several new initiatives, with half of the plan outlay being reserved for new institutions at the high-end (92), new centres for research and training in frontier areas (50) and new colleges and polytechnics in uncovered districts. Another half is for existing universities and colleges, including those that are not covered by the UGC for funding so far.

However, as seen in Table 4.5, Eleventh Plan allocation of Rs 306.82 billion for new institutions is merely a small fraction of Rs 2147.60 billion. This amount has been estimated to enhance support to existing institutions/programmes/schemes for expansion, quality upgrading and for making higher education inclusive; establishing new institutions, and centres for training and research in frontier areas; and effecting long overdue academic, administrative, governance and financing reforms. This only covers half of the colleges. To cover the remaining colleges, another Rs 600 billion would be required, and to have a university in each district, an investment of another Rs 1,000 billion would be required. This does not include cost of land and recurrent expenditure.

Financing and Management

TABLE 4.5   Central government—Eleventh Plan outlay

	No. of institutions	Unit cost	Total amount	11th Plan outlay
			in Rs billion	
General Higher Education				
• New central universities	16	6	96	30
• World class central universities	14	10	140	45
• New colleges in low GER districts	370	.10	37	7.82
• Development of uncovered state universities	150	2	300	70
• Development of uncovered colleges	6,000	.10	600	
• Additional assistance to covered universities	160	1.60	256	30
• Additional assistance to covered colleges	5,500	.05	275	
• Hostels for women	1,000	.05	50	10
Subtotal			1,754	192.82
Technical Higher Education				
• New IITs	8	8	64	20
• New NITs	20	1	20	5
• New IIITs	20	2	40	9.40
• New IISER	5	5	25	9
• New IIMs	7	2	14	6.60
• New SPAs	2	2	4	2.40
• New centers in frontier area	50	.50	25	1.50
• Upgradation of state engineering colleges	200	.50	100	9.10
• Upgrading technical institutions	7	2	14	7
Subtotal			306	70
Polytechnic Education				
• New Polytechnics in uncovered districts	300	.12	36	13.20
• Strengthening of existing polytechnic	400	.05	20	10
• New community polytechnic	580	.02	11.60	5.80
• Support to colleges for diploma courses	200	.05	10	10
• Women hostel in 500 polytechnic	500	.02	10	5
Subtotal			87.60	44
Total			2147.60	306.82

Source Planning Commission, New Delhi.

Efforts are being made to fill in gap by mobilising private resources through public–private partnerships.

Funding in Terms of GDP

The amount of funds allotted to higher education in a country determines both its size and quality. There are several ways to measure the overall level of financial commitment to higher education, each with its own strengths and weaknesses. In cross-country comparisons, public expenditure on higher education expressed in terms of percentage of gross domestic product (GDP) is often used.

Against a global average of 4.2 per cent of GDP spent on education, India spends 3.80 per cent of its GDP on education. Higher education spending is 0.70 per cent of the GDP. Comparing public expenditure on higher education as a percentage of the GDP is not a good measure. In such comparisons, it is seen that there are few differences between the developed and the developing countries. The differences in the level of GDP and also different participation rates in higher education mask the relative efforts of different countries towards higher education. Both the developed Scandinavian countries and poor African countries like Lesotho and Barbados spend a high percentage of their GDP on higher education. Whereas the public expenditure of 0.70 per cent of GDP on higher education in India is larger than that of Korea (0.50 per cent), China (0.50 per cent), and Japan (0.54 per cent), it is lower than the US (1.30 per cent), France (1.10 per cent), and UK (0.80 per cent), as noted in Table 4.6. It is seen that in a range of countries (Australia, New Zealand, Korea, Canada and the USA), high private spending goes with high participating rates. There are a few countries like Sweden and Finland that combine high participation with little private spending. These countries have very high level of public spending on higher education—levels that might be unsustainable in most other countries given other budgetary demands.

Another measure is to compare the public expenditure per student across countries. As seen in Table 4.6, whereas developed countries spend close to USD 10,000 per student per year, developing countries spend less than USD1,000 per student. India spends merely USD 400

Financing and Management

TABLE 4.6   Higher education expenditure in 2005, or latest year available

Country	% of GDP	Public expenditure per student PPP US $	Public expenditure per student as % of GDP per capita
Finland	1.70	9,996	34.1
Sweden	1.50	13,035	44.1
USA	1.30	10,365	27.6
France	1.10	9,996	34.1
India	1.00	400	94.7
UK	0.80	8,100	27.7
Australia	0.80	7,041	23.2
Brazil	0.70	2,938	35.9
Russia	0.62	1,024	10.8
Japan	0.54	4,830	17.0
China	0.50	2,728	53.0
Korea	0.50	1,841	9.0
Philippines	0.40	575	12.4
Indonesia	0.20	465	13.3

Source UNESCO Global Education Digest, 2007.

per student. Even at purchase point parity, it works out to be much lower than the developed countries and China (at USD 2,728 per student). Here again, at the very top of the list of countries with the highest per student spending is an odd mix of developed and less-developed countries. High fixed costs in universities result in very high cost per student in very small higher education systems (Hauptman, 2006).

A better measure is to use an indicator that factors in both student enrolment and how higher education spending relates to the overall economy. Thus, government expenditure on higher education per student as a percentage of GDP per capita is often used for international comparison. Usually, it is less than 50 per cent for developed countries, while for developing countries it is generally more than 50 per cent; in some cases it might even exceed 100 per cent. As seen from Table 4.6, this ratio is very high in case of India.

This ratio is 26 per cent in US, 31 per cent in the UK, 17 per cent in Japan and merely 5 per cent in Korea. Despite the relative effort of the governments of Korea and Japan on higher education being small, these countries have already achieved universal higher education. In these countries, there is a sizeable private higher education, and large part of higher education spending comes from private sources, mainly from the households. The USA is a unique case, where despite two-thirds of all expenditure being met from private sources, the government spends a huge amount on higher education (Usher, 2006).

Public expenditure on higher education (including technical education) has increased from 0.19 per cent of GDP in 1950–51 to 0.66 per cent in 2004–05 (Table 4.7). It is now close to 0.70 per cent. Of the total government support for higher education, only about one-fourth comes from the central government. The contribution of the central government to the overall expenditure (including household expenditure) is around 10 per cent compared to more than 30 per cent by the federal government in the USA.

TABLE 4.7   Education/higher education expenditure in terms of GDP

Year	Total education % GDP	Higher education %GDP	Higher education % Education
1950–51	1.20	0.19	20.0
1960–61	1.52	0.39	22.0
1970–71	2.11	0.77	27.0
1980–81	2.98	0.98	29.0
1990–91	3.84	0.77	20.05
2000–01	4.33	0.89	20.55
2001–02	3.84	0.69	18.06
2002–03	3.79	0.70	18.42
2003–04	3.50	0.62	18.08
2004–05	3.68	0.66	18.00

Source Selected Educational Statistics, MHRD, Govt. of India, 2004–05.

Funding Arrangements

Source and Agencies for Funding

While departments of higher education are primarily responsible for higher education funding, there are other ministries and departments and several agencies responsible for funding higher education. The government budget is either plan or non-plan budget and capital or revenue budget. Day-to-day expenses, including salary expenses, are recurrent expenses usually provided under the non-plan budget, while capital investment comes from the plan budget. Since higher education institutions are autonomous entities, all financial support to them is GIA under the revenue account. Thus, almost all expenditure on higher education is on revenue account—capital expenditure is negligible.

Both the central and the state governments share the responsibility of financing higher education. There are four major strands of higher education: general higher education, technical education, medical education and agriculture education. Each of them is separately funded. Medical education and agriculture education are funded by the Ministry of Health and the Ministry of Agriculture respectively. There are similar arrangements at the state level. Both general higher education and technical education are funded by the Department of Higher Education. General higher education is funded through a buffer body, namely the UGC, while technical education is funded directly through the Department of Higher Education at the national level. At the state level, funding is directly by the state governments. The UGC also provides plan grants to state universities and colleges. The Indian Council of Agriculture Research (ICAR) discharges similar functions in respect of agriculture education. There is no buffer body for funding medical education at the national or the state level. The All India Council for Technical Education (AICTE) provides some funding support to technical institutions. Table 4.8 provides an overview of funding arrangements for higher education institutions in the country.

In addition, there are other ministries at the national and state level and several other that support specialised institutions under their jurisdiction or provide some financial assistance to higher education institutions generally. There is a network of the National Institutes of Fashion Technology (NIFTs) under the Ministry of Textiles; the multiple-campus National Institute of Design is under the Ministry of Commerce and Industry; Indian Statistical Institute under the Ministry of Statistics and Programme Implementation, and so on. The Ministry of Science and Technology has a network of institutions with a focus on research, and the ministry also provides research funding to other

TABLE 4.8 Funding of higher education institutions

Type of institutions	Funding agency (source)
Central technical institutions including IITs (7), IIMs (6), NITs (20), IIITs (3), IISER (3) and Others (3)	Department of Higher Education (Govt. of India)
Central Universities, majority of colleges affiliated to Delhi University, colleges affiliated to Allahabad University and Banaras Hindu University	UGC (Govt. of India)
Central medical institutions including AIIMS	Ministry of Health (Govt. of India)
Central agriculture universities	ICAR (Govt. of India)
Deemed universities (other than private deemed universities)	12 by the UGC, another 12 only plan assistance, some directly by the concerned government and remaining about 70 receive no public funds
State universities (other than private universities)	Department of higher education (state governments); UGC provides some plan grants
State technical universities and colleges	Department of technical education (state governments); AICTE provides some support
State health universities and colleges	Departments of Health (state governments)
State agriculture universities and colleges	Departments of Agriculture (state governments)
State government colleges	Department of higher education of state governments (UGC provides some plan grants)
Private aided colleges	Concerned department of the state governments (usually support towards salary grants only)

Source Author.

institutions of higher education as well. As noted in Chapter 1, post-1980, a large number of private colleges have come up. Such colleges receive no grants from the government. In recent years, there has been a rapid increase in the number of private deemed universities. More than a dozen private universities have been set up by the state governments. In all, funding arrangements are extremely complex.

As seen in Table 4.9, even among the institutions funded by the central government, certain institutions like the IITs are more liberally funded than others. 85 per cent of the total central funding to higher education (including technical education) goes to support only about 3 per cent of students, enrolled in about 130 higher education institutions. Though the UGC is seen as the main funding agency of the government for higher education, yet the fund flow through the UGC is a small fraction of the overall funding of higher education.

TABLE 4.9 Funding of higher education from the central government

Agency	Institutions (type and number)	No. of students	Funding (2004–05) Rs in billion		Per student funding (average) in Rs	
			Plan	Non-plan	Plan	Non-plan
University Grants Commission	16 Central Universities + 12 Deemed Universities and 59 Colleges	150,000	2.0	1,100	13,350	73,300
Central Government	42 University level Institutions (IITs, IIMs, NITs etc.)	50,000	5.0	750	100,000	150,000
State Governments	180 Universities and 10,250 colleges	6,644,000	4.0	Nil	602	Nil
Self-financing Sector	70 Universities Level + 7,650 Colleges	3,637,000	Nil	Nil	Nil	Nil
Total		**10,481,000**	**11.0**	**1,850**	–	–

Source Estimates by author based on budget documents of Ministry of HRD and UGC.

It is clear from above that the spread of public funds is uneven. Nearly one-third of the institutions do not get government funds at all. Of the remaining, only about one-half get funds from the central government. A small number of central institutions that cater to less than 3 per cent of the student population get 85 per cent of the central funds; the amount of central funding received by the rest is very small. A majority of the universities and almost all colleges (with exceptions of some colleges in Delhi) depend on the state governments for funding. Overall, the role of the central government in funding higher education is very limited. Only about one-fourth comes from the central government with the remainder coming from the state governments. With many state governments facing financial crunch, public funding level per student is inadequate and declining.

Public funding has increased across countries in absolute terms, as a percentage of GDP, but in fewer cases on student basis. The fact that higher education in India is severely under-funded is corroborated in a recent study by Tilak (2004). He found out that with the increasing enrolments in recent years, there has been a decline in per student expenditure in higher education. This decline has been drastic in the 1990s. He estimated this decline at 28 per cent points over a 12–year period from the year 1990–91 to 2002–03.

Funding from the UGC

The UGC was set up on the pattern of the University Grants Committee in England. The purpose of the buffer body arrangement was originally to avoid any suggestion that the government might use the power of the purse to interfere and that judgements and decisions are not taken with an eye on short-term political considerations. It is also the main funding agency of the central government. Whereas, around 42 technical institutions are funded by the central government directly, all others are funded through the UGC.

Nearly 65 per cent of the budget of the UGC is meant for meeting the operating expenses of the central universities and the Delhi colleges. The remaining 35 per cent plan budget is spent for the system at large. With only Rs 6 billion for about 5,500 institutions, the level of funding is insignificant. It is also skewed in favour of the central university system.

Financing and Management

Somehow, there is an impression that only the central university system is the primary responsibility of the UGC and the central government. This is evident from the fact that an additional amount of nearly Rs 5 billion allocated by the Planning Commission in 2005–06 was almost entirely provided to central universities. With a view to increase capacity in higher education institutions to accommodate students from other backward classes, an investment of nearly Rs 80 billion has been planned. This amount will again go mainly to the central institutions.

In terms of its mandate, the UGC is expected to inquire into the financial requirement of the universities (and colleges affiliated to them) and advise the governments to provide the same (a role that the UGC never performed, perhaps because such exercise would end up being futile, due to the inability and unwillingness of the governments to meet the genuine requirements of higher education institutions in the face of financial constraints). The private unaided universities and colleges are expected to be self-financing institutions and are expected to meet all their expenses from their own revenue sources, which is mostly from tuitions. They are not eligible for any public funding or UGC grants.

Only about 14,000 colleges come under the purview of the UGC system, and with permanent and temporary affiliations and UGC assists only 40 per cent (5,625) of the colleges that meet its minimum eligibility norms, mostly in terms of physical facilities and infrastructure. The UGC's policy on the eligibility for grants, that had become restrictive because of fund constraints, is likely to be reversed during the Eleventh Five Year Plan.

Only 130 institutions of higher education get recurrent grants from the UGC or the central government. More than 90 per cent of the grants are against operating expenses such as salaries, pension and other pre-emptive claims like water, electricity and rental charges, and so on, and very little is left for library, laboratory and other academic activities. Other institutions eligible for UGC grants get only the plan budget support for capital expenditure, and even that is not substantial. On an average, a college gets merely around Rs 0.2 million or so each year whereas a university gets Rs 5 to 7 million per year as a development grant. Box 4.1 and Figure 4.2 show that UGC funding of higher education is grossly inadequate and skewed in favour of selected universities and colleges.

FIGURE 4.2   Universities and colleges with/without central and public funding

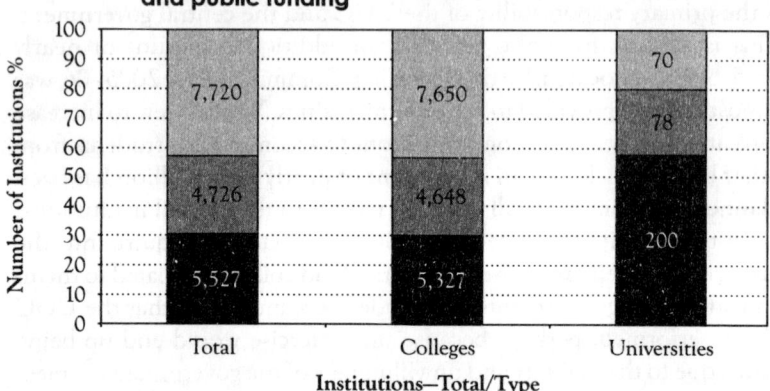

Eligible for central funding   Not eligible for central funding
Not eligible for any public funding

BOX 4.1   UGC funding—inadequate and skewed

During the five year period from 2000–01 to 2004–05, 73.5 per cent of the total grants were disbursed to the central universities, 8.37 per cent to the deemed universities and 19.15 per cent to the state universities (113 state universities eligible to receive UGC grants). Nearly 50 per cent (46.7 per cent in 2004–05) goes to the Delhi–based universities and colleges.

Merely 28 universities (out of a total of 350 universities) received operating funds (also referred as non-plan or maintenance grants) from the UGC. None of the state universities receive maintenance grants.

Student-based grants (scholarships and fellowships) are just about three per cent of the maintenance grants. Of the total non-plan grants given to the Central Universities, Delhi-based universities (three central and two deemed-to-be universities) account for nearly 30 per cent. Only Delhi colleges (other than 50 per cent grant to four BHU colleges) get maintenance grants (non-plan grants) amounting to about Rs 2.9 billion in 2004–05.

Share of state universities under plan grants over the last five years was 53.12 per cent for 113 universities, against 39.69 per cent for 16 central universities and 7.19 per cent for 23 Deemed-to-be Universities.

Source UGC Annual Statement of Accounts 2004–05 (based on analysis by the author).

Most public funding for higher education is institution based. It is on input-based deficit financing basis. This is not only inefficient, but promotes status quoism. On an average, nearly 85 per cent of all public spending on higher education institutions is on salaries and allowances. Many old institutions have huge pension bills. Very little is spent on academic activities. In many institutions, the number of non-academic support staff far exceeds the number of academic staff. Policies adopted by most funding agencies in India adjust income from internal resources—mainly tuition fee income from the annual grants, leaving no incentive for institutions to raise internal resources or raise tuition fees.

In addition to general development grants and maintenance grant, the UGC operates over 100 schemes—providing a wide range of development grants to institutions, running day care centres for children, promotion of sports, travel grants for VCs and researchers, area studies, cultural exchange, adult education, women's studies, academic staff colleges, hostels for women, innovative programmes in frontier research and career oriented education, and so on. The schemes implemented by the UGC are rarely by any external professional agencies. The Eleventh Plan has suggested that there is an urgent need for such in-depth evaluation and streamlining the range of schemes, and rationalising the procedures and delivery mechanism including the disbursal of grants.

In sum, majority of higher education institutions are not eligible for central funds. Those who get central funds find that the amounts are very small. A large number of institutions do not get any public funds at all.

Private Funding

Earlier, the government provided funds for setting up of new institutions, their extension and improvement as well as maintaining such institutions by providing them with operating expenses. In many cases, the government maintained privately set up institutions by providing financial support for meeting salary charges. Such institutions are referred to as private-aided institutions. Now the government neither sets up nor maintains most of the new institutions. These are the private unaided or simply private institutions. Now these institutions are increasingly funded by private sources, mainly, the households in India. Chapter 3 has dealt with such institutions in detail.

Thus, accounting for only public expenditure on higher education misses out on an important and growing component of higher education spending that is the private spending. In many cases, private contributions as tuition fees in public or government dependent private and independent private institutions are significant. Direct estimates of private spending are not available. Based on estimates by compiling data on the share of tuition fee income in the annual budgets of higher education institutions, it is seen that the contribution of households as tuition fees is around Rs 186.75 billion per year. The sources of revenues other than tuition fees being small are inconsequential. These have been ignored in the estimates. The total annual expenditure on higher education works out to be Rs 376.75 billion per year. Thus, against a desired expenditure of Rs 629.8 billion, Rs 376.75 billion (around 60 per cent) per year is being spent by the government and households together. Thus, there is a shortfall of about 40 per cent. This shortfall would obviously get reflected in the poor standards of higher education in the country.

While estimating the shortfall, an average unit cost of Rs 60,000 has been used. This is a conservative estimate based on the author's own assessment of handling university finances in India. In 2004, a group of vice-chancellors had estimated the unit cost at Rs 100,000.[1] Cost of higher education in India varies very widely across institutions and by discipline and subject of study. In some cases, the unit costs are as high as Rs 200,000 per student and in other cases this is as low as few thousand rupees. The average unit is therefore indicative.

Direct estimates of private spending on higher education, as already noted, are not available. Based on estimates by compiling data on the share of tuition fee income in the annual budgets of the higher education institutions, it is seen that the contribution of households to the revenue stream of higher education institutions is at least as much as public expenditure on higher education. This is not surprising considering

43 per cent institutions are private institutions, and 30 per cent of enrolment is in private institutions; many public institutions have self-financing courses and most public institutions offering professional degree programmes have high tuition fees.

Another way of estimating private spending on higher education is using NSS data. As per the NSS (2003), there has been a sharp hike in private spending on education over the last decade or so. The per capita private expenditure on education almost quadrupled from 1.2 per cent in 1983 to 4.4 per cent in 2003. In urban areas, the growth was a strapping 200 per cent from 2.1 per cent in 1983 to 6.3 per cent in 2003. The rural sector showed a high growth of 262 per cent from a mere 0.8 per cent in 1983 to 2.9 per cent in 2003. In absolute terms, households spent nearly Rs 335 billion on education in 2003. It is estimated that almost half of it goes into higher education. This works out to be comparable to the figure mentioned above.

There are, however, wide interstate variations. Private spending is higher in the richer states, where government spending also tends to be high. Interestingly, private spending as a proportion of the total spending on education tends to be higher even in poor states. The reason is possibly due to the fact that government spending on education in poor states is so low that households need to spend more to fill in this gap. It would be fair to expect that a significant amount of this flows to the higher education sector (Table 4.10).

Based on data compiled by UNESCO, Table 4.11 gives expenditure on education at different levels from public and private sources as percentage of GDP. It is seen that in advanced countries, namely US, UK, Australia and South Korea, public spending at lower levels of education is much higher, while in India public spending on higher levels is more. It appears however that this data does not capture the recent trends in growing private spending for higher education in India. Across a range of countries, a significant amount of expenditure on higher education is through private financing. It is seen that 84 per cent of all expenditure on higher education in Korea and 57 per cent in Japan comes from private sources. As per analysis done by the author, nearly 50 per cent of the higher education expenditure comes from private sources in India (Agarwal, 2006a). This is in fact more than many

TABLE 4.10 Relative expenditure on education by major states

States	Share of population %	Education expenditure as percentage of SGDP %	Per capita expenditure on education (in Rupees)	
			Private (2001–02)	Government (2000–01)
Andhra Pradesh	7.4	3.5	368	567
Assam	2.6	9.6	153	778
Bihar	10.7	6.2	168	44
Delhi	1.3	2.0	693	809
Gujarat	4.9	3.7	272	812
Haryana	2.1	3.2	609	737
Karnataka	5.1	4.0	245	674
Kerala	3.1	4.3	434	902
Madhya Pradesh	7.9	7.0	210	838
Maharashtra	9.4	3.5	323	1,070
Orissa	3.6	5.4	182	515
Punjab	2.4	3.7	604	845
Rajasthan	5.5	5.0	225	591
Tamil Nadu	6.1	4.1	364	784
Uttar Pradesh	17	3.9	291	387
West Bengal	7.8	3.9	354	1,749
All India			299	705

Sources For share of population–Registrar General of India (2001 Census); For education expenditure–Analysis of budgeted expenditure on education (2002-03), Ministry of HRD; and for per capita expenditure–Household consumer expenditure and employment–unemployment situation in India (NSS–58th round, July–December 2002, Report no. 484).

of the developed nations. For instance, only around 29 per cent of the funding for higher education in UK, around 14 per cent in France and less than 10 per cent in Germany comes from private sources in India. Estimates of expenditure from private sources in other South Asian countries are not available, but it would be safe to guess that these would also be significant, particularly if one looks at the large and growing independent private sector in these countries (Agarwal, 2008b).

Jongbloed (2004) notes that the countries such as the United States, Korea, Canada, and New Zealand that have been able to channelise a higher percentage of GDP into higher education raise substantial share

Financing and Management

**TABLE 4.11 Expenditure on education as a percentage of GDP
by source of fund**

	US	UK	Australia	South Korea	India
Public sources					
Pre-primary	0.3	0.4	0.1	0.1	–
Primary	1.9	1.4	1.6	1.6	1.2
Secondary	2.1	2.5	1.8	1.9	1.4
Higher	1.3	0.8	0.8	0.5	1.0
Subtotal	**5.6**	**5.1**	**4.2**	**4.4**	**3.8**
Private sources					
Pre-primary	0.1	–	0.2	0.1	–
Primary	0.2	0.1	0.2	0.3	0.6
Secondary	0.2	0.5	0.5	0.6	0.4
Higher	1.9	–	0.8	1.9	0.2
Subtotal	**2.4**	**–**	**1.7**	**2.9**	**1.3**
Total	**8.0**	**–**	**5.9**	**7.2**	**5.0**

Source UNESCO, Institute for Statistics, Global Education Digest, 2007.

of funding from alternate sources. These alternate sources are mainly students' contribution or private sources. Private finance is primarily tuition and fees. While, there is a trend towards additional cost recovery from public institutions, new arrangements for public–private partnerships are being explored to raise private finance.

Public–private Partnership (PPP) Model

In June 2008, the Planning Commission held a consultation on public–private partnership (PPP) models to explore possibilities of raising additional resources for higher education. Under the PPP model, the government remains accountable for service, quality, price and cost-effectiveness, while the private service provider takes responsibility of design, financing, building and operating the facilities, the risks and rewards associated with the project are shared. This ensures efficiency gains through cost-effectiveness and efficient use of resources, modern technologies in design, development and operations.

It is expected that private financing through the PPP model will supplement public efforts. It will ensure optimal risk allocation through risk sharing and accelerated and improved delivery of quality service with clear customer focus. It will promote accountability and institutional autonomy by reducing dependence on public funds, avoiding undue political and bureaucratic interference.

It needs to be accepted that PPPs would work only for programmes and projects with revenue generation potential. It will free public resources to that extent at least and may correct the present imbalance in higher education. User charges and additional cost recovery may make higher technical education unaffordable and access inequitable. While through efficiency gains operating costs may be reduced, PPPs will still have to be supported by liberal provisions for cross-subsidisation, means-tested scholarship, student loan programme, industry sponsorship of students and earn-while-learn arrangements. This would lead to changes in statutes of the universities, in order to create enabling provisions for contractual engagement with private service providers, leasing out land resources for 25–30 years and outsourcing of non-core services (even core services in some cases).

Tuition and Fees: Second Stream

Globally, responsibility of bearing the cost of higher education is shifting from the governments (or taxpayers) to the parents and the students. The limitations of public finance make charging of tuition fees inevitable. In some countries like Australia and the UK, this shift is deliberate or policy driven. In other countries like India, this is happening on its own, as the consequence of resource crunch faced by public institutions on one hand and the emergence of a significant private sector on the other. This shift is making higher education opportunities beyond the reach of a large section of the population.

Bulk of the private financing for most higher education systems comes through tuition and fees. Faced with fiscal pressure and growing acceptance of the private benefits of higher education, there is a tendency in nations around the world to shift some of the costs of higher education from the state to students, graduates or their families. Cost of higher education is shifted from exclusive or near exclusive dependence on the government or taxpayers to some reliance on parents and/or students.

Financing and Management

Although tuition and fees have been established in the US in the public as well as the private sector, they have generally been absent from the European higher education system till the late 1990s. Now most countries have introduced some form of tuitions and fees and others are planning to do the same. Experience from across the countries has been that introduction of tuition fees does not affect equity, provided it is linked with well-designed student financial aid arrangements that may include targeted grants and student loans.

This shifting of the financial burden of higher education attendance from the general taxpayers to the students and their parents, 'cost-sharing' as Johnstone (2005) calls it can take different forms. Seven types of cost-sharing arrangements are seen worldwide. These are—

1. Introduction of tuition fees (in China in 1997, in Britain in 1998, in Austria in 2001, and most recently in Germany in 2005);
2. Introduction of a dual tuition track with high level of fees for less meritorious students with capacity to pay (practiced in Russia, most of Eastern and Central Europe, India,[2] Uganda);
3. Sharp rise in tuition fees (public universities in the United States increased their in-state fees by an average of 10 per cent in 2001–02. Several institutions in India like the IITs and the IIMs have increased their fees sharply in recent years);
4. Imposition of user charges (happening in China, several African countries like Ethiopia, Mali and Guinea and the Nordic countries);
5. Diminution of student grants or scholarships (done in Britain, Russia and most of the Eastern and Central countries);
6. Increase in the effective cost recovery of student loans through various measures; and
7. Encouragement of a tuition-dependent private higher education sector. This has happened in Japan, Korea, Philippines, Indonesia, Brazil and some other countries in Latin America. This has increased the participation of parents and students in cost-sharing, and even in profit-making institutions.

This takes the form of either tuition fees or 'user charges' to cover the living cost of students. In the face of the financial crisis faced by higher education systems worldwide, cost-sharing is no longer an option but an imperative. However, the designing of an effective cost-sharing programme is essential to mitigate the risks that may be associated with it. Cost-sharing in the form of introduction of tuition should ideally be preceded by the provision for means-tested financial assistance programmes, as well as generally available students' loan programmes. Concerns relating to cost recovery are different in public institutions compared to that in private institutions. In public institutions, there is a need to raise tuition fees in order to supplement public funds. In tuition-dependent private institutions, there is a need for some form of regulation of tuition fees. This issue of fee regulation in private institutions has been discussed in Chapter 7 on regulation.

Since the early 1990s, several committees have examined the need to raise tuition fees in the public institutions in India. Prominent among those were the Punnayya Committee on UGC Funding of Institution of Higher Education (1992–93), the Pyle Committee on the Unit cost of Higher Education and other related matters (1997), the Anandakrishnan Committee to review the maintenance grant norms for Delhi Colleges (1999) and the Mahmood-ur-Rahman Committee to formulate revised fee structure in the Central and Deemed Universities (2000).

These committees have generally recommended upwards revision of tuition fees and its periodic adjustment with inflation. It has been suggested that tuition fees should constitute at least 15 per cent (and enhanced to at least 25 per cent after 10 years) of the total recurring expenditure. It has also been felt that the fee structure should be simplified and the number of items be grouped to make the fee collection easier with lesser accounting work involved. But the progress on this front has been tardy so far.

For the time being, 15 per cent of the total recurring expenditure has been fixed as a goal, which is both practical and achievable. There would, however, have to be exceptions made for universities/colleges located in disadvantaged areas. All universities and colleges have been allowed to increase their capacity by 20 per cent for catering to foreign students over and above the total capacity available to them.

This supernumerary category of students could be charged steep fees, usually in foreign currency, which could be considerable higher than the standard payment seats.

Section 12A(2) of the University Grants Commission Act puts responsibility on the UGC to lay down limits for revising fees. However, it has refrained from specifying any such levels. The individual universities also have powers under the relevant university acts to increase fees, but the general trend has been against increasing fees. This is obvious because of fear of the opposition from the student community. Thus, while the universities look to the UGC to take responsibility and issue directives, the UGC tends to pass on this responsibility to the government and the fees remain at the same unrealistic levels. Yet another reason for lack of initiative in increasing fees is that such a measure would not only be a thankless task, but universities in many cases do not have any incentive to increase fees since the income from fees gets adjusted from their annual grant.

Notwithstanding the lack of political will and clear policy, higher education costs have gone up significantly in recent years. Full costs are recovered for most of the professional programmes whether these are offered in the private or public institutions. While fee levels may continue to be low in central universities, which form a very small part of higher education in India, the fee levels are quite high in many state universities, particularly those in Tamil Nadu, Karnataka, Kerala, Haryana, Punjab and Rajasthan.[3] Figure 4.3 shows that nearly 50 per cent or more of the operating budget of many state universities (Madras University: 50.4 per cent, Bangalore University: 63.7 per cent and Punjab University: 50.4 per cent) in 2004–05 comes from fee income. In addition, living expenses have also gone up with inflation. In all, but for a very small section of public institutions mainly under the central government and in a few northern states in India, higher education in India is beyond the reach of students from poor background.

The Eleventh Plan notes that given the limitations on public funds to subsidise higher education, it is necessary to encourage public universities to charge at least 20 per cent of the operational costs of education. The plan suggests that this level of fees could be achieved gradually over time. There is ample evidence that the majority of the

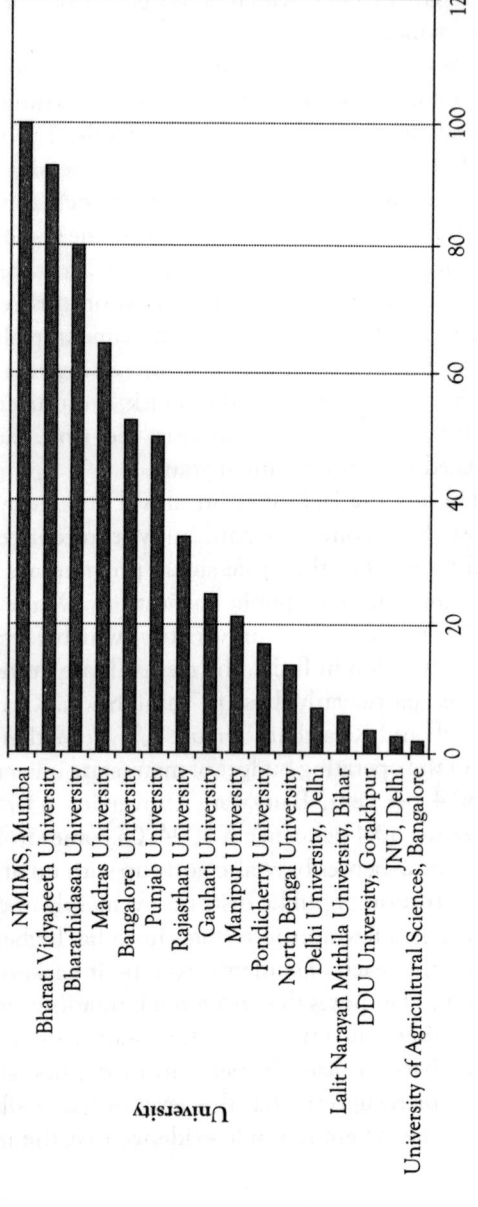

FIGURE 4.3 Per cent cost-recovery through tuition fees (2004–05)

141

students have the capacity to pay for higher education, but for those who cannot pay there should be a system of scholarships-cum-loans. It is for the universities to decide the level of fees but as a norm, fees should meet at least 20 per cent of the total expenditure in universities. This should be subject to two conditions: first, needy students should be provided with a fee waiver plus scholarships to meet their costs; second, universities should not be penalised by the UGC for the resources raised from higher fees through matching deductions from their GIAs. The fee structure of the universities also needs to be rationalised.

While clarifying its stand on fee revision, the NKC suggested that the increase should be gradual. Those who can afford to pay should do so while education should be subsidised for those who cannot pay. On an average, fees constitute less than 10 per cent of total expenditure in our universities. And, in most universities, fees have remained unchanged for decades. In theory, universities have the freedom to decide on fees. In practice, however, universities have not exercised this freedom in part because of some genuine concerns about access but in larger part because of the rhetoric and populism in the political process. The problem has been compounded by the UGC method of providing GIAs to bridge the difference between income and expenditure. Consequently, there is no incentive for the universities or colleges to raise income through higher fees as that sum would be deducted from their UGC (or state government) grants.

The NKC points out that low tuition fee in public universities, without any means test, have meant unquantifiable benefits for unintended beneficiaries. But private players and foreign institutions have not been restrained in charging fees that the market can bear. The time has come to rethink, as we have no choice but to rationalise fees. It is, as mentioned earlier, for the universities to decide the level of fees but, as a norm, fees should meet at least 20 per cent of the total expenditure in universities. In addition, fees need to be adjusted every two years through price indexation. Such small, continuous adjustments would be absorbed and accepted far more easily than large, discrete changes after a period of time. This rationalisation of fees should be subject to two conditions: first, needy students should be provided with a fee waiver plus scholarships to meet their costs; second, universities should not be penalised by the UGC for the resources raised from higher fees through matching deductions from their GIAs.

A key issue therefore is to devise sustainable tuition fees policy. In this regard, it would be instructive to draw lessons from experience of Japan, where the public sector did not have a tuition-free policy but controlled the tuition charges and fees at costs below those of the private sector. Thus, there was a level playing field between the public and the private sector that competed for students' enrolment. Over time, the private institutions began to respond to market forces by controlling the rise of tuition charges. Consequently, the gap between the two sectors gradually faded away (Arimoto, 1997). Such a mechanism would be useful in India. Currently the difference between the tuition fees between the public and private institutions in the country is so large that simple market mechanism is unlikely to put pressure on the private sector to lower their fees. It is only by gradually increasing fees for students of public institutions that private institutions will respond by lowering their fees. This will slowly equalise the disparity between the two, making it possible to prevent further widening of differences between students according to their socio-economic backgrounds.

Funding from the 'Third Stream'

Access to liberal funding is not a panacea for improving the health of higher education. As seen from the experience of the United Kingdom, a system that was slipping down on its performance turned around when financial cuts were imposed by the Thatcher government. The UK universities looked for alternate sources of funding. Like the UK, in most countries around the world, government funding has steadily decreased as a share of institutional revenue; tuition and fees have risen to replace the lost funding, but not without controversy. Institutions are therefore increasingly turning to revenue sources other than tuition and fees. Several institutions now aggressively pursue alternative revenue streams called the 'third stream'. The third stream could either be a wide range of entrepreneurial activities or donations. Such diversification of income sources is seen as a strategy to achieve greater institutional autonomy. This trend away from single source dependency has spread internationally. Many universities are moving from 'reluctant income diversification' to 'enthusiastic income diversification' and now to 'unique business models' wherein they are looking at available business opportunities from activities other than their core functions of teaching and research.

Entrepreneurial Activities

Entrepreneurial activities may include various kinds of franchising, licensing, sponsorship and partnering arrangements with third parties, technology transfer, business incubator, research parks, testing services, executive education, venture capital investment, investment in real estate, and so on. Entrepreneurial practices are on the rise in many countries. In UK alone, 25 universities have earnings of USD 10 million or more from technology transfers alone. Income from executive education, research and technology parks, sponsorships and advertising are significant sources of revenue. Many universities are run as businesses and their peers are not other universities, but private research organisations and consultancies. Cranfield University, a public university in UK is an interesting example. Faced with financial adversity a decade ago, the university organised itself as a group of independent business units, each responsible for its own revenue having a market view of life. And now it is a rich, reputed and much envied university in the country. While in India such entrepreneurial activities by institutions of higher education are not common yet, in Russia and China factories and firms are owned and operated by higher education institutions.

Donations

Philanthropy has played a significant role in the development of higher education in the United States. But in much of the rest of the world, educational institutions have only recently begun to incorporate philanthropy into the financing of higher education. Many countries are turning to philanthropy in an attempt to fill the gap between the rising costs of higher education and limited state funding. Examples can be found around the globe, including the establishment of endowments at African universities, the initiation of fund-raising campaigns at universities in Europe, Australia, and China and the establishment of mechanisms for corporate philanthropy in support of research in Europe.

Endowment incomes are substantial in the United States. As per the 2007 NACUBO (National Association of College and University Business Officers) Endowment Survey, 76 American Universities have endowments of greater than USD 1 billion with Harvard having an endowment of over USD 34 billion, and 65 universities have announced campaigns to raise USD 1 billion or more in the next few years. Another 700 universities have endowment values of less than USD 5 million to USD 1 billion. The remaining universities have small endowments. In terms of endowment income, public universities have traditionally been the laggards. The highly reputed state university, University of Berkeley, has far smaller endowment compared to top privates despite its very high reputation and huge enrolment. All UK universities together have an endowment of USD 12 billion. The government in the UK is assertively supporting the universities in their fund-raising activities along American lines. A matching funding scheme has been initiated to help universities set up fund-raising office and staff in the sector. In Australia, initial corpus for endowment came from the cash surplus generated from mining lease operations by the government.

Donation for higher education is not a universal phenomenon and plays an insignificant role in financing higher education in most countries. This is mostly found in the United States and the United Kingdom, and in a limited way in a few elite institutions with wealthy alumni in other countries. Like the rest of world outside the US and the UK, donations in higher education are yet to become popular in India. Outside the reputed IITs, very little donation is received by Indian institutions. Even for these institutions, much of their donations come from their successful alumni, who are either based in the United States or have studied there. It is thus influenced by tradition of philanthropy in the United States.

Currently, there is an implicit disincentive in both tax laws and trust laws for donation to higher education institutions in India. In 1998, the central government made it even more difficult by requiring donations to be received only through Bharat Shiksha Kosh, a trust set up to encourage and facilitate donations. Though this requirement was later waived, it caused a setback to the culture of philanthropy that was slowly building up in the country. The NKC has recommended that laws should be changed so that universities can invest in financial instruments of their choice and use the income from their endowments to build up a corpus. It has suggested that the country should nurture the tradition of philanthropic contributions through changes in incentives for universities and for donors. It may be a good idea to support potential institutions to set up fund-raising offices as initiated by the UK government recently. While this may help in raising donations for higher education, such donations are unlikely to be a significant part of finances for higher education on short or even medium-term basis. Thus, the potential of philanthropy is often overstated in the Indian context.

Fund Allocation Mechanism

While there has been a rise in private financing, higher education will continue to have significant dependence on public revenues. Public funding policies often see whether it is a public good being supplied or private good. In case of higher education, both the public and the private institutions supply public and private goods and thus need similar treatment in terms of public money. In several countries including the United States, significant funds flow to the private sector. Not only the non-profit, but also the for-profit higher education institutions in the US depend significantly on pubic money. Funding, however, is through different streams, research grants and students' financial aid, while in public institutions, funding is through institutions. Different models of funding are used with a view to achieve various end objectives. Efficient use of public funds is one such important objective. It is thus increasingly realised that it is not just level of funding but also the basis and criteria according to which public funds are available that can improve the quality and accessibility of higher education (Jongbloed, 2004).

There is a traditional budgetary process involved in funding of higher education institutions in India. Allocations are based on requests (activity plans; budget proposals) submitted to funding authorities.

Budget allocation is often based on the previous year's allocation of specific budget items. Separate budget items then are negotiated between representatives of educational institutions and the funding authorities. Annual changes (usually increases) in each budget item are treated individually, with discussion taking place on the basis of cost projections. In this case, budget items are likely to include categories like staff salaries, material, requirements, building maintenance costs, and investment. Funding is line item based, and shows the different expenditure items as separate lines of the budget. These line items are determined by referring to norms with respect to indicators such as unit costs or capacity in terms of number of funded students. In the recent years, in place of scrutiny of each item of budget, block grant is provided based on a percentage increase over previous year.

There are several problems with this kind fund allocation mechanism. Austerity measures to control unproductive expenditure in the government are often extended to higher education. This results in absurd consequences. Despite government policy to encourage institutions to raise internal resources, fund allocation is done on deficit financing basis and such resources when raised are adjusted from the annual grants leaving them with no incentive to raise resources. This neither promotes cost-effectiveness nor internal resource generation.

The Punnayya Committee (1992–93) pointed out that the existing mechanism of funding for higher education perpetuates inefficiency and suggested that the GIA system should be suitably modified to reward quality, efficiency and innovativeness. The committee recommended the replacement of the existing practice of negotiated block grants based on historical allocations by policy-driven funding based on unit cost method. In 1997, the Pylee Committee was set up to develop a mechanism for computing unit costs. Apart from changing the funding mechanism, both the committees also advocated cost recovery by suitably revising, rationalising and enhancing tuition fees. Later, the Anandakrishnan Committee that examined the issue of maintenance grants to Delhi colleges funded by the UGC recommended that annual grants for the colleges should be based on faculty strength guided by optimum student–teacher ratio and teachers' work load.

Financing and Management

Despite specific recommendations of these committees, the funding of higher education institutions continues to have a historical or political basis. The amount of funding that an institution receives is based largely on what they received the year before or how powerful their friends are in the government or funding agency. This approach tends to be more input-based, taking care of staff costs and institutional infrastructure needs (Hauptman, 2006). Whereas in many countries there is a shift to policy-driven funding by introducing policy variables into funding process (as in UK) or performance-based funding that recognise outputs rather than just inputs (as in US), the funding process followed in India continues to be negotiated funding mechanism.

With a view to achieve specific targets in order to improve quality, spur innovation and develop the management of higher education institutions, several countries have effectively used the competitive funding process. The US was one of the first countries to introduce a competitive fund in 1972, with the creation of a Fund for Improvement of Post-Secondary Education (FIPSE). Later, many other countries followed. In India, the UGC provides competitive grants to the eligible universities and colleges (those covered under Section 12B of the UGC Act) under various schemes to promote equity, relevance, excellence and research. Though these competitive grants have helped the universities and colleges in taking up many new activities, no objective evaluation of such competitive grants has been made. The amount of such grants is not only meagre but is often cornered by a small number of eligible institutions.

With the increasing cost of higher education, strategies to help students and their families to pay for higher education have become an increasingly important component of financing higher education. These strategies include aid, which is funded or sponsored by the government, provided by the institutions themselves, or given by private individuals or organisations. In many countries (such as the US), student financial aid is a major responsibility of the government. In India, such an arrangement is nearly absent. A further analysis of the same occurs later in this chapter. In addition, in several countries, governments support individuals rather than institutions, particularly researchers, through competitive research funding.

In sum, revisiting the fund allocation mechanism for higher education is as important as increasing the allocations. There is a need for creating clear incentives for enhancing institutional efficiency and improving productivity. Public funds should be used to address concerns relating to affordability due to rising cost of higher education.

Institutional Management

Closely related to the fund allocation mechanism is the issue of strengthening institutional capacity to deliver against outcomes. While state support has decreased noticeably, performance and accountability expectations from institutions have increased. Public institutions are striving to maintain and enhance competitiveness. They have to meet the increased expectations of different stakeholders. They are required to do more with less (be more efficient) and do it better (be effective). They have to be transparent in their functioning. The Right to Information Act, 2005 imposes new requirements of transparency on them. Though transparency enables institutions to build trust amongst its various stakeholders, it also brings their workings under public scrutiny and puts immense pressure on them.

There are now efforts to bring in new management practices and an entrepreneurial culture in universities around the world. Such efforts are often opposed to by the traditionalists and the academia claiming that this would erode the university's ethos. Such conflicts may not be highly visible in the public universities in India. However, in many countries the world, even the most reputed universities are not free from them. Recently there was turmoil in the nine hundred year old Oxford University over bringing in outside business expertise to raise financial resources and promoting stronger ties with the government (*The Indian Express*, 2007a).

Whereas governance refers to decision making, administration is more about the execution of those decisions. There have been changes in the organisation and structure of both the governance and administration of higher education institutions in recent years. These changes are reflected in three distinct approaches that are in use. These are: new public management, entrepreneurialism, and academic capitalism.

Financing and Management

New public management is an extension of the experiences with the public sector in general to academic institutions for making them more efficient and effective. There are several examples of universities using new public management principles. Faced with financial crunch, the University of Maryland took up a drive to save USD 100 million through various cost-reduction measures. Entrepreneurialism is driven by making different units of the university more autonomous in the quest for diversified sources of funding. Finally, the academic capitalism is the shift of higher education from a social institution to an industry. One can see a combination of all the new approaches being adopted by some higher education institutions that are adapting themselves to the changing circumstances.

In this context, three specific areas—staff development, procedural simplifications, and computerisation efforts are discussed. There is the issue relating to rightsizing of administrative support, particularly in public institutions. It is seen that non-academic staff in many public-funded institutions is several times more than the academic staff, resulting in inefficiency of operations. The Indian Institute of Science, Bangalore had tried a special voluntary retirement scheme to reduce the non-academic staff. The Expenditure Reforms Commission suggested that academic to non-academic ratio needs to be brought down.

There is a need for training and development of academic administrators and support staff in the universities and colleges throughout the country in a structured manner. The activity need not be confined only to the development of generic skills but should also focus on development of specific skills required by different groups of academic administrators in the system. A coordinated plan for the same through empanelled training providers could also be considered. Higher education institutions could be encouraged to earmark a specific budget for this purpose each year. Each institution could have a training cell or a suitable mechanism to identify the training needs and conduct and arrange programmes for the same. The key to improved institutional governance is the simplification of internal procedures on a continued basis, which needs special attention. The institutions can benefit by sharing of the best practices on improved institutional management.

The computerisation of administrative systems and streamlining of back office processes provides efficiency and promotes transparency in the functioning of institutions. The track record of such use of computers in the higher education institutions has been poor. Early efforts to introduce computers were limited to standard packages for word processing, simple spreadsheet for calculations or isolated databases to store information of a section or a department. Now there is a need for a system that will integrate all the functions—academic, financial, building and works, personnel, hotel management, alumni affairs. The system should be able to interface with the government and government agencies seamlessly. The efforts for computerisation are likely to be successful now as there is an increasing acknowledgement of the ability to use computers and the availability of a large 'computer ready' workforce in the higher education institutions. Considering the new computer-enabled technologies now available, a web-based model is suggested. This would be both reliable and scalable.

Since the way educational institutions function and the requirements of the institutions vary only marginally, a single packaged solution with flexibility for customisation may be possible. A set of standard modules could be created (with more than one version for some modules if necessary) that will cover all the functions and which could be customised for each institute.

The rapid growth of enrolments in universities and colleges has not only led to concerns about financing, but has also raised the issue of related costs. Consequently, there is an interest in strengthening institutional governance and management as a way of improving institutional efficiency and effectiveness. These concerns are addressed both through interventions within the institutions and through responses in its external environment.

Information management at the systemic level would not only enhance efficiency and effectiveness of the interface between institutions between the funding and regulatory agencies, but also bring about a paradigm shift in the management of higher education. The Indian higher education system is a loose configuration of heterogeneous organisational units—universities, colleges, professional councils, the UGC, and so on. Information management in such a complex system is tricky, yet necessary. Such a system has to provide for an efficient mechanism for data collection, compilation and dissemination, improving targeting and monitoring of funding, promoting collaboration between higher education institutions themselves and with the industry and the society through sharing of expertise and facilities, providing credible information about higher education institutions and programmes and catering to many other related needs.

With the above objective, a Higher Education Information Systems Project (HISP) was conceptualised with various modules for the purpose of grants management, statistics collection and compilation, recognition management, research projects management; information on expertise and facilities, students' information, knowledge repository and university and college admission management.[4] This could be built and offered as an open source educational Enterprise Resource Planning (ERP) package in an Application Service Provider (ASP) model. This would enable even the remotest colleges with a dial-up connection to integrate with the system. For its implementation, a policy document on electronic records management could be developed. This shall cover legal issues; information security including authentication and audit; issues relating to privacy, records preservation and disposal and strategies for incorporating metadata tags in various electronic documents.

Students' Financial Aid

As the tuition and fee levels rise, either driven by policy or on their own (as in India) due to resource crunch faced by public institutions and the emergence of the private sector, higher education becomes beyond the reach of a large section of the population. Equity in access to higher education thus becomes central to debates on funding higher education. Equity in access is the ability of the brightest students to study at the most intellectually demanding universities, unrelated to their socio-economic background. To ensure this, higher education has to be free at the point of use. Thus, an increase in fee levels is usually accompanied with the introduction of suitable grants and loan programmes that are designed to be, as closely as possible, both need-based and generally available to the academically prepared students without regard to the wealth or credit-worthiness of their parents or their individual career and earning prospects. There can be a variety of grants and loan options designed to address this problem.

Apart from grants and loans, many countries find tax cuts rather than tax increase as a good solution. The people who would benefit the most from this are the middle class families who are overburdened with education costs. It would cost the government revenue in the short term, but a college-educated worker has significantly more taxable income than he or she would have otherwise. Taxing the moneyed individuals' spend on education is not the government's best source of tax revenue. In India, there are tax incentives for spending on higher education. However, their impact is limited due to the low proportion of people covered under the tax net.

Student financial aid is mainly in the form of grants and loans. In India, there are several government schemes of scholarship and free-ships. These usually target the disadvantaged students belonging to the scheduled castes, scheduled tribes, other backward classes and even women. Recently, the merit-cum-means scheme and post-matric scheme for students from minority communities have also been started. Many of the schemes are funded by the central government, but there are some initiatives of the state governments as well. In a few cases, schemes to support the weaker sections of society have also been started by the institutions themselves. In spite of several such schemes, their overall coverage is insignificant. An amount of merely Rs 450 million has been earmarked for scholarship for college and university students during 2008–09, with the objective of covering at least 2 per cent of the student population pursuing higher studies.

The amount spent on scholarship schemes is very small. It is less than half a per cent of the total expenditure on education and has been declining over the years. This was merely Rs 250 million in 2003–04 (CABE Committee, 2005b). Most scholarship schemes are needs-blind. These do not necessarily cover the poorest students. The amount of scholarship does not even cover full tuitions in many cases, particularly for professional courses. In many cases, due to cumbersome disbursement procedures, the assistance is not received in time. There are also reported leakages in disbursement. In sum, despite rising cost of higher education making it beyond the reach of a large section of Indian society, there are few efforts to make higher education affordable to all.

Student Loans

Education loans have not been particularly popular in India. A National Loan Scholarship Scheme started by the central government in 1963 was discontinued in 1991 because of its dismal performance, very low rate of recovery, unrealistic rate of scholarship and thin spread. Several commercial banks had been operating education loan schemes on their own. Almost all loans needed security, and the amounts were small while the rates of interest were high. Thus, the number of students taking loan was negligible. Banks had been operating education loans in haphazard manner. On the Supreme Court's intervention, the central government, in consultation with the Reserve Bank of India and the Indian Banks Association, framed a comprehensive education loan scheme in 2001. In pursuance to this, several banks have started their own student loan schemes and now most public sector banks have student loan schemes broadly based on the model scheme with minor variations. The scheme was further revised in 2004-05.[5] Currently, education loans up to Rs 1 million (revised in 2007 from 750,000) for studies in India and up to Rs 2 million (revised from Rs 15 million) for studies abroad are available.

Till about 2000-01, the education loan portfolio remained small. It was from the year 2001-02, when the Government of India announced a new comprehensive educational loan scheme to be implemented by the public sector banks that the education loan portfolio has grown. See Table 4.12 for growth trend in students' loans over the years.

By September 2007, more than 1 million students had availed of education loans and education loan portfolio stood at Rs 145 billion. Though growth in new loan accounts at 35-40 per cent is robust, yet less than 1 per cent students avail of education loans. Thus, financing through student loans is still small. In comparison, 85 per cent students in UK and Sweden, 50 per cent in USA and Canada and 77 per cent in Australia had availed of students' loans in recent years (Usher, 2005b). Tax concessions are available against interest on education loans. Its impact, however, is not significant.

TABLE 4.12   Growth of student loan portfolio (1990–91 to 2005–06)

Year (as on March)	Loan accounts		Amount outstanding	
	No. ('000s)	Per cent growth over previous year	Rs million	Per cent growth over previous year
1990–91	70	−2.78	770	14.93
1995–96	74	5.71	1,830	15.82
2000–01	112	40.00	5,430	0.00
2001–02	157	40.18	10,280	89.32
2002–03	239	52.23	28,700	179.18
2003–04	347	45.19	41,790	45.61
2004–05	470	35.45	63,980	53.10
2005–06	641	36.38	108,040	68.87

Source Ministry of Finance (various years) taken from Tilak (2007).

I-Tenable, a market research company, conducted a comprehensive study of the students' loan performance in the country. The study covered more than 350 branches of 78 banks covering public and private sector banks including foreign and cooperative banks in 20 cities in Maharashtra and Delhi. The study showed that more than half of the banks did not offer student loans at all. In the remaining banks, the student loan portfolio was only about 3.77 per cent of their entire loan portfolio. The major part of the total portfolio constitutes personal loans, automobile loans and home loans. On analysis of the 7,751 student loan cases of various banks across the state, it was found that the average loan amount was around Rs 300,000 and the interest rate at about 12.5 per cent. The majority of students who availed these loans were pursuing professional degree programmes with 46.17 per cent studying engineering, 22.64 per cent pursuing MBA and 12.71 per cent doing medical programmes. Around 12.1 per cent of the students took loans to pursue higher studies abroad. Only about 19 per cent of the students who took loans were females. Surprisingly, the default and delinquent levels in student loans were found to be extremely low with 1.1 per cent and 0.7 per cent figures respectively.

I-Tenable also conducted a survey on the perceptions of the students towards education loans. The company interviewed more than 5,000 students. It was noted that most of the students (around 81 per cent) would take loans if these were available. Though the students found the amount of student loan adequate and the requirement of collateral fine, they were wary of the time-consuming and complicated processes of disbursement of loans, untrained bank staff, constraints of documentation, high rates of interests, and incomplete information with the bank branch's staff regarding students' loans. To address these problems, simplification of the banking procedures and documentation and training of bank staff would be required. The central government plans to start the Education Loan Interest Subsidy Scheme for pursuing professional courses during 2008–09. The scheme would require about Rs 40 billion during the Eleventh Five Year Plan (*Business Standard*, 5 May 2008). This might make student loans more popular in future.

Though agreeing that education loans may require a 'sweetener' like interest subsidy to begin with to make them politically acceptable,[6] but Nicholas Barr of the London School of Economics strongly opposes interest subsidies for reasons of efficiency and equity. According to him, the optimal interest rate on education loans should be broadly equal to the government's cost of borrowing, that is, the long-term risk-free rate. This would be particularly true when repayments are income contingent and repaid through temporary increases in the income tax. In such a situation, the money can be continuously recycled to finance the education of future students. The best system is one where students can obtain sufficient but difficult to default loans. This way, all students would have the opportunity to obtain a higher education degree.

Income Contingent Loans

Student loans in conventional format are high risk loans with a lot of uncertainty. Banks therefore charge a risk premium. They cherry pick students with low risk and lend only to students who can provide security. Though India has seen a rapid growth in education loans in the conventional mode, its further growth and equitable access to all sections is doubted. As per global experience, there is inefficiently low borrowing and lending under conventional loans for education. These are also inequitable (Barr, 2004).

Income contingent loans (ICLs) are increasingly used to finance education. Income contingent repayments ensure that low earners make low or no repayment. People with low lifetime earning do not fully repay. A larger loan (or higher interest rate) has no effect on monthly repayments, which depends only on a person's income; instead, a person with larger loan will repay for a longer period. Income contingent loans are designed to protect the borrowers from excessive risk. They are equitable because there is built-in insurance against inability to repay. First started in Australia, there is now a rich experience on ICLs. When introduced to cover a newly introduced tuition charge in Australia in 1989, it was feared that there would be drop in participation rates due to ICL. Participation rates did not drop, on the contrary there has been an increase in overall participation, women's participation grew more strongly then men's, and the system also did not discourage participation by people in the lowest socio-economic groups (Chapman and Ryan, 2003).

Given the above background, there is a need to introduce a scheme of ICLs in India. This loan arrangement has built-in insurance against the inability to pay and therefore helps low earners. The provision to write off a fraction of loan for each year of service in the rural areas or national research system could be provided. This also takes care of the problem of student indebtedness. ICLs could be provided through a wide range of private and public sector lenders with a third party servicing of loans. This is a mature and tried concept where lenders outsource their student loan servicing function to an outside specialised agency. This results in better recovery, effective use of funds, efficient student financing supply chain right up to improved and timely collection of repayments. An appropriate framework can facilitate securitisation of student loans so that fresh money keeps flowing at relatively lower costs.

Since student loans are inherently risky, the government is required to share a part of the risk of a student loan programme. Such loans should be widely available to all or most students in need. Risks can be lessened through a judicious use of cosignatory requirements, with the government as a primary guarantor only for families with insufficient collateral, and then a secondary guarantor for families who are able to co-sign the loan and bear part of the risk. This can provide the much-needed impetus to public and private lenders to lend money to students based on market forces. Multilateral and bilateral agencies like the World Bank, Asian Development Bank, and so on have been partners with the governments all over the world for a similar initiative. A Student Loan Clearinghouse will have to be created to link all stakeholders through a transparent, data driven, credible and validated system. This would be an essential information infrastructure for the success of any large scale student loan scheme. Basic building block for this would be a National Graduate Student Repository that would maintain unit records of all students in the higher education system.[7]

Of late, there has been some thinking in the government on loan guarantee and an ICL-like mechanism in India. As per media reports in July 2007, the central government could soon become a guarantor of education loans given to needy students. According to the details reported, the loan guarantee is likely to cover 75 per cent of the amount. All students enrolled in government or private institutions and confirming to certain quality standards would be covered. Those who are able to repay would repay; for others, there will be an arrangement to write off the loans. Eligibility would be based on economic rather than caste basis. Interest subsidy will bring down the interest to one-third the existing rate for economically weaker students. For those students who cannot afford collateral, the government will act as the guarantor. However, no more has been heard on this since then.

With a large informal sector and limited capacity to collect tax, mimicking income contingent repayments as in advanced countries may be problematic in India. It may therefore begin with a select group of institutions and expanded gradually to include more institutions. Viability means testing is also a contentious issue. Therefore indicators such as home ownership, or fee level in the school last attended could be used. A good starting point for ICL could be the centrally funded professional institutions. Currently these institutions operate at low fee levels. Tution fees in initially funded institutions have risen significantly in recent years. Allowing the option of either upfront or deferred payments, the equity issue can be addressed. By exempting deferred payment in certain cases like students opting for Indian science and technology establishments or opting for faculty positions in technical education, bright graduates could be encouraged to make more desirable choices in national interest. The entire money collected through upfront or deferred payment should be spent on further consolidation and expansion of the technical education system (Agarwal, 2005). This would free resources and promote access.

Sustainable Financing Arrangement

Kothari Commission (1964–66) had suggested that the government should have minimum commitment to finance up to 6 per cent of GDP on education. The CABE Committee on financing higher education and the NKC's note on higher education (29 November 2006) reiterated the same. It was suggested that the government support for higher education should be at least 1.5 per cent of GDP. Over time, it has become a matter of faith without much rationale. It is seen in Table 4.6 that there are examples of countries that provide greater access to higher education with much lower levels of funding in terms of GDP, and thus this argument for increased funding based GDP cannot be pushed too far. The Mazumdar Committee Report (2005) suggested that the outlay on higher technical education be increased gradually to Rs 683.61 billion by 2011–12 (that is, the last year of the Eleventh Five Year Plan). Though this may be desirable, for reasons of competing priorities for public funds, it may not be feasible.

Increase in the level of funding is not in itself a panacea for improving the health of higher education. As seen from the experience of the United Kingdom, a system that was slipping down on its performance turned around when financial cuts were imposed by the Thatcher government. United Kingdom universities looked for alternative sources of funding and as a result became more competitive. In India, nationwide agitation mainly against, but also for the numerical-based quotas in central higher education institutions created a crisis that almost went out of control: it required the Supreme Court's intervention to contain it. Skill shortages were seen as the binding constraint in the country's sustaining its high growth trajectory (Agarwal, 2006d). In this backdrop, there has been an unprecedented increase in allocations for higher education.

Financing and Management

Increased funding from the Planning Commission largely goes for capital expenditure that too for a limited number of central and new institutions. For maintenance of reasonable standards, there is a need for an optimal level of funding to meet the recurrent costs. This may vary from subject to subject and institution to institution across the country. Average cost has been computed as Rs 18,750 to Rs 21,250 per student for an average quality institution and Rs 33,333 to Rs 37,750 per student for good quality institution in a recent study by NUEPA. For 13.7 million students in 2006–07, requirement to bear recurrent costs would be Rs 325.34 billion against Rs 179.29 billion with 25 per cent good quality institutions and other average quality institutions. Thus, there is a shortfall of around 45 per cent. These are only indicative figures since; per student cost varies very widely. With an average of Rs 150,000 in an IIT to Rs 86,000 in a central university, Rs 35,106 to Rs 59,582 for a deemed university and Rs 1,422 to Rs 7,450 for a state university. In any case, shortfall in recurrent expenses is large.

A large part of recurrent expenditure (that is, current expenses) goes for salaries (as seen in Table 4.13). In India, current expenses may not be as low as 0.1 per cent as noted in the Global Education Digest, 2007,

TABLE 4.13 Expenditure on higher education by nature of expenditure (per cent)

| Country | Current | | | Capital |
	Salary	Other current	Total	
Sweden	62.2	39.8	100.0	0
Australia	54.2	36.7	90.9	9.1
Finland	59.7	34.4	94.1	5.9
United States	55.6	33.8	89.4	10.6
Israel	58.0	30.7	88.7	11.3
Germany	64.8	26.4	91.2	8.8
Brazil	72.2	24.5	96.7	3.3
Philippines	79.0	18.7	97.7	2.3
Korea	44.6	3.5	82.1	17.9
Indonesia	81.1	0.8	82.0	18.0
India	98.8	0.1	99.0	1.0

Source Global Education Digest, 2007.

but in most universities and colleges, salary expenses comprise 90–95 per cent of the current expenses. In the Indian case, even investment in new infrastructure and facilities for expansion of enrolment are included in current expenses, since funding to most institutions is as GIA and thus even capital cost is classified as revenue expenses in the budget. Further, living and transport expenses are borne by the students and parents directly.

There are apprehensions that a good opportunity would be squandered if the increased funding does not go along with complementary institutional reforms that are required to improve performance. Discussion on funding higher education is often flawed. Finer nuances and understanding of the way higher education is financed are usually ignored. While the government has to continue to take primary responsibility for the financing of higher education, gaps will have to be identified and strategies thought of to fill in these gaps. According to Barr (2004), a good funding arrangement for higher education rests on three legs: variable fees (that is, prices), which assist the efficient allocation of resources within higher education; well-designed loans, that provide consumption smoothing, thereby assisting efficient allocation over a person's life cycle; and measures to promote access and improve equity.

Inadequate and declining public funding of higher education is reflected in its falling standards. This is endemic in the country. The role of the government in funding higher education is getting marginalised. Budgetary support for higher education did not increase to commensurate with expansion of enrolment in higher education. A large part of the higher education system is not even eligible for public funding, making the situation worse. The funding mechanism also requires a re-look.

The role of the central government in funding of higher education is limited and uneven. With a handful of central institutions that cater to less than 2 per cent of the students getting nearly 85 per cent of central allocation for higher education while other institutions that cater to much larger numbers are starved of funds, there is something unjust about the current system of allocation of central resource for higher education. State governments are required to provide the bulk of the public funding for higher education. Faced with a financial crunch, state governments are tightening their purse-strings for higher education and advocating upward revision of fees. Even states like West Bengal support the view that colleges should try to be self sufficient.[8]

It is seen from experience of the last two decades that the expansion of capacity in higher education has been largely through private initiatives. This will continue to be so. Government funding has to be used for revitalising the starved public higher education system. Public higher education would require significant one time investment and continued support. It needs to be realised that in a knowledge economy the size and growth of quality higher education would be the main differentiating factor between a dynamic and a marginalised economy. Therefore larger public investment in higher education is vital. Considering the above reality, it needs to be realised that the private sector would play an important role in increasing the capacity of higher education in the country. Public financing of higher education would fill in the critical gaps. To enable this, public funding has to increase significantly. It is equally important to improve the quality of expenditure by targeting it better.

In future, little capacity creation and enrolment expansion is likely through government support. Most of it would be through private initiatives. However, public funding for higher education facilities in the underserved areas, such as in the far-flung states in the North East and Jammu and Kashmir shall continue to be required. Further, public funding shall continue to be necessary for academic programmes that the market may not support. These could include programmes that have strong social and cultural value and those that are aimed at promotion of science and scholarship to enhance the country's competitiveness on a long-term basis.

There is a need to substantially enhance the level of funding for higher education in the country by both augmenting support from the government and ensuring greater contribution from the households. Funding agencies should gradually shift to a more transparent, rational and formula-based mechanism of funding of public-financed higher education institutions.[9] Institutions should be given adequate financial autonomy within a framework of greater accountability. Both teaching and research need to be supported separately. Funding mechanism needs to facilitate and encourage higher education institutions to raise internal resources, particularly to raise tuition fees to realistic levels.

A larger share of public funds, particularly central funds need to be assigned for student-based grants for providing access to students from poor backgrounds. This not only ensures better targeting of public funds by guaranteeing equal access opportunities for all, but also ensures a more efficient and demand-driven system of public funding. Student-centred funding should also be extended to accredited private institutions.[10] This would provide equal opportunities for all providers, be they public or private. This would lead to adequate balance in sharing of costs and benefits and enhance competition on the basis of quality. This would also encourage private investment in higher education.

Competitive grants to leverage change need to be increased manifold. The number of schemes for disbursement of such grants should be reduced through review and harmonisation of guidelines with a view to minimise the burden of implementation and enhance the impact through outcome focus. A greater objectivity and transparency in disbursements should be ensured by introducing a system of online submission and tracking of proposals for grants. Competitive and general development grants should be admissible to all public and genuinely not-for-profit private institutions. Perhaps accreditation may be made a condition precedent to their eligibility for the same.

Higher education institutions supported by the state governments face an acute problem of deteriorating infrastructure and facilities and a large number of vacancies in the faculty. Adequate and continuing support is required to bring up the level of these institutions to minimum standards. Public funding, both to individuals and the institutions, may be provided to groups to promote collaboration and cooperation. To encourage working together, mobility grants would be essential. It may be concluded that public funding for higher education, both at the central and the state-government level, need to be increased significantly. Public funds should be utilised where the private sector may not enter. The public funding mechanism needs to be reviewed in order to ensure that performance is rewarded, higher education institutions are encouraged to raise fees and other revenues by themselves and collaboration is promoted.

Though there has been some significant amount of private investment in higher education in India, until recently the big corporate sector has shied away from this due to cumbersome procedures. Similarly, the prestigious foreign universities have not entered the higher education sector in India. These universities usually get confused signals and an impression that they are unwelcome. There is a merit in proactively enticing the big corporate sector and prestigious foreign research universities to set up research universities/campuses for post-graduate education and research in science and engineering in India to raise the standards of research for long-term competitiveness of the country. For this purpose, India could begin to work with prestigious foreign universities (say, 500 universities in the SJTU's list of research universities) and big corporate houses in the knowledge sector. Single point contact and a time-bound approach could be adopted to facilitate high quality institutions of higher education to come up with bare minimum regulations.

In the final analysis, it must be noted that higher education spending would not necessarily translate into faster (economic) growth or better higher education (Wolf, 2002). The nature of funding and the way it is spread over the system is important. Also, the quality and relevance of higher education is central: the level of spending is relevant, but so is the responsiveness of the system to the needs of students, employers and other stakeholders.

Conclusion

Recent debate on financing Indian higher education is primarily con-fined to increasing the funding levels. Public spending as a percentage of GDP in the country is often compared with that in the advanced countries. Estimated at 1 per cent (with almost the same contributed through private finance), level of spending is not low. At the same time, given the differences in country systems, levels of development, size of the country and in definitions, comparisons should not be pushed too far. Relative effort expressed in terms of per student expenditure as a proportion of per capita GDP at 95 per cent is one of the highest in the world. However, in absolute terms and on per student basis, funding levels are still low.

There has been a quantum jump in outlays for higher-technical education in the Eleventh Plan, but with limited capacity how much would be absorbed is not known. There is a large gap in requirement and outlay. Actual allocations at the end of second year (2008–09) would be far less than proportionate five year outlay. The funding is primarily for some new institutions and a small number of central institutions, support for infrastructure and faculties to accommodate increased intake in the wake of reservations for the other backward classes and one time grant for half of the state universities and colleges that constitute the bulk of the system. There is already a wide disparity in level of funding of institutions funded by the central government and the state governments. This would further exacerbate this disparity.

The above central funding recurrent expenditure, particularly for financing of academic activities (other than salaries) is likely to be a major concern. This does not fall within the purview of the Planning Commission. While one time assistance would help in creating and expanding facilities, if the posts of teachers continue to remain unfilled and laboratories and libraries are not sufficiently provided for, such one time assistance would not be of much help. With the limited scope of increasing non-plan grants that provide for recurrent grants, a sustainable funding arrangement would be to have user charges or additional cost recovery from the students and parents. Though, at present, about one-half of the finance comes from private sources, yet level of fees in a majority of universities and colleges continue to be low. Both public and private funding is going in for professional education only.

With growing number of households capable of and willing to pay for higher education, there is scope to rationalise tuition fees in public institutions and raise resources. This would have to accompany with well-funded schemes of freeships and scholarships for students from poor families. There is a larger scope for student loan programmes, but these have to be properly designed. Public spending (particularly central expenditure) on students aid schemes for poor students needs to be substantially raised with simplified procedure for disbursement. Students loan financing has to become a major source of funding higher education. More specifically, student aid schemes in the form of deferred payment of fees on graduation and employment, with risk of unemployment/under employment transferred to the government could be initiated. ICLs could be provided through a wide range of private and public sector lenders with a third party servicing of loans and government guarantees and attractive tax cuts against money spent on education would promote increased spending on education.

In sum, there is need for more funds for higher education. This has to come from the government, and the students and parents. Private initiatives need to be encouraged to enhance capacity since they bring in upfront investments. Public funds are required to provide for the basic minimum infrastructure and facilities that are lacking in a large part of public-funded higher education. Though the central government could share a larger responsibility, since a major part of public higher education is with the state governments, their sustained funding support is critical. Public-funds are also required to set up new institutions in areas or for subjects where the private sector may not be interested; for research funding, particularly in the sciences and other technical fields; funding for collaborative activities; and competitive grants to reinforce accreditation and promote excellence. Apart from increased public funds, there is a need to make fund allocation mechanism objective, so that it is outcome focused and performance based. The much publicised increased outlay will have little impact on increasing access or improving the quality for bulk of the higher education system unless these are accompanied with wider institutional reforms.

◆

5

Workforce Development

I have always found that plans are useless, but planning is indispensable.

—Dwight Eisenhower

DESPITE rhetoric about the traditional moral, civic and intellectual goals of higher education, the rationale for growth and mass expansion of higher education has been its ability to provide a workforce for a technologically-driven knowledge economy. Ironically, as enrolments in higher education grow, so does the problem of unemployment and underemployment of graduates across a wide range of countries, including India. Graduate unemployment is much higher than overall level of unemployment. In China, explosive growth of higher education in recent years has resulted in skyrocketing unemployment.[1] More often than not, in such cases, higher education is blamed for not equipping students with skills required in the job market. This makes quality and relevance of higher education and its ability to adapt to changing economic conditions critically important.

Recent focus on higher education in India has been in the context of mounting skill shortages. Such shortages co-exist with the rising graduate unemployment and underemployment. This concerns employers, education policy makers and students alike. This phenomenon is not unique to India. However, given the numbers involved, and the high growth path on which India is engaged, it takes a particularly acute form here. There is, though, an aspect peculiar to India: by skipping the manufacturing stage and going straight to the services sector, India upsets the conventional path to growth, and has taken the supply of graduates in certain segments by surprise.

In the above context, the focus of this chapter is to assess the role of higher education in developing workplace skills and to deconstruct skill shortages in the Indian context. The chapter begins with explaining the linkages between higher education and economic growth on the one hand and with labour market on the other. It examines the dynamics of the demand and supply of qualified manpower in Indian economy as it integrates with the world economy and shows signs of structural change. Based on its talent pool, India is perceived to be a frontrunner in the global knowledge economy. However, there are concerns that the country's antiquated higher education and training system might derail the growth process. The chapter analyses these concerns and suggests ways to address them.

Higher Education and Economic Growth

Education promises public benefits ranging from economic growth to political coherence and social order. Among them, the evolution of the economic purposes of education is seen as the single most important educational development of the 20th century. Developments—first marked by a wave of industrialisation in one country after another, and then with the emergence of knowledge economies—endowed education explicitly with an economic value by forging both direct and indirect, backward and forward linkages between education and economy.

Until quite recently, the contribution of education to economic growth lacked any real evidence. In the 1960s, while measuring various components of economic growth, economists found that often 50 per cent or less of the growth in gross domestic product could be attributed to the stock in capital and the amount of labour. The residual factors were responsible for most growth.[2] These factors are closely linked to the way knowledge is used in better way or more productive use of inputs. Technological progress, or advances and human capital, the various forms of education and training that make workers more productive were two main components of the residual factors (Harberger, 1998). While the issue of technological advances shall be discussed in the next chapter, the focus of this chapter will be on education and training of people that increases their productivity.

Education and training enhances the skills and capacities of people, and therefore, their productivity, and the employers award such people with higher earnings. People therefore invest in education and training by making rationale estimates of returns of education. This has been the central idea of the human capital theory that dominated the discourse in the economics of education since the 1960s. Recognition of human capital as an agent of growth transformed not only development economics but also led to a new field in the economics of education. Since then, the productivity enhancing effect of education and its differential impacts on income in accordance with differences in educational attainments of workers attracted attention of policymakers and analysts. With this, *learning to do* has become a vital function of education, particularly higher education that usually connects formal education to the world of work.

There are serious reservations to this limited view of higher education that human capital theory advocates. According to the UNESCO's report of the International Commission on Education for the 21st century, education must be organised around four fundamental types of learning: the four pillars of knowledge—learning to know, that is, acquiring the instruments of understanding; learning to do, so as to be able to act creatively in one's environment; learning to live together, so as to participate and cooperate with other people in all human activities; and learning to be, an essential progression which proceeds from the previous three (Delors, 1996). The role of higher education in developing human capital to foster economic growth fails to take a holistic view.

At the same time, the public benefits of higher education through economic growth are ambiguous in several ways. There is evidence to suggest that investing in education by itself does not automatically cause growth; other conditions are necessary to realise potential productivity increase associated with education.[3] In addition, higher education, the way it is pursued, may in fact exacerbate inequality. Further, differences

170

in earnings of individuals could be due to some kind of irrational credentials that higher education provides. Such credentials are merely a signal of higher ability rather than actual productivity differences.

In 1973, the economist Michael Spence propounded the screening hypothesis in education. This hypothesis assumes that education does not enhance the employee's productivity at all. The value of formal education is not so much in what has actually been learnt (provision of new knowledge that enhances human capital) but as an instrument for the selection of the most gifted employees by the employers. Education acts as a signalling device in the job market. Employers do not have much information about the potential employee's quality and use markets to judge quality: a higher educational qualification is treated as an indicator of ability, and sustained unemployment is regarded as mark of disability (Spence, 1973).

Based on a contradictory set of assumptions, the human capital approach and the screening hypothesis differ in their policy implications. While the former makes a case for greater investment, including public investment, in higher education, the screening hypothesis suggests that since higher education merely enables employees to get higher wages and not make them more productive, therefore public investment in higher education is wasteful. Despite these differences, the two are found to be valid in different contexts and complement each other to understand the public and private benefits of higher education.

In addition, formal education is seen as a way of helping students to develop socially acceptable norms of behaviour and such traits are valued either explicitly or implicitly by all employers. Thus, the role of formal education in the socialisation process along with the two approaches above help in understanding the link between education and the world of work in a holistic manner. It is, however, difficult to separate out the signalling value of education from its productivity enhancing effects, and its impact on building social and emotional skills. Thus, the measuring value of education both for computing the private and social returns of education is difficult.

The link between formal education and work is usually established through what is termed as qualification. This qualification could mean the skills required to do a job, the skills that a worker possesses linked mainly to his or her education (as per the human capital approach), or the skills that are recognised in the labour market with qualification merely provide a signal in the job market (if we follow the screening hypothesis). These concepts are not identical. Thus, they fail to establish any concrete correlation between education and employment and make it difficult to define the objective standards of qualification (Bertrand, 1998). As a result, creating a fit between the supply of graduates from the higher education system and demand for graduates from the job markets is not easy.

Higher Education and Labour Market

Demand for higher education could either be private demand from the students and their parents or the demand from the labour markets for specific skills—very often the two are unrelated. Higher education, which was viewed primarily as a social experience earlier is now seen as a way to get ahead in life. This culture of aspiration is continuously pushing up the private demand for higher education. The policymakers are required to respond to this rising demand. Exalting the public benefits of higher education, policy usually has an expansionist bias resulting in over-education, leading to unemployment and underemployment of graduates, a phenomenon common throughout the world in varying degrees.

Since the link between fields of study and occupational areas are relatively loose in most countries and the process of transition from higher education to employment has become more complex and protracted, it has its own dynamics of raising and dashing hopes (Gibbons, 1998). The formal higher education does not necessarily equip students with skills required in the job markets. This creates a problem of unemployment on the one hand and skill shortages on the other.

Public policy is required to create a fit between supply of skilled people by the education system and the demand for skilled manpower from the labour market and to ensure provision of adequate number of places in the higher education system to meet students' demand. This requires coordination at two levels: between the demand for qualified manpower and places in higher education system on the one hand, and places in higher education and students' demand on the other. Ideally, the two should relate to each other; poor labour market outcome of graduates should dampen the demand for places in higher education system. In reality this does not happen, because the feedback mechanism and coordination system is often weak. Coordination is required for different types of education, at different points in time and at different locations. Given the enormity and complexity of the task, this multi-level coordination is not easy to achieve. Central planning would not be very useful.

The nature of work has changed and is continually changing with technical changes. With increasing integration of the job markets, the national context is no more relevant. These aspects need elaboration in order to understand the dynamics of coordination between higher education and labour market. In this complex scenario, market forces usually do a better job than central planning in matching the skills of the graduates with their own preferences and the demands of the labour market, though some planning may be desirable.

Changing Nature of Work

While much of the technical change during the early 19th century has been skill replacing, the 20th century has been marked by skill-biased technical change. Rapid increase in the supply of skilled workers has induced the development of skill complementary technologies. The skill-biased technical change has altered work environment. It has transformed the nature of work and its content.

Earlier advances liberated people from strenuous and dangerous work; the current wave of technological change driven by new information and communication technologies frees people from tedious, repetitious and mindless work. Its impact is sweeping. It also promises potentially limitless access to information. New ways of acquiring, analysing and presenting information have reorganised work and created new jobs and products. New technologies have enabled greater mobility of both work and workers across borders enabling an efficient division of labour across nations. The changes are at an individual as well as an organisational level. This has impacted employment structures and labour markets.

At the individual level, there are two undeniable trends: the decrease of workers in industrial and manual jobs and the rise in tertiary employment. Tertiary employment requires a large number of people who do intellectual work. The work content of jobs has changed, leading to new demands in terms of knowledge, skills and behaviour. There is a demand for a more abstract form of thought. It gives priority to analytical and problem solving ability, adaptability and capacity for innovation and written expression. In view of rapid technical changes, the focus is now on attitudes and behaviour of people, rather than their technical capacities that in any case need to be renewed continually.

At the organisational level influenced by new technologies, distributed work has become the dominant form of work organisation. It overcomes the challenges of working across organisational boundaries in different time zones or flexi-time at different physical locations and often transcends national boundaries. This has altered the basic rules for organising and managing work, particularly knowledge or intellectual work (Ware, 2002).

There is a growth in the demand for analytical and managerial work like that of scientists, engineers, attorneys, executives and perhaps economists that have strong complementarities with new technology. There is a growth in the demand for services workers, such as security guards, truck drivers, housekeepers, waiters, salespeople, etc. But the demand for 'middle-skilled' white collar jobs like that of secretaries, bookkeepers, insurance adjusters, bank tellers, telephone receptionists has collapsed. In such jobs, direct substitution with computers is feasible. These changes have resulted in a polarisation of work—the hollowing-out of the distribution of job tasks (Autor, 2006). Table 5.1 shows how computerization is having an impact on routine, abstract and manual tasks.

While the impact of the above changes has been greater in the advanced countries, signs of transformation are clearly visible in the developing countries as well. The changing nature of work has obvious implications on the expectations from the education and training system. The pace of change is, however, often exaggerated by the rhetoric of knowledge economy, and as a consequence there are unreal expectations

Workforce Development

TABLE 5.1 Computerisation and three task categories

	Task description	Example occupations	Potential impact of computerisation
Routine Tasks	Rules-based, repetitive and procedural	Book-keepers, assembly line workers	Direct substitution
Abstract Tasks	Abstract problem-solving requiring mental flexibility	Scientists, engineers, attorneys, managers and doctors	Strong complementarities
Manual Tasks	Environmental and inter-personal adaptability	Truck drivers, security guards, waiters, maids and janitors	Limited complementarities or substitution

Source Adapted from Áutor (2006).

from the education and training system. This issue is discussed in details later in this chapter.

Integration of Job Markets

Increased trade in both goods and services across national borders has paved way for an integrated global economy. National context is often not very relevant now. Three recent developments having implications on increasing integrated job markets are worth noting. The first relates to a larger pool of global workforce. With the end of the Cold War and collapse of the socialist economic system, two global economic systems, with very separate labour forces, trade patterns and investment pools, merged into one. The labour force of the formerly socialist economies in Russia, China and Eastern Europe is being slowly incorporated into the global production system. This is also true in case of India, which shifted from an inward domestic focus to an outward focus from the early 1990s. As a result of this integration, the global supply of labour increased significantly without a corresponding increase in the capital for investment.

The second relates to a dramatic increase in the productivity due to technological changes, in both manufacturing and services. According to Polaski (2004), though in the long term, productivity growth is good because it creates the possibility of higher wages and incomes in countries that experience it, in the short term, it contributes to a dis-equilibrium in supply and demand for labour.

The third relates to the growing offshore outsourcing of a wide range of work. Routine cognitive tasks, mostly services, were formerly almost non-traded across borders. These required real-time communications and coordination and massive information flows. Revolutionary advances in telecommunications have lowered the costs of sending vast amounts of information rapidly and have improved coordination in real-time basis across continents. As a result, there is an emergence of off-shoring industries. A large part of services work can be sliced up and sent abroad to low-wage destinations. It started with business operations, computer programming, call centres, product design and back office jobs like accounting and billing. The next wave of outsourcing is likely to be consumer services, an array of potential services beyond tutoring and personal assistance like health and nutrition coaching, personal tax and legal advice.

These developments have turned a segmented global labour market into an integrated whole. Increased trade and rising mobility of financial capital, demographic shift are continually changing the dynamics. There is an intense competition for an expanding array of jobs.

In the backdrop of the above discussion, adapting higher education to future work is difficult since it is almost impossible to foresee how the nature of work is going to evolve over a period of time. Earlier, countries adopted manpower planning approach that projected demand occupation-by-occupation over a given timescale and created education capacities accordingly. In these uncertain times, creating this fit is found difficult and of little use. The fact that a large percentage of jobs are filled up through job mobility renders this approach even more meaningless.

As a result, the manpower planning approach has been by and large abandoned and replaced by a study of signals from the labour markets. This requires a dynamic system of providing the job market information on placement, unemployment rates by levels of competence, job offers and employers' estimation of their needs in terms of manpower to the higher education institutions on a continuing basis. These signals from the labour market help the educational institutions to make adjustments in their capacities and adapt their curricula to emerging changes in the job market and also assist individuals to make correct choices. Rather than an inward domestic focus, these developments have to be viewed in global context in a manner that best serves the national interest. The rest of the chapter looks at the Indian case—the employment patterns and trends, education and skill profile of the workforce, employment prospects of graduates, supply-side perspective, skill shortages and the way this has to be addressed.

Employment Pattern

In India, a majority of the workforce is engaged in agriculture and allied activities and has low productivity levels. A large proportion of non-agricultural workers are also engaged in low productivity and low-wage jobs. More than 90 per cent of the workforce is in the informal sector and work in poor conditions. Despite changes in the economic structure in terms of value added by different sectors to the gross domestic product, the employment pattern has not changed much over the years.

There were 402 million workers and 626 million non-workers as per Census 2001.[4] Of the total workers, 313 million were main workers and 89 million marginal workers. These included 127 million cultivators and 106 million agricultural labourers. While agriculture contributes just over 20 per cent to the GDP, its share in employment was 58.4 per cent in the year 2004–05. The services sector that contributed nearly 58 per cent to the GDP employed only 23.2 per cent of the workforce. Between 1991 and 2001, though the share of services to GDP increased by about 10 per cent, its share in terms of employment increased only marginally.

The decade from 1991 to 2001 saw a marginalisation of workforce in agriculture—the number of main workers declined, while there was a significant increase in the number of marginal workers. Growth in the agriculture sector did not keep pace with the growth in labour force resulting in division of the available job opportunities and causing marginalisation. Fragmented land holding, with the average size[5] going down made this sector unviable for most farmers.

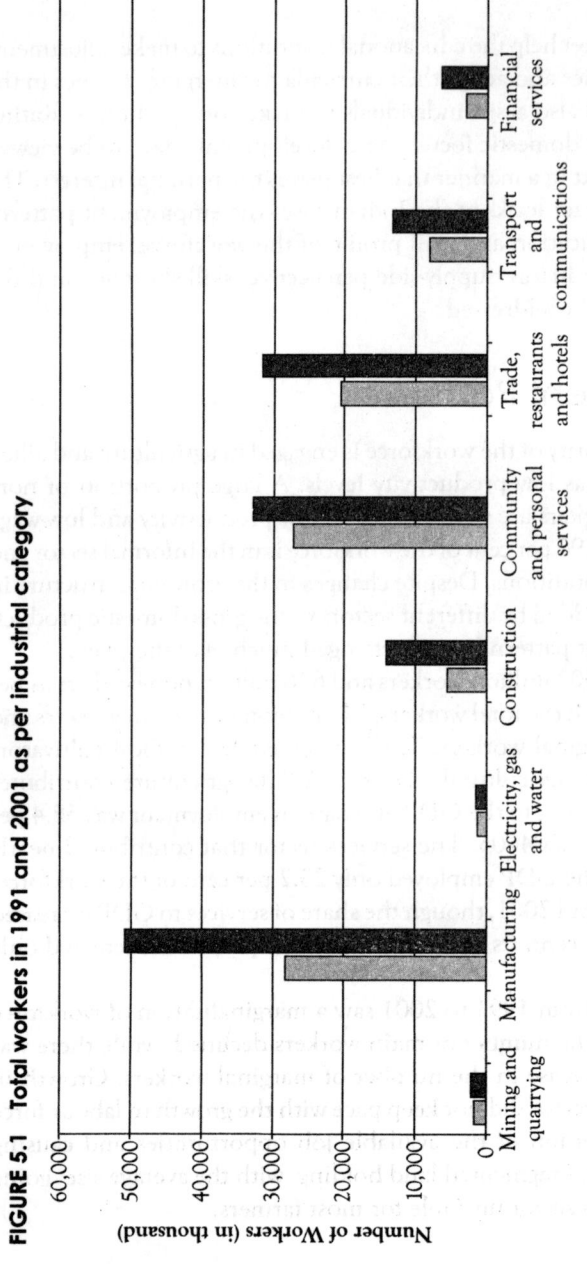

FIGURE 5.1 Total workers in 1991 and 2001 as per industrial category

Number of Workers (in thousand)

Industrial Category

Mining and quarrying · Manufacturing · Electricity, gas and water · Construction · Community and personal services · Trade, restaurants and hotels · Transport and communications · Financial services

▨ Total workers (in '000s) 1991   ■ Total workers (in '000s) 2001

Source Compiled by the author based on Census of India, 2001.

Workforce Development

While globally the services sector has displaced agriculture as the main sector for employment, with 42 per cent of the global workforce employed in the services sector against 36.1 per cent in the agriculture sector, in India agriculture still employs 58 per cent of the people and is only below Sub-Saharan Africa where 63 per cent of the workforce is in agriculture.

As seen in Figure 5.1, the non-agricultural sectors (except mining and quarrying) saw growth in absolute as well as percentage terms and in both the main and marginal workers. This suggests some shift in occupational pattern from agriculture to other sectors in the country, but the shift has not been very significant.

As seen from Table 5.2, the services sector employed 107 million workers, the industry sector employed 83 million and the manufacturing within industry merely 53.5 million workers in 2004-05. In recent years, growth in services has preceded growth in manufacturing. This, along with the fact that there is growth in skill-intensive rather than labour- intensive manufacturing within the manufacturing sector, share of services in employment has grown much slower than its share in GDP suggests that Indian economy is following a non-traditional pattern of development. Services that accounted for over 57 per cent of GDP in 2006-07 contribute only about 24 per cent of the employment. Banga (2005) pointed out that within the services sector, fastest growth is in the communication and business services sectors that absorb less labour compared to labour-intensive construction and transport sectors. As a result, the capacity of the non-agriculture sector to create jobs is limited.

Many people have raised doubts about sustainability of this growth pattern. On detailed analysis, Handsa (2001) has concluded that the services sector, with its backward and forward linkages, will induce growth in manufacturing and improve its productivity. This is a positive signal since low labour productivity is a major concern. Labour productivity in India (at USD 6,587 per worker) is one of the lowest in the world right above Sub-Saharan Africa. It is one-third of the global average (at USD 19,834) and almost one-tenth of that in the developed economies. Good news though is that it is improving faster than most countries except East Asia and certainly more rapidly than advanced

TABLE 5.2 Employment by sector/industrial category (various years)

(in million)

Sectors	1993–94	1999–2000	2004–05	2009–10
I. Agriculture, forestry & fishing	242.46 (64.8%)	237.56 (59.8%)	267.57 (58.4%)	296.62 (56.0%)
II. Industry	58.23 (15.5%)	69.18 (17.4%)	83.23 (18.2%)	104.94 (19.8%)
Mining & quarrying	2.7 (0.7%)	2.27 (0.6%)	2.74 (0.6%)	3.19 (0.6%)
Manufacturing	42.5 (11.3%)	48.01 (12.1%)	53.51 (11.7%)	61.9 (11.7%)
Electricity, Gas & Water supply	1.35 (0.4%)	1.28 (0.3%)	1.37 (0.3%)	1.5 (0.3%)
Construction	11.68 (3.1%)	17.62 (4.4%)	25.61 (5.6%)	38.35 (7.2%)
III. Services	73.76 (19.7%)	90.30 (22.7%)	107.02 (23.2%)	128.31 (24.2%)
Trade, hotels & restaurants	27.78 (7.4%)	37.32 (9.4%)	47.11 (10.3%)	79.56 (15.1%)
Transport, storage & communication	10.33 (2.8%)	14.69 (3.7%)	17.38 (3.8%)	Included in above
Financing, insurances, real estate and business services	3.52 (0.9%)	5.05 (1.3%)	6.86 (1.5%)	9.94 (1.9%)
Community, social & personal services	32.13 (8.6%)	33.20 (8.4%)	35.67 (7.8%)	38.81 (7.3%)
Total	374.45 (100%)	397.00 (100%)	457.82 (100%)	529.87 (100%)

Source Based National Sample Surveys compiled by the author from different sources.[6]
Note Figures in parentheses denote sectoral share in total employment.

countries. Productivity rose by 3.7 per cent per annum between 1996 and 2006. With a current low base, there is scope for improvement and hence sustained economic growth (ILO, 2007a).

The overall quality of jobs is declining. Debate in the country on the quality of jobs centres around formal or organised sector employment. The estimates of employment in the organised sector vary widely. The Directorate General of Employment and Training (DGET) collects data on employment in the public sector and the non-agricultural establishments employing more than 10 workers. According to these

Workforce Development

estimates, this sector constitutes merely 7 per cent of the total workforce. Other estimates put the figures somewhere between 11 and 14 per cent. The DGET data shows that employment in the organised sector has remained flat or even declined since 1990. While there is a drop in public sector employment, employment in the organised private sector has marginally improved in recent years.

Another key feature of the Indian labour market is its very large informal sector. The informal sector in India comprises small, non-capital intensive enterprises run by self-employed persons, often with family support and/or employing a few temporary hired workers. This also includes casual wageworkers, contract labourers and piece-rated home-workers constituting a large, fluid labour market. As noted in Table 5.3, the informal or unorganised sector employed 92 per cent of the total workforce; though its contribution to the GDP was merely 59 per cent in 1999-2000. In contrast, contributing 41 per cent of the GDP, the formal sector employed a little above 8 per cent of the workforce.

According to a National Council of Applied Economic Research (NCAER) study, around 30 per cent of the workforce in the informal sector is in the home-based segment comprising mostly invisible workers. It needs to be noted that skill acquisition in the informal sector is substantially hereditary or through apprenticeship with master craftsmen. According to the Economic Census (1998), 94.2 per cent of the enterprises in the Indian economy employed between one and five persons.

Employment in the formal or the organised sector is not only small, but it is primarily in the public sector—70 per cent employment is in the public sector. Due to capital deepening and technology adoption, employment elasticity of organised sector has been very low at 0.066 during 1993-94 to 1999-2000, whereas it has been 0.213 for the informal sector (Table 5.3). Because of its very small base and major portion of this being in the public sector, prospects of the organised sector emerging as a major employer even in a long-term perspective are bleak. In fact, employment in public sector and government has been stagnating since 1994 (Planning Commission, 2002).

TABLE 5.3 Output, employment and productivity in various sectors

(Organised, unorganised, private and public sectors at 1993–94 prices)

	Organised				
	Total	Public	Private	Unorganised	Grand total
Value Added (GDP) (NET) in Rs billion					
1993–94	2,568.49	1,808.43	760.06	4,411.43	6,979.92
	36.80%	25.9%	10.89%	63.80%	
1999–2000	4,189.20	2,665.19	1,524.01	6,004.25	10,193.45
	41.10%	26.1%	15.0%	58.9%	
Growth in per cent	8.5%	6.68%	12.30%	5.27%	6.52%
Employment in million					
1993–94	27.18	19.3	7.88	288.66	315.84
	8.61%	6.1%	2.51%	91.39%	
1999–2000	28.11	19.42	8.69	308.64	336.75
	8.34%	5.8%	2.54%	91.66%	
Growth in per cent	0.56%	0.10%	1.64%	1.12%	1.074%
Employment elasticity	0.066	0.015	0.133	0.213	0.165

Source Report of special group on targeting 10 million employment opportunities a year in the Tenth Five Year Plan, Planning Commission, 2002.

Under competitive pressure due to globalisation and consequent rationalisation and retrenchment, there is sub-contracting, outsourcing and casualisation of work. Though the 60th round of the NSS shows that there is a recovery in share of self-employed workers and decline in casual workers, the shift is not large. The survey showed that quality of jobs is an issue since regular jobs are not being created, though the working conditions of the top cohort of self-employed workers matches that of the regular workers.

Recent *OECD Employment Outlook* points out that the country faces several challenges on the employment front. The country has a huge surplus labour (130 million) in the rural India and faces the problem of finding jobs for women and the youth. Employment to population ratio at 50.5 per cent is poorest compared with at least 66 per cent in other BRIC (Brazil, Russia, India, China) countries. Another area of concern is high proportion of the workforce is in the informal sector.

This is much higher than other BRIC countries. There is faster growth in informal sector than in organised sector salaried jobs (OECD, 2007).

In overall terms, there is an acute problem of unemployment and underemployment. Based on workers' usual principal status (UPS), the number of unemployed persons in India increased from around 7.78 million in 1983 to 10.6 million in 1999–2000, placing the unemployment rate at around 2.8 per cent. This counts only those people who spend more than six months in a year looking for work. The other approach to measure unemployment is based on the current weekly status (CWS) that corresponds to the international definition of unemployment. Measure on the basis of current daily status (CDS) both of underemployment and short-term unemployment is even bleaker. Based on CWS, the unemployment rate was about 5 per cent and as per CDS the unemployment rate was around 9 per cent in 2004. Underemployment is estimated at 13 per cent on average for all workers and 25 per cent for casual workers.

In recent years as per the World Factbook, open unemployment rate (based on CDS unemployment rate) at 9.2 per cent for India is comparable to that in the European Union (9.5 per cent) and China (9.8 per cent). Like India, there is a substantial underemployment in China, which was estimated at 20 per cent in 2003. While the countries in East Asia—Vietnam, Malaysia, Thailand and South Korea—have low unemployment rate, the advanced countries such as Germany and Spain have high rates of unemployment.

Employment Trends

In the 1990s, employment trends indicated a grim scenario marked with jobless growth. Between the years 1993–94 and 1999–2000, employment growth rate had slowed down from 2.1 per cent to 1.6 per cent per annum; wage inequality had increased with real wages growing rapidly in the top two deciles between 1983 and 1999–2000 (World Bank, 2006b). However, as per the 61st round of NSS, between the years 1999–2000 and 2004–05 employment growth rate rose to 2.89 per cent, while labour force (people available for employment) growth rate rose to 2.93 per cent. Making projections based on sectoral employment and using values of elasticities of employment growth with respect to growth of sectoral value-added, Rangarajan and others (2007) have claimed in a recent paper that with the current 9 per cent growth rate, workforce will match the labour force eliminating unemployment.

The recently released *OECD Economic Outlook* has also concluded that India outperformed Russia, Brazil and China in creating jobs during 2000-05. The country generated 11.3 million net new jobs annually between 2000 and 2005. Real wages have also risen (by 2.7 per cent) during 1995-2000, through the growth in wages is slower than in China and Russia.

This is a positive development. It debunks the notion of jobless growth in the post-reforms period as normally believed, but there are serious concerns. It is noted that agriculture, forestry and fishing would continue to absorb 56 per cent of the workforce even in 2009-10, as seen in Table 5.2. The bulk of employment is being created in the informal sector where wages are low. Though wages have risen marginally, these are still low, therefore wages and not jobs are the issue. Further it is estimated that about 150 million workers are caught in low productivity employment. Therefore full employment in any meaningful way might be almost two decades away. The small base of employment in non-agriculture sectors where higher productivity can be achieved is a matter of concern and will continue to be so in near future.

Tracking the evolution of labour market conditions, it is seen that more jobs are being created, but these are not necessarily better jobs. With acceleration in growth, there are signs of picking up in employment. The size of the informal economy is growing rapidly with steady labour accruals. This is accompanied with decline in real wages in some sub-sectors, leading to marginalisation. The trends reflect the bleak employment scenario in the country, though a recent World Bank report suggests that labour market outcomes in the 1990s have been better than commonly perceived. According to the report, wages and labour productivity grew faster in the 1990s, and the workforce has been deployed more efficiently (World Bank, 2006b).

Despite declining job opportunities in the public sector, a large number of people register themselves with the employment exchanges. As on 31 December 2005, around 39.3 million persons were on the live register in 939 employment exchanges and waiting for jobs. Around 5–5.5 million job seekers register each year. Vacancies notified vary from 220 to 420,000 over the past few years and placement is even lower at 138,000 in 2004 and 173,000 in 2005. More than 80 per cent of job seekers (4.2 million) during 2004–05 were educated, that is, passed grade 10 or more.

Women's participation in the workforce in India is low—women are usually responsible for household activities not classified as economic activities, while the men work outside. Therefore, while the male participation rates are roughly comparable to those in other countries, the female participation rates at about 30 per cent are low. Recent global employment trends for women show that women still work as unpaid contributing family workers or low income workers, particularly in South Asia including India, where they are still struck with the lowest paying jobs, often in the informal economy with insufficient legal protection (ILO, 2007b). However, a positive trend of participation of educated women in the workforce is seen and with this the gender gap is now closing.

With technical change, there is hollowing-out of the middle all over the world. This phenomenon has been noted earlier in this chapter. Most jobs are now clustered at the low productivity end and only some at the high productivity end. This trend is visible in India as well. Employment in both manufacturing and services sector is showing signs of this kind of dualism.

While the country's growth rate has gathered momentum, manufacturing industries have failed to create unskilled labour-intensive jobs in manufacturing to absorb low productivity marginal farmers. As a result, too many people are bottled up in the low productivity rural sector. Overall employment in manufacturing has not changed over the years. Generous depreciation rate for investment in machinery and equipment and rigid labour laws encourage firms to be capital intensive. Manufacturing sector is concentrated in large firms or small units leading to the problem of the missing 'middle'. International experience shows that this missing middle is the most enterprising and dynamic in employment generation. Annual Survey of Industries (2000–01) showed that the organised manufacturing sector, dominated by large units, employed only 13.85 per cent of the manufacturing workforce, while contributing more than three-fourths of the manufacturing output.

In the year 2006-07, the manufacturing sector grew by 14 per cent, the highest growth rate for any part of Indian economy for more than a decade. This expansion has been however based on using high tech automated equipment rather than recruiting large numbers of new employees. Employment in manufacturing stands at 60 million (compared to 56 million in 2004). The growth came mainly from the small businesses employing 20 or fewer people, with larger businesses growing their workforce only slowly or not at all. It is estimated that the number of jobs added per unit of extra manufacturing output in India is now just 70 per cent of the figure a decade ago. The future of manufacturing in India is about employing more capital, equipment, and not more humans as per a report by Global Insight, US Economic Consultants (*The Business Standard*, 17 July 2007).

In the services sector, jobs were created in trade, transport, hotels and restaurant sectors with low productivity levels as also in the financial and business services sector with mid-level productivity during the 1990s. It is now accepted that India has a strong revealed comparative advantage (RCA) in services, particularly software services (World Bank, 2004). It has leveraged its large pool of human resources with English-speaking population to achieve very high growth rates in the IT–ITES sector. Over the past decade, there has been a surge in employment in IT and IT-enabled services sector. This has created highly skilled jobs with high productivity level. The surge in growth and its overall impact on Indian economy is so large that it warrants special attention in discussion on employment trends particularly for the graduates.

Surge in Growth of IT/IT-enabled Services Sector

IT and IT-enabled services sector has seen a surge in growth over the past 10 years. According to National Association of Software and Services Companies (NASSCOM), in the year 2006-07, revenues from this sector were USD 39.7 billion. Out of this nearly four-fifths (USD 31.3 billion) is revenue from exports. Projected to grow at 24-27 per cent over the next few years, this sector is expected to reach USD 50 billion target, more than ten-fold increase over the revenue of USD 4.8 billion reported in the year 1998. By 2009-10, revenues from this sector would touch USD 60 billion.

This sector has created a large number of jobs for educated people with very little capital investment. In the year 1997, there were just 190,000 people working in this sector. The 2001 census reported 200,000 computer professionals. This number quadrupled by 2004 in the next three years to 830,000. Between the year 2004 and 2007 as seen in Table 5.4, it has doubled. This sector now employs 1.63 million persons directly—72 per cent of them are graduates, mainly engineering graduates.

TABLE 5.4   Employment in software and services sector

Sector	FY 2004	FY2005	FY2006	FY2007
IT Services	215,000	297,000	398,000	562,000
ITES-BPO	216,000	316,000	415,000	545,000
R&D and Products	81,000	93,000	115,000	144,000
Indian Market*	318,000	352,000	365,000	378,000
Total*	830,000	1,058,000	1,293,000	1,630,000

Source NASSCOM (quoted in *The Financial Express*, 29 January 2007).
Note   * Including user organisations.

IT professionals earn high disposable income at a relatively young age. They have fewer liabilities, leading to higher spending. Large disposable income of a relatively young section of people in the sector is fuelling consumer demand and contributing to demand in other sectors. Estimated turnover of the sector was Rs 1,342 billion in the year 2005-06 and it employed 1.3 million people with an average salary of Rs 540,000 per annum. Of this, Rs 634 billion is spent on the domestic economy including consumption spending. It is estimated that employees spent Rs 260 billion on domestic consumption. It is therefore not surprising that each IT job creates four more jobs in areas such as construction, transportation, security, entertainment and retail, catering and housekeeping services. It is estimated that the IT sector has created indirect employment opportunities for nearly 6 million people engaged in transport.

IT and IT-enabled services, pharmaceuticals, biotechnology, automobile and next-generation manufacturing are the country's sunrise sectors. These have succeeded mainly on the basis of lower cost and an abundance of technically qualified human resources and resulted in the country's atypical growth pattern. However, India, with its large informal economy, is faced with the problem of employing a growing unskilled labour force and managing increased wage disparity. In a recent study, Kochhar and others (2006) analysed the challenges and concluded that policies to boost the supply of skilled labour would be essential not only to further consolidate gains but also to attract investment in labour-intensive activities in order to reduce income gaps. The study suggested that availability of skilled manpower both for its growing services sector and skill-intensive manufacturing sector would be important even to attract investment in labour-intensive activities and made a strong case for expansion of higher education and training sector.

Employment Prospects

The country is on a new growth trajectory, registering sustained economic growth. The acceleration of economic growth over the past two decades has been driven by rising investment and savings rates and rising domestic consumption. Growth of Indian enterprises and a global workforce of Indian youth are the main reasons behind this virtuous cycle of growth.

The job market, particularly for the educated and skilled people, has also been transformed. Till about mid-1980s, it was the employers' market. There was little job-hopping; engineers, doctors and civil services were most coveted. After that, till about 1995, job opportunities expanded as multinational corporations came in; MBA became a middle-class dream degree. Between 1995 and 2000, there was a boom in the services sector; manufacturing shed jobs and the multinational corporations continued to be big hirers. After 2000, manufacturing has rebounded, exports are doing well and the services sector is continuing to boom.

While IT continues to be the most visible sector, there are signs of growth in the other knowledge sectors such as pharmaceuticals, biotechnology and engineering design. The country's manufacturing is has become competitive in niche areas such as the automotive sector. Many of these growth sectors need qualified skilled people. Seen differently, growth in these sectors has been enabled by a large pool of qualified people. Educated people have never had it so good. Engineering graduates now get placements a year ahead of completion of their course. In a globalised world, India is attracting investment in sectors that require the best educated workforce, as Martin Carnoy (1999) would argue that globalisation 'increases the pay-off to high level skills relative to low level skills....because interdependence between globalization and education presupposes competitiveness and efficiency which is achieved upon the latest technology or knowledge accessibility of the system.'

Recent manpower employment outlook surveys conducted by Manpower Inc (India) have reported positive hiring intentions across a range of sector with finance, insurance, real estate and services sector showing strongest increase in hiring intentions. Services sector that includes software and BPO lead the headhunting game. Offshore outsourcing of services that was earlier confined to business operations, computer programming, call centres, product design and back office jobs like accounting and billing have now expanded to consumer services, tutoring and personal assistance like health and nutrition coaching, personal tax and legal advice. There are efforts to extend it to help with hobbies and cooking, learning new languages and skills and more. These have created new opportunities for educated people. For instance, TutorVista, a tutoring service founded in 2005, helps educated people to earn up to USD 200 a month after a 60 hour training course.

Manpower Inc's Talent Shortage Survey, 2007 shows that 41 per cent of the employers worldwide are having difficulties in filling position due to lack of suitable talent available in their markets. Talent shortage at 9 per cent is reportedly least in India. India is amongst the top 10 (at 10th position) of the world's leading countries for nurturing and developing talent over the next five years (by 2012) as per the Global Talent Index (GTI) recently developed by executive search firm Heidrick & Struggles and the Economist Intelligence Unit. Thus, India has the potential to transform itself from an outsourcing hub into a repository of talent that can feed the global demand for skilled workforce.

Global Mobility

The country has the potential to provide workforce for the knowledge economy beyond the national borders. Recent developments have moved the country from a 'working power' based on supply of low-cost labour to a brainpower comprising skilled and educated workforce. It is estimated that the country could possibly generate direct or indirect job opportunities for 10–24 million people by providing an increasing array of services to advanced countries that currently face skill shortages. By servicing overseas consumers of services such as medical, tourism and education, an additional 10–48 million jobs could be created (AIMA, 2003).

The country has a large diaspora of more than 30 million people spread in 130 countries around the globe. A country's well-being is its talent pool spread globally. This contributes to the country's interests abroad and to the home country's economy through infusion of funds and cutting-edge ideas. Even citizens who study abroad come back if there are opportunities here. Those who stay abroad also contribute to the country's welfare. The notion of losing talent to other countries had a meaning when nations were seen as geographically bounded entities. In a globalised world, this idea has become meaningless. In a borderless world, people and ideas are not trapped by geography.

With its large population and huge capacity to generate skilled professionals at home and by education abroad, out-migration of professionals for India is now seen as an opportunity and not a threat (Bhagwati, 2004). In a global world, countries compete for markets by creating and attracting highly skilled people and the advanced countries have a big appetite for them. A large part of such flow is through education abroad and India sends a very large number of students to the United States and other developed nations. Freeman (2005) sees that India with large population and sizeable number of scientists and engineers could threaten the North's monopoly in the high-technology sectors by producing innovative products and services. It could become a magnet economy attracting high skilled and high-waged investment capital and offer high value-added services to the rest of the world.

There is a huge demand for nurses in Ireland, Great Britain and the United States. This demand is sweetened with offers of fast-entry permits and a pay several times that a doctor gets in India. As a result, a large number of nursing schools and colleges have come up. Leading the pack is Karnataka, where 656 nursing schools and 320 colleges came up in the past few years. DLF intends to bring 20,000 skilled workers —carpenters, bar-bender and electricians from West Asia for its construction projects in India. There are already 4,000 Chinese blue collar skilled workers are used by Reliance Industries at Jamnagar.

Currently about 9 per cent of the TCS workforce comprises foreign nationals. By 2012, one-fifth of its workforce could comprise foreign nationals. For Infosys and Wipro, this could be about 15 per cent. Some companies like Microsoft believe in hiring the best, irrespective of where they come from. With a large Indian diaspora of about 30 million people in around 130 countries of the world, there is huge potential for employment overseas. The European countries with shrinking population like Germany, Belgium, Poland, Sweden, Italy and France require skilled people like engineers, construction workers, health workers and semi skilled professionals like drivers, janitors and agriculturalists. For Indians, the European Union is a good hunting ground given the stiff immigration laws in the US and the UK and the tough working conditions in the Gulf. The Ministry of Overseas Indian Affairs (MoIA) has signed MoU with International Organisation for Migration (IOM) to facilitate legal migration of Indian workers to EU. The IOM will fulfil the gap in five countries and train Indian workers before sending them there.

With sustained high economic growth and demand from a wide range of sectors seen by positive hiring intentions, there is big opportunity for new jobs being created outside the farm sector. New job openings will require a trained workforce of adequate quality at a reasonable cost in sufficient numbers. Many sectors of the Indian economy are facing skill shortages. In many sectors of the economy, the labour market is now integrated at the global level. Supply constraints may not only hinder the growth prospects, but the people at home would lose jobs to others and the country will miss out on an opportunity to ease pressure on the farm sector and bring about a structural transformation of Indian economy. Before the issue of skill shortages is discussed, it is useful to examine the education and skill profile of the workforce and the supply-side scenario.

Education and Skill Profile of the Workforce

Education and skill level of India's workforce is low and primarily responsible for its low productivity. Though education enrolments are significance—more than 90 per cent in primary classes, around 60 per cent in middle classes, more than 30 per cent in higher secondary and about 11 per cent in higher education—yet percentage of people having marketable skills is woefully low. As per the National Sample Survey on Employment and Unemployment (1993–94), only 10.1 per cent of male workers and 6.3 per cent of female workers possessed specific marketable skills. The percentages were marginally higher in urban areas.

The situation has not improved much over the years. The 61st round of the NSS, conducted during July 2004 to June 2005, shows that out of 260 million persons in 15–29 years age group, only about 30 million are trained in any of the formal or the non-formal ways. Only about 2 per cent had received formal vocational training while about 3.4 per cent had received so-called hereditary training, that is, learning the trade of the family. This mostly includes farming, fishing, handicrafts, etc. Over 3.8 per cent of the surveyed age group acquired training through other means like working with a skilled person in a factory.

The levels of vocational skills of labour force compare poorly with other countries. Only 5 per cent of the labour force in the age group 20–24 had vocational training compared to 96 per cent in Korea and varying between 60 and 80 per cent in industrial countries.

Work participation rates by levels of education in Figure 5.2 shows that the participation rate increases with the level of education, though the pool of workers decreases sharply with increasing qualifications. Non-workers seeking work or available for work also increases by level

FIGURE 5.2 Work participation by education level, India, 2001

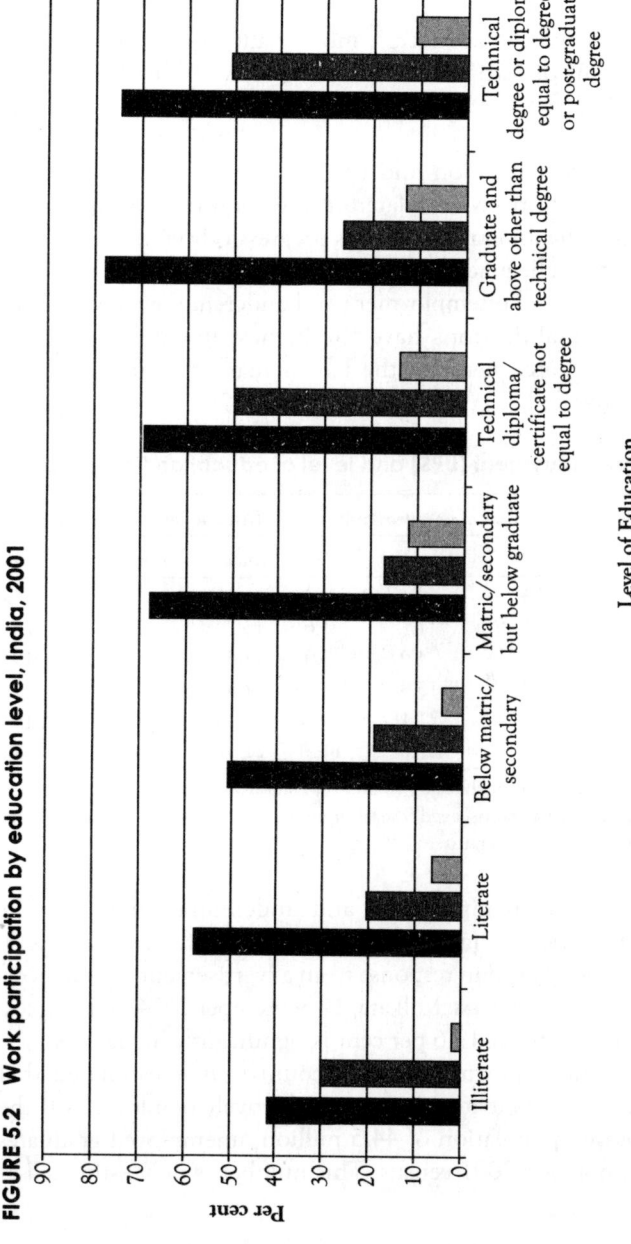

Level of Education

■ Males ■ Females ■ Non-workers seeking or available for work

Source Census of India, 2001.

of education. In percentage terms, more graduates and people with technical diploma or certificates are seeking or available for work than those with below matric qualifications, though in absolute terms their numbers may be small.

It suggests that education and unemployment as well as underemployment are positively correlated in the country. Unemployment is lowest among the illiterates, but rises progressively with education as seen in Table 5.5. The graduates with more than 12 years of education have the highest rate of unemployment and underemployment. Persons with technical qualifications have the highest unemployment rate suggesting a mismatch between the labour market requirement and the training provided.

TABLE 5.5 Unemployment (UPS) and level of education (in per cent)

Years of education	Rate of unemployment			Distribution of underemployment		
	Male	Female	All	Male	Female	All
0	0.4	0.1	0.3	5.1	3.8	4.8
1–5	1.7	1.3	1.6	15.2	7.7	13.3
6–8	3.7	4.9	3.8	21.5	11.5	19.0
9–10	5.4	15.8	6.5	21.5	23.1	21.9
11–12	7.6	21.1	9.1	15.2	15.4	15.2
More than 12	8.5	27.0	11.3	21.5	38.5	25.8

Source Reproduced from Ghosh, 2004 (Based on Data from NSSO-2000).

Note   Unemployed are persons, aged 5 years or more, who are unemployed according to the usual principal status.

The problem of unemployment and underemployment is more acute for graduates. Several MBAs and engineers figured in 10,000 odd applications received in response to an advertisement for two posts of peon (*The Financial Express*, Kolkata, 16 September 2004). Unemployment rate of graduates at 19.6 per cent is significantly higher than the overall rate of unemployment in the country. It is estimated that nearly 40 per cent graduates are not productively employed. Of the total unemployed population of 44.5 million, unemployed graduates are 4.8 million as per 2001 census. This number is now estimated at 5.3 million.

Ghose (2004) points out that educated young people do not want to engage in low-productivity, low-income work in the informal sector. They look for non-manual work, preferably in the organised sector. The very fact that they have some education also means that their families have some capacity to support them. This aggravates the problem of educated unemployment. Visaria (1998) noted that many of the unemployed have rather poor qualifications in terms of their performance at the examinations and have little aptitude or the capacity for the type of work they aspire for. Many of the unemployed are also perceived as unemployable by the industry.

This is corroborated by the fact that a large majority of job seekers are educated freshers who are inexperienced who and do not possess employable skills. As per DGET (2006), 56.2 per cent of them are Grade 10 pass, 25.9 per cent Grade 12 pass and 17.9 per cent are graduates. The proportion of educated job seekers has increased from 67.5 per cent in 1995 to 72.3 per cent in 2004. 72.5 per cent job seekers not being classified by any occupation. Seventy per cent job seekers are young, below the age of 29 years.

Earlier, a classic study by Blaug (1973) showed that higher education in the country expanded, despite high levels of unemployment among the graduates, long waiting times for first jobs, and the first jobs when obtained were not much more than that of high-level clerks. According to Blaug, this was in part due to even higher unemployment of people with secondary level education and in part due to low tuition fees in higher education. Many graduates accept lower paid jobs incompatible with their qualifications. While fat salaries enjoyed by a few tend to get highlighted, the plight of the vast numbers who remain jobless for long periods goes unnoticed.

Looking at the sectors in which graduates are employed, it is seen that the agriculture sector employs very few graduates. More than 40 per cent of the graduates work in the community and personal services sector (Figure 5.3). This includes government, defence, education and health services. More than 30 per cent of the main workers in this sector are graduates. The manufacturing sector employs the second largest number of graduates, but of this only about 10 per cent of the total workforce is in manufacturing. This is not surprising, since about 40 per cent of

FIGURE 5.3 Total workers and graduate workers by sectors

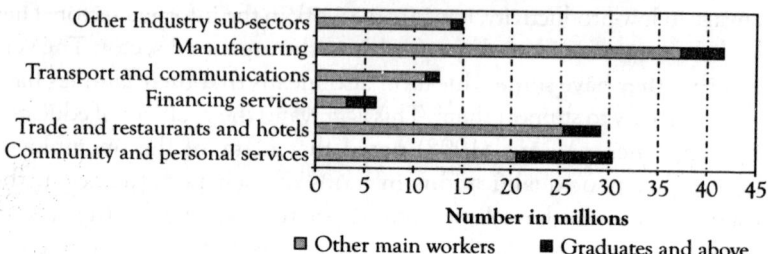

Source Census of India, 2001.

them (16.9 million out of 41.6 million) are in the household industries and may not require higher education qualifications.

In the financial services sector that includes insurance, real estates and business services and also scientific and research services, nearly half of the workers are graduates. 166 million workers in the agriculture and allied activities sector are either agricultural labourers or cultivators with small farm holdings and subsistence agriculture. Most of them do not require graduate degrees. Even amongst the other workers, around 9.7 million, that is, in this sector, only 3 per cent, are graduates.

Analysis based on the number of workers in each sector and the proportion of graduates in each suggests that most sectors have a small proportion of graduates (Table 5.6). It is not even sure if graduates in these sectors are performing jobs that would require graduate skills. Taking into consideration the employment base of various sectors, proportion of graduates among them, projected growth rates and elasticities, it is seen that while financing, insurances, real estate and business services would have high demand of graduates, manufacturing, trade, hotels and restaurant, transport, storage and communication, community, social and personal services would have moderate demand. Other sectors would have small or very small demand for graduates.

Looking at advanced or even transition economies where the agriculture sector is not large, as evident from Table 5.7, skilled work-force is relatively small compared to unskilled labour. Percentage share of skilled workforce (usually requiring higher education qualifications) is less than half of the GER in higher education across a range of countries.

Workforce Development

TABLE 5.6   Projected graduate demand in various sectors

Sectors	Employment base	Proportion of graduates	Projected growth rate	Projected elasticity	Graduate absorption
Agriculture, forestry & fishing	Very large	Very small	Low	High	Very small
Mining & quarrying	Very small	Very small	Low	High	Very small
Manufacturing	Moderate	Small	High	Low	Moderate
Electricity, Gas & Water supply	Very small	Average	Average	Low	Small
Construction	Moderate	Very small	High	High	Small
Trade, hotels & restaurant, Transport, storage & communication	Large	Very small	High	Average	Moderate
Financing, insurances, real estate and business services	Small	High	High	High	High
Community, social & personal services	Moderate	High	Average	Low	Moderate

Source Author.

TABLE 5.7   GER and skill distribution

(various countries for 2002–03 or most recent year available)

Country	GER in HE	Skill distribution of labour force		
		Agriculture labour	Unskilled labour	Skilled labour
USA	83	2.0	63.7	34.3
China	15	43.6	48.9	7.5
Japan	52	3.8	79.0	17.2
India	11	59.2	35.4	5.4
UK	64	4.1	69.0	26.9
Brazil	20	16.1	73.1	10.8
Russia	65	14.3	61.6	24.0

Source GER from *Global Education Digest, 2007* and skill distribution from LABORSTA database, http://laborsta.ilo.org.

This broadly suggests that in many countries workforce is overeducated. In the United States, it is noted that while many Americans are undereducated for specific work, at least a third are overeducated for the jobs they hold.

Occupation-wise population data on the basis of Census 2001 is now available. The data is as per National Classification of Occupation (NCO), 2004. This classification is based on two concepts: the kind of work performed in an occupation and the level of skills involved in the performance of the occupation.

As per this data, there were 402 million workers. Out of them 127 million were cultivators and 107 million agricultural labourers. Other workers were 167.8 million. This included 16.9 million workers in household industries. Main workers amongst them (145.5 million) have been classified by occupation. Numbers of workers in each occupation category, growth pattern since 1991, main occupations and qualifications required have been summarized in Table 5.8. It is seen that there were merely 12.5 million workers in the category of legislators, senior officials, managers and professionals that might require graduate degree or above.

Trends suggest highest growth in elementary occupations with large base and high growth in legislators, senior officials, managers, and professionals' categories but with low base. Lowest growth is in the clerks' category. This includes customer services. Past trend does reflect manpower requirement in the organised retail sector. Most categories of workers do not require graduate qualifications. Development in the last few years show the need for manpower in new and emerging areas like animation services, aviation sector, organised real estate and infrastructure sectors. Large manpower is required in these sectors. People in these sectors need not necessarily be graduates, but require specific skills.

Supply-side Perspective

In the matter of supply, both the university (referred to higher education) sector and the vocational education and training sector are taken together to take a holistic view and to see how they relate to and supplement each other in catering to the skills needed in the economy. This is critical to the understanding of the issue of skill shortages. In addition, India has the advantage of its young population and a large pool of workers with excellent English language skills. While the country's demographic

TABLE 5.8 Main workers by occupations, qualifications required and growth

(in million)

Occupation category	Qualification required	2001	Main occupations	Growth 1991–2001
Legislators, Senior Officials and Managers	General/professional degree	4.77 (3.28%)	Legislators –0.11 Senior officials –0.72 Corporate managers –3.81	52.7
Professionals	Professional degree	7.73 (5.10%)	Teachers (above middle) –2.55 Engineers –0.92 Lawyers –0.4 Computer professionals –0.2	50.6
Technicians and Associate Professionals	Professional diploma	9.26 (5.52%)	Health professionals –1.18 Teachers (up to middle) –4.04 Art & entertainment –0.3	33.7
Clerks	School certificate	6.93 (4.76%)	Office clerk –6.25 Customer services –0.68	10.3
Service workers and Shop and Market Sales Workers	School certificate/training	28.86 (19.84%)	Sales persons –18.89 Policemen –1.33 Hairdressers and beauticians –1.15	33.6

(Table 5.8 continued)

(*Table 5.8 continued*)

Occupation category	Qualification required	2001	Main occupations	Growth 1991–2001
Skilled Agricultural and Fishery Workers	Vocational education/training	6.95 (4.78%)	Dairy and livestock –4.28 Forestry workers –0.48 Fishery workers –1.18	41.6
Craft and Related Trade workers	Vocational education/training	33.87 (23.28%)	Masons –2.77 Carpenters –1.89 Mechanics & fitters –1.53	26.5
Plant and Machine operators and Assemblers	Vocational education/training	13.15 (9.04%)	Machine operators –4.52 Drivers –5.87	17.6
Elementary occupations	Functional literacy	24.74 (17.00%)	Street vendors –2.21 Domestic helpers etc. –3.25 Messengers, porters –2.43 Labourers –13.48	115.2
Total		145.5		43.0

Source Census 2001 and author's estimates. Total includes 9.25 million (6.36 per cent) workers that are not classified by occupations.

advantage and competence with English are discussed in Chapter 9, the focus here will be on the university and vocational education and training sectors.

University Sector

The university sector in the country comprises the universities and the university affiliated colleges. It had an enrolment of 10.4 million students with an outturn of 2.65 million in 2004–05. The total stock of graduates was estimated at 51.14 million in 2005. As seen in Table 5.9, graduates in the general stream outnumber those with professional qualifications. More than 82 per cent of the total enrolment is in ACS programmes with little occupational focus. As noted in Chapter 1, the government, in its effort to expand access created large capacity in the ACS programmes.

As the purpose of higher education began to be defined more in terms of preparing people for the world of work, few students entered higher education purely for academic pursuits. Therefore, the aforementioned expansion did not reflect students' preferences, and a void in terms of a large unmet demand for professional education was created. A larger proportion of students could pay for their education, and hence private professional education flourished.

As seen in Table 5.9, almost four-fifths of enrolment, outturn and stock relate to ACS. Outturn and stock are a little less than 80 per cent, while enrolments are above 80 per cent since one-third of the undergraduates go for post-graduate or for second degree programmes— more than half of these are professional programmes, such as MBA, MCA or B.Ed. and LLB. Duration of each of these programmes varies, therefore outturn and stock rather than enrolment reflect the correct situation from the labour market point of view.

While in terms of size, general higher education form the largest proportion of Indian higher education, professional higher education, particularly engineering and education have witnessed rapid growth in capacity in recent years. Since the growth is of recent origin and the capacity continues to grow, actual enrolment in professional programmes are understated by the UGC. Though this may not much change the

TABLE 5.9 Stock, enrolment and outturn of graduates and above, India, 2005

(in thousands)

Education level/subject	Enrolment (2004–05)	Outturn (2004–05)	Stock (2001)	Stock (2005)
Graduate and above	10,430	2,654	37,670	51,140
General Stream	8,556 (82.04%)	2,095 (78.94%)	30,015 (79.7%)	40,490 (79.1%)
Graduate other than technical degree (B.A., B.Sc and B.Com)	7,886	1,760	24,065	32,865
Post-graduate degree other than technical degree (M.A., M.Sc and M.Com)	770	335	5,950	7,625
Professional Stream	1,744 (17.96%)	559 (21.06%)	7,655 (20.3%)	10,650 (20.9%)
Management	100	50	800	1,050
Law	319	150	1,800	2,550
Engineering and Technology	754	160	2,588	3,388
Medicine	330	60	769	1,069
Agriculture, dairying and veterinary	77	20	127	227
Teaching	154	154	1,548	2,318
Others	10	5	23	48

Source Compiled by the Author (various sources[7]).

overall situation, yet a few observations would be in order. While the UGC recorded an enrolment of 161,000 in teacher education programmes, the Annual Report (2005–06) of the National Council for Teacher Education (NCTE) noted that enrolment in teacher education institutions stood at 594,000 as on 31 March 2006. Similarly, as per UGC data, the intake in engineering programmes at the undergraduate level is about 200,000 (corresponding to an enrolment of 795,120), whereas AICTE data gives an intake figure of 595,000. Like the rest of the professional higher education, most of the fresh capacity both in engineering and education has been created in the private independent sector.

Globally now, higher education is no longer dominated by the arts and the sciences. Core subjects are covered by layers of professional education: first, by the liberal professions; then by technical professions, principally the many branches of engineering and the technical sciences that accompanied the successive waves of industrialisation including the latest wave of the information sciences; followed by the caring professions which were stimulated by the growth of the welfare state and most recently by a new upsurge in enterprise professions, centred upon management and accountancy. The shift from liberal education to professional training that was observed in other parts of the world reshaped higher education in India. Though the professional higher education sector is growing faster than before, yet the gap between the general and professional stream is huge. The graduates from the general stream will continue to form the bulk of the stock of graduates in the country in the years to come. There is a misconceived notion that private higher education with focus on professional courses is creating an imbalance and arts, humanities and sciences are getting neglected. In fact, private higher education is correcting an undesired bias and enabling adaptation of higher education with labour market needs.

Bias for the arts and humanities in Indian higher education is evident from the comparative analysis of data of graduate numbers by field of education for various countries in Table 5.10. Though data for India is based on enrolment rather than graduate numbers, this is broadly indicative since proportion, rather than actual numbers, are being compared. It is seen that the Indian system produces far less number of graduates in health and education and it is skewed in favour of the humanities and arts. While science is adequately represented, there is further scope for increase in numbers of engineering and social sciences (mainly business and law) graduates.

The way the Indian system is structured, students have little choice. As noted in Chapter 2, about 87 per cent of enrolment is in affiliated colleges that have little academic autonomy in matters of curriculum and courses. A majority of them (14,000 out of 18,500) are ACS colleges and offer B.A., B.Com. and B.Sc. programmes teaching a fixed and often outdated syllabus provided by the parent university. Neither students nor teachers have much choice. A large majority of these colleges are small, enrolling just a few hundred students and have less than a dozen

TABLE 5.10 Graduates by fields of education (as per cent of total)

Field of education	US	UK	Germany	Japan	France	Finland	Malaysia	Brazil	India
Science	9	14	11	3	12	9	21	7	20
Engineering	7	8	16	18	15	21	23	5	8
Education	11	11	7	7	2	7	11	26	2
Humanities & arts	13	15	10	15	12	13	13	3	45
Social science, business and law	38	31	24	25	42	23	22	36	21
Agriculture	1	1	2	2	1	2	3	2	1
Health & welfare	13	18	24	12	12	19	5	12	3
Services	6	1	4	11	4	6	1	2	0
Unspecified	0	1	0	5	0	0	0	6	2

Source UNESCO, Institute for Statistics, *Global Education Digest*, 2007 and *UGC Annual Report*, 2005–06 (for India).

teachers. Therefore, these colleges are offering a fixed menu and are incapable of providing any meaningful choice.

Over time, occupations have become increasingly different. As a consequence, students demand a greater choice in the provision for education to cater to expanded occupational choices. Unfortunately, the Indian system fails miserably on this account. While most of the institutions offer no choice, student choices are limited even in the elite institutions that have a choice-based credit system in place. In contrast, a typical undergraduate of a university in the United States can chose from a catalogue that offers 3,000 to 5,000 courses. Even at the much smaller colleges, the number of courses range from 800 to 1,500.[8] The power of student choice in the United States is seen in the graduation trends. Twenty-two per cent of the undergraduate degrees are awarded in business studies, 8 per cent in education and 5 per cent in health. In comparison, fewer than 4 per cent of college graduates graduate in English, and only 2 per cent graduate in History. There are more bachelor's degrees awarded in parks, recreation, leisure, and fitness studies than in all languages and literature (Menand, 2007). The agility shown by the US system to respond to changing times is its main strength, while the Indian system appears to be in some kind of a time warp.

Responding to declining interest in liberal arts, the Carnegie Foundation for Advancement of Teaching that classifies institutions of higher education no longer uses the concept of 'liberal arts'. Like the US, while the tradition of liberal arts is on decline elsewhere, India continues to hold on to it with a significant proportion of its graduates in general or liberal arts stream. Most students acquire a degree for its symbolic value for they study subjects without much occupational focus. Some of them get jobs that require generalised skills such as those required in government organisations or teaching; the number of government jobs is however dwindling.

But there is good news for ACS graduates. In a knowledge economy marked with rapid change, proponents of liberal or general education often argue that technical education provides firms with short-term response to their needs, but are limited in developing skills beyond entry-level functions. The long-term needs are met better by employees with a combination of technical and general skills who can translate abilities learnt in one setting to other settings. Liberal education should therefore stress on cognitive skills (for instance, the ability to think critically and distinguish between valid and invalid inferences) on the one hand, and breadth of knowledge on the other. For instance, some familiarity with the sciences, some knowledge of human achievement of the past, philosophical and religious concepts would be desirable. Apart from the acquisition of the values of responsible and modern citizenship, liberal education is to be valued because if done right, it allows an understanding of the nature of learning itself. This is necessary foundation for a lifetime of relearning, a key attribute to survival in a knowledge-based economy.

With a view to integrate technical skills with general education and address growing concern related to rising graduate unemployment, the National Policy on Education (NPE), 1986 advocated a systematic and a well-planned programme of vocational education at the undergraduate level. It was a distinct stream intended to prepare students for identified occupations. In pursuance to this, a scheme for vocationalisation of education at the university and college level was started in the year 1994–95 by the UGC. This was redesigned in the year 2003–04 to bring in greater flexibility. This now allows students to pursue both their regular programmes and utility oriented certificate/diploma courses together. Since inception, 2,769 colleges and 39 universities have been provided assistance amounting to Rs 2.44 billion. For want of any systematic study, the effectiveness of this initiative is not known. In overall terms its coverage is small and the impact has not been significant. Across the country, there are several private initiatives that address the employability issue of graduates.

While the issue of relevance, structural problems in terms of limited student choice and rigidity have been discussed earlier, the issue of quality is of paramount importance. In recognition of this, Chapter 8 is entirely devoted to quality. Here it would be sufficient to say that usually there is heterogeneity in the quality of higher education institutions and the quality of graduates that they produce. In the Indian context, this heterogeneity is huge. Universities and colleges use archaic teaching methods and outdated syllabi, and their emphasis is on rote learning that produces graduates who know little about their field of study and even less how to relate that knowledge to the outside world. Recognizing this, the NPE, 1985 noted:

> Against the small minority of quality products, the preponderant majority come out of institutions of higher education, perhaps with a little more of book learning and of course a degree, but with very little capacity for self-study, poor language and communication skills, a highly limited world view and hardly any sense of social and national responsibility. (Ministry of Education, 1985: 8)

Non-university Sector

The non-university sector comprises formal and informal sector of vocational education and training,[9] and the private training sector. Vocational education as a stream was also started at plus-two level in schools in 1988.

Formal Sector

The formal vocational education and training sector comprises institutions imparting supervisory (diploma) level training—1,244 polytechnics with about 1,800 AICTE-approved programmes of three-year duration and 295,000 seats; craftsmen training—5114 institutions in 57 engineering and 50 non-engineering trades with 773,000 seats; and apprenticeship training—158,000 apprentices in 254 industries in the formal sector. Over the past two decades, a major part of this capacity has been created through private initiatives. Currently, about 50 per cent of the polytechnics and 63 per cent of the Industrial Training Institutes (ITIs)/Industrial Training Centres (ITCs) (with 46 per cent seats) are in the private sector.

The polytechnics, ITI/ITCs primarily focus on engineering programmes. 90 per cent of the diploma-level programmes and 80 per cent of certificate programmes are in engineering trades. With an explosive growth of degree programmes in engineering, students opt to go for degree programmes. Now that engineering degree-holders are easily available, industry employs graduates in place of diploma holders. With very little mobility from diploma to degree programmes and diploma institutions suffering, it is not surprising to note that several polytechnics are getting themselves upgraded as engineering colleges. Thus, diploma-level education is adjusting itself to changing students' demand and demand from the job markets.

Though ITI/ITC certificate holders have relatively better labour market outcomes than Grade 10 and Grade 12 completers, yet more than 60 per cent remain unemployed even three years after completion of their course as per study of ITI certificate holders in Karnataka (World Bank, 2002). An ILO study in 2002–03 found that ITCs were more efficient than ITIs. Despite poor student–teacher ratio (9.6 in ITCs compared to 5.5 in ITIs), student retention, graduation rate and capacity utilisation have all been better in the case of ITCs. However, surprisingly, the labour market outcomes of ITI certificate holders were better than that of the ITC certificate holders. This could be due to the ITIs' better screening mechanism for admission of students and also strict grading regime.

Lasting from six months to four years (depending on the trade), on-the-job training is imparted under the Statutory Apprenticeship Training Scheme. During the year 2006, over 254,000 training seats in 20,700 establishments in 153 designated trades were available. A majority of this was confined to engineering related trades. While three-fourths were for the craftsmen from the ITIs/ITCs, the remaining were for degree or diploma holders or persons from the vocational education stream. Though the regulation requires all public and private sector employers in designated industries to engage apprentices in set ratios of apprentices to workers for prescribed trades, there are major shortfalls. Private employers are not particularly enthusiastic. Of the total, only about 10 per cent (1,900 out of a total of more than 25,000 private establishments registered under the Employees Provident Fund) were registered for the Apprenticeship Scheme in 2001.

Private Training Institutions

Government efforts to provide training have been found to be inadequate. Many private and non-governmental efforts emerged to fill in this gap. There is a lack of credible information on the size and activities of private training institutions (PTIs). These are mainly seen to offer short, non-formal, non-standard courses, focusing on a few types of skills and occupations, typically associated with information technology. Based on a survey conducted in 2003, it was estimated that around 0.8–1.0 million students are enrolled in such institutions. Though some of them are accredited by a government agency (like the DOEACC Society), a majority of them are unaccredited. A bulk of these institutions offer training in IT-related and non-engineering trades, such as travel and tourism, hospitality, media and journalism, animation, aviation, event management, fitness consultancy, fashion designing and even clinical research.

The growth of PTIs has been entirely demand driven. They adapt quickly to change in demand. This is evident from the way the private IT training and education sector initially grew slowly and then very rapidly before its growth again slowing down after 2000. Starting in the year 1980, by 1995–96 this sector generated annual revenues to the tune of Rs 4.58 billion. Pioneering the franchising route for growth, IT training and education expanded fast and became a popular option for tapping the geographically dispersed demand rapidly. Between 1995–96 and 2000–01, the sector posted a compounded annual growth rate of 41 per cent and stood at Rs 25.94 billion in 2000–01.

The private training sector is growing and is increasingly popular. With the gap between training and education getting narrower, this is the eroding the traditional monopoly that universities have enjoyed in providing training and granting credentials with good currency for jobs in the job markets.

Informal Sector

Considering that over 90 per cent of employment is in the informal sector, the government has taken up several programmes for training of the workers in the informal sector. Community polytechnics as an add-on feature of the polytechnics offer training programmes of three to nine months duration. A total of 675 community polytechnics train about 450,000 people a year. This is being extended to all AICTE-accredited polytechnics in a phased manner. Under its National Literacy Mission (NLM), the Indian government has established 172 Jan Shikshan Sansthans (formerly known as Shramik Vidyapiths) for improving vocational skills and quality of life of neo-literates and unskilled and unemployed youth. During 2004–05, around 1.4 million people participated in the Jan Shikshan Sansthan activities. There are several other training programmes, such as Training for Rural Youth for Self-Employment, Support to Training and Employment of Women of the Department of Women and Child Development and the training centres (51 in number) run by the Khadi and Village Industries Commission.

There are several non-governmental initiatives for training in the informal sector. Taking a cue from the community college movement in North America, more than 200 community colleges have been set up over the 10 years.[10] These colleges have flexible entry norms with no prior formal academic qualification requirement. A one year standard curriculum integrating life skills (21 weeks), work skills (21 weeks), internship and hands-on training (8 weeks) and preparation for employment and evaluation (2 weeks) has been developed. This has been a resounding success with more than three-fourths of the students from these community colleges reportedly finding employment. The scheme of community colleges has now been recognised by IGNOU to provide associate degree programme with direct entry into third year degree programme.[11]

Vocational Education at the School Level

With a view to enhance individual employability, reduce mismatch between the demand and supply of skilled manpower and provide an alternative for those pursuing higher education without particular interest and purpose, a scheme funded by the central government to have a separate vocational education stream at plus-two level at schools was started in the year 1988. Targeted to cover 25 per cent students at the plus-two level by 2000, only less than 3 per cent are currently enrolled in vocational stream. By 2006, 9,583 schools catering to about 1 million students had the vocational stream in their curriculum. Not only coverage, but even capacity utilisation is poor at 42 per cent. Along with the conventional schools, the vocational stream has been introduced in the open school system as well. The National Institute of Open Schooling introduced vocational education of 6 month to 2 year duration through more than 700 accredited private training providers.

Due to its poor image, the vocational stream at the school level fails to attract good students. Students take up the vocational stream as a last resort. Usually students who perform poorly in Class 10 join the vocational stream. It also suffers from inadequate numbers of trained teachers and training materials. Instructional materials have been developed for only a quarter of the courses. Outcomes have also not been very encouraging. Though there is no recent data available, a study by Operations Research Group in 1998 reported that only 28 per cent of the vocational stream pass-outs were gainfully employed and 38.3 per cent were pursuing higher studies. Despite poor outcomes, the government is keen to expand vocational education in schools, even though the global trend is towards increasing generalisation of vocational curricula and integrating technical and vocational tracks in general education content. By blurring the boundaries between general and vocational stream, many countries are addressing the 'image problem' with vocational courses.

In the informal sector, there are several government initiatives and a large and dynamic private training sector catering to 0.8–1.0 million students. Vocational training is also provided to nearly 0.4 million students at the higher secondary level in the schools. Overall, training capacity is around 3.1 million seats. Though large in absolute terms, it is grossly inadequate.

In all, the non-university sector is now huge and plays an important role in skills development in the country. A major proportion of this is financed by students and their parents. It responds more directly and usually more effectively to the needs of industry and the labour market. With the gap between training and education getting narrower, this is the eroding of the traditional monopoly that universities have enjoyed in providing training and granting credentials with good currency in the job markets.

Overall Supply Scenario

India has a distinct advantage in terms of a large and young labour force. A large pool of workers possessing English language skills is another advantage. But unless the people are productively employed and trained for the purpose, this large pool can become a liability. Even the large pool of English skills on closer scrutiny is found to be shallow. Though university system is large, yet almost four-fifths of the graduates have no employable skills. In the area of vocational education and training the country is far behind.

There are serious concerns about the relevance and quality of higher education. With large enrolments in liberal arts and humanities, there is a mismatch between the available capacity and the skill requirements. There is limited student choice. There is a lack of agility. Quality higher education sector is tiny and a major bottleneck.

The vocational education and training sector is not only small, but faces two major problems.[12] One that it is largely supply driven and second that there is social stigma associated with vocational education and blue collar jobs. The country faces a situation where there is a shortage of skilled personnel for blue collar jobs and rampant unemployment of those with higher education degrees.

The provision for private training is becoming increasingly popular. Many students pursue training courses along with their degree programmes, enhancing their employability. Students and their parents finance such training courses. Such courses respond in more direct and usually more effective ways to the needs of industry and the labour market.

Each segment of higher education and training—public, private, formal and informal—has grown independent of the other. There are no pathways. Rather than aptitude, it is the academic performance that segregates those who opt for higher education from those who are forced into the vocational stream. Not only capacities are limited, the quality of vocational education and training and its relevance are major bottlenecks.

Skill Shortages

While unemployed graduates still vastly outnumber available positions, several sectors of the economy face skill shortages. The industry routinely laments about the acute shortage of qualified people, unacceptable attrition rates and their rising wage bills. It is argued that the country with its tiny quality education sector cannot sustain its leadership in global knowledge economy. A study based on the perception of human resource managers worldwide concluded that only one in four Indian engineering graduates is actually employable. The rest lack fluency in English, the ability to work in teams or the ability to deliver basic oral presentations, as well as technical skills. Skill shortages are not only a major domestic issue, but in recent times there has been a lot global interest about it.[13]

Concern about skill shortages is not unique to India. Complaints about skill deficits are in all countries. With global competition for science and engineering (S&E) talent intensifying, the United States is worried about its continued dependence on international S&E labour market to fill unmet skill needs. According to the US Commission on National Security/21st Century (2001), not being able to manage science, technology and education for the common good poses a critical national security challenge, second only to a weapon of mass destruction detonating in an American city (NSF, 2003). UK's apex industry association, the Confederation of British Industry in its 2007 employment trends survey found that 52 per cent of employers are dissatisfied with the basic literacy of school leavers and 59 per cent with their basic numeracy.

As people become prosperous, they would not like to do labour-intensive jobs unless such jobs are far more lucrative. It is therefore difficult to find unskilled labour, workers for entry-level construction, for picking fruits and vegetables and cleaning in many advanced countries. Such jobs are often done by the immigrants from the developing world. Not only low end jobs, advanced countries face problem in terms of getting people as nurses, doctors, computer programmers, teachers (particularly for maths, science, accounting, finance) and for armed forces. These jobs require hard work, which many people in the advanced societies are unwilling to put in.

Skill shortages could either be real or perceived. Skill shortages are often based on impressions of individuals and expressions of interests of interest groups and their lobbyists. The media usually perpetuates and exacerbates such fallacies and inconsistencies and misses the reality.[14] A recent study suggests that while there is a glutted market for early-career scientists in the United States, numerous prestigious reports call for training and importing even more scientists to meet the looming shortage. Numerous labour market experts have found no such shortage, but the highly publicised perception of a dearth, often linked to inadequate school education, persists (Benderly, 2008). Thus, understanding the issue of skill shortages or skill imbalances in the Indian context requires detailed analysis.

The basic concern is that graduates are not always employable. A recent survey in South Africa revealed that firms are not always able to use graduates to meet their skills requirements because graduates have the qualifications but not the practical skills and experience. Furthermore, wrong types of graduates are being produced. There are too few technical graduates, and usually the graduates are not suited to fill shortages at the management level. Skilled staff is often poached by other companies or emigrate and the graduates are not always of high enough quality. Such concerns are almost universal. It is essential to look at the nature of skill shortages, problems of transition from higher education to workplace and related issues in order to examine the matter in details.

Individuals are generally not fully prepared to start work when they finish their education. The industry complains that though the students are equipped with graduate degrees, they lack employable skills. This has opened up a yawning skills gap between academic output and industry expectations. The employers usually have unreal expectations from their employees and prefer them to be productive as soon as they join. Due to the fear of poaching and due competitive pressures, employers are unwilling to invest time and money in induction training. There are differences between work skills and academic skills. These differences are not only unavoidable, but desirable, since different outcomes are expected from workplace and academic institutions. Thus, the disjunction between 'education skills' and 'work skills' needs to be understood. This will enable smooth transition from academic to work environment.

Education Skills and Work Skills Disjunction

Usually, the abilities acquired in education are referred to as education skills or competencies. These individual skills are transferable from one setting to another. Work skills on the other hand, are context specific and dependent on the work setting and on the interaction of individuals in particular setting. It is argued that preparation for work is a process of socialisation into a work environment, starting with a peripheral participation of a novice and expanding over time with competence acquired in the new work environment.

The distinction between the two skills also shows up in the conflict over general versus specific skills. Education usually aims at imparting general skills, such as literacy skills, numeracy skills or higher order skills, such problem solving, judgement and communication skills, whereas the firms often prefer to hire individuals who have specific skills—knowledge of using a certain machine or specific software package—because they can be put to work with little additional training. Even though, firms may value general skills, they may not invest in it because other firms may hire the trained individuals away—the problem of poaching.

There are other important differences. While cognitive competencies are important in education, depending on the nature of work, various non-cognitive competencies may be required at work. In the education system, where individuals are judged, graded and promoted, there is an individualistic conception of skills, while people often work in teams. Traditional pedagogy practice has emphasis on conveying facts and procedures through drill and repetition. This could be appropriate for routine work of an industrial society, but flexible skills with meaning-centred and problem-based pedagogy are required in the new work environment. Finally, the text studied in the educational setting—the academic subjects—are different from work-based texts such as instruction manuals, charts, and so on. Despite efforts like the adoption of a different pedagogy and introduction of applied academic courses, the traditional pedagogy and continuation of academic subjects continues to have a powerful influence on higher education, making transition from academic to work environment difficult.

In terms of work skills, WIPRO, an Indian IT major, has identified four sets of skills—behavioural skills, cross-cultural skills, process skills and technology-skills for its workforce. These are to be embedded in the company's value system to make its employees likeable, flexible, scalable and capable. According to company sources, it has identified a set of 12 transitions that a student makes when he moves from a college campus to the corporate world. These are given in Table 5.11. As per their experience over decades, it is found that five of these transitions are more difficult: from individual-based to team-based working environment; from self-planned to project-planned approach; from last minute preparation to day-to-day work discipline; from prescribed syllabus to each day's activity is unique mindset; and from understanding theory to activity based learning.

TABLE 5.11   Transition from campus to corporate sector

Campus	Corporate
Individual based to	Team-based
Self-planned to	Project planned
Last minute preparation to	Day-to-day work discipline
Answers available and known to	Solutions not known
Remember the answers to	Arrive at an answer
Marks based to	Productivity based
Evaluated by someone else to	Starts with self evaluation
Deadlines not all that tough to	Very strict deadlines
Canteen behaviours to	Corporate etiquette
Home and college to	Alone and corporate
Prescribed syllabus to	Each day's activity is unique
Understanding theory to	Activity based Learning

Source D. Selvan, Wipro Limited, *Sharing of Replicable Best Practices–Talent Transformation*, presentation at the FICCI Higher Education Summit in 2007.

While the older moral, civic and intellectual purpose of education has been relegated to the background and there is greater occupational focus in higher education, there is still increasing concern across countries that their education system is failing to provide 'key' or 'core' skills for the 21st century. These skills, variously defined in different countries, are much beyond the traditional basic skills (the three R's—reading, (w)riting and (a)rithmetic—plus speaking and listening), thinking skills (creativity, decision making, problem solving, conceptualisation, reasoning, knowing how to learn), personal qualities like individual responsibility, sociability, and self management.[15] Great Britain is searching for 'key' or 'core' skills for its graduates; Germany is trying to develop key qualifications for its workers. All over the globe, there are similar concerns and countries are struggling to make their education systems more relevant and develop 'skills for twenty first century'—higher levels and new form of human capital for competing in the new millennium (Grubb and Lazerson, 2004: 6).

Many sectors have come up with a set of skills required in the new work environment. According to the KPMG report on Global Skills for Graduates in Financial Services, the financial sector requires a portfolio of soft skills including the right attitude, commitment to learn, teamwork, communication, client relationship management, customer services, business acumen, problem solving and achievement orientation skills to operate on a global platform in a fast paced environment.

Despite the shift towards programmes with occupational focus, a vast majority of academic programmes even today are not equipping the students for the world of work. It is seen that the notion that the learning should take place without reference to the economic and social needs has been under attack even in the United Kingdom, from where India inherited its university system. A white paper on higher education in 1972 noted:

> If [these] economic, personal and social aims are to be realized, within the limits of available resources and competing priorities, both the purposes and the nature of higher education...must be critically and realistically examined. The continuously changing relationship between higher education and the subsequent employment should be reflected both in the institutions and in individual choices. (DES-UK, 1972)

Skills agenda is again on the top in the UK. In this context, it must be realised that perception of skill shortages will continue to exist because of differences in education and work skills. A recent Duke University study based on actual hiring experience however established that India continues to be the country with the best availability of entry-level engineers. Yet the common perception is that there is a huge shortage of engineering graduates in the country. Even when they are available, only one out of four is employable.

Supply Constraints

While the disjunction between education and work skills explains a part of the phenomenon of perceived skill shortages, there are at times actual supply constraints. This could be due to inadequate number of qualified people, quality thereof or a mismatch between demand and supply. These are usually location-specific and often short-duration or cyclic. There could be three reasons for skill shortages. First, the basic reason could be the employer not being able to fill or facing considerable difficulty in filling up vacancies for a post. The second reason is when existing employees do not have the required qualifications, experience and/or specialised skills—this is often referred to as skill gaps. Third is when recruitment difficulties exist due to various reasons, such as the characteristics of the industry, occupation or employer, relatively low remuneration, poor working conditions and poor image of the industry. Unsatisfactory working hours, a location that is hard to commute to, inadequate recruitment or firm-specific and highly specialised skill needs are similarly important considerations. The distinction between the three is usually blurred. They often co-exist together and a generic term 'skill shortages' is used to define all three types of supply constraints.

Difficulty in filling up vacancies for an occupation could be due to inadequate supply of certain skills or a sudden requirement that the system is not able to meet and will eventually meet, particularly if the supply side is not inelastic. In India, a large majority of jobs require vocational skills, while a majority of graduates only possess bookish knowledge. The vocational education and training system is small, its output even smaller and its quality indifferent. This supply-side constraint and the case of Indian IT sector discussed later will fall in this category. People's skills have a shelf life. Many firms face the challenge of shelf life erosion due to employees stopping to innovate and learn and employers ceasing to provide for career development. This would obviously result in skill gap.

The third form of skill shortage is due to recruitment difficulties for a variety of reasons. This is most common, yet least recognised. Since the solution to this has to be firm or industry specific and often location specific, one has to get into details to address this form of skill shortage. For instance, garment units in Tirupur require 30,000 trained persons, leather units near Chennai are short of 10,000 to 15,000 trained workers and 50,000 skilled workers are required by hosiery units at Ludhiana. At the high end, there is a shortage of engineering talent in chip design. It is estimated that engineering colleges meet only 20 per cent of the current demand. With the recent focus on climate change, the three-year old carbon trading sector is now worth USD16 billion and there is an acute shortage of climate change analysts and managers for carbon trading. All these are industry and location-specific and require customised responses. While there is general concern about skill shortages, a popular newsmagazine through its in-house research has identified specific business sectors that are facing skill shortages, the nature of skill that is in short supply and the way industry is responding to it (see Table 5.12).

Poaching is noted as the most widely used strategy. This suggests that most industry sectors would rather hire experienced staff from related sectors than train staff on their own. However, some of them have started hiring staff with lower qualification level (in some cases even higher qualification levels like M. Tech who were not hired earlier, since the M. Tech degree was considered as adding no value) or from lower ranking colleges and training them on their own.

Supply Constraints in the IT and ITeS Sector

Supply constraints are reportedly acute in the IT and ITeS sector. IT/ITeS sector employs 1.63 million people. It has been growing by 25 per cent each year. The top six IT companies quadrupled the headcount between from 91,987 in June 2003 and 368,963 in 2007 (as seen in Table 5.13). In September 2007, TCS crossed employee strength

TABLE 5.12 Coping with skill shortages

Business	Skill in short supply	Adopted solution
Retail	Sales, marketing, supply chain, floor and category management, merchandising, overall business leadership	Poach from BPO, aviation, hotels for customer interface; hire managers from FMCG and bring in retail specialists from abroad; engage students and housewives on part-time basis
Real Estate	Project management, finance management, design & engg.	Poach from hospitality, construction, design, and finance companies
Aviation	Pilots, cabin crew, sales, marketing, maintenance, overall leadership	Import pilots, technicians and managers; groom service staff
Hospitality	Food & beverage preparation and serving; customer care; marketing	Hire youngsters just out of school and train them; supplement regular staff with housewives and the disabled
Media	Editors, designers	Hire Indians with experience of working with foreign publications; bring in designers from abroad as consultants
Banking & Finance	Sales, marketing, treasury management, wealth management	Set up schools for banking and finance schools; design banking and finance curricula for business schools and universities
Construction	Engineering, project management	Hire engineers from lesser colleges; hire diploma holders and train them

IT	Software and systems solutions; special knowledge of the served businesses	Offer proprietary software free to engineering colleges; hire non-engineers; poach domain specialists from served businesses
BPO	Customer relations; Domain knowledge of served businesses	Remote voice tests and training; resume collection in colleges and malls; hire retirees and housewives for part-time
Health Care	Global marketing, R&D, doctors	Hire specialists abroad; bring back Indian working abroad
Accounts & consulting	Accounting, taxation, special knowledge of served businesses	Hire non-chartered accountants and training them for accounting and taxation work; hire domain specialists
Manufacture	Engineering	Hire engineers from lesser schools; hire diploma holders and train them; hire M. Techs

Source Adapted by the author from BW Research, *Business World*, 16 April 2007, p. 42.

of 100,000 (*The Economic Times*, 29 September 2007). Even the multinationals have huge operations in India. IBM has increased headcount from 4,000 in the early 2000s to 53,000 in 2006. It intends to increase this number to 120,000 by 2008. Accenture, one of the biggest consulting and IT service providers in the world, will increase Indian staff from 27,000 to 35,000 making India its biggest employment hub overtaking its US hub with 30,000 employees.

TABLE 5.13 Hiring of computer professionals by top six companies

	June 2003	June 2004	June 2005	June 2006	June 2007
TCS	25,514	36,639	52,038	71,190	94,902
Infosys	17,977	27,939	39,806	58,409	75,971
Wipro	21,174	31,517	41,911	56,435	72,137
Cognizant	6,689	11,920	19,258	29,675	45,550
HCL	10,041	16,358	24,090	32,626	42,017
Satyam	10,592	15,631	20,505	27,634	38,386
Total	**91,987**	**140,004**	**197,608**	**275,969**	**368,963**

Source Compiled by the author from various sources.

With growth and outward focus, the appetite of the Indian industry has increased enormously. IT industry is sometimes resorting to hoarding as well, which is not bad, since this signals their positive future outlook. NASSCOM projects that the technology jobs would double to 1.7 million in the next four years and forecasts a shortage of 500,000. Tata Consultancy Services plans to add another 30,000 people to its pool of 72,000 people. It is unrealistic for the industry to expect the system to feed into such large expansion without enlarging the pipeline for quality graduates.

Net additions were 24,597 in 2002–03, increased to 92,412 in 2006–07 and declined to 89,868 in 2007–08. Campus placements are likely to go down by 15–20 per cent during the current year. According to experts, while earlier IT companies were under constant pressure to hire more and more, now they are hiring more prudently with focus on utilisation, efficiency and ways of reducing the number of employees on the bench (*The Economic Times*, 2008c).

On the supply side, more than 1,700 engineering colleges will produce about 500,000 graduates this year and most of them will land up in the IT sector. Adding almost half a million a year, there is no reason for supply constraints in the IT sector. The problem however is that while earlier the IT companies could meet their requirement from the top 100 colleges, now they have to source manpower from a much larger pool. And as one goes down the list, the quality deteriorates rapidly.

IT companies are adopting a variety of strategies to remain competitive, in the face of wage inflation and currency appreciation. Many companies now have adverse bulge mix,[16] meaning high proportion of midlevel employees as compared to entry level. This is regarded as undesirable for the industry. IT service companies are struggling to manage their bulge mix. Tata Consultancy Services has about 52 per cent of its employees in less than 3 years experience range and it is hiring fresh science graduates and providing them 3–4 months' training. It had already deployed 500 such candidates by 2007. To cut down on costs, Infosys is hiring third year engineering students and putting them on internship for 17 weeks, saving three month salary bill and making them billable faster when they join (*The Economic Times*, 2008a).

The facts and data above clearly show that the supply constraints in IT/ITeS sector were due to the explosive growth of this sector. Sudden unanticipated increase in appetite of the IT sector has taken the higher education system by surprise. This resulted in rapid growth of engineering colleges offering computer and related courses. Now that the demand from the sector may plateau, such constraints may not exist, however competitive pressures may force companies to expect new hires with exactly the right skills at the lowest possible price or take people with lesser skills and train them up.

Shallow Base of English Language Skills

The country's historical legacy and colonial past helped India to build a large pool of people with English language skills and gave a competitive advantage to Indians in the global economy (see Chapter 9 for more details). However, explosive growth of job opportunities has raised concerns about the shallow pool of people skilled in English and poor proficiency levels of the large section. With the boom in medical transcription and call centres, English language proficiency began to be seen as a key skill. With this there is a burgeoning demand for people with English language skills. This has blown apart the myth about the unrestricted supply of people with English language skills in India.

With only an insignificant number of people having English as their mother tongue, English proficiency levels are often poor. Though English is the main medium of instruction in the universities, most of the interaction amongst the students and between the students and the teachers, both inside and outside the classroom takes place in Hindi or the vernacular medium. Professional education has little focus on developing English language skills. Unlike in China, where students have to clear a compulsory exam in English for entry to higher education, entry exams, even for elite engineering schools, do not test English language skills. Therefore, test preparation does not hone the English language skills of the Indian students.

Rather than actively promote learning English as a part of the country's strategy for economic development in the context of globalisation as in case of China, English language instruction in India has been victim of linguistic chauvinism. As a result, many states had abolished English at primary education level. Recognising the importance of English not only as a means of communication and access to higher education and better paid jobs, but also as a determinant of access, the NKC, in its communication to the prime minister on 20 October 2007 has recommended that teaching of English as a language should be introduced along with the first language (either the mother tongue or the regional language) of the child, starting from Class I in school. Nine states (of which six are in the north-east) and three Union Territories (UTs) have already introduced English as a compulsory subject from Class I onwards. Another 12 states and three UTs have introduced it as compulsory at different stages in primary school. However, the progress is slow and the quality of English language teaching is not good enough.

Seeing a large potential, the private training sector has also got into the fray. English language training market is estimated at Rs15 billion per annum and VETA is the largest private English teaching institute with over 115 centres in 85 cities in the country. Such efforts are, however, nowhere close to efforts made in China. One-fifth of the Chinese are learning English. China has emerged as the world's largest market for English language training. Apart from education and training in the public system, there are around 50,000 private language schools that enrol 2.5 million students. Not only adults, but even children at very young age are enrolled in these schools. Parents in China are willing to spend more than half of their income for their children to learn English (Aiyar, 2007). Because of the long history of the English language in the country, India is currently ahead of China in English language skills, but after having embraced English as a key to its economic prosperity and with massive efforts underway, China will soon close the gap. Other populous countries like Philippines, having about 45 million English speaking people, and Vietnam where people are learning English fast, are emerging as India's competitors. Therefore, any complacency about its large pool of English language skills may cost the country dear.

Quality Deficit

Thus the problem is not so much about numbers, but about quality. With the economy growing rapidly and showing signs of structural changes, there is likely to be a greater overall demand for qualified manpower in the years to come. There were 23.6 million graduate workers in 2001 as per Census 2001, mainly in the four sectors as seen in Table 5.14. Based on average sectoral growth over the past five years and assuming same proportion of graduates, this number stood at 33.3 million in 2005. Using the projected sectoral growth over the next five years with same proportion of graduates, this number would swell to 50.8 million in 2010. The estimates and projected figures are likely to be underestimations since an increasingly large portion of new jobs created in recent years require higher education qualifications. If these numbers are compared with the data in Table 5.8, it is seen that only about 12.5 million workers may actually require graduate qualifications. About 62 per cent graduates are in jobs that do not require graduate qualifications.

With 33.3 million graduates in the workforce out of a graduate pool of 50.7 million, it appears that there is no shortage of graduates. However, it needs to be realised that a significant proportion of them is not

TABLE 5.14   Graduate workforce—estimates and projections

(in million)

Industrial category	Actual 2000–01	Estimated 2005–06	Projected Annual growth rate (2005–06–2010–11)	Projected 2010–11	Addl. jobs (2005–06–2010–11)
Community, social and personal services	9.7	13.0	7.0	18.3	5.3
Manufacturing	4.3	6.0	8.0	8.8	2.8
Trade, hotels, transport and communications	3.7	8.2	11.0	14.5	6.3
Financial services	2.9	4.2	9.0	6.5	2.3
Others	1.7	2.1	8.0	2.7	0.8
Total	**23.6**	**33.3**		**50.8**	**17.5**

Source Actual based on Census 2001; Estimated 2005–06 based on actual growth rate in each sector; Projected based on growth rate projected on average growth rate for last five years.

available for work. While the women comprise nearly 40 per cent of the graduate pool, only about 3 out of 10 women are available for work. A sizeable number of graduates are old people not available for work. In the year 2000–01, only about 46 per cent of the graduates were in the workforce. This has increased to 66 per cent in 2005–06 and is likely to increase to 77 per cent in the 2010–11. A sizeable portion of the remaining comprise women and elderly—not looking for job or those who are seeking job, but not finding one in absence of requisite skills or due to limitations of mobility.

While graduate numbers are sufficient, but growing job opportunities require employers to go deeper into the graduate pool as is evident from Figure 5.4. Graduate quality is heterogeneous, with a small number of quality institutions at the top and a base with a large number of institutions of indifferent quality. Going deeper into the graduate pool would mean getting graduates of poor quality. This is seen in the recruitment of engineering graduates in the country. Seventy per cent of the engineering graduates are picked up by no more than 10 leading

FIGURE 5.4   Going deeper in the graduate pool for employment

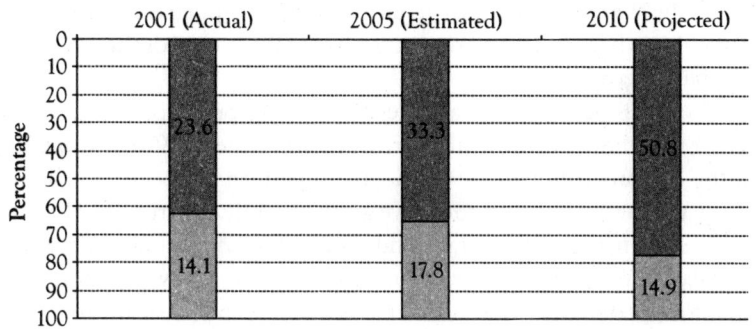

☐ Graduate and above not available for work (elderly or women)
   or seeking work (in million)
▣ Graduate and above in workforce (in million)

Source Author (From Table 5.14).

companies, most of them in the software sector. All other potential employees have to compete for the remaining 30 per cent, and many engineering graduates at the bottom of the pile are not employable.

Public funding is inadequate and skewed and funding mechanism is ad hoc. In real terms unit costs have fallen and there is a steep fall in expenditure on critical inputs. While a small number of institutions are well funded, a large majority gets very little. As a result public institutions are usually underfunded and face the problem of deteriorating infrastructure and facilities, large vacancies and falling standards. Funding mechanism fails to ensure quality and instead perpetuates status quoism.

Addressing Skill Shortages

Abilities developed in universities and colleges and the competencies required in work are often mismatched. As a result, while many graduates are undereducated for serious work, a large number are overeducated for the jobs they hold. The country's employment structure has been impervious to economic growth and its changing

227

structure. Despite sharp decline of agriculture in terms of its share in GDP, the share of agriculture in employment dropped only marginally. Agriculture has continued to employ over 60 per cent of the workforce for many decades.

The organised sector with the dominating presence of the public sector has a limited potential to provide employment. With the opening of the Indian economy, the employment pattern has begun to change. Many non-agricultural sectors have grown rapidly. Apart from IT/ITES services, there is growth in trade and transport services, financial services, construction and health and education services. Many sectors require qualified people in large numbers. While the initial steam to propel the country on a high growth trajectory has come from its large pool of English knowing qualified people, now the country is running out of this steam. It is felt this vacuum may retard the growth momentum unless the supply side is better managed.

Perceptions regarding the country running out of a skilled pool of workers, as stated in the previous paragraph, are not reinforced by evidence. There is large and growing unemployment and under-employment of graduates. It is self-evident that further expansion could amount to over education. This could be a waste of resources with many workers possessing a higher level of education than their job requires. A recent research, however, suggests that unemployable graduates seeking work may be the result of restricted mobility and skill mismatches in the labour market. A bigger pool of qualified people may actually facilitate the development of a competitive and dynamic knowledge-based economy (Büxhel et al., 2004).

A detailed examination of the skill shortages based on the existing education and skill profile of the workforce, taking into consideration the actual growth sector by sector and projecting the growth until 2010 shows that there is no general shortage—shortages are specific in some sectors and for some kind of skills. There would always be shortages in newly emerging areas, but the private sector, if active in such areas, would come up and fill in the gap. It may, however, take time.

Ideally, the supply of graduates has to adjust to the demand for skills in the job markets. However, the link between higher education and the world of work is relatively loose and the process of transition from higher education to employment is complex and protracted (Gibbons, 1998). As a result, students' demand for higher education is often based on their aspirations, societal and parental expectations and not necessarily based on signals from the job markets. Mismatch is therefore a primary concern. To address this concern, the focus has to be on enhancing employability and aligning higher education with labour markets.

This apart, in a changing economic environment with a dynamic labour market, it is necessary that higher education continuously adapt to the labour market. Adaptability has to be ensured both at the systemic level and the institutional level. While at the systemic level there are issues of capacity, diversity and structure, at the institutional level there are issues of continued relevance of curriculum and quality of teaching-learning process. New institutional arrangements may be required to enlarge the pipeline of quality graduates in the country.

In India, affiliating colleges form the bulk of the higher education system. They follow curriculum and offer courses set by the affiliating universities. They hardly have any flexibility to innovate and experiment. The standards usually get set to the lowest common denominator. The affiliating system that represents the higher education system in the country therefore brings in rigidity.

The large public sector that grew in the first four decades after the independence provided education in the general stream. General stream graduates hardly have any employable skills. Students acquired degrees for their symbolic value. Though some of them found jobs that required generalised skills such as those required in government organisations or teaching, the number of such jobs has been decreasing. This resulted in a large pool of unemployable graduates.

There is however now evidence that there is higher demand for workers with general skills as compared to vocational skills in industries where technology is changing rapidly. General course work can increase students' mental flexibility and demonstrate to potential employers that the student can deal with new situations. Berman et al. (1998) have gathered substantial evidence from the past 15 years on technology-skill complementarities to make a case for general higher education in changing technology environment.

229

Generalised skills enable workers to develop and implement new technology more quickly. In contrast, vocational education based on narrow skill sets is useful when technology is less rapidly changing. Therefore, good quality general higher education, rather than becoming less relevant, is likely to become more relevant in the time to come. It is now realised that generic skills with flexibility, adaptability and opportunities for lifelong learning, will provide young people with the best basis for a career in any area and for the unforeseen needs of the future. The large capacity in general stream may therefore turn out to be a blessing in disguise. However, quality thereof has to be ensured. Several companies have started recruiting general graduates for jobs that traditionally went to professional graduates.

A majority of universities and colleges use archaic teaching methods and outdated and heavily theoretical curriculum. With emphasis on rote learning, graduates know little about their field of study and even less how to relate that knowledge to outside world. They lack 'key', 'core', 'transferable', and/or 'generic' skills, such as communication, numeracy, IT and lifelong learning skills required in many jobs today. The institutions have a momentum of their own—courses once started cannot be easily discontinued; faculty once recruited on permanent tenure cannot be removed and is difficult to retrain; and putting infra-structure and facilities to alternative uses has its own limitations. There has to be far greater flexibility in starting and shutting down departments and programmes, and innovative processes must to be put in place to respond to the needs and opportunities of a fast-changing country.

Aligning higher education to work place typically includes modifi-cations to existing course content (sometimes in response to employer suggestions), introduction of new courses and teaching methods and expanded provision of opportunities for work experience—all intended to enhance the development of employability skills and/or ensure that the acquisition of such skills is made more explicit. In some cases, university departments have sought to 'embed' the desired skills within courses; in other departments, students are offered 'stand-alone' skills courses which are effectively 'bolted on' to traditional academic programmes. Usually a mix of embedded and stand-alone teaching methods in their efforts is used.

230

Sometimes structural adaptation policies like integrating the university sector with the non-university sector is used to improve efficiency and effectiveness of the system as a whole. Short-cycle courses are also introduced. Apart from structural adaptation of the system, the curriculum and content of the courses has to change on a continuing basis in order to accommodate a new body of knowledge that gets created with changes in economy and society.

While most universities in the country have not changed their curricula for decades, a few universities have taken initiatives on their own to restructure curricula and incorporate vocational element in the curricula so as to make it job-oriented. Such efforts are, however, few and far between. The process for changing curricula in the universities in India is painfully slow. Rigid academic structure and cumbersome process for change in curriculum are often blamed for it. The fact that the colleges that enrol nearly 90 per cent students have no freedom to change curricula and are at the mercy of their affiliating universities makes the situation worse.

In 2004, Delhi University restructured its BA (Pass) course that now has both theoretical and applied components. Restructured course provides ample scope for employment opportunities, a marked departure from the old one. In third year, applied papers ranging from computers, tourism, tax management, film studies, theatre and music have been introduced (*The Times of India*, 23 April 2005).

In many cases, the universities do not have dynamic leadership or capacity to initiate such changes. Creating communities of academics across the nation for sharing good practices and providing incentives to universities and faculty to champion such changes can accelerate this process.

Improving Average Quality

The country has a tiny quality sector. The number of quality institutions is small and remains so—this is considered a major bottleneck. An interesting fallout of the tiny quality sector, though, is the competition it spurs because of the tough entry requirement into these institutions. It has raised the overall standards by promoting self-directed learning

231

and raises the level of student learning. Tiny quality sector also results in a large number of Indian students going abroad for studies. This is now seen to be building a strong base of high-quality human resources both within and outside the country.

Overall quality of graduates produced is highly uneven. As the industry goes on to recruit a larger number of graduates, there is a sharp fall in quality. For instance in the engineering segment, 70 per cent of the graduates are picked up by no more than 10 leading companies, most of them in the software sector. All other potential employees have to compete for the remaining 30 per cent, and many engineering graduates at the bottom of the pile are not employable. By the year 2010, 77 per cent of the people with graduate and above qualifications will have to be in the workforce against 62 per cent in the year 2001.

The country has a small capacity for education at the doctoral level and its quality is also poor. A good PhD in most fields now commands a global market. The salaries in Indian universities lag behind the prices available elsewhere in the world and in the Indian private sector. This has sharply curtailed the supply of good researchers who are willing to work in universities. There is selectivity bias where the best people are leaving universities or not joining them at all. Not only does this impact the quality of teaching, but also a small outturn of doctorates is resulting in acute faculty shortages.

The country has a large and growing private sector. The private sector growth has been rapid over the past two decades. Though this growth has been tentative and occurred in a policy vacuum, private higher education is the most dynamic sector of higher education today. The private institutions are mainly confined to the professional stream. Quality and accountability in private higher education is often uneven. There is an accreditation system in place; however, its reach, particularly amongst the private institutions is limited. With poor coverage and without much consequence, accreditation has failed to create incentives to enhance quality.

Competition among providers has the potential to spur quality enhancement. However, distortions persist due to large supply constraints and for reasons of information asymmetry. Burdensome regulatory arrangement and its poor compliance has erected entry barriers for new providers and prevented the existing ones from being creative to meet the quality challenge.

Private institutions that depend primarily on tuition fees have to cater to students' demand. This forces them to change their offerings according to it. These are, therefore far more adaptable. Within the private sector, the non-formal training providers are even more flexible since no regulatory framework binds them. They respond to the changes taking place in the job markets far more quickly. This makes a case for mix of public and private as well as formal/non-formal system of education and training each fulfilling a different need.

Public–Private Mix

From a small, elite and largely public-funded higher education and training system, the country now has a large and complex system having public and private, formal and non-formal institutions. A suitable mix of the public and the private, the formal and the non-formal provision for higher education and training provides an optimal solution and would meet the changing needs of economy and society. Yet, institutional arrangements to govern the system have largely remained unchanged. They fail to recognise and address new concerns.

Each segment of higher education and training—public, private, formal and informal—has grown independent of the other. There are no pathways. Vocational education and training suffers from an image problem. Rather than aptitude, it is the academic performance that segregates those who opt for higher education from those who are forced into vocational stream. Not only are capacities limited, but the quality and relevance of vocational education and training are also major bottlenecks. Developing a National Framework of Qualifications (NFQs) would be an important step. This would enable vertical and horizontal pathways between formal and non-formal education and training sector.

In each field of study, there could be a network of teachers referred to as Teaching and Learning Support Networks (TLSNs). They would not only restructure the curriculum, redesign course sequences, but also evolve policies and develop framework to strengthen teaching, learning and research in different subject areas that are in tune with global practices. These networks could be open-ended communities of academics and other stakeholders. New technologies could be leveraged for collaboration. The work of these networks could be coordinated through an independent body—the National Qualification Authority that could also be responsible for the NFQ.

Engagement of Industry with Institutions

Industry is no more dependent on government efforts, but is now engaging with education institutions directly and more meaningfully. They are doing in-house talent development. It started with IT sector at the top end of the value chain with engineers and science graduates. It is now trickling down to the manufacturing and construction sector, at the bottom end of the labour pyramid, touching now even rural un-educated unskilled workers. From the bottom to the top, companies have put together differentiated strategies to enlist, groom and deploy talent at every stage of their staff needs. RPG Enterprises has set up 12 centres for Pragati, a grassroots level school that picks up and trains 300 students from government schools in tier-II cities

A large part of corporate manpower today comes from private institutions. Because of the dysfunctional government regulatory mechanism and accreditation system governing higher education, these institutions have no incentive to improve their quality. Consequently, Gresham's Law kicks in and the bad drives out the good. However, there are many creative ways in which industry could contribute towards reversing the trend. For instance, it could foster competition between the institutes of higher learning by setting standards on things like contact hours for effective teaching–learning, computing, library and laboratory facilities and enlisting institutions that publish these details. Enlisted institutions could then become preferred choices for industry to recruit from. This would reduce their search cost and provide an incentive to educational institutions to improve the standard of teaching. The industry could thereby create mechanisms for raising quality and constructively meet their increased appetite for qualified manpower.

Effective industry–academia partnerships could help address skill shortages. Industry is already finding ways to address this concern. TCS under its 'Talent Transformation Program' is training science graduates to be industry-ready IT professionals. TCS would then hire them at salaries less than the salary of an engineering graduate. TCS has accredited 350 colleges for the purpose and plans to hire 2,000 science graduates during the year (*The Times of India*, 23 November 2006). Under its Campus Connect Program, Infosys is working with 334 universities and colleges to produce industry-ready recruits since 2004 by providing courseware for industry-specific subjects, projects for students, and sabbaticals for professionals and holds seminars in colleges.

CISCO Network Academy program runs in 46 universities and 110 engineering colleges to overcome shortages of professionals with advanced networking skills in the areas of network security and new areas like IP telephone and wireless networking (*The Times of India*, 25 February 2007). Wipro CodeZap Guru Program helps develop code-writing skills of final year engineering students and supports them with training materials. Accenture has a Campus Corridor Program that helps the company to hire from select colleges and engages with them by supporting them in areas like curriculum development, faculty training, student seminars and sponsorships.

National Skill Development Mission

Vocational education and training sector has small capacity is largely focused on engineering trade. Even this small capacity has been under-utilised and the rates of unemployed are high due to mismatch and quality gap. The development of centres of excellence in the ITIs with industry participation is aimed at removing this mismatch and addressing the quality issue. A more comprehensive approach, however, is required. The issue of skills development cuts across allocation of work of many line ministries at the centre. While some ministries are responsible for education and training, others need adequate numbers of skilled people for growth. The states are major stakeholders in terms provision as well as financing. At the same time, it is important that skilled manpower is available within the state for development. Therefore the issue of skilled manpower is critical to a large number of stakeholders. Despite its importance, efforts towards skills development lack focus, coordination and suffer from many implementation bottlenecks. Often public investment in schemes for skills development is either not monitored or is monitored only in terms of expenditure or disbursement with little focus on its end use and outcomes.

The proposal to set up a national mission for skills development is therefore timely and crucial. As per the Eleventh Plan document, the mission would adopt a multi-pronged and innovative approach, involving different ministries of both the national and state governments and industry associations for significantly scaling up the vocational education and training efforts. Over the next five to eight years, vocational education and training capacity is proposed to be increased from the current 3 million to 15 million, in order to meet training needs of the entire annual workforce accretion of about 12.8 million and train a large section of existing untrained labour force.

For the engagement of higher education institutions with the industry and employers, sector-specific membership based networks could be created. Time and resources have to be committed from the industry and the employers as well as by the higher education institutions for these networks. These networks would also compile and collate high-quality labour market intelligence and make it generally available to all for making informed decisions. These could also ensure that specific skills (including generic skills) required in particular sectors are met on a continuing basis. This would be an important platform for sustained meaningful interaction. One can learn from the enterprise-led approach through clusters and financial participation of the government that has been extremely successful in Ireland (see Box 5.1).

With a massive outlay of Rs 31.2 billion, a very ambitious skill development mission is planned during the Eleventh Five Year Plan. Government initiatives, mainly in the public–private partnership mode will be supplemented with private initiatives. The mission will operate through four sub-missions, namely, Industrial Training Sub-mission, which will look after ITIs, ITCs and related central and state institutions; Polytechnics and Vocational Education Sub-mission will take care of community polytechnics/colleges, vocational education schools;

BOX 5.1   Enterprise-led approach to skill development in Ireland

Ireland is using a networked enterprise-led approach for training of workforce since 1999. 'Skillnet', a training network is a group of three or more enterprises clustered either by sector or region for cooperation in training suited to enterprise needs and cost efficient. Training occurs where companies choose and is therefore flexible and accessible eliminating one of the most oft-cited barriers to workplace training. So far, 114 networks involving 6,122 companies have participated, benefiting 35,315 employees. Government has provided Euro 24.24 million of grants to the networks while the participating companies have contributed Euro 12.76 million. This entire activity is being managed by Skillnets Limited—an independent employer-led body. This has raised the profile of enterprise training in Ireland and has been a source of national competitiveness for the country. The Irish economy has seen the most rapid growth of the EU and OECD countries for many years.

Source Skillnets Limited (Ireland).

Unorganised Sector and other Government Initiatives Sub-mission to cater to the rural farm and non-farm sectors of the economy; and the Private Skill Initiatives Sub-mission to develop tailor-made skills required for the industries and coordinating the efforts in the private sector to align them with national goals.

There will be sector-specific initiatives with respect to the 20 sectors identified as high growth sectors. Other aspects of the mission are shifting from institution-based to student-based funding, establishing the NFQ to facilitate mobility between various forms vocational education, technical training and academic streams at more than one career points and setting up the National Skills Registry and Database for Skill Deficiency Mapping and converting employment exchanges to career counselling centres. It is expected that these initiatives would help fill in 58.6 million jobs in the domestic economy and 45 million jobs in the global economy (Planning Commission). With commitment from the top and good conceptualisation, the mission can make real difference if implemented properly.

Short-cycle Programmes

Short-cycle programmes, either on standalone basis or in conjunction with regular programmes with focus on employable skills, are now on offer. These programmes bridge the gap between the theoretical curriculum in universities and colleges and practical specific skills required in workplace. Faqir Chand Kohli, the doyen of the Indian IT sector and former chairman of TCS, suggests a simple solution to the problem of skill shortages in the IT sector (Kohli, personal communication, December 2006). He considers that out of the nearly 3 million youth graduating from the Indian higher education system, one-third are employable with some training but without any supplementary education. Another one-third at the bottom can get jobs that are routine and work up the ladder by learning on the job. The middle rung, the remaining one-third can be converted into employable assets. They need supplementary education. This education should enable them to think in problem-solving mode, logical understanding, programming skills, and skills in rapid reading, writing, speaking and some exposure to operation research. Assuming that they have studied mathematics at the 10 + 2 level and possess basic English language skills, a two-semester course work covering system engineering and system modelling, logic, operation research, programming skills, programming style, proof of correctness and extensive coding structure, rapid reading to achieve speed of 300–500 words per minute, writing essays and proposals and making presentations would suffice.

According to him, such supplementary education could be provided at selected colleges. Expenses could be as little as Rs 30,000 to Rs 50,000 per student for which financing could be worked out including innovative loan schemes for the students. NIIT is undertaking initiatives to generate skilled manpower in small towns and villages. It has set up a model district learning centre (DLC) at Chhindwara in Madhya Pradesh creating talent and skilled manpower for global readiness. The graduates would be equipped with various skills, such as IT, communication (verbal and written) and business etiquette that enable them to acquire gainful employment.

Context-specific Solution

Supply constraints in retailing and pharmaceutical industry are two cases of skill shortages that are industry-specific and require context-specific solution. There has been an explosive growth of organised retailing in India. Modern format retail is manpower intensive, and most jobs are on the shop floor require skills that can be acquired by short-term training. They are poorly paid and have high aspirations, and therefore face high attrition rates. Globally, retailing is a high staff turnover industry, with even the larger retailers facing attrition rates of between 40 and 60 per cent a year. To address manpower constraints, many retail players are setting up their in-house training facilities or tying up with other education and training institutions for preparing retail workforce. In the pharmaceutical industry, where a science degree or degree in pharmacy was considered essential, many companies are now hiring matriculates as medical representatives. Salary level of medical representative is around Rs 5,000 a month and a maximum of Rs 100 per day as allowance.

The aviation sector is growing at the rate of 35-40 per cent with potential to provide direct employment to 3 million people by 2020. Several new airlines have come up. 400 new aircrafts are likely to fly in the Indian skies over the next four to five years. The central government has set up an expert group to chalk out the Aviation Sector Manpower Plan for the next 20 years. India need not only meet the domestic requirement, but could also become a preferred source of skilled manpower—pilots, engineers and technicians, air traffic control and airport management—for the global aviation sector. There are training institutions with a wide franchise network for training of cabin crew. Four institutions for pilot training are being set up.

Certification or Benchmarking by End-users

Certification or benchmarking by the end users or their associations could effectively raise the quality and constructively meet their needs for qualified manpower. This could either be done for individuals or for institutions. When this is done at the institutional level, it helps to reduce the search cost for the employers and provide an incentive to educational institutions to improve the standard of teaching.

End users could also set up certification programmes with their specific needs in mind. For instance in 1998, the National Stock Exchange (NSE) started the National Certificate on Financial Management (NCFM) to measure the knowledge of a person for many roles in the financial industry. At present, nine different certification tests are offered under this umbrella. Tests take place at locations all over the country, and roughly 55,000 persons appeared in the tests in 2004 (Shah, 2005). NASSCOM has initiated a pilot project for assessment of competences of professionals for the BPO sector and maintains the National Skills Registry of IT manpower. Since academic degrees fail to provide a signal about the quality and suitability of person in the job market, private companies have entered the business of skills assessment.

Community Colleges

An interesting development in recent years has been the setting up of community colleges, primarily through non-governmental initiatives in the country. About 200 community colleges, mainly in South India, have been set up over the past decade. These colleges have flexible entry norms. No prior formal academic qualifications are essential. But for a few of them, all others are non-governmental initiatives. The curriculum comprises 21 weeks each of life skills and work skills with eight weeks of internship and hands-on training and two weeks of preparation for employment and evaluation. With more than 75 per cent students finding employment on passing out, it is a resounding success and needs replication and support. These community colleges are distinctly different from the community colleges in the United States and Canada as seen in Box 5.2.

Manpower Forecasting

Manpower forecasting in India is weak and based on assumptions of the past. Disjointed efforts to provide long-term forecasts and post-mortems are of little use. Assessment of skills required within the country, its supply and dynamics has to be done keeping the future in mind. Dissemination of such information would enable the higher education and training system to create new facilities or adapt the existing ones to bridge the demand–supply gap. A system is required to take charge, create and motivate the entire supply chain of skills required dynamically and ahead of the curve.

BOX 5.2   Community colleges in the United States and Canada

The United States and Canada have their unique system of community colleges that fulfils certification needs for vocations and skills required in communities. Anyone, regardless of prior academic status or college entrance exam score is allowed to join a community college. Community colleges are as popular with students attending high school (who can enrol under concurrent enrolment policy), as with working adults (who attend classes at night to complete their degree or gain additional skills in their field). These not only provide a cheaper option than the expensive higher education, but provide pathways for entry to a regular four-year college. Research shows that students who begin their higher education with a community college are more likely to transfer to better quality four-year institution. Low fees, focus on vocational skills with easy transfer to regular higher education programs makes community colleges a preferred option particularly for students with mediocre academic records. In the United States, low-cost community colleges focus on vocational skills with open admission policy on one side and highly selective and very expensive research universities on the other are a part of an integrated and coherent higher education system. This system provides for high degree vertical and horizontal mobility and has a lot of flexibility and variety.

Source Author, based on literature survey.

Manpower planning is poorly organised in the country. There are a few disjointed efforts, built on the assumptions of the past. National Technical Manpower Information System (NTMIS) manpower forecasts and information dissemination is limited to technical education. It has become irrelevant with the unanticipated development of a major proportion of degree and even diploma holders in engineering taking up jobs in the IT sector. Long-term forecasts, post-mortems and staid reports that are occasionally produced are of little use. Efforts are required to assess skill requirements within the country, the supply and the dynamics of outflow, and then feed this information effectively to user markets. Such information will enable setting up new infrastructure that will help bridge the demand–supply gap. This would also help development of skills with the dynamism needed so that the expectations of India's population dividend and human capital do not prove short lived.

This requires a dynamic system of providing the job market with information on placement, unemployment rates by levels of competence, job offers and employers' estimation of their needs in terms of manpower to the higher education institutions on a continuing basis. These signals from the labour market help the educational institutions to make adjustments in their capacities and also adapt curricula to emerging changes in the job market and also assist individuals to make correct choices. Rather than an inward domestic focus, these developments have to be viewed in global context in a manner that best serves national interest.

In all, there is a need to enlarge the adaptive capacity of the higher education system so that it is more responsive to the changing world of work and meets the diversified needs of economy—both domestic and global. For that purpose, diversification of the Indian higher education and training system has to be pursued as a goal. This can be achieved by having a proper mix of public and private, formal and non-formal institutions. Special initiatives are required to enhance employability. Curriculum and content have to be continually renewed through teaching and learning support networks and specific skill development network may be set up. Collection of data on job market trends, its analysis and dissemination are important.

Conclusion

Higher education helps people develop skills to gain access to higher status and better paid jobs and enables the nation's economy to be competitive. However, matching of graduates skills with their own preferences and the demands of the labour market is a complex affair. Changing nature of work and its content and growing integration of labour markets at a global scale makes it even more complex. Due to technical changes, most jobs in both manufacturing and services sector are now clustered at the low productivity end and some at the high productivity end, and there is a hollowing-out of the middle.

A majority of the workforce is engaged in low productivity and low wage jobs. After remaining unchanged for decades, of late there have been some positive signs. More and better jobs were created in the 2000–05 period debunking the notion of jobless growth in the post-reforms period. Some jobs are being created at the high end. Led by the IT and IT enabled services sector, high skill jobs are being created in pharmaceuticals, biotechnology and engineering design. A much wider range of jobs are now being off-shored to India, creating new job opportunities. Several new economy sectors such as finance, insurance, organised retail, aviation, hospitality, animation, media, real estate and infrastructure are creating new and larger variety of jobs. Indians are hired for jobs overseas, and several Indian companies are hiring foreign nationals reflecting emergence of a truly global labour market. Ordinary graduates that the country's higher education system churns out are unfit for the new jobs being created.

Despite the above positive development, the unemployment rate of graduates at 19.6 per cent is significantly higher than the overall rate. Most sectors have small proportion of the workforce as graduates and more than 60 per cent of graduates perform jobs that do not require graduate skills. While fat salaries enjoyed by a few tend to get highlighted, the plight of the vast numbers who remain jobless for long periods goes unnoticed. Graduates may have restricted mobility and their skills may not match with the labour market, hence rather than 'tight fit', a bigger pool of qualified people may actually facilitate the development of a competitive and dynamic knowledge-based economy.

The recent focus on higher education has been in the context of mounting skill shortages. Such shortages co-exist with the rising graduate unemployment and underemployment. Most of the discussion around skill shortages is often based on impressions of individuals and interest groups and their lobbyists, with the media usually perpetuating and exacerbating fallacies and inconsistencies and the reality is thus missed out. Such perceptions are usually wrong and unnecessarily alarmist. The Indian system is skewed in favour of humanities and arts, and almost four-fifths of the graduates it churns out has no employable skills. With rigid academic structures, there is little student choice and large heterogeneity in terms of quality.

The vocational education and training sector is very small and faces the problem of low quality and mismatch. There is also social stigma attached to blue collar jobs. As a result, there is a large shortage of blue collar workers, and a glut of those with higher education degrees. There are also perceived skill shortages due to differences between work skills and academic skills. Such differences, however, are not only unavoidable but also desirable, since different outcomes are expected from workplace

and academic institutions. There are few education and training opportunities in the formal sector for jobs that the new and emerging economy
sectors have opened. With many inadequacies in courses and curricula,
higher education institutions do not provide skills for the 21st century
worker. The pool of English language skills is found shallow in the face
of large demand for these skills in a variety of jobs.

It is seen that from the labour market perspective, overall enrolment
levels are adequate—relevance and quality are the main issues. Thus,
modifications to existing course content, sometimes in response to
employer suggestions, introduction of new courses and teaching
methods and expanded provision of opportunities for work experience,
all intended to enhance the development of employability skills are
required. Due to the rigid academic structure, process for changing
curricula in the universities is painfully slow. The number of quality
institutions is small and seen as a major bottleneck. Tiny quality sector, however, spurs competition among students due to tough entry
requirements that help to raise the overall standards through self-
directed learning.

There is a high unmet demand from students due to large supply
constraints. Information asymmetry is large. Regulatory arrangements
and their poor compliance has erected entry barriers for genuine new
providers and prevented the existing ones from being creative to meet
the quality challenge. As a result, there is little competition that could
spur quality enhancement among the institutions.

Private institutions that depend on tuition fees have to cater to the
students' demand. This forces them to change their offerings according
to it. These are, therefore, far more adaptable. Within the private sector, the non-formal training providers are even more flexible since no
regulatory framework binds them. Thus, a suitable mix of the public
and the private, the formal and the non-formal provision for higher education and training provides an optimal solution and would meet the
changing needs of economy and society. However, with a view to build
pathways, a national qualifications framework is required. Managing
public–private mix and devising policies that ensure healthy growth of
both the public and the private sectors would be a challenge.

Workforce Development

There are several initiatives to address the skill shortages. Several companies have taken up in-house talent development. Short-cycle programmes, either on standalone basis or in conjunction with regular programmes with focus on employable skills, are now on offer. These programmes bridge the gap between the theoretical curriculum in universities and colleges and practical specific skills required in workplace. Industry-specific and context-specific solution is being tried in many sectors. Certification and benchmarking by end users is being used to raise quality and meet needs for qualified manpower.

A national skill development mission, aimed at sector-specific initiatives in 20 high growth sectors to fill in 58.6 million jobs in the domestic economy and 45 million jobs in the global economy, has been proposed. This mission adopts a multi-pronged and innovative approach, involving different ministries of both the national and state governments and industry associations for significantly scaling up the vocational education and training efforts. With commitment from the top and proper conceptualised, the mission can make a real difference, if implemented properly.

While there may not be an acute problem of supply of graduates in terms of absolute numbers, the problem lies in their uneven quality. This is getting aggravated with an increased appetite of the industry in recent years with the country's rapid economic growth, investment boom and structural changes. The skill shortages are at the low end, where graduate skills are not required, or of blue collar skilled workers. Thus skill shortages are not general, but specific and often temporary due to recent developments. The solution may not lie in large scale expansion of higher education, but in identifying the shortages and finding context-specific solutions.

Overall, this calls for intervention to make the connection between higher education and the jobs more efficient as a means for reducing unemployment and underemployment of graduates on the one hand, and addressing the problem of skill shortages on the other. Linkages between higher education and the labour market are tenuous. Supply-side responses are required to be in sync with the demand side impulses. The challenge lies in multi-level coordination with speed and flexibility to accommodate a large variety. For big countries like India, given the enormity and complexity of the task due to a large labour market and a huge higher education and training system, multi-level coordination through central planning is less useful and the market forces can usually do a better job.

◆

6

Research and Higher Education

*Whoever acquires knowledge but does not practice it is
one who ploughs but does not sow.*
— Sa'di

KNOWLEDGE has always been a key factor in economic development. Societies that realised this and were able to produce, select, adapt, and commercialise knowledge had better chances of achieving sustained growth and better quality of life. The ability to create economic value through the creative application of knowledge is innovation. There are three inter-related mechanisms: division of labour, capital accumulation and innovation involved in economic growth. Innovation is the most fundamental mechanism—it is self-perpetuating and pushes economic growth on a continuous basis. Each new innovation triggers further innovation in a kind of chain reaction that fuels long-term economic growth. Thus, in several science-based, technologically-advanced economies, economic growth has continued for several decades without running out of dynamism, or even slowing down (McArthur and Sachs, 2002).

In discussions on the role of knowledge and innovation on economic development, several terms are loosely and interchangeably used. Data is quoted out of context and comparisons made across nations. As a result, the debate on it is often superficial. This chapter briefly explains some key concepts and analyses Indian research in the global context, using several key indicators. It then summarises major developments that define the role of innovation in economic growth and explores its linkage with academic research. Finally, the chapter outlines the manner in which Indian higher education could be organised to create and transfer knowledge in an effective manner to foster and sustain innovation and economic growth.

Concepts and Issues

Science, in a broad sense, is the unfettered search for knowledge for the sake of understanding. The process of this search is referred to as research. Research may be basic, with the intention of advancing science, or applied, with an orientation towards some practical end. These are the two ends of a continuum of problem solving, as basic research suggests avenues of inquiry that are advanced by applied research and likewise, research is enriched, made more complex and significant, as applied work creates the need for more theoretical work and suggests new avenues for further basic research.

While basic research (could also be referred to as pure science) may require no justification outside itself and its usefulness has no bearing on its validation, it is now widely accepted that the fruits of applied research follow the careful nurturing of pure science. Therefore, pure science is not only important by itself, but it also has an important role in laying the foundation for applied research that leads to innovation.

With the blurring of boundaries between them, various distinctions have been made between basic and applied research. The OECD defines pure basic research as experimental and theoretical work undertaken to acquire knowledge without looking for long-term benefits; strategic basic research is defined as experimental and theoretical work undertaken to acquire knowledge in the expectation of useful discoveries; applied research refers to original work undertaken to acquire knowledge with a specific application in view; and experimental development is systematic work, using existing knowledge gained from research or practical experience, directed to producing new materials, products or devices (OECD, 2002).

Knowledge is non-rival (a person's use does not impede another person's use of it) and non-excludable (once known it is difficult to prevent others from using it). As a result, the creator of new knowledge is not able to capture its full value—a classic case of externality. For this reason, it is classified as a public good in economics, justifying government funding. To provide incentives to creators and businesses to invest in new knowledge creation, the intangible intellectual property needs to be protected to capture value from it. The ability to legally protect useful knowledge becomes the basis for commercialisation. The new useful knowledge takes form of either software or hardware or a combination of the two and could be anything that enhances the efficiency and quality of our lives. This is broadly referred to as technology and technology transfer is the communication of such technology.

It is commonly held that pure science, applied science and technology development and transfer follow one another in a linear sequence and higher education institutions are at the earliest stage of knowledge cre-ation, with university research focused on the generation of new ideas. In practice, however, university research involves a wide range of activity starting from scientific discovery to clinical trials, beta testing and prototype development. Strong complementarities between university research and industrial research have been shown by several studies, particularly in the advanced countries. These would be stronger in areas such as biotechnology and information technology, where science plays an important role.

Substantial investments are required to transform abstract ideas from basic research into commercially viable products. It also requires the universities to be pro-actively engaged with industry. Success in technology transfer efforts and commercialisation of scientific research depends upon close and continuous engagement with the industry along with an effective intellectual property rights (IPR) regime.

Looking at the technology trends, it is seen that some of the most significant technologies of the future are likely to be at the intersection of disciplines that are now just beginning to flourish. Technology, unlike science, is a group activity; it is not based on an individual's intelligence but the interacting intelligences of many. This has implication on the way university research is to be organised in future. It requires the formation of inter-disciplinary research teams not only from within the higher education institutions, but also collaboration with researchers from other institutions and public research laboratories and also from the industry.

The term 'research and scholarship' is also used sometimes in the context of higher education. This usually refers to a wide range of activities, from uncovering or generating new knowledge to solving particular practical or theoretical problems. More specifically, while 'research' means systematic and rigorous enquiry leading to research outputs, 'scholarship' is seen as the means by which academics keep themselves up-to-date with changes in their own disciplines so that they can communicate the latest knowledge on the discipline to their students and peers. The focus of this chapter is primarily on research and not scholarship.

Research is a vital function of the higher education systems world-wide. Higher education institutions are dedicated to advanced learning, sophisticated research and public service important for the functioning of a modern economy. While an important function of higher education is to create a pool of qualified people with a wide range of skills in-cluding skilled human resources for the Research and Development (usually abbreviated as R&D) system, it is also often the lead player in public research arena. R&D activities are aimed at making scientific discoveries and inventions that are commercially attractive and higher education plays an important role in supporting a nation's R&D efforts (Harman, 2006). University research forms an important component of the technological base of a country. With a rapid pace of change with globalisation, the role of the higher education institutions in fostering R&D is becoming important. In the USA, which has the most vibrant and the largest R&D system in the world, higher education plays a vital role.

Understanding the linkages between pure and applied research, appreciating the need for an effective mechanism for technology transfer for its commercialisation, the existence of a proper IPR regime, recognising the importance of interdisciplinary research and understanding of process of technology diffusion—all would help in providing a foundation for shaping public policy for supporting academic research in the country.

Indian Research in Global Context

As evident from the concepts and the review of developments in the previous section, R&D covers a range of issues too complex and too broad to be defined by any single parameter. However, input measures, such as the number of trained personnel carrying out R&D work, the level of national expenditure on R&D and output measures, such as the number of scientific and technical articles published, patents filed, revenues from royalties and licenses, high technology exports are indicators that reflect the technological capability of a country. At times, various combinations of these indicators are used to develop indices to depict the innovative capacity of a nation. In addition, several ranking methods have been evolved to show relative research performance of countries and higher education institutions.

This section analyses the present status of research in India in terms of various input and output measures. Comparisons with other countries are used to benchmark India's performance. These comparisons have been made with big economies and a few other countries to make a specific point. In many countries including India, a lot of research is done outside the higher education system. Since getting disaggregated data on academic research is often difficult, therefore the discussion in this section is on the total research enterprise rather than merely academic research.

R&D Expenditure

Until recently, research, particularly academic research, had been relatively isolated from the demands of economic utility. Research was considered to have high externalities. It was, therefore, largely publicly funded. However as the private benefits to individuals and firms started accruing due to the emergence of IPR, private investments in research began. It was realised that the producers of ideas respond to incentives: if they are granted no rights in their creations, they will create less, or not at all.

Today, research is funded both from public and private sources. Expenditure on R&D by a nation is often used as a proxy to the importance given by a nation to develop its technological capacity. The share of R&D expenditure from private sources is a good indicator of the dynamism of the private sector. It shows as to how the private sector uses innovation to drive national competitiveness.

Table 6.1 shows recent trends in global spending on R&D. It is seen that R&D spending in India is a little over 1 per cent. In comparison, it is 2.76 per cent in the United States, 3.40 per cent in Japan and 1.88 per cent in Europe. China's research spending at 1.61 per cent in 2006 is picking up and is catching up with Europe, which lags behind the US and Japan. In India, research spending had declined from a peak of 0.98 per cent in 1988 to 0.66 per cent in 1997 before increasing marginally to reach 0.81 per cent in 2001. Since then there has been a secular increase. The government has announced its intentions to raise research spending to 2 per cent of the GDP,[1] but this would definitely take time.

TABLE 6.1   Global R&D spending

	R&D spending as per cent of GDP	Per cent share of global R&D spending			R&D PPP in billion US$
	2006	2006	2007	2008*	2008*
Americas	2.47	35.7	34.4	33.1	401.1
U.S.	2.76	32.7	31.4	30.1	365.0
Asia	2.02	36.9	38.8	40.8	494.4
China	1.61	13.5	15.6	17.9	216.8
Japan	3.40	13.0	12.8	12.4	150.4
India	1.03	3.7	3.7	3.7	45.0
Europe	1.88	25.2	24.6	23.9	288.8
Rest of the World	1.11	2.2	2.2	2.1	25.9
Total	2.08	100	100	100	1,210.2

Source Battelle and *R&D Magazine*, Global R&D Report, 2007.
Note *Estimates.

Research and Higher Education

Trends in global share show decline in the case of the United States and Europe and an increase in China, while India's share at 3.7 per cent has remained the same over the past three years. In absolute terms, India has the ninth largest spending on R&D on PPP basis. It is, however, still very low, and much smaller than China, which is already the world's second largest R&D spender in PPP terms.

As per data compiled by the Ministry of Science and Technology, the country's R&D spending increased from Rs 180 billion in 2002-03 to Rs 197.27 billion in 2003-04 and then rose to Rs 216.4 billion in 2004-05. 79.7 per cent of the research spending came from the government, with private sector spending merely about 20.3 per cent. Of the government appending, 80 per cent is spent by the central government, 10 per cent by the state governments and about 5 per cent each by the higher education institutions and the public sector. Twelve major scientific agencies—Council of Scientific and Industrial Research (CSIR), Defence Research & Development Organisation (DRDO), Department of Atomic Energy (DAE), Department of Bio-technology (DBT), Department of Science and Technology (DST), Department of Space (DOS), Department of Ocean Development (DOD), Indian Council for Agricultural Research (ICAR), Indian Council for Medical Research (ICMR), Ministry of Communication and Information Technology (MCIT), Ministry of Non-conventional Energy Sources (MNES) and Ministry of Environment and Forests (MOE&F) account for 84 per cent of the total R&D expenditure incurred by the central government, and the remaining is spent by other ministries, departments and public sector units. A large portion (30.3 per cent) is spent by the DRDO (DST, 2006).

About 17.8 per cent expenditure is on basic research, 41.7 per cent on applied research, 34 per cent on experimental development and remaining 6.6 per cent on supporting activities. In the state sector, 92.9 per cent of the total expenditure (Rs 15.28 billion) in 2002-03 was on agriculture and allied areas with Maharashtra, Gujarat, Karnataka and Punjab incurring more than one-third of total state sector expenditure. Thus, overall trends show a small share of higher education institutions, state governments and the private sector with the bulk of research spending coming from the central government through its 12 major scientific agencies. There has been substantial increase in outlay of the central government from Rs 237.6 billion in the Tenth Plan to Rs 733.04 billion in the Eleventh Plan, but this would still fall short of 2 per cent target (Planning Commission, 2007: 208).

In view of its high positive externalities, research is primarily funded by the government. Though there is an increasing share of the private sector in funding research, particularly for funding applied research and technology development, most of the basic research is funded by the government. In India, nearly 80 per cent of research is funded by the government. In contrast, a bulk of the R&D spending (about 50 to 60 per cent) is made by the private sector in most developed nations. Even in China, more than 65 per cent of the expenses are made by enterprises. In many countries, part of research is funded by the government but carried out by private sector. In India, this system is slowly emerging (as noted in Table 6.2). Providing incentive in the form of tax breaks to foster private investment in research is a strategic option that countries use to raise overall research funding levels. India needs to review and use this option more effectively. But as per the trends now, research in India will be primarily funded by the government in the short- to medium-term basis.

TABLE 6.2   Contribution of private sector in research

Source	North America	European Union	Nordic countries	India*
Private sector financing	59	53	59	20
Private sector carrying out	71	62	67	25
Universities carrying out	16	21	23	5
Public sector carrying out	10	16	10	70

Source *UNDP Human Development Report, 2001*, p. 37.
Note   *Author's estimates for 2002–03 based on DST data.

While research funding as a per cent of GDP is seen as an indicator of national commitment to scientific research, it has little meaning unless it is seen in terms of how that investment contributes to the growth and welfare of a country. It is important to note that the data on the total R&D that is performed in a given country will actually tell you everything while at the same time telling you nothing. The more important data are of the kind that tell you who is providing the funding, who is doing the work, how the money is being spent and what the priorities, thrusts and directions are. In brief, it is the internal structure of the R&D enterprise and the roles and interplays among the different sectors that have a bearing on the manner in which the investment in R&D has the desired societal benefit outcomes of economic security, improved health care and the like.

Table 6.3 provides research outlays by economic objectives for a few selected countries. It is seen that priorities shift from one country to another. Of the 27 countries (which exclude China and India) for which this information was collected, the field of energy research received only one reference as a priority item (from Poland), and in fact was found to be at the bottom of the list of five priority R&D concentrations for the other countries. Almost all governments provide support to higher education, basic research, industrial technology, human health and agriculture. Defence has the highest priority in Germany, but also in the UK, the US and France (it appears that defence research forms a part of defence budget and is not separately indicated in these countries). Based on budget analysis, scores have been given with respect to five top socio-economic objectives for India. It is seen that defence and space receive highest priority in India.

There are huge upsides to an increased R&D expenditure. In a highly integrated globalised world, innovation through investment in R&D has the potential to transform the economy in a very significant way. As Finland increased its R&D spending to 3.22 per cent from 1.5 per cent of its GDP, its exports, mainly high tech exports, increased manifold. As per available trends, investment in R&D is poised to increase in India. However, there is no guarantee that it would translate into improving research outcomes. For progress to be made in this regard, not only the amount spent on R&D, but also the quality of expenditure on R&D need to improve.

Research Manpower, Doctoral and Science Education

In terms of the number of researchers and technicians engaged in R&D activities, India has merely 119 researchers, whereas Japan has 5,287 and

TABLE 6.3 Research outlays—by socio-economic objectives

(importance on 1 greater to 5 lesser scale)

Country	Non-oriented research	General university funds	Industrial production and technology	Human health	Agriculture	Defence	Social structures and relationships	Space programmes	Other civilian research	Energy	Infrastructure and land use planning	Earth exploration and exploitation
United States	2		4	1	5		3					
Germany	4	5	3		2	1						
United Kingdom	3	4	1	2	5							
Japan	3	5	2	4			1					
South Korea			1	2								
India*	5			4	3	1		2				

Source Battelle and *R&D Magazine*, Global R&D Report, 2007.
Note *Author's estimates based on budget analysis.

Research and Higher Education

the US has 4,484 researchers per million of the population. It is seen from Table 6.4 that even in absolute terms, the number of researchers in India is much smaller compared to the US, China, Japan, Russia and Germany. The number of technicians in India, however, is not as small. It suggests that R&D establishments in India have more technicians per researcher compared to most of the other countries.

TABLE 6.4   Research manpower, 2000–04*

Country	Researchers per million people	Researchers Number	Technicians per million people	Technicians Number
US	4,605	1,316,951	–	–
China	708	859,380	–	–
Japan	5,287	675,678	528	67,478
India	119	128,484	102	110,129
Germany	3,261	269,032	1,089	89,842
UK	2,706	162,089	–	–
France	3,213	194,065	–	–
Italy	1,213	69,868	1,347	77,587
Brazil	344	63,261	332	61,054
Russia	3,319	477,272	557	80,096
Canada	3,597	115,104	770	–
Korea	3,187	153,294	567	–
Australia	3,759	73,767	–	–

Source UNESCO Institute of Statistics from WDI (2007).
Note   *Data for the most recent year available.

The numbers of doctoral degrees awarded in science and engineering in India is a little over 8,500 doctorates, compared to 9,000 in China and 25,000 in the US. It increased rapidly from a little over 1,000 in 1990 to over 9,000 in recent years in China. In comparison, there has been a modest increase in India. The National Science Foundation's (NSF) Science and Engineering Indicators, 2002, show that in the US, about 4 per cent of the science and engineering graduates finish their doctorates; this is about 7 per cent for Europe and in India this is not even 0.4 per cent.

From a low base of 183 in 1953–54, the number of PhDs in science and engineering has increased to over 8,500 in 2005–06 (as seen in Table 6.5). With only about 6,500 doctorates in science and engineering each year and the low current base of researchers at 128,500 compared to 860,000 in China, the country would take nearly 100 years to reach China's level of research workforce even if all 8,500 sciences and engineering doctorate join the research workforce in case of India, and China freezes its research science workforce. The status of doctoral education in India is disturbing. Its numbers are not increasing to meet the growing demand from the public sector research labs and higher education institutions. There are a small number of university level institutions that produce a decent number of doctorates. Even among them, there is a suspicion about the quality of doctoral education, especially in the institutions that are not known to be reputed yet contribute to a significant number of doctorates. Table 6.5 gives the number of PhD degrees awarded in the country over the years.

TABLE 6.5 Number of PhD degrees awarded

Subject	1953–54	1973–74	1993–94	2003–04	2004–05	2005–06*
Science	164	1,515	3,504	5,408	5,549	7,605
Engineering	19	266	348	908	968	1,058
Total	183	1,781	3,852	6,316	6,517	8,663

Source UGC Annual Report, 2006–07.
Note *Provisional.

There is waning interest in science at the school level. Bright students are not opting for science at the degree level and beyond. Though there is an increase in the absolute numbers of students enrolled in the science stream at the graduate and post-graduate levels, its percentage in overall enrolment has declined. At the undergraduate level, it has declined from 33.2 per cent in 1971 to 21.7 per cent in 1997, and at the post-graduate level from 26.1 per cent in 1971 to 22.2 per cent in 1997 (Powar, 1999). This has further declined since then. This drop in students opting for science reflects added opportunities for the better prepared students in professional courses in engineering, medicine and so on. Some students prefer commerce or law to science. This is not unusual. In today's market driven social order, good students are rarely interested in taking up basic science as their career. This trend is seen in almost all countries.

However, declining enrolment in science has a cascading effect in India. According to experts, India will not be able to attract talent from outside; rather it will lose nearly all talented students who happen to study basic sciences on their own (rare) or who drift (majority) to such courses in the absence of their preferred professional subjects (Lakhotia, 2005). Overall, the state of science education is dismal, with declining numbers and low quality. The base of doctoral education is very small. Though scientific manpower in absolute terms appears large, but normalised by population this is very small.

Research Publications and Citations

Publication count in refereed scientific and technical journals is often used to measure impact of research. For this purpose, the Institute for Scientific Information (ISI) has developed a methodology and identified and classified sets of journals for Science Citation Index (SCI) and Social Science Citation Index (SSCI). The databases used by the ISI for SCI and SSCI have their limitations. There is some bias towards English language journals. These exclude several journals with regional or local focus. For want of alternate measures, despite limitations, citation analysis using these databases serves a useful purpose for measuring research performance in global context.

The Research Handbook published by the UGC undertook benchmarking of research performance for various countries based on citation analysis using ISI databases.[2] Table 6.6 shows the number of papers and the number of citations for top 10 countries by the size of the economy and a few other countries for a 10-year (1994–2004) period. It is seen that the top seven countries in research publications are also the world's seven largest economies—the G7 countries. This suggests that research publication count of a country is related to their economic performance.

India stands at the 13th position in terms of the number of papers published; it ranks 21 in terms of number of citations with citations per

TABLE 6.6 Publications and citations, 1994–2004 (10-year period)

Country	Citations Numbers (rank)	Citations % share	Papers Numbers (rank)	Papers % share	Citations per paper (rank)
United States	33,212,308 (1)	62.7	2,698,434 (1)	38.5	12.31
China	799,415 (18)	1.5	271,032 (9)	3.9	2.95
Japan	5,264,781 (4)	9.9	722,512 (2)	10.3	7.29
India	573,792 (21)	1.1	180,783 (13)	2.6	3.17
Germany	6,102,642 (3)	11.5	666,104 (3)	9.5	9.16
United Kingdom	6,373,300 (2)	12.0	604,397 (4)	8.6	10.54
France	4,338,642 (5)	8.2	488,585 (5)	7.0	8.88
Italy	2,709,842 (7)	5.1	320,667 (7)	4.6	8.45
Brazil	433,772 (nr)	0.8	98,747 (18)	1.4	–
Russia	870,485 (15)	1.6	282,027 (8)	4.0	3.09
Canada	3,587,966 (6)	6.8	358,176 (6)	5.1	10.02
Korea	504,634 (nr)	1.0	126,438 (nr)	1.8	–
Netherlands	2,206,097 (8)	4.2	197,426 (12)	2.8	11.17
Switzerland	1,823,353 (9)	3.4	140,164 (15)	2.0	13.01
Australia	1,821,757 (10)	3.4	216,819 (11)	3.1	8.4
Spain	1,529,708 (12)	2.9	219,404 (10)	3.1	6.97
Israel	864,214 (16)	1.6	96,890 (nr)	1.4	8.92
Finland	733,391 (19)	1.4	73,068 (nr)	1.0	10.04

Source UGC Research Handbook,[3] 2005.
Note   nr—not ranked.

paper being as low as 3.17 (119 rank out of 149 countries), compared to 12.31 in case of the US. The US has the largest share of papers and also the citations. Even smaller countries like the Netherlands and Switzerland have large citation and publication counts compared to India.

Arunachalam (2004) analysed the trends of publication counts over a 10-year period (1993-03) for a selected group of countries. The trends show that India's scientific output is on the decline or has remained very nearly the same over this period whereas countries like Brazil, China and South Korea have outperformed India and have improved their performance significantly (as seen in Figure 6.1).

FIGURE 6.1 Percentage share of world publications

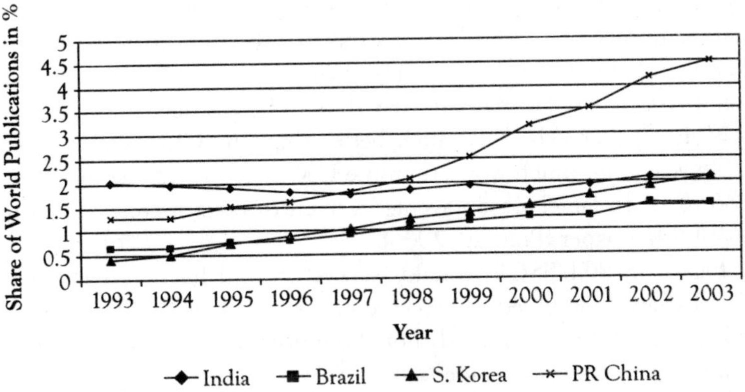

Source Arunachalam (2004).

A recent study that tracked publications indexed in major international multidisciplinary subject databases shows that India's publications growth rate has been relatively fast in the recent years. Compared to 2.51 per cent annually during 1985-05, it more than doubled (5.4 per cent) annually in 10 years (1995-05), and quadrupled (10.1 per cent) in the recent five years (2000-05). India's publications indexed in Web of Science alone have grown from 14,405 papers in 1990 to 28,603 papers in 2005 and is expected to reach 38,000 papers by 2010. The study further noted that higher education institutions contribute the largest share (52.2 per cent in 1985–86) on account of their large numbers. Their share has now declined by 5.56 per cent in 2001–02, while the share of mission-oriented R&D increased from 28.3 per cent to 37.86 per cent. The contribution of institutions of national importance (IITs and IISc) increased from 17.2 per cent to 20.2 per cent and that of industry increased marginally from a low base of 1.78 per cent to 2.1 per cent (Gupta and Dhawan, 2006).

While the number of institutions participating in research has almost doubled from 1,734 institutions in 1985–86 to 3,443 in 2001–02, yet less than 10 per cent (310) contributed almost 80 per cent of the publications and a mere 24 institutions published 300 or more papers. This suggests that a bulk of the system is not productive enough. Not only this, Indian scientists are on an average less efficient. Using the average number of years a scientist takes to publish an SCI paper as a proxy for the scientific efficiency of the nation's science workforce, scientist Gangan Prathap showed that Indians take 13.84 years to publish a paper, which is much better than the Chinese, who take 30.46 years, but much worse than the US, where a scientist takes only 5.86 years. In Israel, on an average a scientist takes merely 1.53 years to publish a paper (Prathap, 2006).

Based on SCI/SSCI, Ronald N. Kostoff and his colleagues have analysed and compared the science and technology (S&T) literature of India and China. The study noted the dismal state of scholarly publication from India and added:

> In 1980, India was light years ahead of China in volume and breadth of published research. For almost two decades, India's research output production stagnated. During that period, China's research production increased exponentially. Presently, China outperforms India substantially both in quantity and quality (as measured by the impact factor and relative citations of research output). The gap is widening and shows no sign of abating, if present research policies are continued. (Kostoff et al. 2007)

More recent trends suggest an upturn. According to a white paper released in November 2007 by Thomson Scientific, the owner of

SCI/SSCI, the number of publications from India had been stable at around 15,000 papers per year until 2000, when there was a pronounced upturn. In the latest five years, it increased to just over 25,000 papers per year. This is a 45 per cent increase. The impact of this research has also been increasing over this period of time, as illustrated by the citation rate of Indian research publications. From the late 1980s onwards, the citations India receives has increased constantly. Research papers from India received 256,253 citations in the latest five years—this is four times as many citations as received in the early 1980s (Stembridge, 2007). This is corroborated by the report of the Steering Committee on Science and Technology for the Eleventh Five Year Plan. Thus, there is a silver lining to the grim scenario as far as publications and citations are concerned.

Global and Domestic Patenting

An indicator often used to measure quality of innovative work done in a country is the number of patents filed by it annually. Though the grant of patents is the exclusive domain of individual countries or patent unions, however, with a view to facilitate the filing of patents in multiple countries, an application process was introduced through a Patent Cooperation Treaty (PCT) under the aegis of the World Intellectual Protection Organization (WIPO) in 1978. For cross-country comparison purpose, the number of PCT applications filed by a country is a good measure of the relative innovative capacity of a country. Table 6.7 gives PCT applications filed by nationality of first applicant. It is seen that one-third of the applications are filed by US citizens. There has been rapid growth (67 per cent growth) of PCT applications filed since 2000.

Indians file a very small number of PCT applications. After reaching 764 in 2003 from 190 in 2000, this number has been around 700–800 for the past four years. Of the 156,100 international patents filed in 2007, only a paltry 686 were from India dropping from 831 in 2006, while China filed 5,456 applications, increasing from 3,951 a year earlier. A notable feature of PCT filings in 2007 was the impressive growth in applications from China and Korea. East Asia now accounts

TABLE 6.7   PCT applications (by nationality of first applicant)

Country	2000	2006	2007 E	Percentage share 2007	Growth over previous year
USA	38,007	50,941	52,280	33.5	2.6
China	784	3,951	5,456	3.5	38.1
Japan	9,567	27,033	27,731	17.8	2.6
India	190	831	686	0.4	−17.4
Germany	12,582	16,732	18,134	11.6	8.4
UK	4,795	5,090	5,553	3.6	9.1
France	4,138	6,242	6,370	4.1	2.1
Italy	1,394	2,716	2,927	1.9	7.8
Brazil	178	333	384	0.2	15.3
Russia	533	695	507	0.3	−27.2
Korea	1,580	5,944	7,061	4.5	18.8
Switzerland	1,989	4,529	4,186	2.7	−7.6
Netherlands	2,928	4,529	4,186	2.7	−7.6
Overall	**93,240**	**149,156**	**156,100**	**100**	**4.7**

Source WIPO website.
Note E—Estimate.

for more than a quarter of all international applications. The Republic of Korea overtook the United Kingdom in 2006 to become the fifth biggest country of PCT filings.

Despite growth in East Asia, the United States and Europe (members of the European Patent Convention) with about one-third applications each continue to be most important country/region in international filing of PCT applications. Even smaller countries like Switzerland and Netherlands file large number of PCT applications, though in 2007 the numbers declined. Researchers from Russia, like India, file a small number of applications and in both countries, there has been a fall in numbers during 2007.

In contrast, there has been a significant growth in patent applications in India. Over the past three years, the number of patent applications increased threefold and more importantly patents granted grew several-fold. The Indian patent office granted 15,262 patents in 2007–08, more than double the 7,539 granted previous year (2006–07) and 1,911 patents granted three years ago, in 2004–05. Government has set a target of 72,000 applications by 2011–12, for which an ambitious patent awareness campaign has been planned. This campaign will rope in universities, laboratories, state-level chambers of commerce and industry, patent attorneys and the scientific community. Planned at an estimated cost of Rs 200 million, this would establish a correlation between intellectual property, innovation, productivity and competitiveness. A National Institute of Intellectual Property Management to handle training, education, research and think-tank functions in intellectual property rights has been planned (*The Economic Times*, 19 May 2008).

Revenue generated by IP offices have gone up eightfold in the last three years. This is 10 times more than the expenditure in these offices. The number of patents filed by foreigners in India has increased substantially. Eighty per cent applications in Indian patent offices are from foreign companies and individuals. Despite an uptrend in patent activity by Indian institutions in India, we significantly lag behind many other countries including China where the number of patent applications now exceeds 100,000.

Though the track record in patenting of some of our academic institutions, such as University Department of Chemical Technology (UDCT) under the Mumbai University and the Indian Institute of Science, Bangalore, is quite impressive, yet overall patent filing by Indian higher education institutions is low. Only nine institutions were engaged in filing of patents in 1995; this number increased to 22 in 1999 and 29 in 2000. Altogether during 1999–2002, 315 applications were filed. Of these, 183 were from IITs and IISc and the remaining 132 from other institutions of higher education (Ganguly, 2005). A positive development, however, is that the Council of Scientific and Industrial Research (CSIR) from India was among the top 10 users of PCT from the developing countries.

The CSIR has also been a leader in patent activity in the country. CSIR dominated the research activities from 1968–2004 as per ranking of patent assignees for all Indian inventions. However, during 2006, Microsoft Corporation India toppled CSIR from the top slot in receiving patents for research done in India. Microsoft bagged 584 patents in India during the last year against CSIR's 476. This shows the rising power of the private sector in investment in research and innovation in India (Stembridge, 2007). Despite this setback, CSIR share amongst the Indian applicants continues to be about 20 per cent. The CSIR also enjoys half of the market share in terms of US patents granted to an Indian entity.

Though India has been a laggard in global patent filing, it has seen a significant activity in domestic patenting in the recent years, with multinational companies and foreign innovators providing the lead. While this reflects an increasing interest by the foreigners in the Indian economy; but this could also be a matter of concern when seen as a form of intellectual colonialism by the multinational companies.

Competitiveness Ranking

The World Economic Forum (WEF) has been measuring national competitiveness and producing Competitiveness Reports for over two decades. Since 2001, WEF started providing Growth Competitiveness Index (GCI) for 75 countries. This index is based on the quality of macro-economic environment, the state of the country's public institutions and the level of its technological readiness. It further separates the countries as core innovators and non-innovators, based on the number of US utility patents. For the year 2005, India was at a low rank at 50, though this was an improvement over its previous year's position at 55. Various other indices like innovative capacity index, innovative policy index, cluster innovation environment index, linkages index, etc. have also been developed. It is noted that in all these indices India fares poorly.

In the World Bank's Knowledge Economy Index (KEI), India's recent rating at 2.71 is lower than the global average (5.59) and well below the advanced countries rating (8.5). Yet another measure of innovation is the Global Innovation Index (GII) developed by the INSEAD Business School on behalf of World Business magazine recently. Eight pillars underlay this index. Five input pillars (institutions and policies, human capacity, infrastructure, technological sophistication, business markets and capital) represent aspects that enhance the capacity of a nation to generate ideas and leverage them for innovative products and services. Three output pillars define the benefits of successful innovation to the citizens and organisations of the country. India's decent rank at 23 amongst 107 nations in GII is largely on account of its high score on competitiveness (Rank 5; score 4.72 out of 7) and human capacity (Rank 7). A further analysis shows that Asian nations—Japan (Rank 4), Singapore (Rank 7), South Korea (Rank 19) and China (Rank 27)—will drive the global innovation in future (Dutta and Caulkin, 2007). Thus, India's competitiveness rankings send out mixed signals.

Global Ranking of Institutions

Fascination with rankings does not stop at the national level. There is now an emerging trend of global ranking of universities that form a key component of the national innovation ecosystem. With a large and growing number of globally mobile students and a highly mobile workforce, formal global ranking of higher education institutions is very popular and done by various organisations around the world. Two popular rankings are done by the Institute of Higher Education at Shanghai Jiao Tong University (SJTU)[4] in China and the Times Higher Education Supplement (THES) in the United Kingdom.[5] The Shanghai Jiao Tong ranking system emphasises publications, citations and academic prizes, especially in science and technology. In contrast, the Times Higher Education Supplement system relies heavily on peer evaluation.

The SJTU publishes its annual rankings since 2003 with the top 500 world universities while the THES has started its rankings in 2004 with the top 200 world universities. While the SJTU ranking uses criteria as alumni and staff winning Nobel Prizes and other prestigious awards, articles published in particular periodicals such as *Nature* and *Science*, the THES ranks institutions on the basis of the broader parameters such as peer reviews, international citations, staffing levels, international students and faculty. Though, none of these criteria are very comprehensive, yet these rankings are good indicators of relative quality of higher education institutions in different countries.

In the SJTU academic ranking of world universities, only three universities, namely, the Indian Institute of Science (Bangalore), IIT Kharagpur and the University of Calcutta figured in the world's top 500 for the year 2004. However, in 2006, only two universities from India remained in the list. Table 6.8 gives scores on these two universities

TABLE 6.8 Academic ranking of world universities, 2006: top 500

World rank	Institution	National rank	Score on alumni	Score on award	Score on Hi-Ci	Score on N&S	Score on SCI	Score on size	Total score
16	University of Wisconsin-Madison (USA)	14	41.5	35.5	53.3	45.1	68.3	29.3	48.8
22	Kyoto University (Japan)	2	38.3	33.4	36.9	36.2	72.4	31.7	43.9
23	Imperial College London (UK)	3	20.1	37.4	40	39.7	64.2	40.2	43.4
201–300	Shanghai Jiao Tong University (China)	2–5	0	0	0	8	51.1	17.5	–
301–400	Indian Institute of Science (India)	1	0	0	10.9	8.4	33.1	16.3	–
401–500	Indian Institute of Technology, Kharagpur (India)	2	0	0	10.9	4.9	25.4	12.8	–

Source Institute of Higher Education, SJTU, 2006.
Notes Hi-Ci: Highly Cited Publications; N&S: Publications in Nature and Science; SCI: Science Citation Index.

compared to a few other universities of comparable size and standing. With most of the world's universities showing a zero score on alumni and awards, too much need not made out of these rankings.

From India, the Indian Institute of Technology (IIT), the Indian Institute of Management (IIM) and the Jawaharlal Nehru University figure in the top 200 universities and are ranked at 57,68 and 183rd positions respectively in the THES-QS World University Rankings. Here it may be pertinent to mention that the Jawaharlal Nehru University, which ranked 192 in 2005, has moved to the 183rd rank this year, while IIM from rank 84 in 2005 has now moved to the 68th position. The IIT meanwhile had slid from the 50th rank in 2005 to rank 57 in 2006. The United States, the United Kingdom and Australia have the largest number of universities in this list of the top 200. Among the Asian universities, 34 universities, comprising six universities from China, 10 universities from Japan, two universities from Singapore, four from Hong Kong, three from India, three from South Korea, one from Taiwan, two from Israel, one from Thailand and two from Malaysia, have made it to the top 200 list.

Indian institutions fared very poorly in terms of international students and faculty. On the other hand, the THES ranking of technical institutions based on peer review of 2,375 academics ranked the seven IITs above other global technical institutions like Stanford and Georgia Tech. The IITs were ranked at the third spot, after MIT and the University of California at Berkeley. Even here though the IITs had a high peer score, yet they fared poorly in citation counts. In the world's 100 best technology universities survey for 2006 published by the THES, the IITs have retained their number three ranking, largely based on their high peer review scores.

It is a matter of concern that only a few universities in India compete favourably with the world's best institutions. Their number is not only small, but there is also the fact these are not in top rung. A country of the size of India needs a much larger number of higher education institutions that can compete with the best in the world. Based on a careful statistical analysis of these rankings, it is seen that while there is broad consensus about the first 10–12 universities, the lists begin to diverge after that. The lack of an absolute set of performance criteria may mean that 'world class' standing will probably be based more on academic reputation than on a set of formal standards. Thus, too much importance to such rankings may not be desirable.

India's Overall Research Standing

India's research performance is depressing based on the above input and output measures. This would have a sobering effect on the irrational exuberance about India becoming a global knowledge power. It is seen that despite a very large system of higher education and a significant number of science and engineering graduates, research output of India in terms of publications, particularly its quality and patenting is poor. Very little is being spent on research through higher education institutions. Even in terms of high technology exports and royalties and license fees from technology licensing, India's performance is dismal. It is the lowest amongst all the top 10 economies and other selected countries. India also ranks rather low on various competitiveness indices. India's position on various input and output measures for research performance have been summarised in Table 6.9.

There is a lack of adequate linkages between universities and research laboratories on the one hand and universities and businesses on the other. While the required infrastructure and experimental facilities for research do not exist, it is a pity that even the existing facilities are not being optimally utilised due to lack of collaborative work and absence of the culture of sharing of facilities. These concerns are real. In spite of poor rankings on various indicators, India has performed well in recent years. Efforts are required to improve the country's performance on these measures; an understanding of the research–innovation–growth linkage in the new environment is needed to build on the existing strengths.

Research–innovation–growth Linkage

Despite India's poor performance in basic research (as measured by publication and citation counts) and applied research (as measured by patent counts), there is general optimism about India's potential

TABLE 6.9 S&T indicators for four top economies (various years)

	United States	China	Japan	India	Remarks
R&D Expenditure					
–As percentage of GDP, 2007	2.47	1.61	3.40	1.03	2.64% of GDP spent on R&D in Korea and 34.9% R&D through HEIs in Canada
–Percentage performed by HEIs	16.8	10.1	13.9	4.1	
Research manpower					Russia also has a relatively large number of researchers
–Researchers (per million population)	4,484	663	5,287	119	
–Technicians (per million population)	–	–	528	102	
Rank–Growth Competitiveness Index	2	49	12	50	Finland is ranked at No.1
Patent–PCT applications, 2007	52,480	5,456	27,731	648	33.6% of applications on PCT from the US
Publications/Citations, 1994–2004					38.5% papers and 62.7% citations are from the US
–Number of papers–Rank	1	9	2	13	
–Number of Citations–Rank	1	18	4	21	
–Citations per paper–Rank	1	121	11	113	
High technology exports					33% of Korea's manufactured exports is high tech exports
–Volume (US$ billion)	216.02	161.60	124.04	2.84	
–As percentage of manufactured	32	30	24	5	
Royalties and license fees					UK also has sizeable receipt and payment under this head
–Receipts (in US$ billion)	52.64	0.24	15.70	0.03	
–Payments (in US$ billion)	23.90	4.50	13.64	0.42	
Institutions in SJTU's Top 500 University list	161	18	36	2	Highest from India is Indian Institute of Science in 251–300 range

Source Compiled by author from various sources.

in the new knowledge-based economy. According to Virmani (2005), there could be several reasons for this optimism, such as continued growth of the business services sector, demographic transition and demographic bonus, indigenous entrepreneurship, large institutional and social capital, the ability of Indians to manage diversity and huge pool of underutilised brain. All these factors helped in maintaining a sustained growth momentum. He adds that the innovative capacity of a nation matters only after a country reaches the high income category. India's performance in high technology research would not really matter in the catch up stage.

As per UNDP's *Human Development Report 2001*, not every country needs to develop cutting-edge technologies, but every country needs the domestic capacity to identify technology's potential benefits and to adapt new technology to its needs and constraints. However, everyone does not seem to agree. They argue that India cannot continue to piggyback for long on the dynamic and vibrant knowledge base of the West. It has to invest in blue sky and original research to become a truly innovative nation by 2020. Imperatives to foster a nationwide culture of innovation would depend on the stage of development of a country. In developing countries like India, the capacity to absorb and make use of new technologies throughout the economy is weak. According to a recent World Bank report, while technological progress is now faster in the developing world than the high income countries, yet the technology gap between them remains wide. As a result, while few sectors and some firms have technologically sophisticated operations, a majority of the population and most firms work in a low-tech environment. This is true of India, where technological advancement in the IT sector is at par with the advanced countries, but economy-wide level of technological achievement is not very different from that in other countries at similar levels of development (World Bank, 2008).

In the above circumstances, technology diffusion to other sectors and firms offers opportunity to raise productivity levels through out the economy. While some of it is happening through the market mechanism, the government could facilitate this by creating an enabling environment. Today it is not critical to aspire to achieve technological self-reliance. Exposure to new technologies through import of high-tech equipment and rising levels of foreign direct investment often brings with it the knowledge of important process technologies. A highly skilled diaspora in advanced countries exposes the home country to new technologies through regular contacts, and even coming back when there are economic opportunities (World Bank, 2008). However, this is not to suggest that continued poor performance of basic research and technology development in India should not be a matter of concern. The fact is that there are several restrictions in transfer of strategic technologies. Thus, country needs to develop indigenous technological capabilities.

In addition, there is now, a new understanding of the manner in which innovation drives growth. Several nuances of these new developments are not adequately represented through various science and technology indicators that are often used in international comparisons on competitiveness. The importance of gradual and experimental innovation in comparison to breakthrough inventions,[6] environment for rapid diffusion of technology facilitated by new information and communication technologies, the power of disruptive innovation, and migration of skilled people from universities to businesses are all important features of technology driven growth. Of all of these, the new information and communication technologies are the most important in recent years and have helped build up momentum for innovation-led growth.

There is often a focus on big ideas and breakthrough innovations; the experience has however shown that gradual and experimental innovations bring in the greatest gains in productivity that drives economic growth. Romer (1993) points out that it is not only the big ideas that are important, but also the millions of little ideas produced and put to use are of equal importance. This places a premium on the diffusion of technology in society where the higher education institutions could play a vital role.

Reaching out the benefits of technological innovation to the masses is an important policy goal in the developing world. There is a huge demand at the bottom of the pyramid—from people who need and want new goods and services but cannot afford them. This requires disruptive innovations that could bring in a different value proposition—typically cheaper, simpler, smaller, and frequently more convenient to use. Disruptive innovations can open new opportunities in such circumstances creating a win–win situation leading to accelerated growth.

Though IP protection and its licensing for commercialisation is important, there is evidence to support that a more effective form of technology transfer is the migration of skilled people from universities to businesses. The technical know-how that researchers carry with them is significantly more valuable than the legal right to commercialise inventions. Therefore a strategy based on creating environment for training of highly skilled manpower is more sustainable. This requires a people-centric approach to be adopted in the national innovation system.

The new information and communication technologies offer vast opportunities for progress in all walks of life. These offer opportunities for economic growth, improved health, better service delivery, improved learning, and social and cultural advances. Not only India's information and communication technology expenditure is a decent 3.8 per cent of the GDP, but ICT products and services are quite afford-able in India. This has helped in rapid increase in its their usage. This increase is having a large spin-off in fostering innovation throughout the society and contributing to growth.

Thus, traditional measures of research outcomes and aggregate competitiveness scores hide critical details and micro-realities that are vital in grasping the idea of competitiveness and devising a roadmap for the country to become competitive. In recent times, India has achieved success in several brain-intensive services and manufacturing. Indian software industry is considered top-class. Starting from low-end software, Indian companies have risen fast and very competitively up the ladder into high-end products and services.

India is doing well in the pharmaceutical and automotive sector. Brain-intensive manufacturing has made India world class in small cars and auto ancillaries. Hyundai, Suzuki and now Nissan have made India a centre for global export production. India has emerged as a force in global biotechnology and Indian companies are engaged in cutting-edge stem cell research. The Open Source Drug Discovery Project to develop new drugs at a fraction of their cost by roping in brightest young minds the world over is being steered by Indian scientists. Many global corporations are setting up their research centres in India. This has helped attract many scientists who had earlier migrated back to India.

India as a Global R&D Hub

Large corporations are now increasingly adept at managing global innovation networks to draw on pools of relatively cheap but highly qualified brainpower. These are in diverse fields, and not only confined to the IT sector. Though these are mainly confined to development research and not in the cutting-edge technology areas, yet this is a healthy development for India. The reason for this development is the low-cost manpower available in India, around four to six times cheaper than the advanced countries, and the country's huge talent pool in English. It needs to be realised that the total investment in these R&D centres is not huge. These centres may also not create jobs in huge numbers. Their direct impact on national income may not be significant, and yet when R&D flourishes, the growth in manufacturing and other services would follow.

This development has improved the job market for science and engineering graduates. India is tipped to be among the top three destinations where the multinational companies (MNCs) plan to spend their R&D budgets over the next three years, according to a 2004 survey by the Economist Intelligence Unit. A recent UNCTAD survey corroborates this. India was number three in terms of R&D location attractiveness—close behind China and the US and way ahead of UK, Germany and Japan.

According to Mitra (2006), India was host to about 150 multinational R&D centres in 2006, more than 100 of which were opened since 2002. A Technology Information, Forecasting and Assessment Council (TIFAC) survey showed that foreign companies invested USD 1.1 billion in R&D in India between 1998 and 2003. The 100 FDI companies in the R&D sector surveyed by TIFAC employed 22,980 workers comprising scientists, software engineers and other support staff (TIFAC, 2006). Recent reports suggest that the number of R&D centres of MNCs is now over 300. India has witnessed a significant increase in private R&D expenditure. The total private R&D investment is estimated to have risen from Rs 32 billion in 2002 to Rs 164 billion in 2005. This has led to a corresponding increase in total R&D spending from Rs 160 billion in 2002 to Rs 340 billion in 2005 with total private spending is estimated to have risen to 48 per cent. Table 6.10 shows headcount, patents and investments in a few big research centres in India.

A recent survey by PricewaterhouseCoopers found that 35 per cent of multinational chief executives were likely to do business in India because of the available talent pool, compared with 22 per cent for China and only 12 per cent for Russia (PWC, 2006). This helps the country to take a new trajectory of growth. It is now seen that under the pressure of the global competition, even the domestic private sector is keen to invest in the technology development.

TABLE 6.10   Major multinational R&D labs in India, 2007

Company	Year set up	Headcount		Patents	Investment in US$ million
		Current	Future		
GE	2000	3,500	5,500	600+	120
Unilever	1958	250	–	670	–
Dupont	2007	90	600	–	40
Monsanto	1997	60+	70+	–	–
Dow Chemicals	2008	–	500	–	25
Motorola	1990	3,500	–	–	–
Intel	1999	3,000	–	50 (+800 invent disclosures)	1700
Yahoo!	2002	1,500	–	–	–
Microsoft	1998	1,400+	–	180 (since 2004)	–
Texas Instruments	1985	1,300+	–	415	–

Source BW Research, Business World, November 2007.

Given the history of the past 20 years, there is every reason to believe that the globalisation of R&D will continue to grow, and that the competition for research funds will become more intense. According to Jules Duga, a senior researcher at Battelle and world-renowned expert on R&D trends, the US will continue to dominate for up to the next 10 years or so, but after that decade R&D activity is likely to be split into thirds with North America, the European Union (EU) and Asia—dominated by China and India—holding approximately equal shares (Krishnadas 2007). Outsourcing and off-shoring of R&D is becoming increasingly prevalent among all players in the R&D enterprise. The long history of R&D interactions among the US, Western Europe and Japan has been growing to include the rest of Asia, which is not a surprising trend to those who closely track the R&D enterprise. This growth has been unlike any other in recent years, and it foretells the approach to a new equilibrium in global scientific and technological practice.

A 2006 study by the technology consulting firm Booz Allen Hamilton and the French business school INSEAD reveals that by the end of year 2007, India and China together would account for almost a third (31 per cent) of the global R&D staff, up from 19 per cent in 2004. But China leads in absolute numbers. India has between 117,528 and 300,000 scientists, researchers and engineers while China has three times as many at 926,252. Over the next three years, more than three-quarters of the new R&D sites to be set up will be in China and India. As investment and output in China are mostly for local consumption, India with its local and global focus could emerge as the dark horse and become the number one knowledge destination by 2020.

With private research opportunities increasing, there is a sudden demand for researchers. A decade ago, the difference between industry salaries and salaries in government labs used to be 2-3 times—this has now gone up to 10-20 times.[7] Hence, there is flight of researchers from the public lab system to the private sector. Dream salaries and challenging research opportunities are making them prefer industry research in the private sector. The demand for researches is particularly large in the life sciences, computer sciences, electrical and electronics and mechanical engineering.

In these circumstances, the issue of science talent is important. Low numbers and poor quality of PhDs is a major handicap for the R&D centres currently. Hence several research centres have a majority of their senior level researchers from the US universities, who mentor junior team members (mostly B.Tech and M.Tech) that form the bulk of the workforce in R&D centres. This is one of the several ways that the research centres are addressing the issue of talent storage and inadequacy of the Indian higher education system. Institutions of higher education are the key component of the national innovation system. From the discussion in this section, it is clear that though academic research may not be very important, yet migration of skilled people from universities to businesses is an important feature of technology driven growth. The rest of the chapter deals with research in higher education.

Academic Research and Higher Education

Academic research and higher education are important in fostering innovation through creation of new knowledge and developing trained manpower to use that knowledge for creating wealth and enhancing public good. The data in the earlier sections paint a grim picture of the status of research in India. A matter of greater concern is poorer performance of the university sector. The performance of university sector was quite significant in 1950s and 1960s. It has fallen significantly in recent years. In the OECD countries, research from academic institutions accounts for about 15–35 per cent of the overall R&D effort of the country. In basic research, as much as 60 per cent or more is contributed by the academic institutions. In the US there is a very strong relationship between undergraduate/post-graduate teaching and research. In the well-known universities of the US, the undergraduate students have a good exposure to eminent research scientists, which is lacking in the Indian system.

Low and Declining Standards

Academic institutions in India are severely under-resourced and have insufficient linkages amongst themselves and with the society at large. They suffer from cronyism and academic in-breeding that prevents cross-fertilisation of ideas and is an impediment for good science. It is seen that the researchers in India emulate topics of the developed economies, often to the neglect of local need and national priorities, in order to get published and gain respectability.

Though all universities are expected to have research focus and be comprehensive in their focus both on teaching and research, data on doctorates, particularly in science, engineering and medicine suggests that only a few institutions have real research focus. In engineering there were merely 650 doctorates awarded in 2001–02. Of these 80 per cent were from just 20 top universities. In science, 65 per cent of the doctorates awarded were from the top 30 universities.[8]

Sustained research efforts made by the faculty are eventually reflected in recognition of their work at the national level. Such recognition includes membership of science academies. Even here, it is seen that the distribution is skewed. According to the analysis done in the UGC Research Handbook, only about 20 out of the 120 traditional universities have a fellow in one of the three science academies, namely—Indian National Science Academy (INSA), Indian Academy of Sciences (IAS), Bangalore and National Academy of Sciences (NAS), Allahabad.

There is a serious and growing concern about the quality of PhDs in the country. The requirement of a PhD for appointment and promotion as a faculty member had undesirable consequences. The fact that the highest number of PhDs are awarded not by the most reputed universities suggests widely varying standards of quality control for the PhD degree. In some universities, the student is awarded a PhD degree within 18 months and in others, students take three to five years, sometimes even longer to complete their PhD degree. The Verma Committee, while inquiring about the status of higher education in

Bihar, found out that a single thesis was used by as many as eight students for award of PhD in universities in Bihar (Nath, 2005). There have also been cases of plagiarism.

Research in the social sciences, often considered as a poor cousin of research in science and technology, faces a more serious problems. Poor quality due to lack of accountability and very low levels of funding are key concerns. Doctoral theses in the social sciences often apply a descriptive approach to specific limited topics without really relating it to a wider socio-political and economic context. There is a need for a more analytical and comparative approach in doctoral research and relating it to society, polity and economy. A study conducted on Social Science Research Capacity in South Asia in 2002, showed that the share of the Indian universities in the special articles published in the *Economic & Political Weekly* was only about a 25 per cent. This too was dominated by only three universities, namely, Jawaharlal Nehru University, University of Mumbai and University of Delhi (Chatterjee, 2002).

The science policy analyst, Ashok Parthasarathi, observes that science in India has been afflicted with the 'two box disease' wherein the universities and the government R&D laboratory system have developed independent of each other (Parthasarathi, 2005). The two systems are poorly connected in India and work in isolation. In comparison, in most industrialised countries, these work together in tandem. There is an increasing dichotomy in teaching and research between universities and research institutes in India. It is an accepted fact that research is stimulated, informed and occasionally even germinated as a result of instructional activities, even from teaching undergraduate courses. Being actively involved in research makes one a better teacher, and instructing students makes one a better researcher. These complementarities require that research and teaching to go together. The way new knowledge is created, protected and managed requires new ways of collaboration between the academia, research laboratories and industry. The need for their working together is no more an option, but an imperative.

Signs of Hope

In the midst of these disturbing trends, there are a few signs of hope. Several initiatives have been taken to address various concerns. The consortia approach has been adopted to enhance access to expensive e-journals and e-resources in a cost-effective manner. There is more liberal funding of selected institutions. The IISc at Bengaluru and the seven IITs now receive more funds. In addition, five universities were identified in year 2000 and four in the year 2005 as universities with potential for excellence and each given an assistance of Rs 300 million for upgrading of their infrastructure and facilities. The three oldest universities—Calcutta, Madras and Bombay—received a grant of Rs 1 billion on occasion of their completing 150 years. The strategy, though similar to the selective approach in public funding adopted by China to nurture excellence, the scale and coverage of funding in India is very low compared to the initiatives in China.

Several new institutions with a focus on science and engineering are coming up (see Chapter 2 for details). In 2005, the Indian government has started two new institutes for science education and research at Kolkata and Pune, and the third one at Mohali near Chandigarh came up in 2007. A new institution for design and manufacturing has been set up at Jabalpur. Several other new institutions are proposed. The National Knowledge Commission has also recommended the setting up of 50 national universities that can provide education of the highest standards beginning with 10 in the next three years. These are efforts in the right direction, but for a country of the size of India, much more needs to be done.

Now there are new ways in which innovation is driving development. There are many changes in the way research is being funded and managed the world over. Taking the new developments into consideration, several actions are required to be taken. These would include increasing the level of and improving the mechanism for funding academic research in India, improving infrastructure for quality research, putting in place objective measures for measuring research performance, rewarding performance, and promoting collaboration and competition. Each of these issues is discussed in the following sub sections.

Funding Academic Research

Most countries spend a significant amount of their research budgets through the higher education institutions. In the US, 16.8 per cent of all government expenditure is made through higher education system, in Germany, it is 17.1 per cent and in the UK, it is 22.6 per cent. In comparison, in India, only 4.1 per cent of the total government expenditure on R&D is spent through the higher education institutions. This is very low. Even in China, 10.1 per cent of all R&D expenditure is made through higher education institutions.

Thus while research spending is low, expenditure through higher education institutions is even lower. While a larger budget is needed for research through higher education institutions, it is equally important to adopt policies for selective funding of universities, departments and colleges with orientation for research and to foster competition in research funding. The universities are heterogeneous. Their research profiles and research capacity vary widely. Expecting similar research outcomes on per unit investment from all of them is unrealistic. In recent times, there is a trend in many countries to separate institutional funding for teaching from funding for research. Considering strong teaching and research complementarities, this may not be the best approach.

However, in order to optimise public investment in research, a selective approach in research funding would be desirable. Selective approach is often opposed and rejected, considering it to be elitist and antithetical to the egalitarian ethos of a socialist-democratic polity. For this reason, idea of having 'major universities' recommended by the Kothari Commission did not find favour and even the proposal to expand and strengthen the UGC programme of 'centres of advanced study' has been implemented half-heartedly.

With a view to providing selective funding of selected well-established departments for undertaking academic programmes in specific fields, the UGC's Special Assistance Programme has been gradually expanded. In 2004–05, 477 departments were provided an assistance of Rs 338 million under this programme. Most significant efforts in recent times have been a greater level of funding for 'Universities with Potential for Excellence' and 'Colleges with Potential for Excellence'. Based on the proposals submitted by several universities and presentations made by their vice-chancellors on their achievements and promise, the UGC has so far selected nine universities and given each a development grant of Rs 300 million for five years.[9] While some have definite thrust areas, others have a general spread. The UGC has also selected 100 colleges with potential for excellence and given each a development grant of Rs 10 million. This pales in comparison to the scale and scope of assistance provided by China to build up flagship universities (as noted in Box 6.1).

BOX 6.1   Funding of flagship universities in China

With a view to develop flagship universities that could lead the country into the 21st century, China took up two ambitious projects for substantial funding of selected universities, namely, the 211 Project and the 985 Project. Initiated in 1994, 100 universities were allocated 400 million RMB Yuan (US$ 50 million) each for improvement of teaching, learning and research under the 211 Project.

Under 985 Project, launched in May 1998, a 3-year funding package of 1,800 million RMB Yuan (US$ 234 million) each was provided to two leading universities—Peking University and Tsinghua University and later expanded to cover seven other leading universities—Fudan University, Nanjing University, China University of Science and Technology, Shanghai Jiaotong University, Xi'an Jiaotong University, Zhejiang University and Harbin University of Technology. In both cases, the provincial and municipal governments were expected to supplement this grant and several universities got sizeable additional grants from them.

Source Ma (2007).

Apart from selective funding, performance-based competitive funding is common for public funding of academic research the world over. Performance measures range from use of simple performance indicators like higher degree completions, publication counts, etc.

(as in Australia) to comprehensive research assessment exercise (as in the UK). At times, there is focus on mission-oriented research that is funded on competitive basis. In addition, there is also project funding and funding for special programmes. All these mechanisms are in use in India in some form or the other. There is however a problem of sub-optimal funding, near absence of objective assessment and lack of coordination. There is a need for greater objectivity and transparency in public funding of academic research in the country. This would help improve the quality of its outcomes quality. And finally, the scale of public funding of research through academic institutions has to be significantly enhanced.

Differential and higher level of funding has been recommended by a number of committees and expert groups. In May 2005, the Task Force for Basic Scientific Research recommended creation of 1,000 positions of research scientists and filling up of vacancies, setting up of 10 networking centres in basic sciences, institutionalising formal linkages between academic institutions and R&D laboratories through joint research, joint appointments and training, initiating winter and summer schools, upgrading infrastructure and facilities and investment of Rs 6 billion per year for improving scientific research in the universities (MHRD, 2005).

In July 2006, Report of the Working Group on attracting and retaining young people to careers in science and Technology recommended an investment of Rs 60 billion in the Eleventh Five Year Plan for the launch of high-quality integrated M.Sc. programmes in 20 universities, initiating two-year (post-B.Sc) B.Tech programmes in another 20 universities, special grants for undergraduate programmes, additional funding for the UGC's inter-university centres, infrastructure support for 400 colleges, creation of two new IISERs (in addition to the three already committed), support for technology infrastructure, individual scheme for teachers and students, assured career scheme, scholarship for students and national scholarships for UG and PG students (Government of India, 2006).

In August 2006, Indian National Science Academy (INSA) and the Indian Academy of Sciences in their joint report, *Higher Education in Science and Research and Development: The Challenge and Road Ahead,* recommended an investment of Rs 73.34 billion towards special assistance to 10 premier universities, upgrading of state universities and undergraduate colleges. Several suggestions in all these reports are common and in many simply re-cycled versions of earlier ones, yet the repetitive emphasis has worked and the Eleventh Plan outlay is substantially increased. It is now left to the capacity of the concerned agencies to take up these issues for implementation.

Setting Funding Priorities

An issue closely linked with public funding of research is the priority setting for university research. Various countries use different approaches for setting the priority for public funding of research. In Korea, research in areas that could possibly be the engines of future economic growth are identified, while in the United States, priorities are identified to direct research efforts towards major areas of concern. Korea uses the foresight model, whereas Japan has been conducting periodic technology forecasting exercises using the Delphi method since 1970. In countries such as Japan, Korea, Germany, the Netherlands, a 'top-down' approach is dominant. Several other countries such as the United States, Canada and Sweden adopt a decentralised 'bottom-up' approach for setting research priorities (OECD, 2003). Despite differences in approach, almost all countries set up priorities for public funding of research including research through the higher education institutions. In India, setting up of research priorities is not done in any organised manner. There is a need for streamlining this.

Research Coordination

Research is carried out in a variety of settings and funded by a number of agencies. Research is a collaborative activity. Setting up of priority for research and conduct of research involve a wide range of stakeholders. Considering this, many countries have developed new mechanisms for coordination of research agenda and research efforts. In the US, such coordination is done through the National Science Foundation (NSF) and the National Health Service (NHS) for medical sciences. In India also, the need for setting up such an autonomous body as the NSF has been under consideration for past some time.

The NKC in its report identified a lack of interaction between researchers, absence of a long-term vision, absence of a carrot-and-stick policy in the form of differential remuneration and lack of scientific methods and scientific temper as the four main causes for the current crisis in Indian research. Realising that knowledge is a continuum and the boundaries between disciplines are becoming increasingly blurred, tenuous and indefinable, the NKC has recommended the setting up of a National Science and Social Science Foundation (NSSF). It suggested that the NSSF, apart from being a nodal agency for setting research agenda for the country and ensuing a coordinated approach, with an annual budget of Rs 12.5 billion, should fund 200 to 400 long-term projects that have the potential to make the country a global leader apart from being nodal agency for setting research agenda for the country and ensuing a coordinated approach (NKC, 2006).

In partial acceptance of the NKC's recommendation, the government has decided to create an autonomous body called the Science and Engineering Research Board with greater autonomy and substantially large funding. Currently, the Science and Engineering Research Council, under the Department of Science and Technology (DST), has a budget of about Rs 3 billion. This would be raised to Rs 10 billion. While this might speed up fund disbursal, but officials dealing with the process for many years feel that given the limited absorptive capacity of a large part of the system, this may not really improve research in higher education.

Whereas the setting up of the Science and Engineering Research Board is a desirable move, and may have a desirable impact, there would still be several sources for funding research beyond the board's purview. Hence a research grants portal could be established with a view to address the problem of duplication of research efforts and lost opportunities for collaboration due to lack of communication between different agencies.[10] The aim of such a portal could be to provide centralised access to grants. Rather than having to go through the laborious process of searching grants by the agency, potential applicants can easily search one comprehensive database using a number of criteria, such as date, agency, category, and so on. There could be a system of assigning a unique number to each research proposal to track such grants over a period of time. Applications could be made online through this portal. It should be possible to have simple registration process that could enable researchers to submit applications. The progress of applications could then be tracked online. Increased homogeneity in forms would help to simplify the application process and reduce avoidable administrative burden of researchers. This would also ensure that applications pass through a central contact and enable effective coordination.

Sharing Infrastructure and Facilities

Infrastructure and experimental facilities for research, particularly for science and technology are expensive. Most often these are not optimally utilised. This would call for a strategy on nationally integrated research infrastructure. This has to ensure that existing expensive research equipment, high-end computation and communication infrastructure are accessible to all researchers in the higher education institutions and research agencies, and new research infrastructure can be created where gaps exist by pooling of resources. Whereas, more expensive and less intensively used facilities should necessarily be shared, less expensive and more intensively used facilities need not be shared; and the other facilities could be shared on selective basis depending on the circumstances.

Research Partnerships

Research requires collaboration not only among higher education institutions, but also between these and the research laboratories on the one hand and with the industry on the other. Cooperation is particularly important to achieve critical mass in new fields of knowledge, which is often missing. This often acts as an impediment to creativity and productivity. There are some bilateral linkages. These are primarily for staff and student exchange and rarely for promoting cooperative research. Multiple linkages forming inter-connecting clusters or groupings that are either regional or discipline/subject specific are extremely rare.

Despite this realisation, collaborative efforts are few. Most of these are not very effective. There are five criteria for effective collaboration. These are (i) activities should be jointly designed, implemented and monitored; (ii) resources should be contributory; (iii) organisations need to mutually benefit from collaboration; (iv) people at all level should be actively involved and supportive of the relationship; and (v) collaboration would necessarily require sacrifice of some autonomy of the organisations involved.

Considering the potential for greater synergies between higher education institutions and research agencies, possible models for closer collaboration may be evolved. There is a need for greater focus on commercialisation of research through collaboration and possible alternate funding models to promote excellence across the national research effort. There are inherent gaps in thinking about research in university environment and industry environment. Corporate culture differs from academic and research culture because of its primary focus on profit rather than on disinterested production and transmission of knowledge. Based on detailed analysis by Natarajan (2000), these are summarised in Table 6.11.

TABLE 6.11   University and industry R&D—Different approaches

University R&D	Industry R&D
Essential long-term.	Essential short-term.
Carried out by graduate students under the guidance of faculty supervisors, with the objective of fulfilling degree requirements.	Carried out by professional personnel with objective of satisfying customer needs.
Maintaining continuity is more difficult.	Continuity is maintained in proportion to the industry goals.
Output is more in terms of research papers.	Output is more in terms of products and processes, and patents.
Scope is more deep and detailed.	Scope of solution is determined by the extent of need.

Source Natarajan (2000).

This gap is needs to be bridged in order to have meaningful engagement of industry with higher education institutions. Apart from bridging these gaps, resources need to be committed to institutionalise such partnerships. Academic institutions often face the problem of funding for mobility that is essential for any collaborative activity. Therefore, provision of mobility grants or a 'glue-funding' is perhaps necessary.

Improving Internet Connectivity

Technology is a driving force in the contemporary higher education and academic research. Thus it becomes necessary to connect them through a high speed broadband network. For this purpose, the National Knowledge Commission has recommended a National Knowledge Network (about 5,000 nodes) with gigabit capabilities to connect all universities, libraries, laboratories, hospitals and agricultural institutions to share data and resources across the country.[11] To be initially launched on existing commercial networks, this would involve a recurring cost of Rs 2–4 billion annually for 1,000 institutions in the first phase and capital investment of around Rs 10 billion for a seven or eight node inner core network. While this ambitious project is being considered, the UGC had taken up the task of networking university campuses in 2002 under the UGC–Infonet Connectivity Programme.

Under the UGC's programme, 149 universities distributed across the country have been provided Internet bandwidth ranging from 256 Kbps to 2 Mbps using broadband LL/SCPC/DAMA/FTDMA/RF Open Network Architecture. The task of establishing and maintaining the entire network for the universities is being done by the Education and Research Network (ERNET) India on turn-key basis. The UGC–Infonet is based on an open IP platform, employing state-of-the-art technologies like IP Multicast, TCP Spoofing and other Internet tools that provide interactive education on PC or TV, enabling on-line response to queries. Open systems architecture ensures support for current and future applications. Users from educational institutions now are enjoying high data rates while accessing Intranet and Internet resources. Connectivity for all universities is being upgraded to 2 Mbps depending upon the technical feasibility. The total annual cost on providing differential connectivity to 149 universities is around Rs 120 million.

Improving Access to Information Resources

Easy access to scholarly communication is a critical input for quality research outcomes. Several scholarly journals have become too expensive for most higher education institutions to afford. Scholarly communication in electronic formats has now become popular. With low, almost no cost in distribution, it provides an innovative solution to the affordability problem. Sharing of information resources, putting in place effective document delivery services and open archiving (OA) are becoming popular and alternate solutions to address the affordability issue.

The OA approach by creating institutional archives of research publications from the institution needs to be promoted. According to many recent studies, papers available via open access archives are cited anywhere between 2.5 and 5.5 times more often than papers published in the same source but not made open access. Such archives can be created in all universities and other institutions of higher learning. The software is absolutely free. A Linux server is the major equipment needed, besides an Internet connection. Any computer science graduate or a librarian with some training can set up the archive and run it. This would enhance research productivity by improving visibility of Indian research. This also addresses the problem of research publications from India not getting as much impact as it should because many of them are published in journals that have a small subscription base.

India could also work proactively and get integrated to the worldwide systems of library services and information systems to share resources. For instance, it would be desirable to partner with Online Computer Library Centre (OCLC)—a membership-based, service and research organisation that serves to provide access to the world's information at reduced cost. The OCLC bibliographic database, WorldCat (the OCLC Online Union Catalogue), is one of the most consulted electronic databases in higher education. There is a possibility of developing a separate model for India that may include hosting of OCLC data locally, leasing OCLC's software and collaboration for standardisation of bibliographic records for major Indian universities and creation of bibliographic records for documents in Indian regional languages including Hindi.

Libraries in many institutions of higher education face crisis as a result of rise in cost of journals much faster than the rate of inflation, due to an increase in number of journals and the paucity of funds available to the libraries. This exponential and continuing increase in subscription cost of scholarly journals is referred to as 'serials crisis'. The consortium approach proved to be a recipe for solving the problem for university libraries, which have been discontinuing subscription of scholarly journals because of this crisis. Higher education and research institutions formed consortia to subscribe to large base of journals and databases in electronic format to benefit from discounted pricing due to economies of scale. The consortia are able to obtain attractive terms of agreements for its members through hard bargaining with publishers and aggregators. Such negotiations often involve technical complexities and provide financial options beyond the comprehension of an individual institution.

Though there are many library consortia in the developed countries, this movement has just picked up in India. There are many initiatives in India. Four of these that have significant membership and subscription are given in Box 6.2. Of these, the Indian Digital Library for Engineering, Science and Technology (INDEST)–AICTE Consortium is the largest. This has helped to significantly boost the research productivity of member institutions. An analysis of the cumulative research output of the 37 central institutions from 1975 to 2006 showed a huge increase in number of publications in the block years 1999–2002 to 2003–06 in comparison to the previous periods. While in the previous block years, it declined or remained almost stagnant, after the INDEST came into being, there was a growth of more 50 per cent registered in the number of publications covered under the Science Citation Index (SCI). [12]

There is a need and possibility for the consolidation of the existing library consortia. With the existing four consortia serving as the nucleus, a national consortium could be formed. The national consortium could extend to the institutions falling under various ministries such as the Department of Science and Technology (DST) with 30 institutions, Department of Bio-technology (DBT) with 12 institutions, Defence Research and Development Organization (DRDO) with 44 institutions and Department of Space with 10 institutions. The national consortium

BOX 6.2   Four important library consortia in India

1. INDEST–AICTE Consortium (http://paniit.iitd.ac.in/indest/) subscribes to 21 full-text e-resources and six bibliographic databases and provided access of these electronic resources to 614 academic and research institutions in May 2007. This included 37 centrally-funded government institutions (including IITs, IISc, NITs, IIITs, IIMs), 60 Govt./Govt.-aided engineering colleges (with AICTE support), and 517 engineering colleges and institutions have joined the Consortium under its self-supported category.
2. UGC eJournals Consortium (http://unicat.inflibnet.ac.in/econ/mindex.htm) caters to 120 universities for current as well as archival access to more than 5,000 core and peer-reviewed journals and 9 bibliographic databases from 23 publishers and aggregators in different disciplines. It is funded by the UGC and being extended to other universities and colleges with potential for excellence. It plans to launch its '"Associate Membership Programme"' wherein private universities and other research organisations would be welcomed to join the Consortium for selected e-resources.
3. The Council of Scientific and Industrial Research (CSIR) E-Journals Consortium (http://www.niscair.res.in/http://www.niscair.res.in): funded by the CSIR for its all its 44 labs.
4. Department of Atomic Energy E-Journals Consortium: for 36 institutions under Department of Atomic Energy.

Source Compiled by the author from various sources.

would have a much greater bargaining power. This can ensure greater coverage both in terms of subscription-base and number of institutions. The national consortium can take up collaborative activities such as setting up back file repositories, e-print and electronic theses and dissertations (ETD) repositories, local hosting and mirroring of e-resources, cooperative cataloguing, training, and so on. The national consortium may act as a central agency to coordinate all activities related to acquisition, creation and access to information in digital format. The funds for a national consortium can either be pooled from different institutions or made available directly.

Improving Quality of Doctoral Education

Theses and dissertations are known to be the rich and unique sources of information, often the only source for research work that does not find its way into various publication channels. Doctoral dissertations are the manifestation of result of four to five years of intense research work involving huge investment of resources, mental and physical, infrastructural and other support from the universities. A thesis reflects quality of research work conducted by a student and the ability of an institution to lead and support original work of research in a given discipline.

The process of scrutiny, validation and approval of doctoral dissertations is confined to few experts (identified by the university on recommendation of a theses supervisor). It is not open to the scientific community at large, and therefore, quality is sacrificed. The theses collection in most of the Indian libraries, are kept in closed access, making it difficult for other students to access them. It remains an untapped and under-utilised asset, leading to unnecessary duplication and repetition that, in effect, is the antithesis of research and wastage of huge resources, both human and financial. While several universities and research institutions in developed countries have implemented sub-mission of ETDs, in India the efforts are sporadic and confined to a handful of institutions of higher learning like IITs and IISc. Mandatory submission of theses and dissertation in electronic format under regulatory framework of an agency like the UGC can be an effective mechanism to improve the quality, accessibility and availability of Indian theses to the world community of researchers.

Electronic versions of theses provides greater exposure to research students through greater accessibility. It offers opportunities to use new forms of creative scholarship through use of interactive elements, multimedia, hyperlinks, etc. Recognising the fact that India does not have either a comprehensive database of doctoral theses submitted to the universities in India or submission of ETDs, the UGC has developed a regulatory framework for development of a bibliographic database of theses and dissertation as well as submission of electronic theses and dissertations in universities in India. The UGC regulations are essentially developed to define systematic creation, collection and compilation of cataloguing information, on PhD theses submitted to various universities in a standardised format and to commence the process of submission of theses in electronic format, in all universities.

The UGC has developed detailed documentation with background information, major issues, current scenario, implementation processes, workflow, standards and protocols, and so on.

The first draft of the regulations including requisite parameters for subsequent implementation has already been circulated for inviting comments/suggestions. The UGC is likely to implement the regulatory framework with Information and Library Network (INFLIBNET) as its implementing agency. The implementation of ETD would lead to the streamlining of workflow and save time and labour, as checking of submissions and cataloguing of ETD would be faster, moving and handling of paper copy would be eliminated and delay in binding would be removed.

A major handicap faced by doctoral research in India is its poor visibility and the 'unseen' factor. There is an international trend to preserve and centrally maintain repositories of electronic theses and dissertations and make them generally accessible and improve their visibility. This helps in improving the quality of doctoral research. In this context, there is a need to create a mechanism for collection and compilation of catalogue information referred to as 'metadata' on all theses and dissertations in a standardised format in the country. The universities could also be encouraged to submit full text of their theses and dissertations in electronic format to a central repository. This can then be made available to all researchers in the country to facilitate further research, prevent gaps and overlaps and plagiarism.

There has been an alarming dilution of doctrinal research quality after the insistence of the University Grants Commission for a PhD degree for appointment to senior faculty position. Recent proposals to introduce entrance tests at all-India level for entry into PhD programmes would perhaps help in arresting this dilution.

Rejuvenating PG and Doctoral Education

With a view to move up the value chain in the knowledge intensive global economy, we need to create manpower in the new and emerging areas. This would automatically attract investment. World-class research universities usually have a large number of graduate students and researchers in many new and emerging areas of science and technology. They have state-of-the-art infrastructure and facilities for their research areas. They attract talent from all over the world and have a lot of activities surrounding their research areas. This provides a vibrant environment and makes these research centres sought after by researchers from all over the world. In India, though some good work is being done in new technology areas, in most cases it is nowhere close to world class. Sub-criticality is the main issue. The problem of sub-criticality can be addressed through collaboration. This can either be amongst the Indian institutions or even foreign provision could be used.

These programmes could involve select academic institutions, research laboratories in the public and the private sector and the industry. The focus of such initiatives could be to develop highly skilled manpower in new technology areas. The strategy could be to create a critical mass around a technology area and provide a stimulating environment for academic and research programmes of international standards. Not only graduate and doctoral students, even post-doctoral students from all over the world could be attracted to these programmes by offering attractive scholarships and fellowships. New virtual structures may have to be created overlaid on the existing physical organisational structures to enable this to happen. Such initiatives need to be liberally funded through special focus programmes steered by committed and dynamic persons from the related area.

China and Pakistan are using foreign provision to attract and retain bright people in science. China is providing liberal fellowships to doctoral students (target set at 4,000) to spend 12–24 months in US universities in the preparatory phase of their research work. This would ensure excellent mentoring and guidance by highly qualified academics and overcome the problem faced by China in not having enough faculty to guide a large number of doctorates. Pakistan is funding hundreds of people for doctoral studies in advanced countries. India could also offer such fellowships to attract brighter students to join PhD programmes. This would will help build meaningful linkages with good universities and research groups internationally.

It will help motivate and increase research output of existing faculty, help boost the research output of Indian universities and create a pool of talent for faculty position. For 1,000 fellowships, cost would be around USD 40 million per year. With employment prospects for researchers increasing in India, most of them will return to India, and a degree from an Indian university will make the employment and movement overseas a little difficult. As per current visa regime in the US it would will be difficult for them to stay back (*The Economic Times*, 17 September 2007).[13]

Incentives to Promote Useful Research

Cross-country analysis has shown that countries that have a strong incentive system in place relating to ownership and use of IPR arising out of academic research are more successful in the commercialisation of research (Henrekson and Rosenberg, 2001). The American supremacy in technology is led by major research universities, which under the Bayh–Dole Act of 1980 maintain ownership of all IP intellectual property resulting from federal research grants. The impact of Bayh–Dole Act on patenting activity, technology transfer and its economic fall out are significant. Over 2,200 companies have been formed since 1980 creating economic activity worth USD 30 billion each year providing employment to 250,000 people based on the licensing of an invention from an academic institution.

Legislation on the lines of the Bayh–Dole Act of the United States that would give ownership rights to universities and link such ownership with patents, and the market will make research a much more attractive option. Such legislation is likely to be enacted soon. This would institutionalise incentive system conducive to promoting innovation in India. This would enable a fair portion of the income from publicly funded research to be allowed to be retained by the researchers and provide them a strong incentive to innovate. Higher education institutions in India are yet to catch up with their American counterparts on this. The UGC has framed guidelines and facilitative mechanism for creating awareness, protection and management in the university system.[14] Its implementation needs to be pursued.

Improve Science and Maths Education

Improving science and math education holds the key to sustained competitive advantage in innovative driven global economy. China and Korea have invested prudently in science education and are now beginning to reap rich dividends. In the face of fading eminence in science and technology, and the danger of falling behind nations such as India and China, the US government has taken up a 10-year, USD 136 billion plan effort to promote and keep America competitive in a global economy. A major intervention in the plan is to improve science and mathematics education. More specifically, this includes helping high schools offer more advanced courses in mathematics, science and languages like Chinese, Arabic and Japanese, increasing the teacher count with 70,000 newly trained math, science and critical language teachers in the next five years and quadrupling the number of high school children taking advanced placement tests in math, science and critical languages.[15]

From time to time the national central government and various science academies have examined the issue of science and maths education in the country. Setting of several new institutions focused on science education and research (details in Chapter 2) are based on various recommendations of different committees. Recently, the National Knowledge Commission (NKC), on the basis of nation-wide consultation, has recommended a series of measures to bring about a paradigm shift in science education and research. These include restructuring of masters and graduate degrees (introducing 4-year flexible and modular Bachelor of Science programme and integrated programmes) to promote career flexibility after graduation, dispelling the myth that science graduates are less employable by re-branding and promoting careers in basic sciences, building a critical mass of scientists in each science stream, reforming science curriculum, changing evaluation system, promoting access to quality science educational resources, revamping teacher training and promoting use of teaching aids to retain student attention, and revitalising the teaching profession to attract and retain quality teachers including a mentoring programme for younger members of the faculty (NKC, 2008).

The NKC has floated the idea of setting up a National Science and Mathematics Mission to address the problem of deteriorating standards of teaching and research in science and mathematics. This has been conceived as a massive, well coordinated and well-funded national initiative and will draw up a 5- and 10-year master plan. Interestingly, it is proposed to be led by young, bright people below 45 years of age and even the mission chief is ideally 50 years of age (NKC, 2008).

Setting up World World-class Universities

According to Altbach (2006),[16] each country would require a research university for effective participation in the global knowledge economy. Rather than a mere focus on training and transmission of knowledge, a research university is expected to create new knowledge in the service of the nation in the classic tradition of Humboldt's model of a university. Research universities have laid the foundations of modern industrial nations in the United States and Japan. Research universities follow a tradition of meritocracy. These are not necessarily the most efficient universities. Therefore, these are not likely to be challenged by for-profit providers, though some of them are themselves becoming quasi-for-profit entities with the growing commercialisation of research outputs.

Post-graduate education and research are resource intensive. Normally, this cannot be sustained on tuition fee alone. Therefore, other than the US and Japan, such universities are mostly publicly funded. In the US and Japan, the culture of philanthropy to support research and existence of favourable tax structure has enabled such research universities to flourish in the private sector. Now these universities have built a huge portfolio of intellectual property and earn substantial income from technology transfer and its commercialisation.

In recognition of the need for world world-class research universities to provide long-term competitiveness to the country on a sustainable basis, the central government plans to set up 14 world-class universities. In his remarks before the full Planning Commission meeting on 13 September 2007, the prime minister pointed out that these universities would *ab initio* be targeted to achieve world-class standards. For this, these would be 'more ambitious in terms of infrastructure and facilities and involve higher costs' (Singh, 2007). The location of these institutions should be determined in a manner which 'balances the desire for achieving a greater geographical spread with the potential synergies arising from co-location' (Singh, 2007). Location decisions should not be purely based on land availability, but the states could compete for the location of these prized universities. The scope for private participation in these universities could be explored.

While the states where the proposed world world-class universities would come up have been finalised (see Chapter 3), the next step would be to plan them. There is no single definition of a world world-class university. Though many people talk about it, the concept has remained undefined. According to one definition,[17] a 'world world-class' university would have four characteristics: it should be committed to breadth and excellence in all fields of human inquiry, not simply in a particular niche with real excellence in most fields, most of the time; it must be engaged in cutting-edge research whilst at the same time teaching the next-generation; it should provide freedom to researchers to experiment, succeed, and sometimes fail; and finally, such a university should have permeable boundaries encouraging interdisciplinary research and teaching, foster and encourage partnerships with the private sector and industry and encourage international collaboration.

Referring to world-class university in terms of an emerging global model (EGM) of the research university, Mohrman, Ma and Baker (2008) set out its eight essential characteristics: a mission transcending the boundaries of the nation-state; research-intensive; new roles for faculty members; diversified funding; new relationships with stake-holders; worldwide recruitment; greater internal complexity; and global cooperation with similar institutions. The two descriptions together give us a good idea of how to distinguish world-class university from other types of universities.

Realising that post-graduate teaching and research in science and engineering could be a viable preposition, the private sector in India has shown interest in setting up of higher education institutions for post-graduate teaching and research in science and engineering. A non-profit group (AKRF, based at in Mumbai) plans to set up a major private, self-financing university to provide high-quality post-graduate education in the area of science, engineering and public health. An industry with mining interest in aluminium—Vedanta Resources—plans to set up a world-class university in Orissa with an investment of USD 1 billion, over an area of 5,000 acres with the capacity of 25,000 seats to expand to 1,00,000 seats in due course (*Indian Express*, New Delhi, 19 April 2006). NIIT, an IT training major, plans to set up a research university near Delhi.

The above non-governmental initiatives are different from the usual private higher education. Whereas the traditional professional education at undergraduate level or the post-graduate programmes in management and computer application are low-risk and highly profit-able, the post-graduate programmes in teaching and research in science and engineering are capital-intensive and high-risk. The government needs to treat the two differently. The country should not miss this opportunity the way a similar initiative for setting up of the Global Institute of Science and Technology (GIST) at four locations by a group of NRIs was missed in the year 2000. They were not allowed to set up GIST in India for the fear that they would poach faculty from the IIT system.

To enable the initiatives mentioned in the previous paragraph to bear fruit, the government could proactively woo big corporate sector and prestigious foreign research universities to set up research universities/campuses for post-graduate education and research in science and engineering in India. This would help to raise the standards of research for long-term competitiveness of the country. Prestigious foreign universities, say, 500 universities in SJTU's list of research universities and big corporate houses in the knowledge sector could be identified and approached for the purpose. Single point contact and a time bound approach could be adopted. Instead of subjecting them to a burdensome regulatory system, bare minimum regulatory concerns may be addressed while allowing them to set up such institutions. The fact that big corporate houses and reputed foreign universities would have their own prestige to safeguard would act as a deterrent in preventing them from dilution of standards or indulge in exploitation of students.

This could work better than the most sophisticated regulatory system. This would give the country an edge in international competition in higher science and technology.

Conclusion

To sum up, the story of research enterprise in India is a story of 'hopes' and 'despair'. Many scientists and planners bemoan the decline and fall of science. And it is true that pure science in India is in trouble, but any lay observer would see that Indian technology has come of age. While traditional measures of research performance, input and output measures paint a dismal picture, positive perception about India and enterprise and inventiveness of Indians has given us an edge in certain niche technology areas. Several sectors and many firms have technologically sophisticated operations similar to any advanced nation, though a majority of the population and most firms work in low-tech environment. Technology diffusion to other sectors and firms offers big opportunity in such circumstances.

Despite creditable performance of individual sectors and some institutions, there are serious problems that afflict basic scientific research in India. Overall, the picture of basic science in India is one of declining productivity. Despite India's poor performance in basic and applied research, there is general optimism about India's potential in the new knowledge-based economy. This is largely partly driven by positive perception and partly by upturn in recent years.

Research funding continues to be small, but it has increased in recent years (though not as rapidly as in China). Foreign patenting activity has not picked up, but domestic patenting has grown fast, though it continues to be dominated by patents granted to multinational companies and foreigners. After remaining stable for many years, number of publications has shown a pronounced upturn over the past five years. The impact of research from India has also been increasing over this time. Indian talent is considered top-notch, though there is concern about fewer PhDs graduating from Indian universities and poor quality thereof.

Traditional measures of research outcomes and aggregate competitiveness scores hide critical details and micro-realities that are vital in grasping the idea of competitiveness and devising a roadmap for the country to become competitive. There is often a focus on big ideas and breakthrough innovations; the experience has however shown that gradual and experimental innovations bring in greatest gains in productivity that drives economic growth. In this backdrop, India has achieved phenomenal success in becoming a global hub for brain-intensive services and manufacturing. India has produced the cheapest quality car in the world. Indian software industry is considered top class. Starting from low-end software, Indian companies have risen fast up the ladder into high-end products and services.

There are also signs of hope in academic research. Several initiatives have been taken to address various concerns. The consortia approach has been adopted to enhance access to expensive e-journals and e-resources in a cost-effective manner. Several new institutions with focus on science and engineering are coming up. Differential and higher level of funding has been recommended by a number of committees and expert groups and some of it already in place. The Science and Engineering Research Board with greater autonomy and substantially large funding is being set up. Legislation on the lines of the Bayh–Dole Act of the United States is on the anvil. This would give ownership rights to universities and link such ownership with patents and the market will make research a much more attractive option. There are plans to set up 14 world-class universities in the country as well.

Further action is required on several fronts. Research through higher education institutions needs to be substantially enhanced. Private funding of research needs to be encouraged by evolving a system of incentives. The mechanism for funding should be reviewed to include selective funding of higher education institutions to nurture excellence. Competitive grants should be increased. Research assessment exercise (based on simple parameters to begin with) should be introduced to bring objectivity in research funding and disbursement of competitive grants. A policy for setting priorities for funding research should be put in place. Regarding the issue of research coordination, an NSF-type foundation could be established; initially a research portal could be set up. Existing research infrastructure and experimental facilities should be optimally utilised by putting in place a system of sharing such facilities.

Research partnerships should be encouraged. Various measures are required to improve access to information resources. Steps are required to be taken to improve the quality of doctoral education. Initiatives to create highly skilled manpower through collaborative approach need to be initiated. Incentives to promote useful research should be put in place. Proactive efforts are required to attract private investment and the participation of world-class universities in post-graduate education and research in science and technology.

◆

7

Regulatory Framework

Best laws are self-reinforcing, they create incentives to comply.

—Anonymous

FROM the ancient universities in India to the 12th century universities in Europe, on which the modern-day universities the world over are modelled, all were autonomous and permanent corporate institutions of higher learning. These evolved into immensely flexible institutions, able to adapt to almost any political situation and form of society. Catering to the elite, they enjoyed exalted status, immense clout, autonomy and academic freedom.

Transition from elite to mass and now universal higher education resulted in an explosive growth of institutions of higher education in one country after another. These institutions are not all universities, but a variety of institutions catering to serve the needs of industrial society and new economy. While many depend for resources on the state, others desire credibility of the qualifications that they provide. Thus, universities along with other types of higher education institutions are now an integral organ of the state and economy, losing their autonomy and academic freedom. They are subject to accountability policies of the state and are required to demonstrate explicitly that they are efficient, effective and meet desired standards of performance. Regulatory governance, which was missing in most countries around the world till recently, has thus come to occupy centre stage in the discourse on higher education.

This chapter begins with the examination of the concept of accountability in higher education. Current organisational structure for regulation of higher education is then mapped and regulatory arrangements, particularly the role of the UGC, the apex body for determination and coordination of standards, is reviewed in some detail. As seen in Chapter 4, private institutions, the main venue for growth of higher education now, are posing regulatory challenges as never seen before. The regulatory environment for the private sector has therefore been analysed. While the size and nature of foreign providers for higher education has been mapped in Chapter 4, the regulation of foreign providers is examined here. An overall evaluation of the regulatory framework is then conducted, before suggesting a broad framework for a new regulatory environment and then drawing up conclusions.

Accountability Concept

With higher education acquiring an explicit economic value in today's knowledge economy, structure and delivery of higher education are changing. New types of educational institutions are coming up. There is an increasing use of technology that allows institutions to operate on a national and global scale. These changes are resulting in growing demand for increased accountability in countries across the world.[1]

Historically, higher education institutions had regulatory or compliance accountability based on government statutes. In compliance-based accountability systems, higher education institutions are accountable for adherence to rules and accountable to the bureaucracy. Over a period of time, as educators and in many cases professional practitioners agreed on certain principles and practices, a professional norms approach to accountability emerged. Here the higher education institutions are accountable for adherence to standards and are accountable to their peers. This came to be known as accreditation. The nature of regulatory and accreditation mechanisms vary widely across nations depending on the structure of their higher education systems.

With the emergence of new models of higher education, many aspects of the above two systems of accountability were found inadequate. The compliance-based accountability system in particular failed to meet the growing aspirations of the stakeholders. Dissatisfied with the outcomes, a third accountability system based upon results, where results are defined in terms of outcomes and more specifically in terms of student learning has become popular. Here, the higher education institutions are accountable for student learning and are accountable to the general public (Anderson, 2005).

A view is now emerging that a good accountability system should primarily be based on results while being attentive to the professional norms and the requirements for regulatory compliance. In the private higher education sector, supply and demand for higher education is increasingly the product of autonomous interactions between institutions and individual students, and the competition for students has become fierce. There is a consensus that simply leaving supply and demand to the market will not necessarily deliver outcomes for higher education that represent the best use of resources or that are just and socially optimal (Teixeira et al., 2004). A new set of regulatory practices is now being developed, based on the understanding of the market structure and the nature of competition in higher education, while also taking into account a proper mix of the three accountability systems.

Regulatory Framework

Regulatory structure in India is multi-layered and complex—partly a result of the federal structure of Indian State and partly a legacy of country's colonial past. There are multiple agencies and a complex web of rules and regulations that govern the higher education system with the UGC at the helm. The state governments, the 13 professional councils at the national level and five professional councils at the state level, the state councils and affiliating universities are the key stakeholders in the regulatory system.

Though as per constitutional mandate, all education including university education had been made the responsibility of the states, the centre was assigned the key function of coordination and determination of standards through Entry 66 of the Union List of the Constitution of India.[2] In 1976, education was brought to the Concurrent List as Entry 25 and the centre was brought on equal footing with the states for all levels of education.[3] The exclusive power assigned to the centre as per Entry 66 was, however, retained.

The Constitution, however, does not stipulate that the centre should maintain standards. But, as pointed out by Professor Amrik Singh, realising that neither coordination nor determination of standards is possible without having some control, this role has been assumed by the central government in the course of evolution of higher education system in the country (Singh, 2004). Over the years, the central government has established various statutory bodies for the purpose. In all, the central government has a key role in defining public policy for higher education in the country. In fact, the central government and its various agencies have come to occupy the centre stage of higher education in the country.

Over the years, the central government has established several institutions of higher education. The central government also maintains these institutions in addition to the three universities, namely—Delhi University, Aligarh Muslim University and Banaras Hindu University assigned to the central government under the Constitution. A detailed analysis of role of the central government in financing higher education is given in the Chapter 4 on financing of higher education.

Central government makes key appointments in all central universities, other central institutions of higher education and central regulatory agencies. This enables the central government to have a final say on major issues. In addition, the central government, on recommendation of the UGC, confers on higher education institutions the status of a deemed-to-be-university and specifies the title of degrees to be awarded in the system. In matters of pay scales and career progression of teachers in universities and colleges, the central government has a decisive role.

The central government discharges its responsibilities primarily through the Ministry of Human Resource Development. In addition, there are at least 15 other ministries/departments in the Government of India that either establish, finance or regulate higher education institutions. Whereas medical education comes within the purview of the

Ministry of Health, agriculture education and research is looked after by the Ministry of Agriculture.

UGC

In pursuance to Entry 66 of the Constitution, the UGC was established as a statutory body by the Parliament 'for coordination and determination of standards in Universities' in 1956. While enacting the UGC Act in 1956, two important provisions in the original draft bill were removed. These related to the UGC's prior approval for setting up of a university and power to derecognise a university degree. Thus, the UGC became more of a recommendatory entity (Singh, 2004). This decision was taken keeping in mind that the Constitution required the central government or its agencies to discharge the function only of 'coordination and determination of standards' and not of 'maintenance'. Once the standards were determined, the universities were required to maintain the same by themselves. No formal recognition or approval of the UGC is required by a university in the country. A university is merely required to be incorporated in and established by virtue of a Central Act, a Provincial Act or a State Act.

This arrangement worked fine when the number of universities was small; these were largely public funded, and led by distinguished academic leaders. The universities were supposed to be self-regulating entities. They voluntarily adhered to the standards determined by the UGC. With rapid expansion and emergence of the private sector, many universities were unwilling to adhere to standards determined by the UGC. Soon this infirmity in the UGC structure became evident. Lack of specific provision for UGC recognition or approval has created anomalous situation on several occasions.[4]

Despite the mandate given to the UGC to coordinate and determine standards of universities, the structure and predominant functions assigned to the UGC in India were largely on the pattern of the UGC in England that was set up under the Government Treasury in UK in 1919. While the UGC in UK has been replaced by two independent professional agencies, namely, Higher Education Funding Council for England (HEFCE) and Quality Assurance Agency (QAA) in 1998, the

UGC in India still continues despite its serious limitations in facing new challenges.

The UGC has the national jurisdiction for the determination and coordination of standards in the entire university education in all disciplines. The UGC exercises this role directly over the universities, while the universities exercise this role with respect to the affiliated colleges. Over a period of time, the UGC has devised several instruments to discharge its functions. Some of the rules, regulations and notifications of the UGC are discussed in a subsequent section on regulating academic standards.

Professional Councils

With the growth of higher education in different fields, several other regulatory bodies were set up. A list of such bodies along with their main functions is given in Table 7.1. All but the ICAR are statutory bodies established through an Act of the Parliament. Some of them predate the UGC. None of them, even those set up after UGC, recognise any role for the UGC in their functioning. This has created problems in coordination amongst them and between various regulatory bodies and the UGC.

As noted above, there are significant differences in the mandate, powers and functions of the different regulatory bodies. The councils have rules and regulations of their own. There is an overlap in the functions of the UGC, other professional councils and even those of the universities. In case of MCI, PCI, AICTE, INC and BCI, there are also the state councils, and there are overlaps in functions of the national councils and state councils.

The AICTE regulates a bulk of the professional programmes. It regulates engineering, pharmacy, architecture, town and country planning at both undergraduate and post-graduate levels and management education at the post-graduate level. It is therefore the most prominent of the professional councils. Some professions, particularly those that have public health and safety concerns, require individual practitioners to register themselves to practice that profession. In such cases, approval

TABLE 7.1 Regulatory and statutory bodies for higher education

Name	Main role	Overlaps with the role of
University Grants Commission (UGC)	Funding, recognition of institutions and degree titles, maintaining overall standards	Other professional councils and the Distance Education Council (DEC)
Distance Education Council (DEC) under the IGNOU Act	Funding, maintaining standards of open education	Other professional councils and the UGC
All India Council for Technical Education (AICTE)	Approval for technical institutions and limited funding role for quality improvement	UGC, DEC, PCI, CoA and the state councils for Technical Education
Council of Architects (CoA)	Registration of architects and recognition of institutions for education in architecture and town planning	AICTE
Medical Council of India (MCI)	Registration of medical practitioners and recognition of medical institutions and qualifications	State medical councils and the state governments; UGC and DEC to a limited extent
Pharmacy Council of India (PCI)	Registration of pharmacists and approval of pharmacy institutions	AICTE and state pharmacy councils

Body	Function	Related bodies
Indian Nursing Council (INC)	Accepts qualifications awarded by universities within and outside India	22 state nursing councils with different Acts have registering powers
Dental Council of India (DCI)	Recommend to the central government for approval of dental colleges etc.	Ministry of Health
Central Council of Homeopathy (CCH)	Maintain central register of homeopaths	State councils
Central Council of Indian Medicine (CCIM)	Maintain central register	State councils
Rehabilitation Council of India (RCI)	Recognition of institutions for physiotherapy and related fields	State governments
National Council for Teacher Education (NCTE)	Recognition of teacher education institutions	DEC
Indian Council for Agricultural Research (ICAR)–not a statutory body	Coordinate and fund agricultural education	UGC
Bar Council of India (BCI)	Listing of members of bar	State bar councils

Source Compiled by the author from various sources.

of the professional council becomes necessary. While, where such requirements do not exist, some institutions opt not to seek professional council's approval. For instance, the Indian School of Business (ISB), which offers one of the best management programmes in the country, chose not to apply for AICTE approval.

State Governments

According to the former Vice Chancellor of Punjab Agricultural University and an eminent educationist, Professor Amrik Singh, the state governments are the weakest, though a vital link in the entire higher education chain (Singh, 2004). From the analysis of financing pattern in Chapter 4, it is clear that the bulk of funding for higher education in the country comes from the state governments. As a consequence they also have the main say in all administrative and operational matters. In respect of the colleges, the concerned affiliating university provides academic supervision.

Unlike the central government that discharges its responsibility towards higher education through the UGC and the other professional councils, the state governments carry out most of the functions by themselves through the concerned government department or directorate in the states. Many states, such as Andhra Pradesh, Bihar, Himachal Pradesh, Uttar Pradesh, Tamil Nadu, West Bengal, Tripura, Arunachal Pradesh and Bihar have either state councils or advisory boards for higher education. Kerala has recently decided to set up a state council for higher education. These are largely advisory bodies with little or no operational role. On the whole, the powers with respect to higher education in the states are concentrated in the higher education departments and subject to similar bureaucratic control as other wings of the government, despite the need for the much-touted autonomy norms of the higher education institutions.

Universities and Colleges

The country has nearly 18,600 universities and colleges in the formal system of higher education. This number is more than four times that of higher education institutions both in the US and entire Europe. Higher education in China, having the highest enrolment in the world (nearly 23 million), is organised in only about 2,500 institutions. Whereas the average enrolment in a higher education institutions in India is only about 500–600 students, a higher education institution in the US and Europe would have 3,000–4,000 students and in China this would be about 8,000–9,000. A smaller average size of higher education institution has implication on governance and regulation of system.

Of the 18,600 higher education institutions, nearly 400 are university-level institutions and the remaining are affiliated colleges. The colleges offer undergraduate programmes, whereas the universities offer post-graduate as well and research programmes, though there are colleges that offer post-graduate programmes and vice versa. Though usually universities are larger entities than colleges, yet there are colleges having several thousand students, whereas some universities have student strength of merely a few hundred students. Therefore, in any analysis both universities and colleges need to be taken together. An analysis based on one and to the exclusion of other would lead to wrong conclusions.

From the trends in growth of higher education institutions, it is seen that the number of affiliated colleges has grown much faster than the number of university level institutions. 87 per cent of all enrolment is in affiliated colleges. Affiliated colleges function under the academic governance of a university, whereas these are independent entities as far as administrative and financial matters are concerned. This makes the Indian higher education highly fragmented, much more than any other higher education system in the world. Many institutions are non-viable and under-enrolled, posing serious problems of governance and regulation.

Rules and Regulations

Universities are self-regulatory bodies that determine and maintain their own standards. However, there is a need to put in place a mechanism for comparability of academic standards across universities to enable transfer of students from one university to another. Academic degrees awarded by the universities send signals to the job markets to facilitate the selection process. Such signals should be easy to interpret. As a result, harmonisation of academic standards across universities becomes necessary.

The UGC has the primary responsibility to coordinate and determine academic standards across the university system. The UGC discharges this responsibility through its various rules and regulations. Some of these are listed in Box 7.1.

BOX 7.1   UGC rules, regulations and notifications (illustrative list only)

1. Pay and service related for teachers

- Notification on revision of pay scales, minimum qualifications for appointment of teachers in universities and colleges and other measures for maintenance of standards, 1998 and 2008
- UGC (Minimum qualifications for appointment of teachers in universities and colleges) Regulations, 1991
- UGC (Minimum qualifications for appointment and career advancement of teachers in universities and colleges) Regulations, 2000

2. UGC rules regarding fitness of universities

- UGC (Fitness of Institutions for Grants) Rules, 1975
- UGC (Fitness of Certain Universities for Grants) Rules, 1975
- UGC (Fitness of Agricultural Universities for Grants) Rules, 1975
- UGC (Fitness of Technological Universities for Grants) Rules, 1978
- UGC (Fitness of Open Universities for Grants) Rules, 1988

3. For maintaining minimum standards of instructions

- UGC (Minimum standards of instruction for the grant of the first degree through formal education) Regulations, 2003
- UGC (Minimum standards of instruction for the grant of the master's degree through formal education) Regulations, 2003
- UGC (Minimum standards of instructions for the grant of the first degree through non-formal/distance Education) Regulations, 1985

4. Others

- UGC (Admission to specified Professional Programmes) Interim Regulations, 2003
- UGC (Establishment and Maintenance of Standards in Private Universities) Regulations, 2003

(Box 7.1 continued)

Regulatory Framework

(*Box 7.1 continued*)

- Specification of Degrees (No Notification between 1975 and 1999 and no alternation in the list after August 2003)
- UGC (Recognition of College) Regulations, 1974
- UGC (Inspection of Universities) Rules, 1960
- UGC (Return of information by universities) Rules, 1979
- UGC (Establishment and maintenance of institutions) Regulations, 1985

Source UGC website. Available at http://www.ugc.ac.in.

The UGC Regulations of 1985 on the minimum standards of instruction for grant of first degree through formal education lay down working days, working hours, attendance requirements, supplementation of lectures by tutorials and/or problem-solving sessions, term papers, nature of evaluation, work load of teachers and several other matters. There are similar regulations for non-formal/distance mode of education. All universities and colleges in the country are expected to follow the UGC regulations on minimum standards across various disciplines. Many of the professional councils also have similar standards. This results in overlap and confusion. Universities and colleges blame the UGC to push this extreme form of standardisation and claim that this kills their capacity to innovate at the institutional level.

The UGC, with the approval of the central government, specifies that the title of degrees that can be awarded by the universities. Standard nomenclatures of degrees become necessary for the purpose of comparability of qualifications across institutions and also to ensure that degrees send out unambiguous signals in job markets. In many countries an independent body of experts discharges this important role. Countries like Australia, New Zealand and South Africa have independent National Qualifications Authorities (NQAs) that lay down a National Qualification Framework (NQF). Various academic titles with their duration, content and learning outcomes are specified under the NQF by the NQA.

In India, the process of specification of degrees had been taken very lightly. There is a highly centralised and cumbersome process that has become redundant with the passage of time. The fact that between 1975 and 1999, no new degree titles were specified reflects the lackadaisical approach. Many premier universities find this requirement a blow to their autonomy and continue to award degrees on their own beyond the degrees specified by the UGC.[5] The whole process has been recently reviewed by the UGC, yet the process continues to be cumbersome and centralised—not all universities are willing to oblige the UGC by adhering to it.

An overall review of the scope of UGC rules and regulations and the way they are implemented shows that there is a similar lackadaisical approach. Revisions in these rules and regulations have been infrequent. They either do not reach all stakeholders or are wilfully ignored by them. For instance, the private universities in the state of Chhattisgarh continued for more than year in total defiance of the UGC (Establishment and Maintenance of Standards in Private Universities) Regulations, 2003 before the Supreme Court struck them down in 2005.

The growth of self-financing courses in the public universities has created a divide between the departments in the universities. Those departments that have potential to run self-affiliating courses are better endowed. The quality of such courses is usually questionable. In most cases, these courses were started without adequate facilities and qualified faculty. Since regular appointments cannot be made for running the self-financing courses, such courses are managed through guest faculty from both within the university and outside. Concerned with the quality and the distortion that the trend created in the public universities, the UGC issued regulations for the self-financing courses in 2002. The impact of these regulations is not visible so far.

In sum, the mechanism for determining and coordinating standards are weak in design and poor in implementation. These suffer from the problems of gaps and overlaps. The analysis of funding of higher education in Chapter 4 has shown that with the expansion of higher education, the UGC's role as a primary funding agency for higher education has become marginalised. Therefore, the UGC now neither has the statutory power to direct the universities to do what in its judgement should be done, nor the financial clout to oblige the universities to fall in line with its directives. Added to this is the fact that with the passage of time, higher education has expanded beyond the university sector, leaving an increasingly large portion of higher education outside its jurisdiction.

Regulatory Framework

Closely linked to the norms on academic standards are norms on infrastructure and facilities. These are particularly rigid for professional programmes. Compliance is usually assured through inspections. The results, however, are not satisfactory. For general courses, the norms on infrastructure and facilities are often not laid down at all. These programmes, thus, are run in conditions of sub-optimal infrastructure and facilities.

In some fields of study, there is an overlap between academic standards and professional standards, and one often sees conflicts between different agencies. Box 7.2 lists some of the regulations of the four professional councils to show that there are many overlaps in their functioning. Recently, there was a dispute between UGC and AICTE over their jurisdiction on maintaining standards and obtaining prior approval in respect of technical courses offered in the deemed-to-be universities.

There are several institutions that run programmes that are not approved by the professional council concerned. In March 2007, AICTE identified 273 institutions that were running professional programmes in management, engineering, hospitality and fashion technology. Of them, 104 were running such programmes with foreign collaboration, and the others had no AICTE approval at all (*The Business Standard*, 2007). In response to a notice issued by the AICTE, only 32 institutes have applied for AICTE approval. The rest have not bothered to do so. The AICTE is now approaching the state governments to shut down these institutions. While the AICTE cannot be faulted in principle, yet many people believe that the consequence of such an approach would dampen the growth of professional education. It will kill diversity and innovation. They also argue that there are many AICTE approved institutions that offer a dubious quality of education. This shows that *de facto* AICTE approval is unnecessary.

The country's experience with regulatory bodies has so far been mixed. While these bodies were given very broad mandates, they were usually inadequately empowered and poorly resourced to fulfil their obligations. There have been complaints of nepotism and corruption from almost all of them. In the face of serious allegations of corruption in the NCTE, which was set up in 1995 for planned and coordinated

**BOX 7.2   Statutory bodies and list of their regulations in India
(illustrative list only)**

AICTE

(a) Regulations for approval process

(b) Regulations for admission and fee structure

    — Admission regulations, 1992

    — Admission and fee structure Regulations, 1994

    — Resolution of Govt. of India for Fee Structure, 1997

    — Regulations for NRI/Foreign Nationals/Persons of India origin

(c) Guidelines for constitution of governing bodies of self-financing institutions

(d) AICTE Regulations, 2004 on admission under supernumerary quota for foreign nationals and persons of Indian origin

(e) AICTE Amendment Regulations, 2003

(f) Reservation under Persons with Disabilities

(g) Regulations for Entry and Operation of Foreign Universities/Institutions

(h) Interim Policy Regulation consequent to Supreme Court Judgement

(i) Guidelines for Engineering Admissions

(j) Guidelines for Common Entrance Test(s) for Admission to MBA/

(k) PGDBM Guidelines for MCA Admissions, 2004–05

MCI

(a) Graduate Medical Education Regulations, 1997 (Summary)

(b) Post-Graduate Medical Education Regulations, 2000 (Summary)

(c) Teachers Eligibility Qualifications, 1998 (Summary)

(d) Code of Medical Ethics Regulations, 2002

(e) MCI Regulations, 2000

(f) Eligibility Certificate Regulations, 2002

(g) Screening Test Regulations, 2002

DCI

(a) B.D.S. Course Regulations

(b) M.D.S. Course Regulations, 1983

(c) Rules and Regulations, Curriculum and Syllabus etc. for a one year Post-graduate Diploma Course in eight specialties of Dentistry

(d) Dental hygienists mechanics regulations

CoA

(a) The Architects Act, 1972

(b) Minimum Standards of Architectural Education Regulations, 1983

(c) Council of Architecture Rules, 1973

(d) Council of Architecture Regulations, 1982

Source Compiled by the author from various sources.

development of teacher education and to regulate and maintain standards in teacher education in the country, the central government has recently decided to wind it up and decentralise its functioning, with the universities themselves responsible for teacher education, thereby restoring *status quo ante*.

Reacting to this, the eminent educationist, Tapas Mazumdar noted that though the objectives of NCTE were laudable, but its canvas was vast and it overlapped with the mandate of the UGC and the universities (Mazumdar, 2007). Despite its broad mandate, the NCTE had been provided with unbelievably meagre physical and human resources. This could not hope to play the role of a regulator for teacher education in the country. He noted that the NCTE had to be abolished for these reasons, then several other regulatory bodies need to be abolished for the same reason. Overall, the country's experience with regulation of higher education has been a case of taking one step forward and two steps backward.

The regulatory structure that came up in bits and pieces over the years has resulted in fragmentation of the higher education system in the country. To ensure coordination between them, the idea of a national council for higher education was mooted in the National Policy on Education, 1986. But for some reasons, it has not materialised so far. On perusal of the structure and functions of the proposed National Council, it becomes clear that such a body, when constituted, may create further complications.

The government, through the Ministry of Human Resources Development, has again revived the proposal. It now plans to set up the National Commission on Higher Education (NCHE) through an Act of Parliament. The government wants the Commission to be an overarching organisation to advise the government on policy matters, coordinate the activities of the different regulatory bodies, encourage interface between them and allocate resources as per national needs and manpower planning. This has met with stiff resistance from the Ministry of Health that controls medical education, and the Ministry of Agriculture that looks after agriculture education (*The Times of India*, 29 August 2007). The response of UGC and other regulatory bodies to this idea has also been lukewarm. Many observers find this commission as adding another unnecessary bureaucratic layer in the already heavily regulated higher education sector.

The NKC on its part has recommended an independent regulatory authority (Independent Regulatory Authority for Higher Education—IRAHE) to cut red tape and achieve independence of regulatory functions, as in the other sectors of economy (*The Indian Express*, 24 July 2007). While the intent to coordinate, cut red tape and achieve independence of regulatory functions are all desirable, the real impact of such a body would depend on the way such a body actually functions.

Affiliated Colleges

As seen in the previous discussions, the Indian higher education system largely resides in the affiliated colleges. The affiliating system is based on the practice of affiliation started in the London University (established in 1836). While neither London University nor any other long established universities such as Oxford and Cambridge had colleges other than their constituent colleges on the same campus affiliated to them, the affiliated colleges in India are geographically dispersed throughout the states or regions over several hundred square kilometres. Normally an affiliating university has a defined geographical service area and all colleges located in the area are expected to be affiliated to that university.

Most traditional universities in India are teaching-cum-affiliating universities. They have a central campus housing departments or schools of study that offer instruction at the post-graduate level and undertake research. A large number of colleges that offer undergraduate education are affiliated to them. A major task of such universities is to determine and oversee the academic standards of these affiliated colleges and conduct centralised examinations for the candidates enrolled in them. The curriculum is prescribed by the university and examinations are also conducted by them. These affiliated colleges are dispersed geographically, but are under the jurisdiction of a university as determined by law (Jayaram, 2006). The concept of jurisdiction by assigning a geographical service area within which they are entitled to affiliate colleges limits competition and creates a monopolistic situation for the affiliating university.

Regulatory Framework

Over 18,000 colleges that existed in India in 2006 were affiliated to around 120 universities. The colleges affilitated to a university have common syllabi and the students appear for a common examination usually conducted by the university at the end of the year. For many universities the conduct of examinations has become their most important function. Some universities have more than 400 colleges affiliated to them, rendering them as merely examining bodies.[6]

Many of the ills of Indian higher education are often attributed to the system of affiliation. The affiliating system was devised to regulate and standardise the quality of education. But with a huge increase in the number of institutions, the system has been serenely riding piggyback on the reputation of the mother institution. In the affiliating system, the weak colleges tend to determine the policy of the university with regard to the course of study, teaching requirements, examinations, etc. Good colleges that are capable of rising to a much higher standard con-sequently have no incentive to do so and in some cases are not even allowed. Most people consider that the affiliating system in India is a drag on the better intuitions that could otherwise innovate and excel.

In order to allow the growth of colleges that had the desire to innovate and excel, the concept of autonomous colleges was introduced a decade back. It allows the college to have autonomy with regard to academic matters. However, not many institutions have sought the autonomous status. By early 2006, there were only 214 autonomous colleges spread over 47 universities in 13 states (MHRD, 2006). Many educationists feel that the programme of granting autonomy to the colleges needs to be vigorously pursued, even to the extent of making every college autonomous and responsible for itself. Teachers, particularly the teachers' associations, look upon this innovation with suspicion and often oppose it.

In the process of affiliation, initially, temporary affiliation is granted on the condition that this would be permanently affiliated on meeting certain minimum standards in terms of infrastructure and facilities. It is estimated that 60 per cent of all colleges continue with temporary affiliation even after decades, for want of minimum infrastructure and facilities. Such colleges are not eligible for recognition by the UGC under

Section 2(f) of the UGC Act. This leaves us with a very unusual situation. Though degrees for study in these colleges is awarded by the affiliating university and is recognised (because these universities themselves are recognised), these colleges are not recognised by the UGC. More than two-thirds of all colleges in the country are not recognised by the UGC (UGC, 2005). This defeats the whole process of recognition by the UGC.

Regulating Private Higher Education

While examining the explosive growth of private higher education in Chapter 4, it was noted that there are several charges—pursuit of profit, deception, low quality, inequitable access, against the private sector. There are tendencies in the private institutions to be exploitive, and thus regulation is the central policy issue for the private higher education sector. It is realised that the private sector in higher education is inevitable and is destined to grow, yet the nature of private participation is poorly and ambiguously spelled out. Pseudo-educational ventures have come to dominate Indian higher education. Whereas legitimate return on private investment is justifiable, the greed of private providers that results in exploitation of gullible masses needs to be checked.

There are obvious concerns about private institutions indulging in malpractices. Most of these malpractices, such as not giving valid receipts for fees collected, taking signatures from teachers for fictitious salary payments, collecting donations through dummy foundations, and so on, are in fact criminal offences. These require no special laws and can be handled under the existing criminal laws. A system of proactive disclosure of essential information about the institutions needs to be introduced. This should be applicable to all universities and colleges whether these are public, private or private for-profit institutions. A guide on advertising, promotion and marketing stating as to what constitutes misrepresentation or misinformation would help consumer courts to curb deceptive practices.

There is a general feeling that private higher education in India is highly controlled and the burdensome regulations encourage corrupt practices. A strong case for deregulating this sector is often made in the popular media. Experience has however shown that private providers have done little to build public trust in them. The fact they are not organised could be the reason. The Education Promotion Society of India (EPSI) floated by PHD Chamber of Commerce and Industry (PHDCCI) and FICCI-HEN (Higher Education Network) organised by the Federation of Indian Chambers of Commerce and Industry (FICCI) raise hopes for organising private higher education providers to create public trust in them. Private higher education would flourish and gain respectability only if the providers could organise themselves around ethical practices and earn the trust of the general public. This has the potential to make government regulation irrelevant over time.

Despite the common belief that private providers prefer to operate in an unregulated market, a recent survey by the FICCI about perceptions of higher education in India suggest that these providers prefer predictability and transparency in regulation to no regulation.[7] There is a case for making regulatory regime less burdensome, but it is more important to ensure that it does not change with the change in the government and is uniformly applied to all. Experience in other countries has shown that absence of regulation is not a precondition for growth of private higher education. In terms of regulation of private higher education, the example of South Korea is worth noting (as seen in Box 7.3). Korea has one of the highest GERs in higher education in the world with more than 80 per cent of it being in the private sector. With the higher education system dominated by private sector, Korea faced difficulties in maintaining quality and integrity of higher education, so the Korean government tightly regulated higher education. It was only in 1995 that Korea moved towards liberating the private higher education sector to make it more competitive. This two-step process towards liberalisation might be a reasonable approach for India as well.

In all, it is seen that private higher education in the country has grown in an uncertain environment. Lack of clarity and an absence of consensus have marked its growth. Due to inadequacies in the legislative framework for private initiative, it could not grow in an organised manner. Regulatory bodies have an ad hoc and sometimes negative approach. They have acted as controllers, rather than facilitators of private investment. Policy prescriptions have been symptomatic and

BOX 7.3   Regulating private higher education in Korea

Private higher education in Korea grew in an environment marked with very tight regulations. Until 1995, Korea not only had strict guidelines regarding how to establish and operate a higher education institution, it also controlled the number of students in each department for each school, as well as student selection methods. In most cases, student quotas and school licenses were rationed to those institutions that could demonstrate to the government their capabilities of providing quality education. Naturally, the strict regulations created substantial rent-seeking activities, while leaving little room for individual educational initiatives among institutions. Recognising various problems from heavy regulation, in 1995 the government started to loosen controls. Among other things, private universities were allowed to regulate the number of incoming students as well as the distribution of students within the institution. The rules to establish a new institution were liberalised. The government also gave small incentive grants to reward performance. In short, the government introduced competition among universities and colleges by making them more autonomous and more competitive.

Source Kim, 2005.

brought about reactive changes by treating the issues in isolation rather than taking a holistic approach. As a result, regulation has come in bits and pieces, largely through judicial interventions rather than proactive state policy.

The ambivalent status of these private institutions permitted to operate under the cloak of 'charitable' institutions is the problem. In order to claim the status of charitable enterprises, they should explicitly demonstrate the educational commitment and social responsibility and should be willing to allow prescribed social and academic audit. The suggestion of the Supreme Court in *Unnikrishnan J.P. Vs State of Andhra Pradesh* case, that only public trusts or societies should be allowed to run private professional institutions should be extended to all categories of private institutions. This would help to overcome most of the malpractices (Anandakrishnan, 2006).

An obvious corollary to the above would be to declare all educational institutions managed as private trusts or by private individuals or by families as profit-making commercial entities. They could be free to admit whomever they want, for whatever programme they offer and charge the fees they prescribe but should abide by the regulations applicable to commercial establishments including payment of taxes. They could get their programmes accredited by designated educational accreditation agencies, so that their diplomas and degrees are recognised for further education and employment. This would help in making a clear distinction between for-profits and non-profits. Non-profits by definition can only use money left over after deducting expenses to develop the institution and continue its charitable or other non-profit objectives, while for-profit institutions can essentially do whatever they want with it, including offering rewards to the owners.

The above arrangement would be similar to the practice followed in several other countries, where both the not-for-profit and the for-profit private providers co-exist with public providers in higher education. A key difference between non-profit and for-profit is that only the latter pay full taxes. Considering the fact that many of the legally non-profit institutions are functionally for-profit, countries like Brazil and Peru allowed for-profit higher education in 1990s. For-profit institutions of higher education exist in countries around the world.

In the United States, there are nearly 2,400 private not-for-profit institutions that enrol about one–third of all students, and the same number of private for-profit institutions. For-profit institutions are usually small in size and are non-degree granting, though there are some like the University of Phoenix that are big and grant degrees. Some of the private for-profit institutions also volunteer themselves for accreditation. Two-thirds of Brazil's private institutions are for-profit now. In Malaysia, 90 per cent of the private higher education is reportedly for-profit. In South Africa, the bulk of private higher education is legally for-profit and in Philippines 47 per cent enrolment is in for-profit institutions (Kinser and Levy, 2006). There are, however, some countries like Poland, Russia, Portugal, Tanzania and Uruguay that do not permit for-profit private institutions. In India, though for-profit institutions of higher education in the formal sector are not allowed, most of the private institutions today are *de facto* for-profit institutions. In addition, the main players in the computer-training sector are for-profit franchise operations.

The emergence of for-profit private higher education is a worldwide phenomenon. The bulk of the private higher education growth in different countries during the private boom of recent decades has been in secular institutions that absorb the demand that the public sector could not or would not accommodate. Most private institutions are commercially oriented (though they may claim to be otherwise), and prepare graduates for job markets. Neither prior nor contemporary history has brought many non-US examples of academically-prestigious secular private higher education (Levy, 2006). In India, for over two decades now, private higher education has been the main venue for increasing access to higher education. Like many other countries such as Malaysia (even China), private growth in India has just been allowed to happen rather than taking measures to enable, promote or even steer the private growth.

Private higher education institutions are usually more tightly regulated, particularly in terms of requirement for infrastructure and facilities, admission processes and fees. Regular judicial reviews of decisions on these issues are common. Thus, the policy environment for entry and operation of private institutions is still evolving.

Regulating Fees

Due to its awkward economics, pricing plays a limited role in clearing of demand and supply in higher education. For the fear of market failure, arising primarily from information asymmetry and concern for equity, tuition fees and admission policies are often subject to government intervention. With the exception of the US, in most countries, these are regulated to varying degrees. These are often centralised and determined by the government for all higher education institutions. In some countries, tuition fees are differentiated as per programmes and even location.

Higher education institutions usually enjoy autonomy in matters relating to admissions, though in many countries students are assigned to the universities on the basis of their performance in the national level university entrance tests. Some countries are now moving towards providing greater autonomy to their higher education institutions in matters of deciding on fee and admissions.

The US higher education is a good example of a deregulated system with regard to tuition fee and admission policies. There is a substantial price and quality difference across institutions. Each institution focuses on a particular segment, and competes for students within that segment. The students and their parents have access to reliable information on programmes, quality, tuition fees and future income prospects to make informed choices. The success of the US system is largely attributed to the existence of several reliable information sources, independent nationwide testing services (such as Education Testing Service) that help to objectively determine the merit of prospective students, and a credible quality assurance system.

The deregulated system of fees and admissions in the US has its own problems. Over the years, higher education has become very expensive. Tuitions have risen faster than wages. Students' indebtedness is on the increase. There are serious concerns about the affordability of higher education. The government invests heavily to provide student-based support so that higher education continues to be affordable. The US universities are also able to lure the best and the brightest students from all over the world with fee concessions and attractive scholarships. There is definitely a merit in drawing lessons from the US experience.

In India, tuition fee and admission policies were non-issues when the higher education system was largely publicly funded. Though, there was clamour for increasing tuition fees in public institutions to overcome financial constraints, yet fees continued to be reasonable and admission processes by and large free and fair with institutions enjoying great autonomy in choosing whom to take. With the emergence of private higher education in the 1980s and the continued supply–demand gap, many private providers started charging capitation fees, often ignoring merit. These providers made quick money and inspired a whole generation of edu-entrepreneurs to invest in private professional education. A detailed discussion on the growth of private higher education has been conducted in Chapter 3.

There are two reasons for the government to regulate fees. One, the government would like to ensure that higher education continues to be affordable. Two, pricing alone has little consequence in clearing of demand and supply in higher education. The higher education institutions that are perceived to be prestigious can command high prices. The demand for seats in such institutions is relatively inelastic. Even poor people would pay for a seat in such an institution, even if they have to sell their assets. In the absence of credible information sources about quality of higher education institutions, the perception about prestige can be created by misrepresenting facts and using deceptive practices. Fee regulation, therefore helps in curbing exploitation.

Fee regulation for private institutions is therefore common. The norms are however unclear and the fees vary considerably among the states and within the states for various courses. For instance, an undergraduate course in engineering costs Rs 20,000 (USD 492) per annum in Chhattisgarh but Rs 72,000 (USD 1,770) in Chandigarh. The system of high fees charged for management seats continues unabated. According to one report, capitation fees can range from 200,000 to 800,000 rupees (USD 4,920–19,680) per annum for some of the courses, and are as high as Rs 4 million (USD 98,360) for medical courses (Anandakrishnan, 2006). Some private institutions admit students long before actual start of the academic session. They collect full fees and retain the original certificates. Sometimes, they also advance joining time to pre-empt students from joining institutions of their choice and confiscate the entire fee collected.[8]

There is ambiguity regarding fee regulation with respect to the deemed universities. A survey of fees charged by various deemed universities show wide variations. Private institutions also collect exorbitant and compulsory fees in the name of transport, canteen, library, text books, mark sheets, caution deposits, degree certificates, hall tickets, association fees, etc. and refuse to give valid receipts for such collections. In most cases, fees are collected in advance and are not refundable. Some private institutions capitalise on the anxiety of students and their parents and schedule their admission process to benefit from the non-refundable deposits in the name of blocking the seats. Generally, the state fee committees have not bothered to determine fee norms for management programmes, therefore most private management institutions charge whatever maximum the students and their parents are willing to pay. In addition, the fees in a large number of programmes and training courses that are not approved by any agency is arbitrarily fixed and vary according to paying capacity of the parents.

Regulatory Framework

In sum, the emergence of private higher education has resulted in several aberrations. The competition between them fails to set the prices due to the peculiar nature of education services. They either exhibit monopolistic behaviour or non-collusive oligopolistic behaviour each provider trying to maximise its own profit.[9] Interventions by the courts for over a decade and the government's ambivalence have not helped to check the errant behaviour of scrupulous private providers. As a result even credible private providers are tempted to make money by exploiting loopholes in the existing regulatory environment. The principle of Gresham's Law—bad private providers driving out the good providers—seems to be applicable. Some public institutions have also been tempted to make money by starting self-financing programmes that have high, unmet demand. In absence of credible information sources and objective and transparent processes for determination of inter se merit, providers of higher education (mainly though not exclusively private providers) are bound to indulge in exploitative practices. Apart from tuition and admission related regulations, there have been new challenges arising from the emergence of private providers in the country.

Regulating Admissions

With 37 school boards and nearly 400 universities with varied academic standards, developing a common yardstick to determine inter se merit is not easy. Hence, entrance tests for admissions become inevitable. The issue is only whether these should be held by individual university/college or conducted jointly for an academic programme having similar eligibility criterion. Ideally, each university should be allowed to decide on the criterion for admission and conduct entrance exams if required. Considering the short time for the conduct of such exams and mental and financial burdens due to multiplicity of these exams, common exams are always preferred. Many all-India and state level common exams are now being conducted. However, many universities would like to retain control of these exams. The main reason for retaining control is financial. Both public and private universities generate huge surplus from this activity and would not like to forgo that. Some private universities also manipulate entrance tests and maximise their earnings. A huge coaching industry (according to some estimates with an annual turnover of Rs 100 billion) thrives on this.

There is a need for streamlining the entire process of common entrance tests. The practice of universities and examining bodies making huge sums of money through this mode from harried parents is unethical. There is a need to put in place a system of common entrance exams for professional programmes. These common entrance exams could be held at the all-India level, where admissions are from the all-India body of students and at state levels, where admissions are from the statewide body of students. Admissions through these common exams should be insisted upon unless there is a valid reason for a university not to participate in that for reasons of uniqueness of the programme. On a long-term basis, a National Testing Services (NTS), independent of the school boards, could be set up. Such exam could be conducted several times a year on the pattern of the Scholastic Aptitude Test (SAT) and the Graduate Record Examination (GRE) in the United States.

A majority of privately institutions could be accused of collecting exorbitant capitation fees and other institutional fees, not brought into regular accounts; manipulation of entrance results and admission processes to maximise illicit payments; and disregarding admission norms in favour of those willing to pay more (Anandakrishnan, 2006). Under these circumstances, exempting any private institutions or category of private institutions either on account their minority status (or any other status), or in the name of safeguarding their autonomy could lead to exploitation of students and parents.

The fact that private providers are looking for loopholes to escape the common exam system is evident from the recent experiences. Many deemed universities opted out of the common exam for entrance to undergraduate programmes in engineering as soon as the government gave them this option. Ostensibly, they opted for their own tests to safeguard their academic autonomy; the reality, however, is different. Now they are conducting their own exams; some of them are making huge sums of money though entrance exams. They have unreasonable refund policies that create dilemma for parents. Some of them even manipulate the result of entrance exams conducted by them to maximise illicit payments. A large majority of the applications from 'so called' minority institutions for affiliation to the central universities were received after the provisions of the draft bill on regulation of admission and fee in private unaided professional colleges became known. Both this draft bill and the constitutional amendment exempt the minority institutions from their regulatory cover.

Another issue related to determination of inter se merit is the fragmentation of merit space due to a plethora of reservations. Since there are high stakes in admission to a small number of quality institutions, the issue is highly contentious. Reservation quotas for admissions on the basis of the caste and class are instruments of the affirmative action policy of the government. This issue is discussed in detail in Chapter 2. In addition, there are reservations for sports persons, children of war widows, children and grandchildren of the freedom fighters, and so on. Manipulations in such admissions are fairly common.

Judicial Activism

When private professional colleges came up in large numbers in the 1980s, there was no effective mechanism to control their functioning, nor was there a systematic admission procedure, except in Andhra Pradesh, where all admissions were by merit. In other states, private institutions were able to admit anyone they like up to at least 50 per cent of the seats (AICTE, 1999). They collected large sums of money as donations, which were termed capitation fees.

Over the years, there was a general concern that private professional colleges were charging overly high capitation fees. In response, several state governments enacted laws to regulate admission and prohibit capitation fees in private professional colleges—Andhra Pradesh in 1983, Karnataka in 1984, Maharashtra in 1987 and Tamil Nadu in 1992. The provisions of these laws were challenged in court, initiating an era of judicial interventions, which continues to this day. The issue of fees and admissions routinely comes up before the Supreme Court year after year.

In 1993, the Supreme Court held that the commercialisation of education, including charging of capitation fees was not permissible.[10] However, recognising the inevitability of private self-financing institutions, the Court laid down a framework[11] to regulate admissions based on the principle of merit, with a differential fee structure in which the fees of some deserving students would be subsidised by those paying higher fees.

During the 1980s and 1990s, when most private institutions were colleges affiliated to the state universities under the control of the state governments, most state governments evolved a merit-based admission with differential fee structure in private professional colleges within their respective jurisdictions. Despite initial teething problems, this system was institutionalised over the years and remained in operation until 2002, when the Constitution Bench of Supreme Court determined that this differential fee structure was unreasonable, amounting to compelling one citizen to pay for the education of another.[12] It could, theoretically, result in a situation in which a marginally less meritorious but poor student would be required to subsidise a richer one. The Court therefore declared the 1993 arrangement unconstitutional, but noted at the same time that preventing the private institutions from selecting their students and setting their own fees would be unconstitutional. According to the Court, taking away this freedom would amount to violation of their right to practice any profession, or carry on any occupation, trade or business under Article 19(1) (g) of the Constitution. It decreed that fees could be determined in a manner generating a reasonable surplus for the purpose of institutional development and expansion.

The Supreme Court's decision was interpreted by the private institutions as giving them unbridled power to admit anyone by charging any fee they chose. The judgement had several self-contradictions. There were many practical difficulties in its implementation. The entire system of admission and fee that had evolved over the years started to fall apart. Realising this, another bench of the same court was set up in 2003 to interpret the meaning of autonomy in admission and fees.[13] This Bench endorsed a cost-plus system in private institutions with reasonable fees fixed by a committee in each state, headed by a retired high court judge. It also established the need for common entrance tests for merit-based admissions.

As a result of the 2003 Supreme Court decision, fees had to be determined again in all states. Private institutions were allowed to retain management quota, but while some private providers managed a quota as high as 50 per cent in most cases it was capped at 15 per cent. States like West Bengal, where no management quota existed, are now planning a 5 per cent management quota. Students admitted in the management quota are ostensibly admitted on merit basis, but merit in such cases can be determined through common admission tests conducted by the association of private institutions and are thus susceptible to abuse. Though private institutions are not allowed to charge higher fees from students admitted under management quota, capitation fees seem to be part of the common unofficial practice.

Whilst the government and the private institutions were addressing the challenges posed by the Supreme Court judgement of 2002 and 2003, the Court intervened again in 2005, this time on the sensitive issue of caste-based reservation quotas in private unaided institutions.[14] A detailed discussion on this issue is in the next section.

Tracing the evolution of policy on tuition fees and admissions, it seems that it has been driven more by judicial interventions than by a proactive public policy. These have been the two most contentious issues in higher education, with judicial interventions sometimes contradicting each other and reversing the progress. Judicial decisions seek to serve the poor, yet these often end up serving private interests. Nevertheless, a broad direction for policy on tuition fees and admissions has emerged over the years. It is now established that admissions in higher education should be on the basis of merit, to be determined by entrance exams if required. The fact that tuition fees could be fixed on a cost-plus basis with some surplus for reinvestment is now accepted. The issue is essentially one of implementation.

Regulating Foreign Providers

Attracted by large and growing Indian market, several foreign providers have started their operations in India. This has been discussed in Chapter 3. The entry and operation of foreign providers has been widely debated in India.' Until recently, foreign institutions could enter the country on 'the automatic route' under the rules framed by the Foreign Investment Promotion Board, which is to say that they did not require any approvals to set up their presence but operated outside the domestic regulatory framework. Since a foreign provider was not registered as a part of the national system, local regulatory framework and accreditation system did not apply. As a consequence, foreign providers (bona fide and rogue) were not required to comply with national regulations—however, degrees awarded by them were not recognised in India.

Despite the above, as noted in Chapter 3, a large number of foreign providers have been operating in the country for more than decade now. Concerns have been raised from time to time about such institutions being fly-by-night operations indulging in dubious practices. The hands-off approach of the government prevented any meaningful assessment of their operations. The absence of an appropriate regulatory framework has been felt for a long time. The proposal to regulate them has been under consideration since 1997, when the central government admitted in the High Court at Madras in Writ Petition No.11416 of 1997 that ambiguity existed in the legal arrangements on the issue.

Earlier, attempts were made to regulate foreign providers and stream-line their operations. In 1999, the AIU formulated guidelines to grant equivalence to degrees offered in India by foreign universities. However, only one university applied for the grant of equivalence. The AICTE issued regulations for entry and operation of foreign universities/insti-tutions imparting technical education in India in 2003. These were revised in 2005. Here again, merely six institutions have got themselves registered with the AICTE. Obviously, these were not acceptable to the foreign providers and regardless of their status of recognition with the AIU or the AICTE; these providers continue to attract students.

The AICTE has now taken steps to proactively identify foreign providers and pursue them to get registered under its regulations. The AICTE has issued advisory to students not to join programmes not approved by it, for that may have serious consequences for them in terms of eligibility for employment, higher studies etc. According to the AICTE, 169 institutions were found conducting courses in the field of technical education without its approval in March 2007. 104 of them were conducting programmes in collaboration with foreign universities.[15]

Regulatory Framework

New Law under Consideration

Now after almost a decade the government has come close to the enactment of a law to regulate foreign providers. As per provisions of the Foreign Educational Institutions (Regulation of Entry and Operation, Maintenance of Quality and Prevention of Commercialisation) Bill currently under consideration, all foreign universities in India would be given deemed university status, and the UGC would therefore play a pivotal role in regulating them.[16] A committee under the UGC would decide if certain prominent universities—Harvard, Stanford and the other Ivy League institutions—could be exempted from some provisions of this law, but most or all would have to follow the domestic rules. Such universities would, however, be required to bring in at least 51 per cent of the capital investment and have to invest surplus only for growth and development of their institution in India.

As per provisions in the bill, foreign institutions desirous of entry need to be legally set up and accredited in the country of their origin. They are required to maintain a corpus fund of not less than Rs 100 million. Their deemed university status could be withdrawn, corpus fund attached and penalty up to Rs 5 million imposed for violation of provisions of the law. There are provisions for maintaining comparability of quality of programmes with those offered by them at home. Cultural and linguistic sensitivities of the people have to be taken into account by them and their content should not adversely affect the sovereignty and dignity of the country. Currently, there are no restrictive clauses relating to admission, fees or quota-based reservation, but the fear of the same in future cannot be ruled out. Under the proposed bill, all domestic laws as applied to local deemed universities shall apply to foreign providers declared as deemed universities.

The proposed bill is broadly based on the recommendations of the C.N.R. Rao Committee set up by the government in 2006. The Committee had categorically said that it would not like to welcome foreign providers with commercial objectives nor those that wish to recruit high-quality students for their post-graduate programmes. Accordingly, foreign providers could not be profit-making enterprises with the right to repatriate surpluses.

Despite a fairly strict regulatory regime envisaged in the bill, the Left Block, which was part of the then ruling coalition, was 'principally opposed to opening the higher education sector to foreign providers'.[17] According to them it does not follow the principles of equity and access promised in the ruling coalition's Common Minimum Programme. They demand 'social control' and fear that foreign providers would hurt the cultural sensitivities and educational ethos in the country. The government is trying to allay their fears saying that the bill follows the government agenda of 'inclusive expansion'. At the time of writing this section, there is considerable uncertainty regarding the fate of the Bill. There is much doubt as to whether it will eventually reach the statute book.

The bill does not cover collaboration, partnership or twinning arrangements between a foreign institution and a recognised university or institution of higher education in India. Since almost all the current delivery of foreign degrees in India takes place through some form of partnership with an Indian (mainly private sector) provider, therefore, impact of the Bill on foreign provision is going to be limited (also see section on foreign providers in Chapter 1). Given that many of the current programmes on offer are in professional areas regulated by the AICTE, therefore requirements of registration with the AICTE would probably be required.

In all, while many people are very enthusiastic about the bill, most academics with a traditional outlook are sceptic. According to experts, the optimism is based on overestimations rather than ground realities, and the strong criticism is based on misunderstandings rather than actual facts (Stella and Gnanam, 2005).

International Experience

While regulation of foreign provision continues to be a tricky affair, there is now a rich and varied international experience. While many countries do not have a regulatory system in place to register or evaluate out of country providers either due to lack of capacity or political will, countries like Hong Kong, Malaysia, South Africa, and Israel assess the quality of imported programmes, and the United Kingdom and Australia assure even the quality of exported provision.

Regulatory Framework

Overall, there are six models of regulatory frameworks for foreign providers, as seen in Table 7.2. While most countries have liberal or are moving towards a liberal regime, a few countries have very restrictive policies for foreign providers and in India, policy is perceived to be getting more restrictive.

TABLE 7.2 National regulatory frameworks—six models

Type of regulations	Countries
No regulations	Austria, Denmark, France, Malta and Russia
Liberal regulations	Netherlands, Peru, UK, Canada and US
Moderately liberal	Singapore, Hong Kong, Israel, Jamaica
Transitional moving from restrictive to more liberal	Japan, South Korea
Transitional moving from liberal to more restrictive	India
Very restrictive	South Africa, UAE, Greece and Belgium

Source Line Verbik and Lisa Jokivirta (2005).

China adopted a gradualist approach in dealing with foreign providers. Gaining experience from a restrictive policy, the Chinese government liberalised its policy in 2003. Now China proactively seeks foreign investment and participation in higher education. Singapore, Malaysia and Dubai have been able to attract reputed institutions from the developed countries to build domestic capacity. These countries are also attracting a large number of international students, many of them from India.

Malaysia has a policy of allowing foreign institutions to set up their operation only by invitation. It has invited only high profile, internationally well-known institutions.[18] Singapore used the foreign partnership route to build domestic capacity and is now on the way to reducing its dependence on foreign higher education. Over the next 10 years, only elite foreign providers focusing on full branch campuses (INSEAD, Chicago, New South Wales) or niche R&D (MIT, Technische Universität München) are likely to remain and the mainstream transnational delivery of higher education may come to an end. The Knowledge Village at Dubai is emerging as a major education and training hub in the Middle East for both regional and international learners.

These countries have adopted innovative regulatory practices to balance between liberal policies towards foreign providers on the one hand and safeguarding student interest from the unscrupulous practices on the other. Hong Kong has adopted a two-tier approach, as seen in Box 7.4. While there is a compulsory registration norm, accreditation is voluntary. The regulation through registration is based on the concept of comparability, which is not over-restrictive and does not dampen the market; while the voluntary accreditation sets higher and more restrictive standards.

Analysis

Many aspects need consideration to design an effective regulatory regime for foreign provision. It requires defining the type and nature of foreign providers, decision on the scope of regulation, proper choice of organisation for regulatory role, criteria for approval/registration, choosing whether it should a mandatory or a voluntary system and finally, if the system is to be enacted by legislation or administrative

---

BOX 7.4   Regulating foreign higher education in Hong Kong

The Non-Local Higher and Professional Education (Regulation) Ordinance (that is legally enforceable) requires that programmes offered by an overseas/non-local institution should be of comparable standard and quality as courses offered in the home country. The concept of comparability focuses on the totality of the learning experience. It is not expected that the same features and support should exist for the imported provision as for the home programme. The threshold standard of 'comparability' sets a standard which is easily acceptable to the exporting institutions/countries and in theory at least, poses no extra burden upon them.

Voluntary accreditation is outside the legal framework. The standards of accreditation are local academic standards. The accredited programmes have better status and incentives, graduates of such accredited programmes are recognised as having the same status as those from the local institutions when they apply for government jobs, and students are also eligible for low-interest government loans.

Source Wong Wai Sum (2005).

---

measures. While a system backed by legal enactment could be easier to enforce, legal regulation binds the enforcer as much as the bodies that are regulated, and there is less or little discretion that may be necessary in uncertain circumstances.

In the Indian case, the government, by enacting a law to regulate foreign providers, intends to maintain academic standards, safeguard students' interests allowing entry of only reputed institutions, while checking and controlling sub-standard or fly-by-night operators; many people feel that the Bill is deeply flawed, both in the philosophical premises that underlie it and in the specific institutional measures it proposes. It is felt that in a situation when the country needs greater investment in higher education from all possible sources, government and private, domestic and foreign, regulatory barriers to entry would not augur well with attracting investment.

There is even greater concern about the institutional weaknesses in the regulatory system that might drive away reputed universities and allow entry only to sub-standard providers who are able to manipulate the system. Government failure in regulating private providers in the country is evident. It is felt that rogue private institutions are a far bigger menace than a handful of foreign providers.

In view of the above, it is felt by many that while, the other countries are wooing and facilitating foreign universities, India's restrictive policies might drive them away. Unless India takes proactive measures, foreign investment in higher education may remain a pipedream. The country would be deprived of the some good foreign providers that could supplement domestic supply and add diversity to higher education provision in the country.

A pragmatic approach would be to proactively identify reputed universities, invite and facilitate them to set up their campuses in India. Recently, the Andhra Pradesh government invited the Georgia Institute of Technology to set up its branch campus near Hyderabad. Similarly, prestigious universities based on some objective criterion, like ranking by the SJTU, China, or the THES, London, could be invited to set up facilities in India. Subjecting it to the rigid regulatory policies would not serve the national policy of increasing investment, and thereby capacity, of the higher education system in India.

The Way Forward

While there is a genuine concern that the quality of education provided by the foreign providers is highly variable, sometimes indifferent, there is also the realisation that foreign providers could energise local institutions through both example and competition. The possible negative impacts of foreign provision on under-funded and inefficient domestic higher education institutions operating within a weak regulatory system could be addressed by reforming the domestic provision and not by erecting protectionist barriers.

Finally, it needs to be noted that some of the indecision surrounding the future of foreign institutions seem to emanate from the continuing polarised views over the role of private sector in higher education per se. Until these are resolved it is unlikely that the foreign providers would have a predictable policy environment. It needs to be realised that private or foreign institutions would be interested in investing in higher education in India only if they are assured of adequate returns on their investment. Assuming altruistic motives would be just naiveté.

GATS and Higher Education

The entry and operation of foreign providers has also been subject matter of debate in the context of ongoing negotiations under the General Agreement on Trade in Services (GATS). While cross-border activities in higher education have been there for a long time, these are described in terms of commercial trade only recently. Under the GATS, education is one of the 12 service sectors identified to be liberalised. Within the education services there are five sub-sectors: primary, secondary, higher, adult and others under education services. Since most of the cross-border activity takes place in higher education, the focus of liberalisation to promote further trade is on higher education. Like other services, trade in higher education services could occur in any of the four modes, namely—Mode 1: cross-border supply (programme mobility); Mode 2: consumption abroad (student mobility); Mode 3: Commercial or physical presence (institution mobility); and Mode 4: Delivery abroad (academic mobility).

Barriers

Under the GATS, it is presumed that there are barriers that prevent trade. These barriers could be either tariff or non-tariff barriers. In the services sectors, there are mostly non-tariff barriers. These could be in the form of immigration requirements, foreign currency controls, or non-recognition of degrees obtained abroad into national equivalent. Mutual recognition of qualifications is important not only in educational services, but also in professional services. Thus, clauses relating to mutual recognition of qualifications often find mention in many multilateral, regional and bilateral agreements. However, giving effect to such mutual recognition agreements is not easy. The diversity of academic structures and variety of academic institutions, their recognition, accreditation and approval processes make the process very complicated (WTO, 1998).

It is seen that trading conditions in modes 1, 2 and 4 are not seriously impaired or restrained by governmental measures in higher education. There are, however, many restrictions on trade in mode 3. These include the inability to obtain national licenses (that is, to be recognised as a degree or certificate granting educational institution), measures limiting direct investment by foreign education providers (that is, equity ceilings), nationality requirements, needs tests, restrictions on recruiting foreign teachers, and the existence of government monopolies and high subsidisation of local institutions. Thus, liberalisation of higher education under the GATS negotiations is focused on mode 3 (Agarwal, 2006c).

Negotiations

The negotiations under the Doha Development Round are stuck at a low key, and their progress in respect of services, particularly higher education services is even slower. While final offers and counter offers on services round have been invited in June 2008, little is expected. There is a lack of consensus and many misgivings on liberalisation under the GATS framework. For instance, there is a perception that the commitments under GATS would put an end to the public subsidies, with adverse consequences for the quality and affordability of higher education. It is therefore not surprising that there are few commitments made during the Uruguay Round in higher education. In the current round, there have been several and counter offers. India has offered to undertake commitments in August 2005. As seen in Table 7.3, this offer does not mean much.

TABLE 7.3 India's offer—key elements and comments

Key elements	Comments
• Under mode 1 in market access, condition that service providers would be subject to regulations, as applicable to domestic providers in the country of origin.	• For commercial presence, fee caps discourage foreign investors.
• No foreign equity cap for commercial presence but it is subject to condition that fees to be charged can be fixed by an appropriate authority and that such fees do not lead to charging capitation fees or to profiteering. Subject further to such regulations, already in place or to be prescribed by the appropriate authority. In the case of foreign investors having prior collaboration in that specific service sector in India, FIPB approval would be required.	• Motive for need for FIPB approval for foreign investor having prior collaboration in this sector is not understood. • No mention of education services under mode 4 horizontal commitments, thus inward academic mobility not allowed, but opportunity to get foreign nationals to overcome faculty shortages.

Source WTO Document No. TN/S/O/IND/Rev.1 dated 24 August 2005.

Several of these concerns are misplaced. The role and scope of liberalisation under the GATS framework recognises the right of the national governments to regulate and if necessary introduce new rules to meet national policy objectives. Liberalisation is a means of promoting growth and development by enhancing competition and not doing away with regulation. In higher education like in most other services sectors, most countries in their own national interests have gone for autonomous liberalsation. The GATS negotiations merely bind this liberalisation with a view to bring predictability in policy regime. In addition, foreign provision is also opposed on the grounds of hurting the cultural and educational ethos in the country (Agarwal, 2008a).

Critics of GATS claim that steering capacity of a nation-state in higher education would be weakened due to GATS. In-depth case studies, however, suggest it is still the nation-state, either by its domestic policies or partly by its participation in international agreements (such as GATS) or supranational structures (such as the EU), which ultimately decides how the national higher education systems will function. The choice to deregulate and liberalise the higher education market is a deliberate choice of a national government, which by doing so may intentionally reduce its steering capacity. It is the nation-state as the most important player that constitutes and shapes its steering capacity. It needs to be understood that liberalisation is not deregulation but often requires more regulation.

Despite these misgivings, there is a growth of cross-border activities in higher education. Apart from student mobility, there will be a wide range of exchange agreements, distance education programmes, research collaborations and offshore partnerships. This is happening despite several impediments. These include: the lack of recognition of academic qualifications or concerns over the quality of educational providers and the risk of seeing 'degree mills' sprouting in a liberalised environment. It is however not clear if the GATS could offer the most appropriate setting to tackle these issues or the bilateral, regional or multilateral arrangements would be more useful.

There has been a remarkable pace of change in the higher education in recent years. Much of this change has occurred completely outside a trade policy framework. Many issues related to the possible impact of commercial providers are the same, whether they are national or foreign providers, in terms of impact on the public system and how they are regulated. Rightly regulating the domestic private sector is thus important. It would be a mistake to expect that GATS negotiations would either stop or accelerate this trend. Thus, the GATS negotiations are unlikely to be the driving force behind the continued growth of foreign provision of higher education. Yet, as the GATS negotiations gain momentum, the greater transparency and policy predictability in higher education would help in achieving a higher level of bound liberalisation commitments under the GATS that would be beneficial to all the stakeholders in higher education.

Evaluating Regulatory Effectiveness

In his letter dated 29 November 2006 to the Prime Minister, the NKC Chairman's observations about regulation in Indian higher education are:

> The present regulatory system in higher education is flawed in some important respects. The barriers to entry are too high. The system of authorising entry is cumbersome. There is a multiplicity of regulatory agencies where mandates are both confusing and overlapping. The system, as a whole, is over-regulated but under-governed. NKC (2006)

On a detailed review of the existing laws regulating higher education in India, Kapur and Mehta (2004) concluded that the 'regulation (in India) promotes adverse selection and deters genuine investment, while encouraging those who are adept at manipulating the *license quota raj* in the system.'

In a recent survey of the degree of regulatory control of the major higher education systems in the world, *The Economist* noted that whereas most nations in the world including China are working towards loosening of statutory control over their higher education systems, India is moving in reverse direction and tightening government control on institutions of higher education (*The Economist*, 2005b). A dual control over state universities and colleges dilutes their accountability. While the UGC and professional bodies are expected to regulate higher education, the state governments exercise effective control over them. The institutions are subjected to a multi-layered regulatory and control process involving a number of agencies and bodies. According to Pinto (1984), despite such elaborate arrangements, India higher education has virtually remained an 'unbridled horse'.

The regulations often control supply, limiting choice by erecting formidable entry barriers for new institutions to be set up through private enterprise. Time consuming, non-transparent and complex procedures applied arbitrarily create conducive environment for corrupt practices and patronage. It makes higher education institutions less accountable. There is a widespread feeling that the regulatory bodies have miserably failed to discharge their responsibility towards maintenance of standards.

Regulatory Framework

The NKC, in its note on higher education, points out:

> There are several instances where an engineering college or a business school is approved, promptly, in a small house of a metropolitan suburb without the requisite teachers, infrastructure or facilities, but established universities experience difficulties in obtaining similar approvals. Such examples can be multiplied. These would only confirm that the complexity, the multiplicity and the rigidity of the existing regulatory structure is not conducive to the expansion of higher education opportunities in India. (NKC, 2006)

Thus, it is not surprising that several better known institutions such as the IITs, the IIMs, the NIFTs, the National Institute of Design (NID), the Tata Institute of Social Sciences (TISS) and BITS, Pilani are all outside the conventional university system. The IIMs, the NIFT and the NID do not even have degree-granting powers and offer only diplomas.

The failure of regulatory arrangements raises serious concerns about the credibility of the Indian higher education system. The loss of this credibility could have serious repercussions. The country's competitive advantage as a nation with a huge reserve of highly qualified and trained manpower may be lost. Many countries are shying away in signing mutual recognition agreements with India due to adverse media reports about deteriorating academic standards here. This will become even more difficult in the years to come if we allow any further compromise on the standards of higher education in the country. There is a need to safeguard its integrity and enhance its credibility.

Our review of the organisational structure of regulation and regulatory arrangements in this chapter clearly showed the flawed design and weak practices in regulation of higher education in India. The multi-layered system works towards standardisation in higher education and not for maintenance of standards. All nations require a diversity of institutions: some that educate the bright and others that cater to the not so bright, and all combinations in between; some that are experimental in their pedagogy and others that are traditional. The terms 'uniformity', 'homogenisation' and the like are often used by policy makers, regulators and even the judiciary erroneously.

In a judgement in February 2005, the Supreme Court has defined the power of 'determination and coordination of standards' conferred upon the UGC under Item 66, List 1 as follows:

> The expression 'coordination' used in Entry 66 does not merely mean evaluation. It means harmonisation with a view to form a uniform pattern for a concerted action according to a certain design, scheme or plan of development. It therefore includes action not only for the removal of disparities of standards, but also for the occurrence of such disparities.[19]

Perhaps under a similar confusion, the UGC recently made an aborted attempt to introduce uniform curriculum in all universities in the country. Higher education is fundamentally about distinction. The general goal should be that average quality of education improves. Higher education systems around the world work towards enhancing institutional diversity. Unfortunately, role of regulation in India is straitjacketed best described as one size fits all, inhibiting innovation. It is burdensome and counter-productive. These are often too detailed and diminish the responsiveness of the institutions and do not take into account new developments particularly as they relate to new providers and new forms of delivery in higher education.

Being blamed for all its ills, it is often argued that de-regulation of higher education would serve the public interest best. This argument is based on the simple principle of economics that if the market regulates institutions more efficiently and effectively than the state, then the task of regulation should be left to the market; facilitating oversupply would be the best way to subject institutions to the regulations of the market. However, the manner in which clearing of demand and supply takes place in higher education suggests that leaving higher education to market forces may not be the most viable option. While in the long run, competition could drive the dubious institutions out of the market, short-term consequences could be disastrous.

The academic community would normally object to regulation, especially as it relates to academic quality. But it needs to be understood that due to its very nature, academic standards need to be determined and coordinated across universities requiring some kind of external scrutiny.

This makes regulation important; though equally important is the nature of regulation, the question of who is responsible for the development of regulations and who will implement these regulations.

New Regulatory Environment

As noted by the NKC, a meaningful reform of the higher education system, with a long-term perspective is both complex and difficult. Yet, it is imperative and necessary to overhaul the entire regulatory structure governing higher education. An ideal regulatory system should be based on addressing the minimum set of regulatory concerns. These concerns could be those arising from possibility of market failure or need for market coordination or to address issues of public health and public safety. The system should ensure fair play, transparency and accountability. It should be non-intrusive and student friendly. The new regulatory environment needs to provide adequate space for innovation and experimentation and facilitate growth of the private sector.

The problem of information asymmetries in higher education can lead to wrong and costly decisions by students as well as employers. Such information gaps, related purely to financial matters such as fee levels, refund policy, and so on, can be effectively bridged by enforcing transparency similar to the disclosure norms of listed companies. Information gaps related to academic quality are more difficult to bridge. There is difficulty in measuring the quality of student learning and achievement. The purpose for which people pursue higher education is not clear. This makes matters worse. Since higher education is expected to meet the diverse needs of a huge and varied section of people, therefore, defining national or regional standards for higher education is not desirable at all.

Under the circumstances, instead of a traditional form of regulations, it would be appropriate to promote creation of membership-based self-regulatory bodies that could achieve public goals in a more flexible manner. Self-regulatory bodies being autonomous and independent in their functioning would be able regulate its members more effectively and without undue interference. Drawing on case studies in different areas, Coglianese and Lazer (2003) have shown that self-regulation can be an effective strategy when the regulated entities are heterogeneous and regulatory outputs are relatively difficult to monitor.

The Tenth Five Year Plan document suggested a regulatory arrangement broadly on the above lines. According to Para 3.64 of the approach paper of the Plan:

> Laws, rules and procedures for private, cooperative and NPO (not-for-profit organizations) supply of education must be modernized and simplified so that honest and sincere individuals and organizations can set up universities, colleges and schools. Oppressive controls on fees, teacher salaries, and infrastructure and staff strength must be eliminated. The regulatory system must be modernized based on economics of information and global best practices. Given the weak criminal justice system in our country, the regulatory system must also put greatest emphasis on fraud detection and punishment while letting normal individuals to function normally. (Planning Commission, 1999)

Recently, the NKC has recommended the setting up of the IRAHE at an arm's length from the government, and independent of all stakeholders including the concerned ministries of the government. The NKC has cited four reasons: the need for independence, more appropriate forms of intervention, rationalisation of confusing and overlapping mandates and the need for single window clearance to justify it. According to the NKC, regulators perform five functions (see Table 7.4) in higher education. The NKC (2006) points out that 'India is perhaps the only country in the world where regulation in four of the five functions is carried out by one entity, that is, the UGC. The purpose of creating an IRAHE is to separate these functions.'

According to the NKC, this body would be authorised to accord degree-granting powers to institutions, license accreditation agencies and shall be responsible for monitoring standards and settling disputes. Same norms shall apply to public and private institutions as well as domestic and international institutions. The NKC has suggested that the role of the UGC could be redefined to focus on the disbursement of grants to, and maintenance of, public institutions in higher education. The entry regulatory functions of the AICTE, the MCI and the BCI could be performed by the IRAHE, so that their role would be limited to that of professional associations.

Regulatory Framework

The NKC further states that the issues of access could be governed by state legislation on reservations and other forms of affirmative action. Professional associations could continue to set requirements to determine eligibility for conducting a profession. All other regulatory agencies such as the AICTE need to be abolished while the MCI and the BCI will be limited to their role as professional associations. These professional associations could conduct nationwide examinations to provide licences for those wishing to enter the profession. These are all useful suggestions and require careful consideration. The point about conflict of interest when the UGC discharges both its functions of regulation and funding is valid and these have to be unbundled. But retaining the UGC to disburse grants to public institutions may not be necessary either. As seen in Chapter 4, the UGC's role in overall funding of higher education is small. Even at the national level, more funds for higher education are disbursed by the ministries directly than by the UGC. Thus, if the UGC is to be continued, its role, structure and relationship with the government need to be reviewed, as discussed in Chapter 4.

Further, according to my understanding, as the continuation of the UGC is an anachronism today so would be the setting up of the IRAHE. Such central structures to govern a complex and increasingly diversified system of higher education would serve little purpose. The role of coordination and determination of standards of the UGC needs to be devolved from a single national-level agency to a multiple bodies and agencies that are nationally organised with strong international linkages on the one hand and state or regional chapters on the other. In case of professional education, such bodies already exist like the CoA, the MCI, the PCI, the INC, the DCI, the CCH, the CCIM, the RCI, the NCTE and the BCI. These need to be strengthened rather than abolished. However there may be no need for continuation of the AICTE.

There is no reason for the AICTE to continue to maintain standards for education in architecture and town and country planning and pharmacy for which specialised agencies exist. For management education, a separate membership-based body could be set up to determine and coordinate standards.[20] Similar bodies may be required in respect of travel, tourism and hotel management, fashion design, insurance and actuarial studies and many other new and emerging fields. For engineering education, a body on the lines of ABET (Accreditation Board for Engineering and Technology) of US, could be conceived. For IT and IT services, a separate body could be incubated by NASSCOM, which has started conducting nationwide aptitude tests for IT and BPO professionals. Such professional bodies could also define entry norms and ensure their compliance through accreditation process. The United States has nearly 80 such specialised agencies. With new developments, as more and more professions emerge, new bodies could be formed.

The UGC's role of determination and coordination of academic standards in arts, humanities, social sciences and physical sciences could be assigned to subject-level peer networks. Such TLSNs could review, restructure and recommend curricula, teaching–learning methodology; review and recommend the minimum standards of education for each course including duration of the course and the entry-level qualification; review and recommend from time to time the national qualification framework pertaining to the subject; provide subject benchmark statements describing nature and characteristics of courses, general expectations at each level leaving adequate scope for variety, flexibility and encouraging innovation; review and prescribe areas of specialisation; facilitate development and sharing of quality teaching–learning resource material (including e-material); and ensure coordinated development (including the open system) of teaching and research in respective knowledge area and define research agenda in the subject area relevant to national needs.

These networks would be steered by expert groups comprising the subject experts and other stakeholders including potential employers. These networks could be open-ended communities of academia and other stakeholders. New technologies could be leveraged for collaboration by the networks. Overall, this may be coordinated by an independent NQA. Competitive grants for innovation in learning and teaching and creation of learning and teaching performance fund would help in spurring innovation and experimentation, which is essential in teaching and learning in order to give the country an edge over others.

Compliance to ensure that baseline standards are met would be required. For this, while broad norms for infrastructure, facilities, faculty and staffing may be provided by the professional bodies or subject-level networks, their compliance should be the responsibility of the governments of the states where they are located. No state could be authorised to approve institutions for operation outside their own states. For cross-state provision in distance mode, the need for compliance with regulation issued jointly by the professional body/subject network and the DEC may be required.

Experience has shown that communities of practice are in a better position to evolve policies and develop framework to strengthen higher education than centralised bureaucratic agencies. Comparative performance information, reinforcing peer pressure and public account-ability are often more powerful than legislation and formal regulation in shaping institutional behaviour and strategy. Using codified law as regulatory instrument has limitations with its implementation, partly due to the lack of knowledge and insensitivity, and more due to the binary nature of judicial decisions in comparison with the problem solving requirements of effective policy-making.

Thus, UGC need not be continued. Setting up of the IRAHE may also not be desirable. Such central structures in today's complex world would serve little purpose. The entire regulatory architecture needs to be redesigned keeping in mind the increasing professionalisation of various occupations. Public funding arrangements have to be divorced from the new regulatory framework. Table 7.4 provides a summary of the five regulatory functions in higher education, the current arrangements, the recommendations of the NKC and proposals in terms of earlier discussions.

Previous discussions show that while one may agree with the diagnosis of the NKC on the problems of the regulatory system, the solution does not lie in creation of a super-regulator but in unbundling of various re-gulatory functions, devolution of authority, bringing in role clarity and decentralisation. Once the criteria and process for entry is objectively defined, decision on entry can be taken in a fair and transparent manner by the respective governments. There is no need for the IRAHE for the same reason. Accreditation needs to be organised as stated in Chapter 8 and public funding streamlined as given in Chapter 4.

TABLE 7.4 Five regulatory functions

Regulatory functions	Current arrangements	Proposed by NKC	Proposed
Entry: licence to grant degrees	Though legislature/Parliament or deemed university by national government	IRAHE to set criteria and decide entry	Criteria to be set by the NQF, professional bodies or subject networks and decision by the respective governments
Accreditation: quality benchmarking	Three accreditation bodies, NAAC, NBA and AB	IRAHE to license agencies for accreditation	Respective professional bodies to be responsible for programme accreditation; for institutional accreditation to be organised on regional basis
Disbursement of public funds	National (directly and through the UGC)/state governments	Current arrangement may continue and the UGC be responsible for fund disbursement alone sole	Even the UGC could be wound up may not be essential or even desirable
Access: fees or affirmative action	No clarity	Leave to states	Decentralised, but national government to take larger responsibility for student aid
Licence to practice profession	Concerned professional agency	Concerned professional agency	Many more such agencies required for new and emerging professions

Source Author and NKC (2006).

Regulatory Framework

Ideally, government oversight over the institutions of higher education needs to depend on the type of the institution. In the United States, the state plays advocacy role in respect of top private universities like the Stanford University, where it supports its goals by funding research and student scholarships, but does not interfere in setting policies. In the reputed public universities, the state plays a steering role, though in a limited way: it sets fees and costs in order to shape the market, but otherwise does not interfere with administration once policy has been set and basic strategies agreed to. The lower-tier institutions are usually tightly regulated in order to improve access to less-privileged students. The state determines salaries and fees, sets admission requirements, assesses infrastructure and facilities requirements and ensures that the faculty fulfil their teaching requirements, and that research is less important than teaching (Dossani, 2008: 101–02).

As noted in the beginning of this chapter, universities as public institutions serving the elite functioned well for over centuries with no or little role of the state. As an advocacy state in such cases, the state should provide money without taking an active role in defining or ensuring that priorities are met. This is the model of a truly world-class university that is self-regulating with internal checks and balances. The IITs, the IIMs and IISc, Bangalore, currently not within the purview of the UGC or any of the regulatory bodies, would fall into this category. Their numbers need to be increased. Some of the central universities and several state universities (based on their size and profile) could be given this status.

Thus, rather than having a regulatory system that is paternalistic, there is the need for a flexible regulatory environment that adjusts to growing diversity and modulates itself to varying track records of higher education institutions. However, an important element of regulation should be transparency. Compulsory self-disclosure in the form of returns of information by universities and colleges should be mandatory to address the problem of information asymmetry in higher education.[21] Provisions of the Right to Information Act, 2005 could be used for this purpose. This could even be extended to the private for-profit sector. These rules could also define misrepresentation and deceptive practices in advertising, promotion and marketing by higher education institutions. In the USA, the students' 'Right to Know' requirement under the provisions of the Higher Education Act of 1965 and Freedom of Information Act require the disclosure of financial assistance and institutional information to students.

Tuition fee and admission policies require the most attention. While the private unaided institutions could be given greater flexibility in deciding on fees to be charged within a broad framework, compliance to it should be ensured by enforcing transparency in accounting to curb exploitation of the students and their parents. The practice of each university or institution having its own entrance test needs to be curbed. The multiple entrance tests are the cause of avoidable mental and financial hardships to students and their parents and are subject to manipulation. Over a period of time, there is a need to create a national testing service across subjects and levels. For the time being one (or at best, three to four) test in each subject area may be identified at the national and state levels. All institutions should be obliged to use inter se merit based on these tests. Each university could, however, be allowed a reasonable autonomy to decide on their entrance criteria, subject to the condition that such criteria are fair, transparent and merit-based (a combination of merit on the basis of a specified common test and performance in qualifying exams). Admission processes should not be allowed to be used for generating revenues by any institution, public or private.

Conclusion

On review of role of the state in regulating higher education in India, it was seen that the existing system worked fine when higher education was primarily public funded. Now that there is great variety of providers of higher education, the role of the state has to be redefined. It has to be more sensitive and less intrusive than its current role, best described as one size fits all. The state could have three roles. First is providing money to higher education without taking active role in defining or ensuring that priorities are met (advocacy role). The second is the steering role that focuses on policy outcomes and tries to structure the market to realise those outcomes. The third and the final is the role of the regulator, similar to its current role in regulating fees and cost.

In respect of the top-tier institutions, the state needs to play the advocacy role. In respect of private institutions that do not depend for funds from the government, the state must follow a steering role. Many countries deliberately introduce competition and other market-oriented measures among higher education providers. By doing so, it intentionally limits its steering capacity, replacing it partly by market mechanisms. This is reflected in liberalisation, deregulation and privatisation policies. Economists, the industry, businesses and for-profit providers often support this perspective, while the representatives from the traditional academic world would not be comfortable with it.

Notwithstanding the difficulties above, there is a need to develop a roadmap for streamlining regulation of the higher education sector through decentralisation of central regulation and development of institutional mechanism for effective market coordination. Compulsory self-disclosure in the form of returns of information by universities and colleges should be mandated to address the problem of information asymmetry in higher education. Higher education institutions should have reasonable autonomy to decide on their entrance criteria subject to the condition that such criteria are fair, transparent and merit-based and it reduces burden of admission tests on students. For this, there may be a need to create a national testing service across subjects and levels.

As the continuation of UGC is an 'anachronism' today, so would be the setting up of the IRAHE. Such central structures to govern a complex and increasingly diversified system of higher education would serve little purpose. The entire regulatory architecture needs to be re-designed keeping in mind the increasing professionalisation of various occupations. Rather than a single agency, multiple agencies would be required, each with a clearly defined role and some kind of a tribunal to resolve disputes between them. Public funding arrangements have to be divorced from the new regulatory framework. The role of the UGC needs to be reworked as suggested by the NKC.

A NQA could be set up that would work through peer networks, subject-/discipline-wise, with a mandate to define standards of instruction, curriculum and academic titles in each subject area. The

UGC Act may be replaced by a more comprehensive and umbrella Higher Education Act to provide overall unambiguous framework for development, regulation and financing of higher education in the country. Unnecessary regulations need to be terminated. There is a need to relook at the entire recognition and approval system so that baseline standards are met.

◆

8

Quality Management

Quality is never an accident; it is always the result of intelligent efforts.
— John Ruskin

WITH the rapid expansion of enrolment in higher education, countries around the world face the challenge of ensuring quality. Thus, quality assurance is the most talked about issue in higher education; it is also the least understood issue. This chapter begins with providing a conceptual framework for quality in the context of higher education and then describes quality assurance system as it exists in India today. An objective assessment of the existing quality assurance agencies has been done. The accreditation system in the United States, established more than a hundred years ago, is usually treated as a global benchmark. A comparison of the structure and process of accreditation in India with that in the US has therefore been done. Drawing lessons from the US experience, steps required to make accreditation an effective instrument for ensuring quality of Indian higher education have been suggested. Accreditation and ratings are also seen as branding exercises by many. Brand orientation in higher education and its impact on quality have been briefly touched. While the faculty and its quality has an enduring impact of the quality, new technologies are now being deployed as well to improve the quality of higher education.

Developments on these issues have also been discussed in this chapter before conclusions are drawn.

Quality Assurance in Higher Education

Concept of Quality

There are many stakeholders in higher education, including students, employers, teaching and non-teaching employees, government, funding agencies, regulatory bodies, professional bodies and the accreditation agencies. Each of these stakeholders has a different view about quality, influenced by their own interests in higher education. Their views represent their expectations from higher education and its quality.

When higher education is conceived as the production of highly qualified manpower, the graduates are seen as products whose career earnings and employment will relate to the quality of the education that they have received. When higher education is linked to training for a research career, the performance indicators (PIs) then become the research output of staff and students. The third conception is higher education as the efficient management of teaching provision. In this view, the PIs are efficiency indicators, such as completion rates, unit costs, student-staff ratio and other financial data. Further, when higher education is conceived as a matter of extending life chances, the focus is on the participation rates or percentage growth of students from less represented backgrounds, including adults, part-time students and disabled students (Barnett, 1994).

In 2006, using a Delphi study (a social research method designed to identify future trends in complex subjects my means expert opinion), the Global University Network for Innovation (GUNI) secretariat evaluated various benefits from accreditation process for different stakeholder groups. These groups were higher education institutions; students; and society, governments and employers. Table 8.1 shows the three statements that were given the highest scores for each group and statements that were given the lowest score. Actual scores on a scale of one to five are in brackets after the statements (GUNI Secretariat, 2007).

TABLE 8.1 Various benefits of accreditation

	Benefits for institutions	Benefits for students	Benefits for society, governments and employers
Highest level	Accreditation grants legitimacy and public recognition to an institution (4.22)	Accreditation protects students from fraudulent programmes and institutions (4.26)	Accreditation enhances transparency, provides information and makes institutions accountable to society and stakeholders (4.15)
	Accreditation facilitates the international recognitions of national and cross-border degrees (4.13)	Accreditation assists students in choosing higher education institutions (4.02)	Accreditation provides to a certain extent, protection against low-quality education and fraud (4.02)
	Accreditation is a tool for decision-making in institutional strategic planning as it identifies strengths and weaknesses (3.95)	Accreditation ensures appropriate education in terms of programme content, facilities and services (3.68)	Accreditation creates quality culture in HE worldwide and enhances the educational system as a whole (3.96)
Lowest level	Accreditation increases teaching staff mobility (2.85)	Accreditation facilities greater student mobility at all levels (3.43)	Government ensures that the education provided is in line with government policy (3.30)

Source GUNI Secretariat, 2007.

Therefore, what counts as quality is often contested. Quality may mean different things to different people who would demand different quality outcomes and methods of assessing quality. Quality is also sometimes seen as a 'relative concept'. It is relative to the user of the term and the circumstances in which it is involved. In the context of quality in higher education, three terms, accreditation, assessment and academic audit are often and interchangeably used. These mean different things (Box 8.1).

BOX 8.1 Definitions

> **Accreditation** is an evaluation of whether an institution (or programme) qualifies for a certain status. Accreditation provides the outcome in a binary scale—yes/no or accredited/not-accredited.
>
> **Assessment** gives an idea of the quality of the outputs. Typical outcome of assessment results in a multi-point grade—numeric or literal or descriptive.
>
> **Academic audit** is focused on those processes by which an institution monitors its own academic standards and acts to assure and enhance the quality of its offerings. The objectives of the institution or programme are taken as the starting point for the audit. The audit is usually done by a small group of generalists and it results in an audit report.

Notwithstanding the difficulty in defining quality in the context of higher education, all its stakeholders now demand greater accountability. With the rapid growth of enrolments, there is increase in costs to government. This made the government to adopt a new approach (as practiced in the public sector) to the administration of higher education institutions. There is now a focus on 'value for money'. Recent decades have also seen an emergence of the private sector in higher education, and thus higher education today is more competitive, more diverse in terms of students' population and less well funded. Along with increased expectations from higher education to serve the national, regional and local needs, there is a greater demand for efficiency. These developments have given prominence to quality issues in policy discourse on higher education in different countries of the world.

Quality Management

Emergence of Quality Assurance Agencies

In many countries, the responsibility to see that the academic quality and standards are assured lies with specialised agencies and the process is referred to as quality assurance. The term quality assurance is used in different ways in different countries and contexts. In the United Kingdom, the 'quality assurance' is defined as *the totality of systems, resources and information devoted to maintaining and improving the quality and standards of teaching, scholarship and research, and of students' learning experience.*[1]

Over the past couple of decades, under the pressure of greater demand for accountability, many countries have established quality assurance agencies. On the basis of information collected from 146 countries, 88 were practicing a formal accreditation system of some sort, 40 countries were in the process of adopting formal accreditation mechanisms and another 18 practiced some sort of an evaluation mechanism.[2] These agencies convince various stakeholders that a higher education institution takes its quality assurance seriously, and that the quality of teaching and quality of graduates leaves no room for concern. With the increased mobility of professionals and skilled workers and the greater need for recognition of qualifications across borders, these bodies are now required to coordinate their work and create a mechanism for quality assurance in a transnational context.

Quality Assurance in India

Like elsewhere in the world, the rapid expansion of higher education in India has been at the cost of its quality. Quality varies widely across institutions. Despite the general deterioration of quality, some institutions like the IITs, the IIMs, a few university departments and some affiliated colleges have maintained high standards. The deterioration of quality is most glaring in the state universities in general, and at the undergraduate level in affiliated colleges in particular. Conventional post-graduate education is also facing crisis and performs extended 'baby-sitting' function because of lack of job opportunities for the graduates (Jayaram, 2006).

The Education Commission (1966) noted that the standards of higher education in India did not compare favourably with the average standards in the educationally advanced countries. Since then, the standards have continued to deteriorate and low standards are now endemic and a serious problem. While the NPE was being drafted in the 1980s, serious concerns were raised about this continued deterioration in quality. It was found that the built-in controls were not able to ensure quality. Various options were examined. In line with global practices, external quality assurance was conceived in India as a solution (Stella, 2002).

Presently, there are three agencies that evaluate quality of institutions and/or programmes through an external quality assurance in the country. These are the NAAC, set up by the UGC in 1994 to accredit institutions of higher education; the National Board of Accreditation (NBA) established by the AICTE in 1994 to accredit programmes in engineering and related areas; and the Accreditation Board (AB), established by the ICAR in 1996 to accredit agriculture institutions.

NAAC

Though the NPE in 1986 recommended setting up of a quality assurance mechanism, the NAAC could only be established in 1994. It took another four years for the first institution to be accredited in January, 1998.

Initially, the NAAC was expected to be a self-financing body to be funded entirely from the membership fees paid by member institutions. NAAC accreditation was the recommended eligibility requirement for all central funding. Closure of all non-accredited institutions was also recommended. These recommendations of Gowarikar's Committee (1987) were found too radical. National consultation was held. This culminated in Sukumaran's Report in 1990. Linking of the outcome of assessment with funding was not agreed to. It also suggested that accreditation should be voluntary. Finally, the NAAC was set up on the basis of this report. Keeping in mind the existing regulatory environment and a strong affiliating system, it was decided that assessment and accreditation would be used as an enabling mechanism towards self-improvement (Stella, 2002).

The NAAC adopted core elements common to most external quality assurance systems, namely, assessment based on a pre-determined criteria that combines self-study and peer review that is valid for a specific period of time. Based on this, the NAAC evolved its unique assessment model that combined three basic approaches to quality assurance namely, accreditation, assessment and audit together. The NAAC accredits institutions and certifies for educational quality of the institution based on seven criteria (earlier there used to be 10 criteria for assessment).

The process goes beyond certification and provides an assessment that classifies an institution on a nine-point scale indicating where the institution stands on the quality-scale. The grading pattern adopted by the NAAC underwent two changes. The initial grading pattern with letter grades A, B, C, D and E was replaced in 1999 by letter A to denote the accredited status attached with a number of stars (between one and five) to denote the level of quality. Due to criticism that this promoted a 'hotel' culture, a new grading pattern with nine-point scale that uses a combination of letter grades and pluses, (55–60 = C, 60–65 = C+, 65–70 = C++, 70–75 = B,... 95–100 = A++) was adopted from 15 March 2002 onwards. Further, initial 10 criteria/parameters used for accreditation have been replaced with seven criteria to serve as the basis for its assessment procedures. Taking cognizance of the variance in types of institutions, different criteria have been allotted different weightages. The existing nine-point scale is now being revised to a four-point grading system—A, B and C for accredited and D for unaccredited institutions.

A two-step process is being adopted. The NAAC will make suggestions based on the application for accreditation and then once the improvements are made and self-study done, the peer team would conduct an external review. Universities are being granted a greater role in constitution of peer teams (*The Statesman*, 2 August 2007). External peer review report other than its confidential part is made public.

So far, the NAAC has taken up accreditation of universities and colleges only, though it could take up accreditation of departments or programmes as well. The universities recognised by the UGC or colleges affiliated to them are eligible to volunteer for accreditation. Accreditation by the NAAC is voluntary and is valid for five years.

By October 2006, the NAAC had accredited 129 universities and 2,956 colleges. The NAAC has from time to time set a deadline to cover all institutions, but that has not been possible. From Figure 8.1, it is seen that accreditation activities have picked up only in the last few years. Overall, around 13 per cent institutions of higher education have been accredited by NAAC. The analysis of universities and colleges accredited by NAAC shows that these are mostly government or government aided; private unaided institutions have been less willing to subject themselves to accreditation as noted in Figure 8.2. The fact that many of them were set up in recent years and are still not eligible for accredition could be a reason for fewer accredited private (unaided) institutions.

In terms of grading, 90 per cent of the colleges and around 70 per cent of the universities are of middling or poor quality. Among the 129 universities, only 32 per cent are grade A, 52 per cent are grade B and

FIGURE 8.1   Trend of NAAC accreditation

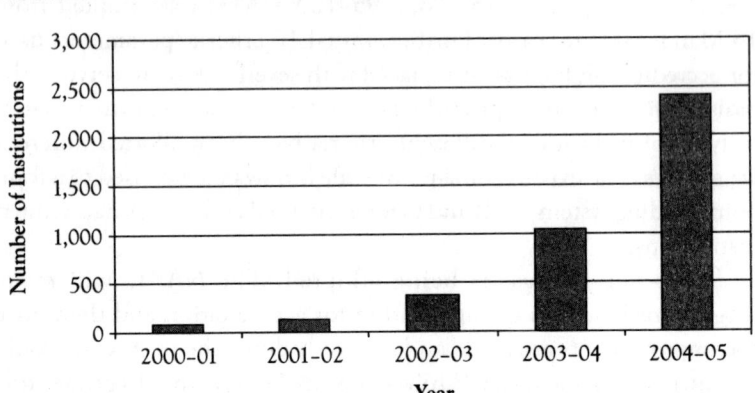

Source National Assessment and Accreditation Council.

FIGURE 8.2   NAAC accreditation status (June 2005)

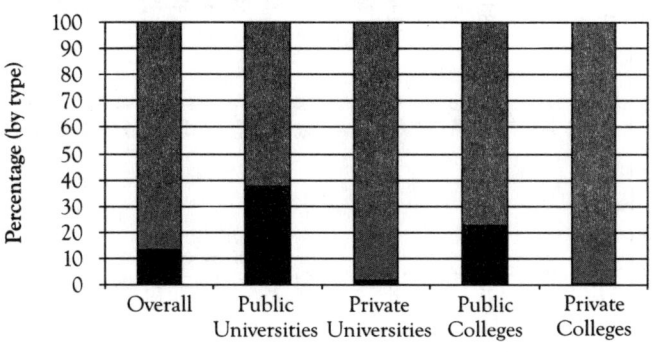

Type of institutions

■ Accredited by NAAC   ■ Not Accredited by NAAC

Source NAAC.

the remaining 16 per cent are grade C. Among 2,956 colleges, only 10 per cent are grade A, 66 per cent are grade B and 24 per cent are grade C. Twenty-five per cent of the faculty positions in the universities are vacant; 57 per cent of the college teachers do not have either an M Phil or PhD (*The Indian Express*, 10 June 2007).

Poor or low quality provision is also linked to the inadequate infrastructure and facilities or fewer and less qualified academic staff. Table 8.2 shows how facilities are distributed across colleges with various NAAC grades.

Though accreditation in India is voluntary, many state governments have mandated it for institutions within their states. The government of Tamil Nadu has decided to submit the government colleges for assessment in a phased manner. Karnataka has made accreditation mandatory for all its professional colleges. Similar moves are on in states like Bihar, Kerala, Goa, Andhra Pradesh and Maharashtra. The UGC is meeting all cost of accreditation of universities and colleges recognised by it. Overall, progress of accreditation across states and regions vary widely (as seen in Table 8.3). While the states in the western region and

TABLE 8.2 Facilities in NAAC accredited colleges, 2002–04

Indicators	NAAC grades					
	A and above	B++ and B+	B only	C++, C+ and C	Non-accredited	Total
No. of Sample Colleges	110	547	298	233	285	1473
STR (Student Teacher Ratio)	20.4	31.8	28.6	28.5	25.2	25.0
STR by Permanent Teachers	29.8	31.8	38.1	35.8	35.6	33.5
No. of Books per Student	9.5	10.7	6.4	7.4	7.0	8.8
No. of Books per College	15215	13921	7019	6504	6748	9882
No. of Journals per College	22.2	13.0	6.1	4.4	4.0	10.0
Students per Computer	145.2	143.8	251.3	546.7	202.7	258.0
Average no. of students per College	1603	1301	954	885	960	1140
Workshops/Seminars Organised	54.5	27.2	17.4	17.4	20.0	24.3
Facilities available (per cent colleges having)						
Library	94.5	91.6	90.9	82.4	90.2	90.0
Computer Centre	86.4	83.7	76.8	64.0	74.7	77.7
Health Centre	74.5	53.7	48.7	36.4	48.1	50.4
Sports Facilities	92.7	88.8	91.6	84.9	88.1	88.9
Hostels	72.7	35.9	39.6	41.9	40.4	48.7
Guest House	44.5	30.9	23.5	21.7	22.8	27.4
Teachers' Housing	47.3	36.9	19.8	18.4	20.7	28.2
Canteen	80.0	77.1	74.8	49.3	64.6	70.1
Common Room (Day Scholars)	30.9	23.8	19.1	9.7	16.1	189.7
Welfare Schemes	49.1	45.5	48.0	35.4	42.8	44.2
Gymnasium	8.2	7.1	3.0	3.6	4.2	5.3
Auditorium/Seminar Rooms	20.9	11.7	7.7	7.1	9.1	10.4

Source Reports submitted with NAAC and NAAC grades.

Quality Management

TABLE 8.3 Accreditation status of universities and colleges–states/UTs

State/UT	Universities		Colleges		Total	
	Total	Accredited	Total	Accredited	Total	Accredited
Andhra Pradesh	20	12	1,255	121	1,275	133
Karnataka	16	08	1,372	443	1,388	451
Kerala	08	06	336	132	344	138
Tamil Nadu	22	18	813	207	835	225
Pondicherry	01	01	25	06	26	07
Southern Region	67	45	3,801	909	3,868	954
Goa	01	01	47	14	48	15
Gujarat	11	04	565	21	576	25
Madhya Pradesh	07	07	623	48	630	55
Maharashtra	27	15	2,064	937	2,091	952
Western Region	46	27	3,299	1,020	3,345	1,047
Bihar	11	03	499	32	510	35
Chhattisgarh	04	02	190	27	194	29
Jharkhand	06	01	148	18	154	19
Orissa	06	03	576	88	582	91
West Bengal	14	07	504	106	518	113
Eastern Region	41	16	1,917	271	1,958	287
Haryana	05	03	221	150	226	153
Himachal Pradesh	03	01	82	17	85	18
Jammu & Kashmir	03	02	69	23	72	25
New Delhi	11	02	84	–	95	02
Punjab	08	04	226	104	234	108
Rajasthan	10	08	364	86	374	94
Uttarakhand	05	04	72	24	77	28
Uttar Pradesh	23	14	733	59	756	73
Northern Region	68	38	1,851	463	1,919	501
Arunachal Pradesh	01	01	06	03	07	04
Assam	06	03	328	191	334	194
Manipur	02	01	60	04	62	05
Meghalaya	01	01	74	06	75	07
Mizoram	–	–	14	05	14	05
Nagaland	01	01	40	02	41	03
Sikkim	01	–	01	–	02	–
Tripura	01	01	22	04	23	05
North-Eastern Region	13	08	545	215	558	223

Source NAAC.

southern region are most pro-active, the response from the states in the northern, eastern and north-eastern regions has been lukewarm.

Other Accreditation Bodies

The NBA, under the AICTE, accredits programmes that come under engineering and related areas. The NBA follows the same process of external peer review as that of the NAAC. Programmes with more than 650 marks out of a maximum of 1000 points are 'Accredited' and those that score less than 650 are 'Not Accredited'. Programmes earning a score of more than 750 are accredited for a period of five years, where between 650 and 750 are accredited for a period of three years. The outcome of the NBA process is not linked to funding.

Though the AICTE has made accreditation by the NBA mandatory for all technical institutions, the progress so far is poor. From Table 8.4 it is clear that although more than 30 per cent programmes in Engineering are accredited, the degree of participation from the other disciplines is very poor. Altogether, only 20 per cent programmes are accredited. Almost two-thirds of the programmes are yet to complete two years after graduating their first batch and, therefore, are not yet eligible for accreditation. The coverage being poor, there is doubt if NBA accreditation serves any useful purpose in the overall context.

The AB, under the ICAR enforces and monitors compliance with norms and standards for agricultural education in India. The AB follows the same process as that of the NAAC and the NBA. The result of AB accreditation process is—'accreditation status', 'provisional accreditation status' or 'no accreditation status'. In each case, the outcome is substantiated with reasons. The accreditation status is valid for a period of five to 10 years. Accreditation outcome is linked to funding. The AB charges no accreditation fees.

Some of the other professional bodies are attempting to establish their own accreditation mechanism. The DEC and the NCTE are working with the NAAC to develop their own accreditation procedures. Overall, the response of the higher education institutions towards the quality assurance movement is lukewarm, though there are significant

TABLE 8.4 Status of NBA accredited programmes

Disciplines	Total Number (approved)		Eligible for accreditation		Accredited programmes	Percentage of accredited programmes
	Institutions	Programmes	Institutions	Programmes		
Engineering	1,617	7,276	1,209	5,310	1,966	36
Pharmacy	736	1,472	345	675	67	10
Management	1,150	1,726	936	1,132	116	10
HMCT	80	80	46	46	04	9
MCA	999	999	995	995	59	6
Diploma	1,766	7,064	1,460	3,996	289	7
Total	6,348	18,617	4,991	12,154	2,501	20

Source AICTE background paper for the National Conference on Development of Technical Education in India, New Delhi, 17–18 December 2007.

regional variations, with the universities and colleges in the southern and western parts of the country proving to be generally more enthusiastic towards accreditation. There have also been initiatives to rope in private professional rating agencies for accreditation in certain segments of higher education.

Private Professional Rating Agencies

In January 2004, the Directorate General of Shipping (DGS), the regulator of maritime education in India, decided to encourage maritime education institutions, both public and private, to get themselves rated by professional rating agencies such as CRISIL, ICRA or CARE. The DGS laid down standards based on global practices for accreditation and allowed the private agencies to do the rest. It did not interfere in determining the fee structure for rating. Initially 24 out of 60 pre-sea institutes voluntarily came forward for grading. There has been an excellent response from the public and aspiring candidates to the institutes that were graded. Based on inputs from the accreditation bodies, the rated institutes have improved their standards. The DGS is now planning to make it mandatory for all maritime education institutions to get themselves rated by the identified private professional rating agencies.

As noted above, the experience of using private rating agencies for accreditation for maritime education in India has been good. Rating by private agencies has helped to improve the quality of maritime education in India. It has also helped in preparing trained manpower that meets global standards for the shipping industry. This experience is however for a niche segment of higher education and it needs to be seen if it is scalable.

Quality Assurance in Transnational Context

There is a growing mobility of students and professionals, programmes and institutions across national boundaries. This requires quality assurance to be seen in a transnational context. While the issues related

Quality Management

to quality assurance are complex, transnational provision makes it even more complicated. On review of transnational activities in higher education in 1999, Philip Altbach noted that there are few controls concerning quality by the universities from the developed countries that were offering 'off-shore degrees', in collaboration with non-educational institutions in other countries. He pointed out that in most cases, programmes were offered not only by respected institutions but also by low prestige schools that simply sold worthless certificates (Altbach, 1999). A recent UNESCO study also highlighted growing concerns, particularly in terms of the quality, reliability and recognition of cross-border programmes (UNESCO, 2006).

Accreditation is used in transnational provision to earn the confidence of prospective students. With global competition for higher education, marketing and branding are strategically important to earn name recognition and increase enrolments. As a result, many accreditation agencies work outside their national territories. For instance, the US national and regional accrediting bodies are providing or selling their services in over 65 countries. The same trend is discernible for accreditation bodies of the professions such as ABET for engineering education from the United States and EQUIS for business education from Europe. There are also initiatives in the South Asia region. See Box 8.2.

In view of the above, addressing quality assurance issues is central to the growth of transnational education. There are many initiatives both at national and international levels to improve quality assurance and accreditation practices in transnational provision. In December 2005,

BOX 8.2 SAQS—a transnational quality assurance initiative in South Asia

The Association of Management Development Institutions in South Asia (AMDISA) has initiated the South Asian Quality Assurance System (SAQS) as a global benchmarked approach to quality assurance for business schools. This is a dynamic system which ensures high standards as also responsiveness to changing concerns of the stakeholders. The AMDISA is a SAARC recognised body chartered in 1988 as a network of management development institutions in South Asia with the generous support from Commonwealth Secretariat and active involvement of leading management schools in the region.

Source http://www.amdisa.org/ (downloaded on 30 May 2008).

UNESCO and OECD have jointly issued non-binding guidelines on 'Quality Provision in Cross-Border Higher Education'. The main goal of this initiative is to protect students against misleading information and low quality provision; to make qualifications readable, transparent and stronger in their international validity and portability; to increase transparency and coherence of recognition procedures and to intensify international cooperation among national quality and accreditation agencies.[3] There is also a move towards an 'International Code of Good Practice'. Whether or not these mechanisms would be appropriate or strong enough to monitor the quality of transnational higher education is yet to be seen.

An International Network of Quality Assurance Agencies in Higher Education (INQAAHE) has been set up as a coordination network designed to help members carry out quality assurance in various countries. More than 80 agencies in over 50 countries have developed formal ties with this network.

The NBA will receive provisional accreditation from the Washington Accord (WA) by the end of June 2007. It will get full membership by 2009. The WA is an agreement among the Engineering Quality Assurance Organisations of 10 countries, namely–Australia, Canada, Hong Kong, Japan, Ireland, New Zealand, UK, USA, Singapore and South Africa. Engineers in these countries have professional legal titles they work under, unlike that in India. Graduates of accredited programmes in a signatory country are recognised by other countries as having met the academic requirements for practicing engineering profession. The WA will help engineers register with official registration bodies in the 10 member countries of the WA and get legal protection.

Presently, graduates holding an engineering degree from India are at times faced with the problem of validity of this degree. This accreditation would thus facilitate and enable mobility of professional engineers. The Institution of Engineers (IE) has also applied for an Engineers Mobility Forum (EMF) certification. The EMF deals with professional engineers who possess minimum seven years of experience in significant engineering activity and who have maintained a satisfactory level of continuous professional development (*Business Standard*, Kolkata, 15 March 2007).

In all, several issues need to be addressed to create trust in trans-national higher education. These include licensing or registering of institutions and providers, quality assurance of the courses or programmes offered, changing the role of accreditation, mutual recognition of qualifications for the purposes of employment and further study. The overall policy and regulatory environment in which programme and provider mobility are operating need to be reviewed in the context of transnational education.

Assessment of Impact

There is now the experience of almost 10 years of accreditation by the NAAC. There is anecdotal evidence to suggest that the process of accreditation had a salutary impact on quality in the institutions that are accredited. There is, however, little solid evidence to say this with certainty. Overall, the impact of accreditation on quality of higher education is yet not quite visible. There is a need for a deeper scrutiny of this. Perhaps the reasons for deteriorating standards of higher education in India are deep-rooted. To address the problems of lack of resources, the issues relating to financing higher education need to be fixed. To address the issues relating to violation of minimum standards, the regulatory system needs to be made more effective. A voluntary accreditation process cannot address these problems.

If one evaluates performance of the NAAC against its intended purpose, we see that the NAAC has been doing a commendable job. The problem lies elsewhere. NAAC accreditation was to facilitate institutions towards self-improvement with the institution as its prime beneficiary. This is beginning to happen. Funding agencies were expected to use the outcome of the accreditation process to target their funding to quality institutions. This is also beginning to happen, yet it has had little impact. The funding agencies have little or no discretionary funding available with them to link it with quality. In absence of clear incentives for accreditation, the higher education institutions do not take accreditation in India seriously.

The coverage of NAAC and NBA accreditation is still small. Many of the reputed universities and colleges have so far not volunteered themselves for accreditation. As a result, accreditation status fails to give any clear signal about quality of institutions or programmes to public at large. In contrast to this ambiguous situation in India, accreditation in the US serves a clear and specific purpose. Accreditation processes in India and the US have the same core elements: institution-based voluntary exercise, self-study, peer review and public disclosure of outcome. Despite this similarity, there are significant differences in the way the accreditation in the two countries is organised. These differences explain different outcomes. A comparative analysis of accreditation in the two countries has been done below.

Comparative Analysis: United States and India

Accrediting organisations in the US play a key 'gatekeeper' role in higher education. Accreditation is used to determine whether higher education institutions and programmes are eligible to receive the over USD 80 billion in federal, state grants and loans available annually (Schray, 2006). In India, there are no such linkages of accreditation to funding. The UGC uses grades of accredited institutions in a limited way as one of the several criteria for competitive grants. As noted in the chapter on financing, the quantum of such competitive grants in India is insignificant to create any real incentives for higher education institutions to get accredited.

Accreditation in the US, though originally started to help students to transfer from one higher education institution to another on the basis of credits earned by them, has evolved into a private, non-governmental 'self-regulation' system. It assures that both public and private institutions of higher education and their programmes meet acceptable levels of quality. It has a wide diversity and enormous reach, as seen in Box 8.3. It involves 100 public and private accrediting organisations that accredit more than 6,400 institutions and 18,700 programmes.

As seen in the Figure 8.3, accreditation bodies occupy the centre stage of the higher education system in the United States. Though the federal government uses the outcome of accreditation for student-based

Quality Management

BOX 8.3   Accreditation in the United States

There are three types of accreditation organisations in the US—regional, national and specialised or programmatic. Regional accrediting agencies operate in six different regions in the US and review entire institutions. Nearly 3,000 regionally accredited institutions cover almost all traditional, non-profit, degree-granting colleges and universities. National accrediting agencies covering around 3,500 institutions operate throughout the country and review the entire institution. Some of them are single purpose institutions. These cover both degree and non-degree granting institutions and also profit and non-profit institutions. Specialised accrediting agencies operate throughout the country and review programmes, departments, or schools in specific fields that are parts of an institution. Sometimes they also accredit single purpose institutions. Some specialised accrediting agencies are government agencies such as those responsible for regulating healthcare professions. These cover 18,713 accredited programmes and single purpose institutions.

Source Schray (2006).

FIGURE 8.3   Linkages between different units in US higher education

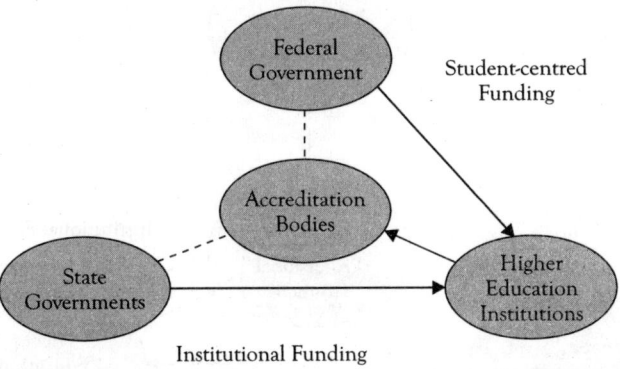

Source Author.

federal grants, the US accreditation bodies do not come under the direct supervision of the government. Accreditation provides the primary means to inform and protect students and parents against fraud and abuse. It helps the students to transfer from one institution to another. States have their regulatory mechanism and provide institution-based funding support.

In India, the central government and its various regulatory agencies rather than the accreditation bodies occupy the centre stage, as seen in Figure 8.4. Accreditation bodies are subordinate to the central government or its regulatory bodies. Though accreditation is voluntary in the US, its coverage is enormous. Almost all higher education institutions are voluntarily accredited and new ones are in the process of getting accredited. In comparison, in India less than 15 per cent of all higher education institutions have been accredited. Many high-quality institutions have not volunteered for accreditation. With the majority of the private institutions yet to be accredited, accreditation does not protect students and their parents against fraud and abuse. Linking of funding with accreditation is tenuous. Mobility of students from one institution to another is highly restrictive.

FIGURE 8.4 Linkages between different units in Indian higher education

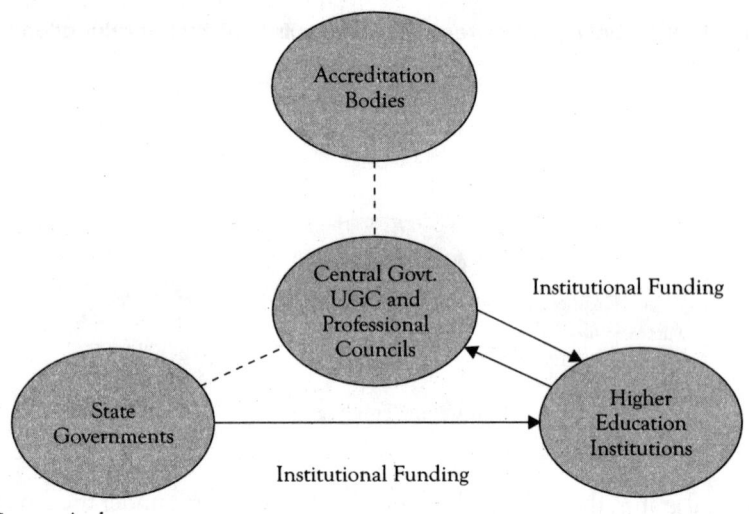

Source Author.

Accreditation agencies in the US are privately organised as not-for-profit membership based organisations. They are financially independent with most of its revenues coming from annual subscription from the member institutions. Institutions pay actual expenses for site visits. In India, the NAAC is organised as an inter-university centre under the UGC, the NBA is under the AICTE and the AB under the ICAR. Accreditation agencies are financially dependent almost entirely on the government. Even the cost of the peer team visit is borne through government grant.

Despite a large number of accreditation agencies in the US, there is a reasonable clarity in roles and functions amongst various accreditation agencies. The two umbrella organisations at the national level—the Committee of Regional Accrediting Commissions (C-RAC) and the Council for Higher Education Accreditation (CHEA) harmonise standards and activities of accreditation agencies and coordinate joint visits (El-Khawas, 2001). On the other hand, in India, despite merely three accrediting agencies (NAAC, NBA and AB), there are often overlaps in their functions. In addition, several regulatory agencies carry out similar functions. Many differences in outcomes of accreditation in the US and Indian system could be explained by how the higher education systems in the two countries are organised. Table 8.5 provides a comparative overview of the two higher education systems.

Voluntary accreditation in the US has evolved as a consequence of a long tradition of cooperation that exists between academic institutions. It grew as its legitimacy was proved and it functioned successfully. Over a period of time, the federal and state governments could trust the outcome of the voluntary accreditation process and used it for a variety of purposes. This reinforced public confidence in voluntary accreditation in the US. Despite accreditation putting a lot of cost and burden on institutions, the academic institutions value it; they value it realising that a substitute for voluntary accreditation would be a more burdensome external scrutiny organised by the government.

Despite the same core elements, each institution is evaluated in accordance with its own stated purpose in the institutional accreditation process in the US. This safeguards the diversity of the institutions, which is considered a hallmark of the strength of the US higher education system. In India, the evaluation for accreditation is done on the basis of standard instruments (largely based on numerical facts). This amounts to

TABLE 8.5 Higher education system in the United States and India

	United States	India
Size and diversity	Large, complex and highly diverse	Large, complex but little diversity
Central government	Maintains arms-length distance from institutions and does not establish and maintain any institutions of higher education, but it shares major responsibility for students' aid. Almost half the students receive financial aid from the central government	Establishes and provides grants to institutions of higher education. It has direct control over some of them. Small central funding for higher education largely goes for maintaining these institutions. Very small central funding for the rest of the system.
State governments	Mainly authorise educational institutions to operate within states and license entry into certain professions; States prevent fraudulent practices of the higher education institutions and provide oversight of the minimum or threshold capabilities.	Most public higher education institutions funded by state governments. States have limited role in maintaining standards. Because of reducing funding role and weak oversight, states are considered as weak links in the Indian higher education system. Many state institutions operate outside the states.
Higher education institutions	Strong commitment to internal accountability through regular programme reviews and systematic activities to assess student outcomes.	Commitment to internal accountability and external accountability (mainly to affiliating the universities) varies widely across range of institutions.
System	The federal government, the state governments and the voluntary accreditation agencies—called the 'Triad' play complementary roles with clear division of labour. Each carry out distinct activities with distinct purposes taking different paths to the same super ordinate goal of providing high quality education with diverse offerings and sound investment of public funds.	The central government, the state governments, largely statutory government controlled bodies like the UGC, professional councils and the universities (particularly the affiliating the afflicting universities) and the voluntary accreditation agencies create a multi-layered burdensome regulatory system trying to achieve often conflicting objectives. Due to poor public funding and weak regulatory mechanism.

Source Compiled by the author.

standardisation. There are now attempts by the NAAC to learn lessons from the US experience.

Based on the comparative analysis of the accreditation in the US and India, it is seen that the success of accreditation in US is in its design, the specific consequences it has and the credibility that accreditation agencies have built over a period of time, while in India voluntary accreditation provides little or no incentives for institutions to go in for accreditation. Accreditation in India is yet to gain full acceptance and credibility. Public awareness about it continues to be low. In its presence form, it is being reduced to a ritual with no clear consequences and needs to be overhauled.

Rankings and League Tables

Rankings and league tables of higher education institutions are popular abroad. These are beginning to be seen in India. These are lists of groups of institutions that are comparatively ranked according to a common set of indicators in descending order. Different from performance indicators, these are designed specifically as a comparative measure, pitting institutions against each other. In most cases, these are produced by commercial publishing enterprises. Most league tables provide a single integrated score that allows an ordinal ranking of entire institutions.

Such rankings provide valuable information to the students, parents, teachers and researchers, policymakers, and to institutions themselves as they compare themselves with peer institutions at home or abroad. However, there are many problems with ranking. Private ranking systems, such as the US News and World Report 'Best American Colleges' use a limited set of data, which is not necessarily relevant for measuring institutional performance or providing the public with information needed to make critical decisions. Many of these rankings are based on data provided by the institutions themselves. Such data is not independently verifiable and is subject to manipulation. Indicators that are aggregated or weighted fail to provide an insight into the actual functioning of the institution. Most rankings are at the institution level and not at the programme level, reducing their value for the students.

There are now approaches to address the problems. Two of these are worth mentioning. Germany's CHE/DAAD (Centre for Higher Education Development/German Academic Exchange Service) rankings that serve to assist international students in coming to Germany are based on faculty surveys and data from third party sources. It does not weigh or aggregate individual indicator scores. Each department's data on each indicator is allowed to stand independently. This allows users to create their own weightings and rankings by selecting a set of indicators and querying the website's database to provide comparative institutional information on that basis. This approach effectively cedes the power of defining 'quality' to the prospective university students and their parents (Usher and Savino, 2006).

Another methodology constructs the ranking of US undergraduate programmes based on how desirable students find them. They have collected data on the college applications, admissions, and matriculation of 3,240 high-achieving students and developed what they call as the revealed preference ranking of more than top 100 colleges in the US (Avery et al., 2004). In India, a similar process is in vogue in respect of institutions where entry is through joint competitive exams. Ranking of the IITs is done on the basis of the choices exercise by the students. Based on choices exercised by top 500 students in 2007, IIT Bombay was rated the most preferred IIT, followed by IIT Kanpur, IIT Delhi, IIT Madras, IIT Kharagpur, IIT Roorkee and towards the end, IIT Guwahati (*The Indian Express*, New Delhi, 11 July 2007).

Despite weaknesses in the existing ranking system, rankings and league tables are essential in an increasingly competitive environment. As in the rest of world, these will have to be done in India by the popular print media. Many of the current rankings are unclear about both the criteria and the methods of rating. The challenge, therefore, is to ensure that they provide accurate and relevant assessments and measure the right things. The government and the higher education institutions could work together to ensure that the media has access to up-to-date and credible data. Further, as Philip Altbach suggests, there could be generally agreed criteria that can be used to do the rankings

(Altbach, 2006). This could be a useful first step towards bringing greater objectivity in rankings and transparency throughout the process is central to its success.

In the above context, the government could well align its information collection system to collect and disseminate institution and programme-related data for comparative analysis, using standard formats, designed for students (and parents) and also policymakers. Availability of sound data in user friendly formats will go a long way in addressing the quality issue in higher education. This could also allow students to create their own rankings of institutions to make informed choices at the time of admission.

Making Accreditation Effective

The standards of Indian higher education do not compare favourably with the average standards in the educationally advanced countries. Low standards are now endemic and a serious problem. Accreditation would hardly serve any purpose if the issues of minimum standards, in most cases arising from poor infrastructure and facilities, are not tackled first. While lack of resources could be primarily responsible for deteriorating standards, there are other reasons as well. The requirements of minimum standards are being violated with impunity. There is undue emphasis on certification rather than the teaching–learning process. This makes examination as 'be all and end all' for all practical purposes. Increasing graduate unemployment arising from supply-demand mismatch is often thought of as quality issue. No quality assurance system can be expected to address the problem of an anaemic, distorted and dysfunctional higher education system. Structural issues related to it need to addresses first.

Currently, the NAAC has monopoly power over accreditation. At the same time it has no capacity to accredit all institutions periodically. A number of accreditation bodies, both public and private, should be empowered. The NKC has pointed out that a rapid growth of higher education, particularly in the private sector, has created a strong need for empowering students and parents with reliable information from a credible accreditation process. This system should be supplemented with creation of self-regulating bodies in the higher education and the freedom to seek recognition from global accreditation systems.

With a view to ensure that the NAAC could undertake accreditation of all institutions periodically, there is a need to develop new methodologies. Currently, only less than 1,000 institutions are accredited by the NAAC each year. With 100 teams, and each team conducting 10 visits each year, it would take 19 years to complete assessment of all institutions. By increasing the number of teams, there is a danger of diluting standards of accreditation exercise. Under the circumstances, a two-stage accreditation process could be adopted.[4] A system could be put in place in all states for collecting the vital qualitative indicators that could form the preliminary assessment. This stage could also be done online. Based on preliminary assessment, considering that only 60 per cent of the institutions are taken up for accreditation, 200 teams assessing 10–12 institutions each per year would be required to complete accreditation in five years. This would require 800–1,000 trained assessors, which should be a manageable number.

Better still would be to overhaul the entire system of accreditation. A properly designed accreditation system could, however, help in making higher education institutions more accountable to its various stakeholders. In its present form, the accreditation system in India serves little purpose. There is a need to initiate and facilitate setting up of membership-based accreditation agencies for institutional accreditation as a means for self-regulation on the pattern of the accreditation agencies in the US. Such bodies may be responsible for accreditation of no more than 1,500 to 2,000 institutions in each region. Such accreditation agencies should be at arms length from the government and totally autonomous in their functioning. There could be a national level body for coordination amongst the accreditation agencies.

There is a need to create clear consequences for accreditation by having suitable and adequate incentives for it. For instance, student-based government grants should be available to students studying in the accredited institutions only. Accreditation of professional courses, particularly for those courses that have licensing and registration requirements may continue to be done by the national level agencies. Duplication and overlap need to be avoided.

Accreditation, in its present form, promotes standardisation, unlike a review against the institution's mission. Maintenance of standards rather than cloning through standardisation should be the objective. Experimentation and innovation in quality assurance mechanism should, therefore, be encouraged. The possibilities of scaling up the accreditation experience of maritime education could be explored.

Quality assurance mechanisms themselves have to be in harmony with global trends so that there is an international acceptance of degrees/diplomas awarded in the Indian higher education system. In this direction, Indian agencies could work towards networking with trans-national and international quality assurance agencies and enter into arrangements for mutual recognition of quality assurance systems. It is desirable to make the quality assurance mechanism in India compatible with UNESCO/OECD guidelines on the issue released last year.

Accreditation agencies in the US are now engaged in aligning their information reporting requirements with other data collection requirements that academic institutions face to make accreditation process less burdensome. An electronic portfolio of information is being designed which would meet accrediting requirements while also informing students, families and the institution's surrounding communities about its activities. Developing a public information system, where information about institutions in comparative perspective and in user friendly standard formats is made available on the web for students (and parents) is, therefore, desirable. Availability of sound data in format will go a long way in addressing quality issue in higher education. This could also allow students (parents and print media) to create their own rankings of institutions to make informed choices at the time of admission.

Finally, there is a need to develop better measures of student achievement by putting in place national level tests. Accreditation bodies should primarily focus on the outcome of such tests and labour market outcomes of the graduates from higher education institution in their accreditation processes.

Brand Orientation

Elite institutions of higher education are some of the strongest global brands and the United States, with a deregulated system of higher education, has many of these strong brands. The US universities such as Harvard, Stanford and MIT are strong global brands that have stood for pre-eminence in higher education for decades. This shows that higher education brands have staying power and make an impact on the public psyche in extraordinary ways that are inarguable. These institutions vie with each other for bright students, star faculty and research grants. According to Kirp (2003), reputation is what matters in such positional warfare that these institutions engage in. Frank (2001) describes higher education as a 'winner-take-all' market. He points out that in higher education market, 'success breeds success and failure breeds failure' Frank (2001).

An institution's actual quality is often less important than its prestige or reputation for quality because it is the university's perceived excellence that matters. According to Garvin (1980), perceived reputation guides the decisions of the prospective students and scholars considering offers of employment and federal agencies awarding grants in the United States. Thus, higher education institutions either implicitly or explicitly undertake extensive brand building exercises. This would be equally true elsewhere, including India.

India has the IIT and IIM brands that are now recognised all over the world. These institutions have helped giving a positive image of India and Indian higher education abroad. These are some of the most selective institutions in the world and like many other elite institutions, these have not increased their intake substantially over the years and thus continue to be very selective (Box 8.4)

And while many people in academics are suspicious of a brand orientation, believing it to be false or superficial, the best brands are, in fact, entirely authentic. The authenticity of the promise conveyed by a brand is particularly important in higher education, where the college or university brand becomes part of an individual's identity, one of the key badges that one wears throughout life. A brand is a promise of an experience; understanding and communicating the validity of that

Quality Management

BOX 8.4   IIT—a global brand

The smartest, most successful, most influential Indians who've migrated to the US seem to share a common credential: They're graduates of the Indian Institute of Technology, better known as IIT. Made up of seven campuses throughout India, IIT may be the most important university you've never heard of ... This is IIT Bombay. Put Harvard, MIT and Princeton together, and you begin to get an idea of the status of this school in India ... With a population of over a billion people in India, competition to get into the IIT is ferocious. Last year, 178,000 high school seniors took the entrance exam called the JEE. Just over 3,500 were accepted or less than 2 per cent. Compare that with Harvard, say, which accepts about 10 per cent of its applicants ... impact of IIT graduates has been on the American technology revolution ... I can't imagine a major area where Indian IIT engineers haven't played a leading role... It isn't just high tech ... Fortune 500 headhunters are always on the lookout for that IIT degree ... And the American companies love the kids from IIT ... Nehru, India's first prime minister, created IIT 50 years ago just after independence to train the scientists and engineers he knew the nation would need to move from medieval to modern. He never imagined India would be supplying brainpower to the whole world.

Source 60 Minutes, CBS News, 22 June 2003.

experience to target audiences is a part of the branding process. Brands do not develop value or authenticity by themselves. It takes time and a great deal of work. Through effective marketing, many institutions have succeeded in aligning or enhancing their images to better fulfil the promise they convey to the constituencies that they already 'own' or desire to attract.

Moore (2004) notes:

> The authenticity of an education brand cannot be taken for granted. If a false promise lures you into buying a pair of acid-washed jeans that you are forever embarrassed to wear, or entices you into the door of a restaurant that serves less-than-average food, your loss is small and your disappointment modest. However, if you choose a college or university and entrust your child to one, based on the promise of a specific experience and then that promise is not fulfilled, the impact can be profound, embittering, and lasting. Therefore, branding in higher education is a two-edged weapon.

Though branding in higher education has always been there, but now there are deliberate efforts to 'market' higher education institutions. These efforts have gone from being a marginal—and somewhat suspect—activity in higher education to becoming a strategic imperative. Heightened competition is encouraging all institutions to take a more market-oriented approach. Since there are a few private institutions with high reputation, private promoters look at branding of their institutions as an important aspect of marketing and realise that their perceived reputation would hold key to their ultimate success. As noted in Chapter 3, private institutions spend heavily on advertisement to attract prospective students and build their brand. This could either be a positive or negative development, depending on the intent of the private sector.

Academic Profession

Of all measures, the faculty and its quality has an enduring impact of the quality of higher education. The condition of the academic profession is thus central to many issues in higher education. Traditionally, teachers in India have been accorded the highest esteem. However, over the past few decades, the academic profession is facing a severe crisis. Rapid expansion of higher education has resulted in severe teacher shortages. Teacher shortages are either due to non-availability of suitably qualified people or arising from the ban on recruitment for financial distress faced by the government particularly the state governments. Most bright people are reluctant to join the profession and those who join, do it as a last resort. They get disillusioned soon after they join when they find that they have no incentive to perform. This section examines the crisis in the academic profession in the changing circumstances and suggests a few remedial measures.

Numbers

Universities and colleges have similar, though not identical structure and ranks in the academic profession. Universities have lecturers, readers and professors. The position of an associate professor also exists in some institutions. In colleges, majority of the faculty are lecturers. In some cases, there are also senior grade lecturers and selection grade lecturers. The latter is equivalent in salary to that of reader but without the title. The rank of an assistant professor exists in some states.

Though recruitment of faculty is done by individual institutions as per their rules and statutes, the minimum qualification and pay scale for the post is prescribed by the UGC in case of general institutions, and other regulatory bodies such as the AICTE/ICAR, and so on for professional institutions. Approximately, there has been nearly twelvefold increase in the faculty strength of the Indian higher education sector, from 40,000 in 1950 to 488,000 in 2006–07 (see Table 8.6).

TABLE 8.6 Number and distribution of teaching staff by category, 2006–07

	In university departments and university colleges	In affiliated colleges	Total	Percentage of total in affiliated colleges	Category-wise percentage
Professors and their equivalent	17,062	24,951	41,258	60.48	8.17
Readers and their equivalent	25,693	107,023	132,716	80.64	26.29
Senior Lecturers	12,405	62,959	75,364	83.54	14.93
Lecturers	23,919	216,979	240,898	90.07	47.72
Tutors/ Demonstrators	1,945	12,631	14,576	86.66	2.89
Total	**81,026**	**423,786**	**488,003**	**83.95**	**100.00**

Source University Grants Commission Annual Report 2006–07.
Note *Includes principals and senior teachers who are equivalent to professors. Part-time teachers/physical training instructors are included in lecturers.

Faculty Shortage and Resource Crunch

The number of academic staff has been seriously affected by resource crunch. There has been either an official ban on the creation of new teaching positions or an unofficial restrictive approach creating hindrance in the process of recruitment of faculty members, even against sanctioned posts. State universities and colleges are not able to fill up even those faculty positions that were sanctioned to them by the UGC under Plan Grants, for they are not able to get commitment of the respective state governments to take them in non-plan maintenance grants. They have resorted to appointment on contractual and part-time basis on a meagre salary, and obviously that has been having adverse effect on the quality of teaching staff. Ban on creation and appointment of faculty position has sent negative signals to the potential candidates and has deterred them from pursuing teaching and research as a career for they do not see any employment and career prospects.

The blanket ban on creation of teaching posts and the recruitment of teaching staff need to be removed urgently. Shortage of faculty members has been a major deterrent in implementing such academic reforms as introduction of semester system, credit based courses, continuous internal assessment, etc. The student–teacher ratio in most universities and colleges are invariably very high. Even out of the sanctioned positions, a large number remain vacant for long time for one reason or the other.

Issue of Teacher Quality

Improving the quality of teachers is the key to improving learning outcomes in all educational institutions including higher education institutions. Hanushek and Rivkin (2004) describe various attempts to estimate the impact of teacher quality on student achievement. Estimates suggest that the differences in annual achievement growth between an average and a good teacher are large. Within one academic year, a good teacher can move a typical student up at least four percentiles in overall distribution (equal to a change of 0.12 standard deviation of student achievement). It is clear that having a series of good teachers can dramatically affect the achievement of any student. In fact, they erase the deficits associated with poor preparation at the previous levels.

In spite of strong empirical evidence and also the commonly held belief that teacher quality is most critical in student achievement, there is a crisis of teacher quality all over the world. This is perhaps the weakest link in the education systems worldwide. Hiring good teachers is not easy. Teaching ability is loosely related to training or experience. Unfortunately, the prevailing salary structures also do not target particularly high-quality teachers (Hanushek, 2005).

Existing evidence suggests that the improvement in teacher quality is more likely to come from selecting and retaining better teachers rather from re-training the existing teachers. This is corroborated by the experience of refresher courses conducted by the Academic Staff Colleges (ASC) and university departments (UGC-sponsored or self-financed) in India. It is observed that these trainings are conducted as a formality. They generally lack the advanced academic orientation expected of them. Teachers attend such courses out of compulsion[5] (Jayaram, 2002). While some in-service training and development courses could be useful and further efforts are required to create a fit between training needs and training courses, it is generally accepted that this strategy would have its limitations. Thus, the focus has to be on selecting better teachers and retaining them. A large proportion of faculty members in colleges and universities do not hold MPhil or PhD degrees.

Now the trend is such that bright students seek employment in the private sector than seek teaching positions. The pay range of a teacher is typically from Rs 20,000 to Rs 40,000 per month, which is much less than what private sector can offer. The problem is more acute in professional areas, where students that pass out earn much more the day they are recruited. In a consumerist society this downgrades the status of a teacher. Students are unwilling to spend many years in getting doctoral degrees, which in many cases is essential for an academic career. There is no monetary growth beyond that point. Promotion schemes are awry. The highest attainable grade is professor in the case of universities and reader for colleges. Many teachers achieve this by an average age of 40 years and beyond that there is nothing to look forward to unless they get involved in research.

Attracting and Retaining Good Teachers

The strategy to attract and retain good teachers is not easy. First, the academic profession has suffered a serious downgrading. Teachers no more earn the same kind of high esteem in society as they used to get a few decades ago. In those times, teachers used to be revered by the society. Even though the economic rewards were inadequate, this sufficiently compensated and attracted people of a high intellect to academic profession. Second, with the advent of knowledge-led economy, students who are better prepared academically have other lucrative alternatives now. Academically, the bright students opt for professional courses at the first degree level itself, with fewer students moving on to post-graduation and the doctoral level, a qualification required for the academic profession. The total enrolment at the post-graduate and doctoral level in India is less than 10 per cent. As a consequence of bright students not opting for post-graduate and doctoral education, the overall standards of these degrees in the country are abysmally low (see Box 8.5). This calls for interventions to improve the standards of post-graduate and doctoral education in the country on the one hand and re-look at the salary structure and career opportunities of teachers on the other.

BOX 8.5   Serious faculty shortages in engineering institutions

With the rapid growth in number of engineering institutions, the non-availability of adequate number of competent faculty has emerged as a serious problem. AICTE Report (2004) estimated a total faculty requirement of 95,924 (comprising 13,703 Professors, 27,407 Assistant Professors and 54,814 Lecturers) on 31 March 2003. This would ideally require 41,110 PhDs and 54,814 M.Techs. With only 7,536 PhDs and 11,983 M.Techs available as faculty in engineering institutions, there was a gap of 33,574 PhDs and 42,831 M.Techs. With further increase in intake now, the situation is worse. The AICTE had to reduce intake in 1,346 approved engineering institutions by 25,335 (from 477,595 in 2004–05 to 452,260 in 2005–06) on the basis of shortage of faculty.[6] Seven institutions with more than 50 per cent shortfall of faculty were not allowed to admit any students. Faculty shortages have been seriously undermining the quality of technical education.

Source Report of the Board on Faculty Development of the AICTE (March, 2004).

Teachers and their associations have often blamed inadequate salaries and unattractive service conditions for the deterioration in the status of the academic profession. The three pay revisions (in 1987, 1998 and 2008) have given the teachers a very good deal. The UGC pay package after the 1998 revision was adequate in absolute terms considering the nature and quantum of work that they do and the little accountability demanded of them (Jayaram, 2002). The teachers were not entirely happy, and were demanding the observance of the principle of parity with Group 'A' services in the government. The UGC pay package has been accepted in principle all over the country, though there are some variations in its implementation. The 2008 pay package has been generous and has given a better deal to teachers than the Group A services in the government.

Special and urgent efforts are needed to attract and retain talent in higher education. Performance-linked incentives to teachers in higher education and allowing them to retain a part of revenue generated by them through research projects, consulting, training programme, short-term courses, management and executive development programmes would help. Since teachers are highly unionised, variable salary structure, though desirable may not be feasible. The recent decision to relax the National Eligibility Test (NET) for appointment in faculty positions may have adverse effect on quality. It is believed that this decision is being reversed.

The Career Advancement Scheme (CAS) has been a boon in attracting and retaining faculty, for it provides opportunities of promotion to faculty members. However, variations in the implementation process of the scheme require certain improvements. The promotion should be based on a rigorous evaluation of publications in peer-reviewed journals. Promotion should be given from the date of the selection committee and not from the back dates. This will require the universities to complete the evaluation process and hold selection committees within a maximum of six months from the date of eligibility of a candidate.

There has been in-breeding in recruitment and selection processes. To curb this, universities and colleges should be given incentives to recruit at least one-fourth of their faculty positions from states other than the one in which the institution in located. In order to promote mobility of the faculty, certain proportion of faculty position should be prescribed to be filled up on contract basis.

Pay and Compensation Issues

The uniform UGC pay package was expected to attract better-qualified persons to the academic profession. On the contrary, it had four un-desirable consequences. First, since the issues arising out of pay revision, particularly relating to career advancement and promotion schemes, retirement age and work load are far from settled, they continue to be the reasons for teachers' protests including strikes. This has been a major cause of teacher truancy and has spoiled the public image of academic profession. There is now less inhibition in not taking classes.

As a result of a series of career advancement and promotion schemes, all teachers, whether they are academically competent or not, rise to the top positions. This has decreased the mobility of individuals who were seeking promotions across universities. This also removed incentives for teachers to perform (Kapur and Mehta, 2004).

Third, with the already deteriorating financial condition, many states could not bear the massive burden of pay hikes for teachers though the central government met 80 per cent of the additional expenditure in the first five years. As a result, there have either been cuts or delays in the payment of salaries. In most states, the teachers are not able to take even the security of their salaries on time for granted. This has demoralised them.

Finally, the financial squeeze has also forced many states to impose an embargo on the recruitment of teachers even against existing vacan-cies. But for exceptional circumstances, new teacher positions against increased enrolment are not being created at all. The ad hoc appointees and part-time teachers outnumber the permanent academic staff in many higher education institutions. The ad hoc appointees, being temporary with little possibility of permanent absorption, have no incentive to perform. Permanent appointments being few and far in-between are subject to intense pressure that is not always fair.

Lamenting on the state of affairs of academic profession in India, Jayaram (2002: 236), himself a distinguished academic, notes:

> Entering the profession with no prior professional preparation other than a postgraduate degree, assured of tenure, doing unchallenging work

without any accountability, with performance being no more than its own reward, teachers at colleges and universities have been largely reduced to the lowest common denominator.

The noted educationist C.P. Bhambhri adds:

There is no internal mechanism of categorising faculty members as performers and non-performers. Every professor is treated as an equal, irrespective of performance and merit. Any demand of their accountability is often opposed by the faculty members who start championing their autonomy to counter this demand. (*The Indian Express*, 2007h)

He observes that the 'UGC has played havoc with procedures to determine the levels of individual faculty members' (*The Indian Express*, 2007h).

In all, instead of improving the teachers' quality and their performance through uniform and attractive pay package, the strategy has led to the lowering of standards and almost a crisis in higher education. Parochialism and inbreeding has become an integral part of higher education in India. It goes on to suggest that governmental intervention in job market for academic profession has resulted in undesirable consequences and calls for a re-look. Rather than a centrally determined uniform pay package for teachers in higher education, there should be a differentiated pay package structure with properly aligned incentives. This should be largely driven by the funding agencies, which would pay according to their means.

There have been suggestions for raising the salary levels of the teachers and increasing their age of retirement. It is being considered that salaries of the teachers should be increased to levels comparable in the private sector so that bright people can be lured to the teaching profession. These measures are desirable and would help in attracting bright people to the academic profession. However, matching the teachers' salaries with the private sector across the board does not appear feasible.

However, several measures have been taken recently to attract and retain quality faculty. The age of retirement has been increased along with age for reemployment. Technical and professional institutions provide opportunities for consultancy and sponsored research. Some

IIMs are also giving cash incentives to the faculty to undertake quality research. For instance, IIM Ahmedabad is giving a cash incentive of Rs 500,000 for a paper published in category 'A' journals and Rs 200,000 for paper published in category 'B' journals. The central government will now allow faculty (and researchers) to set up companies or pick up equity stakes in any commercial ventures while still in-service. This would attract better talent to the academic profession and also encourage commercialisation of innovations.[7]

The teaching profession has to be seen as a package vis-à-vis private corporate job. The kind of intellectual freedom that one enjoys in the teaching profession cannot be thought of in the private sector. The academic profession is much less stressful and can be far more challenging than a career in private sector. Therefore, merely looking at the remuneration package of teachers would be misplaced. Along with improving the conditions of service of teachers, there is a need to link it to their accountability.

Apart from attracting and retaining quality teachers, ensuring that they have the incentive to continue to give their best is important. This calls for aligning their incentives with performance on a continuing basis. There is the need to introduce some kind of tenure system and implement a pay-for-performance system. As suggested by Narayana Murthy,[8] there could be bi-annual student surveys of teachers and all benefits to them including compensation and promotion must be based on the feedback. This would make teachers and the higher education institutions directly accountable to students for student learning.

Of all factors, the availability of committed quality teaching staff is the most crucial, and necessary steps need to be taken urgently to ensure this. Shortage of faculty members has been a major deterrent in implementing such academic reforms as the introduction of the semester system, credit based courses, continuous internal assessment, and so on. Faculty development and preparedness of the faculty to introduce academic reforms is of crucial importance. The ASCs will have to play a most crucial role in academic staff development through continuous updating of knowledge and skills of teaching staff in universities and colleges. Student evaluation and feedback of courses and faculty should be introduced and these should be used for incentivising faculty members. International faculty exchange, inter-institutional faculty exchange within the country, as well as faculty exchange between the industry and academic institutions needs to be encouraged.

Use of New Technologies

Advances in new technologies, particularly the Internet, are now widely used to enhance the quality of higher education provision. The new technologies offer: outreach (the opportunity to reach a very large number of people, in many cases simultaneously); economies of scale (the economic consequence of outreach is lowered unit cost, which has often led to the view of educational technology as a less costly variant of expensive traditional structures); richness of illustration and visualisation; individualisation; access to information (interactive access to worldwide resources of information and archiving); simulation; and an outlet for creativity (Hancock, 1998). Overall, the new technologies can have a profound impact on higher education.

The new technologies can change the teaching–learning process in a way that has not been possible before. Richness of illustration and visualisation and possibility of individualisation could ensure that the most difficult concepts can be understood by all. However, it needs to be realised that the computer will never replace the teacher, but it will change the role of the teacher to increase the time and attention that can be spent on groups of people who are often neglected at present—exceptionally gifted children and those who lag behind. New technologies would have a profound impact on the way the research is conducted. Interactive and easy access to the World Wide Web would ensure that existing base of knowledge is readily available to all at all time. A maze of interconnected computers and huge distributed knowledge repositories sitting in different parts of the world would enable researchers to build new knowledge and collaborate with peers more effectively. New technologies are also known to significantly improve the governance both at the institutional and the systemic level in the higher education system.

Organised efforts are required to reach out to the largest number of institutions to enable and facilitate them to leverage technology in all the three areas of teaching–learning, research and governance. Figure 8.5 shows the framework of using technologies in higher education. In this section, we shall discuss the issues relating to technology infrastructure and the use of technology to enhance the teaching–learning process. Issues relating to use of technology in research and for institutional governance have been discussed in other sections of this chapter.

FIGURE 8.5   Use of technology in higher education—a framework

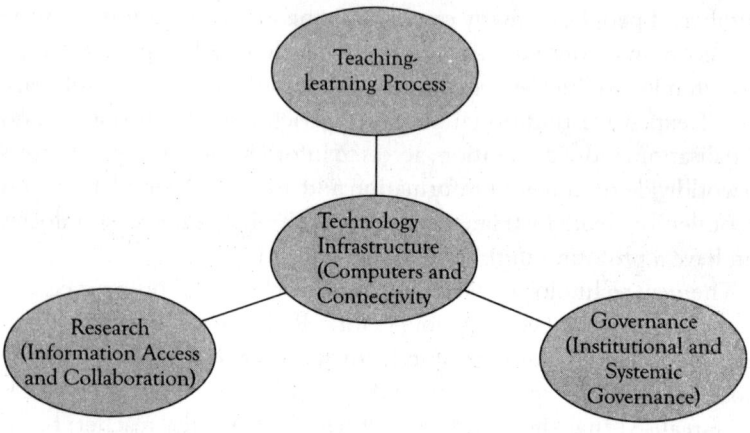

Source Author.

Technology Infrastructure

Good computing, networking and connectivity infrastructure for higher education institutions are essential for the purpose. Considering that the affordability will be an important factor, new technologies that are smaller, cheaper and simpler would be adopted. To bridge the digital divide amongst educational institutions, networked computing at low price-points could be made popular. This would mean a simpler computing environment where upgrading is required mainly on the server-side only. A low-cost thick-server thin-client computing environment with open source software could be considered. To be able to absorb the flow of information at high speeds from external sources, all higher education institutions must improve the internal campus network significantly. In most of the campuses, the application considered earlier was predominantly email access and browsing. As the scene has changed considerably, it is required to redo the bulk of network in every campus. In addition, dense academic areas in every institution could have a wi-fi network.

Reliable connectivity is essential for the technology-enhanced learning initiatives; integration of the efforts to set up digital library of all institutions; bringing together the academic and research community across the higher education institutions using voice over IP and video-conferencing; and to enable easy access to computing resources across the institutions to form a Computer Grid for High Performance Computing. Connectivity is now such a critical infrastructure for a higher education institution that institutions are being ranked according to the bandwidth available on per student basis. Though the central government and the UGC are making some investments in providing connectivity to higher education institutions, in a ranking of universities in Asia, the Indian universities fall far behind.

Technology to Enhance Learning Process

There are many efforts in India to use technology in the teaching–learning process. Their overall impact has not been systematically analysed. Whereas most of them are at the institutional level, there are two major efforts at the national level that have been described below. These are the Consortium for Educational Communication (CEC) and the National Programme on Technology Enhanced Learning (NPTEL). In addition, the IGNOU and other open universities have been using technology to assist learners through its study centres.

The UGC started using the medium of films and broadcast media for knowledge communication in the early 1980s. Countrywide classroom (CWCR) was launched in 1984. Production facilities were set up in six universities. An inter-university centre named 'Consortium for Educational Communication' was set up in the year 1993 to coordinate and provide guidance to the activities of the media centres set up by the

UGC in various universities. The CEC coordinates the development of centres, ensuring the quality of software, coordination of telecasting of the selected films, inspiring and encouraging innovations. During the two decades of CWCR and a decade of CEC, considerable progress has been made.

The system of educational communication has grown to 17 centres. These centres now use computers, the Internet and multimedia extensively and are called Electronic Multi-Media Research Centres (EMMRCs). The average number of education films produced has increased to 500 films from 25 in the beginning. The number of hours of telecast of education films on the national channel has increased from two hours to four hours daily. Now the CEC runs a 24-hour higher education satellite channel known as *Vyas* channel on Gyan Darshan bouquet. The focus of educational films are on the following three types: (i) enrichment oriented films; (ii) subject related series of films; and (iii) undergraduate syllabus-based lectures by eminent teachers. On the side of development of production equipment, the CEC coordinates the acquisition and maintenance of the latest equipment by the media centres.

Over the years, the CEC has developed a huge repository of video films. There are a total of more than 13,000 titles available in 49 subject-areas. Syllabus-based model lessons are available in 47 academic areas. Syllabus-based model lessons in two subject areas, namely political science and economics have also received quality control certifications.

The NPTEL was launched in 1999. The main objective of the NPTEL programme is to enhance the quality of engineering education in the country by developing curriculum based video and web courses. This is being carried out by the seven IITs, IISc Bangalore and other premier institutions through a collaborative effort.

The project intends to provide learning materials, digitally taped classroom lectures, supplementary materials and links to the state-of-the-art research materials in all engineering and core science subjects. So far, approximately 70 courses covering all levels and many subject areas are ready and another 140 courses are in various stages of preparation and distribution using the Internet. The programme ensures harmonisation of curriculum so that the largest number of people can benefit from this initiative. A definite mechanism for assurance of quality and certification of courseware produced under the programme has also been put in place. This is primarily meant for supplementing classroom lectures. Video software developed under the NPTEL is telecast through the *Eklavya* Technology Education channel to reach out to engineering students spread all over the country.

There is a need for the consolidation and scaling up of these efforts. A suitable feedback mechanism is required to understand the impact of using technology. These national efforts could be integrated and monitored at the national level, so that synergies between them could be effectively leveraged.

Conclusion

Quality in higher education is a complicated and hotly debated issue around the world. While the government wants accountability in exchange for more funds and greater autonomy, students want value for money in terms of increased earnings on graduation and the global knowledge economy demands internationally compatible degrees. Thus, quality could mean different things to different stakeholders. In broad terms however, quality higher education is often linked to standards, measurement, assessment and control. In the face of knowledge revolution and the trend towards mass participation, diversified and flexible provision of higher education is increasingly important. In such cases, quality could also mean adapting to change and thinking outside the box. Quality assurance systems thus face the challenge of addressing both goals; hence it has not been easy to come to have a grip over concerns relating to quality in higher education.

Notwithstanding the inherent difficulties in designing an effective quality assurance system, most countries have established or are in the process of establishing quality assurance systems. There are significant variations in the focus of evaluations (institutions or programmes), their scope (territorial jurisdictions and types of institution covered), their initiation (compulsory versus voluntary monitoring) and their frequency (cyclical versus ad hoc). Yet, in terms of process, quality assurance system usually based on accreditation system that evolved over the past century in US. This involves external peer-review on pre-determined criteria and based on a self-study report. Yet, unlike in the US, most QA systems neither perform the 'gatekeeper' role in higher education nor have any consequences in terms of institution or student finance or mutual recognition.

In India quality assurance or accreditation and assessment as it is called in India was initiated in the early 1990s. However, it got established only by 1998. Accreditation is both for institutions and programmes (for technical areas falling within the purview of AICTE). It is organised at the national level. It is voluntary (though at times claimed mandatory) and cyclical. In part due to capacity constraints and largely because of inconsequential nature, its coverage has been poor. While it has definitely helped in sensitising the higher education institutions towards quality, its impact in fostering accountability has been limited. It has weak signalling power and has limited persuasive role in prospective students' choice of an institution. Since there is a parallel regulatory system, though weak with several loopholes, accreditation in India does not play the 'gatekeeper' role in higher education as in the case of the United States. For a large system like that of India, multiple accrediting bodies with sufficient capacity to undertake cyclical accreditation are needed. While institutional accreditation could be organised at the regional level, programme accreditation has to be subject wise involving professionals in respective field of study. Accreditation has to have consequences and the process itself has to be aligned to the regulatory framework to avoid duplication.

Like many other parts of the world, there has been a parallel development of institutional rankings and league tables outside the accreditation system in India over the past few years. These rankings are based on surveys (largely perception) by print media and are often criticised for their arbitrariness, lack of reliability and bias. Despite this criticism, there is a strong evidence of their useful signalling power in perspective standards choice of institution. Though these may be imperfect, they satisfy a public demand for transparency and information and are likely to stay. The way forward would be to evolve 'generally accepted criteria' for rankings to bring greater objectivity in rankings or make information about institutional performance readily available over the Internet to enable various stakeholders to construct their own rankings of institutions and programmes.

Some of the strongest brands are associated with higher education. These brands have been built over a long time. Realising the importance of branding, the private sector is now engaged in branding exercise aggressively. This is both a positive and a negative development. Its impact on quality of actual provision would depend upon the intent of the private sector. Attracting and retaining quality teachers and making them accountable is absolutely essential for quality in higher education. For the rapidly growing Indian higher education sector, this would be a big challenge. The impact of new technologies on higher education, particularly in enhancing quality and improving acess can be far-reaching.

◆ ◆ ◆

9

Perspectives

*The important thing for government is not to do things which individuals
are doing already, and to do them a little better or a little worse;
but to do those things which at present are not done at all.*
— J.M. Keynes

INDIAN higher education landscape is changing rapidly. Demographic
bulge, expanding school education and rising aspirations has put considerable pressure for expansion of higher education. There are greater
expectations from higher education due to the country's rapid economic
growth, rising incomes, outward orientation and growing optimism. In
the previous chapters, the focus has been on facts organised in various
chapters on different topics. These were analysed in international
comparative perspective. Conclusions were reached, which, in many
cases, given the facts, become obvious. This chapter examines these conclusions in the context of changing socio-economic and political realities
and growing optimism.

This chapter begins with an examination of the country's socio-
political and political circumstances and documents various factors
responsible for growing optimism about India in global knowledge
economy. It then examines the challenges faced by higher education
today. In the context of these challenges, three conceptual issues—
purpose, diversity and competition—are analysed. While defining

the purpose of higher education, the key question, whether higher education should be publicly financed or privately funded, is analysed. As the higher education sector is growing, it is becoming more diverse and competition is growing fiercer. Diversity and competition feed on each other and are the quintessential elements of a modern system of higher education. These, therefore, are analysed. Next, the status and prospects of Indian higher education is examined in terms of three key cross-cutting themes: access and expansion, equity and inclusion and quality and excellence. These are also the objectives of the Eleventh Five Year Plan. Finally, the changing nature of policy support and the imperative for systemic governance for effective steering of the system to achieve stated goals are analysed.

Socio-economic and Political Circumstances

India is a large country with high diversity and many contradictions. With a large proportion of children and young people among its vast population of about 1.2 billion, India is seen as an engine of global growth. Though average per capita income and wage levels continue to be low, rising aspirations of the large and growing number of middle income and high income households is creating a huge domestic demand for a variety of goods and services. Its fast growing economy is rapidly integrating itself with the rest of the world, particularly in the knowledge-based sectors. Thus, the country has seen a consistent over 8 per cent rate of economic growth over the past four years. Recession in recent times is likely to have limited impact on this growth story. A large stock of graduates and people with English language skills are feeding this growth.

Economic growth since 1980 has transformed India from the world's 50th ranked economy in nominal US Dollars to the 10th largest in 2005. When income is measured with regard to purchasing power parity, the Indian economy occupies fourth place, after the United States, Japan, and China. Along with growing incomes, India's increasingly outward orientation makes it an important player in the global economy and the growing optimism about India's economy. Several sectors, such as software, IT-enabled services, pharmaceuticals, biotechnology, and dairying and milk processing are globally competitive. Indian software firms have pursued various quality certifications and many of them have secured the SEI CMM (the capability maturity model of the software engineering institute of the Carnegie Mellon University) Level 5 certificate (Roy, 2005).

Changing Socio-political Realities

The country's socio-political realities are being determined by the nature of Indian state. It has two important features: federal structure inscribed in the country's constitution and parliamentary democracy. Both have implications on public policy and the policy process. While some policy arenas are reserved exclusively for the national or the state governments, many others fall in the Concurrent List, meaning that national and state governments have to formulate policy in consultation. Education (including higher education), health, labour laws and power, among other things, belong to the Concurrent List. It is difficult to develop consensus on concurrent policy arenas, especially if the central and the state governments are not ruled by the same political party. In India, the latter has been true since 1967. Until 1967, the Congress Party formed the national as well as state governments. Thus, decision making for higher education has become quite complicated now.

The policy implications of parliamentary democracy in India need to be understood as well. Historically, universal franchise democracy followed the industrial revolution in the West. Britain, the oldest democracy in the world, had only 19 per cent franchise in the 1830s, by which time it had gone through an industrial revolution. East Asia has also followed the Western model in sequencing industrialisation and democracy. In contrast, an independent India was born poor and overwhelmingly agrarian in 1947, but there were no restrictions on franchise. As a consequence, inclusiveness has played a more significant role in Indian policy making than was generally true at a comparable level of development elsewhere.

The focus on inclusiveness in policy making is closely linked to the nature of Indian polity. Though the poor are always talked about in Indian policy circles, the poor are not a united class and thus they are not a politically important group. It is the caste-based politics that ostensibly attack discrimination and denials of dignity, not poverty that defines Indian polity. Ethnicity rather than class, or poverty *per se* drives the policy of inclusive growth to provide social justice in the country. This is based on the argument that the elite upper Hindu castes, numbering somewhere between a fourth to a third of the Hindu society today, have historically enjoyed superior status and have also subjected the lower castes, constituting a majority of Hindu society, to various forms of subjugation and discrimination.

The disadvantaged Hindu groups—the SCs (about 16 per cent), the STs (7.5 per cent) and the OBCs (anywhere between 40 and 52 per cent)—form the numerical majority and are hence important in electoral politics. A large number of poor also come from these groups. Muslims, who form 12–13 per cent of the population, are the largest non-Hindu group amongst the poor. Religiously different from the lower Hindu castes, they are split between their identity as Muslims and their interest as poor people. In a democracy, these numerically large groups realise how voting could be used as a weapon to counter the traditionally instituted status inequalities. Thus, affirmative action (discussed in Chapter 2) is seen as an important and politically convenient tool for egalitarian restructuring of social order in the Indian society.

Evolving Economic Policy

In the decades following independence in 1947, economic planning in India was deeply influenced by the Soviet Union's model of industrialisation through central planning. Despite problems in plan implementation seen in the later half of the 1960s and continued low rates of growth throughout the 1960s and the 1970s, this policy persisted. As per Bardhan (1984), this could be explained by the growing power of interest groups comprising the industrialists, the farmers and the public sector bureaucracy. According to him, all three benefited from dirigisme: industrialists for they were protected from external competition; farmers because they got price and input subsidies; and public bureaucracy for it was well paid, protected and wielded enormous powers. None of them had an incentive to push the government for a change in policy. According to Ahmad and Varshney (2008) low economic growth did not matter so long as the ideology of secular nationalism was in place and the Congress Party was viewed with favour by the upper castes, the dalits, the scheduled tribes and most religious minorities.

With political instability in the late 1970s, policy movement towards the market began. Concerted efforts were made for economic liberalisation and greater reliance on the private sector. During the 1980s, several industries were de-licensed, corporate tax rates were lowered and incentives were given for the development of high technology in several sectors. Exchange rate reform and reduction of quantitative restrictions on imports also happened. By 1991, when a balance of payment crisis hit the country, a blueprint of a larger market-oriented shift in policy was already in place.

The then Finance Minister, Manmohan Singh (now the prime minister), a respected economist, saw an opportunity in this crisis to bring about a fundamental shift in the country's economic strategy. Thus began a whole series of economic reforms with focus on economic liberalisation, privatisation and outward orientation (globalisation), introduced incrementally in the political process. Notwithstanding political changes, the direction of the reform movement has remained the same. While earlier explicit references to foreign models were rare, but now comparisons with South Korea—which had the same per capita income as India in the 1960 and now has a per capita income which is 10 times as much as India's—are often made. More recently, China's size, complexity and monumental economic rise have made it a more acceptable reference point.

Some states embraced reforms early, while the others waited. But now most states have taken the reform path. Even the Left-ruled West Bengal now accepts the fact that they have to follow the path of capitalism while protecting the people against its negative effects.[1] Whilst critics of the left and many people in the academic community may not accept this position, all ruling political parties now recognise the growing role of the private sector in the state's development. As Deng Xiaoping used to say, 'learn truth from facts and not from dogmas' (*The Hindustan Times*, 2007), they have all become pragmatic now.

The emergence of private higher education and the growth of private finance, that began in the early 1980s, coincided with the change in economic policies. Under the state control, universities and colleges produced graduates primarily for employment in the public sector until the 1970s. From 1980 onwards, there grew the demand for people with a variety of skills that the public institutions were not able to meet. Rising prosperity saw growing numbers of families which could afford to pay for higher education. Thus, unmet demand and increased affordability made private higher education a viable preposition. However, public policy on private higher education continues to dither primarily on grounds of equity.

With economic reforms and emergence of the private sector, three kinds of inequalities have grown: interpersonal, interstate and rural-urban. There is an impression that the country's boom has mainly benefited the upper Hindu castes, the cities, and the Southern and Western states. On the whole, the lower Hindu castes, the STs, the large Muslim minority, the villages, and the Northern and Eastern states have lagged considerably behind. As the country moves forward, inclusion has become its greatest policy challenge. Democracy has given the underprivileged a great deal of voice, a voice that can create political instability if ignored.

While the country moves forward with pro-market reforms, tensions between markets and democracy persist. Such tensions arise due to the well-known difference in the organising principles of the two systems. For democracies, the masses are citizens; individually, they have the same weight in franchise as those privileged or the elite. But in the markets, the masses appear as consumers of goods, as labour, or as small producers of low value-added goods. As consumers, the masses matter if they have the purchasing power. Since a large section of people do not have purchasing power, they matter little in the market. In a market-based economy, no assumption of equality of all is made, which is intrinsic to elections, a vital principle of democracy.

Thus, policymaking is strongly influenced by the compulsions of democracy. The process of policymaking itself is quite complex. The complexity, however, can be seen in terms of two important facts: the greatest power rests with politicians and bureaucrats; and politicians are relatively risk-averse on issues that can bring large numbers of people agitating on the streets. They would normally not like the masses to be adversely *and* negatively affected in a big way in the short run. Thus, the country's democracy is incapable of administering shock therapies, even if such therapies expect to improve welfare in the long run. In the context of higher education, absence of any serious efforts to raise tuition fees and continuing discomfort with private higher education are illustrative of this tendency.

In the context of rapid growth and success in few sectors, India has been able to create a perception of being a 'knowledge powerhouse'. The country has several advantages that give it an edge in the global knowledge economy. These are as follows: a young population, a large number of people with English language skills, a large and growing domestic market with a growing middle class, pro-private and outward orientation of Indian economy and a large higher education and training system. While the previous chapters had a focus on higher education and also briefly touched upon the training sector, other factors are discussed here.

Demographic Advantage

India's young population and the declining dependency ratio are considered as a huge advantage. The number of people entering the working age (15–64) population is now 14 million per year. Currently, the largest number of people are entering the workforce in India. Population in the working age group has increased from 619 in 2001 to 699 million in 2006 and projected to reach 957 million by 2026. This will rise from 62.9 per cent in 2006 to 68.4 per cent in 2026. Median age is currently about 24 years. Though this would gradually increase, but even in 2026 this would be merely 31.34 years. Thus, India is a young nation and will continue to be so even on a medium-term basis.

Perspectives

Demographic trends in the country provide a unique 25-year window of opportunity in the form of a demographic dividend. Birth rate has been continually declining. As a result, there are fewer dependent children than before. Very slow improvement in life expectancy would mean fewer elderly people surviving longer beyond working age population. With a change in social norms and modernisation, more women are now entering the workforce. All the three factors contribute to the rapidly declining dependency ratio (ratio of dependent to working age population). As per the Technical Group on Population Projections, dependency ratio for the country has fallen from 0.8 in 1991 to 0.73 in 2001, and is expected to fall further to 0.59 by 2011. This decline sharply contrasts with the demographic trend in the industrialised countries and even China, where the dependency ratio is rising. Low dependency ratio gives India a comparative cost advantage and improves country's competitiveness.

Furthermore, the baby-boomers generation has now crossed the age of 20 and the demographic bulge is occurring at the age bracket of 15-29 years. Thus, India is going through a one in hundred years peak in terms of the number of people entering the workforce.

According to most population projections, the share of working age population in total population will continue to rise for the next 30 years or so, long after the decline has set in other major economies like China, the United States, Western Europe and Japan. These demographics point to a large potential for higher growth through augmented supply of labour and savings and often referred to as 'demographic dividend'. But the demographic dividend is unlikely to materialise unless the country fails to educate its people. Thus, there is a need for thrust on school education and eventually higher education.

All these trends combine to result in the country having world's youngest workforce with a median age way below China and the OECD countries. This would mean that dependency ratio, that is, the ratio of non-working population to working population will continue to be low, giving India a comparative cost advantage over others for another 25-30 years. By that time, the demographic bulge in India would be also reaching the age of superannuation, and India would also be joining the league of ageing economies.

English Language Skills

English is the language for international business and commerce and dominates science, scholarship and teaching. It is the world's most widely studied second language. It has official government recognition in over 70 countries. Thus, importance of English has now universally accepted (Altbach, 2007b). In India, because of its colonial past, English has been the language of the government and associated with the country's elites. After Independence, when the states were organised on a linguistic basis, English became the unifying language of the people. This helped its further spread.

English has continued to be the main language for teaching and research in higher education. English language skills help in access to professional education and white collar jobs. Thus, English language skills are seen as the key to social and economic mobility. Disregarding this fact, the government's ambivalent stand on spread of English education at the school level had been counterproductive. This spawned a large number of English medium private schools. Only a small and well-off section of society could afford such schools exacerbating inequities.

Recent years have seen a dramatic increase in the number of students enrolled in English Medium schools as compared to regional languages in all states. Though only an insignificant number of people (less than 200,000) have English as their first language, over 90 million people know it as an additional language as per the 1991 Census. There is little doubt that these numbers have significantly increased since then. Today, there are more speakers of English in India than in Britain, next only to the United States.[2] Knowing English has given Indians a competitive advantage in global economy. However, the explosive growth of job opportunities has raised concerns about the shallow pool of English knowing people and poor proficiency levels of a large section.

Growing Middle Class

India has a large and growing middle class transforming consumption, production and investment patterns in the Indian economy. Based on surveys by the NCAER, about 100 million people now live in house-holds with annual incomes between Rs 200,000 and Rs 1 million (approximately USD 20,000 to 100,000), compared to about 15 million in 1990–1991. With a lower defining threshold, the size of the middle class would be greater. For example, Bhalla (2007) estimated that the middle class when defined as 'non-poor' by standards of developed economies, 34 per cent of India's population was 'middle class' in 2005 compared to about 10 per cent in 1990. A recent survey of consumption pattern by Mckinsey shows that middle income and high income households will rapidly grow and be almost half of the total number of households by 2025, as noted in Table 9.1.

TABLE 9.1 Middle/High income households (in millions)

Year	Number of households	Very low income	Low income	Middle income	High income
2005	206.9	48.86	44.12	6.42	0.57
2015	244.0	43.44	30.36	24.83	1.35
2025	280.5	17.78	33.19	45.63	3.38

Source McKinsey Study on Consumption Pattern.[3]

Rising aspirations of the growing middle class will create demand for quality higher education. With large disposable income and access to higher education viewed as necessary for upward socio-economic mobility, the middle class is willing to spend and even borrow for better quality higher education.

The Country's Outward Orientation

After Independence, India was an inward-looking mixed economy with a complex system of socialist economic controls and created a large public sector. The government's shift from an inward-looking, command-and-control economy to an outward-oriented, incentive-based, private sector-led economy began after 1980 resulting in an upward shift in the growth path. Some significant pro-market reforms, including attitudinal changes, took place during the 1980–90 period and many others happened after the crisis of 1991. From 1991 to 2006, more fundamental market-oriented reforms took place. A larger share of the growth response in this period came from capital accumulation, although Total Factor Productivity (TFP) contribution remained substantial. Importantly, most researchers agree that without the reforms of the 1990s, the growth spurt of the 1980s could not have been sustained. A large share of the growth impact came from better use of existing capacities reflected in TFP improvement. Today the Indian economy is far more open to external trade, investment and technology than it was 15 years ago. The private investment rate as a share of GDP surged from an average of 10.8 per cent of GDP in 1970–80 to 18.2 per cent in 2000–05. Much of the response, until the late 1990s, came from the domestic private sector.

The policies towards foreign portfolio and direct investment have been greatly liberalised. As a result, the ratio of traded goods to GDP has more than doubled from less than 15 per cent to nearly 33 per cent. Due to sustained boom in software exports and worker remittances, the ratio of current receipts (goods exports plus gross invisibles) has more than tripled from 8 per cent to over 24 per cent of GDP. Net invisibles, including non-factor service exports, worker remittances, income from tourism and travel and investment income flows aggregated USD 55.3 billion in 2006–07, an increase of 30 per cent over that in the previous year. This grew to USD 67 billion in 2007–08. Foreign investment has risen from negligible levels to USD 20 billion in 2005–06.

Economic reforms that resulted in higher rates of growth are thus a combination of attitudinal changes, pro-private sector policies and the country's outward orientation. Despite private growth in higher education from 1980 onwards, India's policy on higher education continued to be focused on public sector and inward-looking.

Apart from the above advantages, many people see interesting factors responsible for the country's success. According to columnist Gurcharan Das:

> India in course of its long and rich history looked at a wide array of diverse paths to human salvation. This made things chaotic but it also fostered an independent, enquiring mind with a bias for innovation which is so essential in the global knowledge economy. (Das, 2006)

He adds that 'the success in education belongs to students rather than teachers' in India and the 'real victory might lie with parents and their middle class insecurities' (Das, 2006). He further adds that 'colonial examination system created a meritocratic middle class society' (Das, 2006) that was obsessed with English and excelling at exams has stayed on with Indian society. This description of the Indian society fits in with the brutal competition for talent now.

Challenges before Higher Education

Technical change, growing integration, demographic shift and rising competition are shaping economies and societies. With this there is a burgeoning demand for higher education and the nature of this demand is changing continually. In this backdrop, higher education faces four key challenges. First, the advances in information and communication technologies and the advent of the Internet have impacted teaching-learning paradigms and more significantly, academic research. We now require more and differently educated people. There are resultant job losses and sometimes shifting of many intellectually-driven jobs from the developed world to the developing countries like India and China, thereby accelerating the process of globalisation. Second is the challenge of globalisation, which is happening at a faster pace than ever before. This is the direct by-product of the Internet era and has made national borders less relevant in today's world, with increased mobility of students and workers alike.

With global competition and the rhetoric of knowledge economy, countries around the world see a close relationship between the education system and their economic well-being. They are vying to get for their citizens as many high-wage high-skilled jobs as possible. Usually, such jobs require formal education beyond school level. Reform of their systems of education, particularly higher education, has therefore become central to their strategy to remain competitive. Though the economic benefits of higher education are mostly assumed, yet the human capital theory developed formally by economists and restated loosely by believers in education has reaffirmed the faith of the policy makers in more and better higher education. Individuals see benefits of higher education in the belief that it would provide them access to better paid jobs. The reality, however, is somewhat more complex.

With rapid technological advances, there are new ways of organising work. Consequently, occupational structure is changing and the job market for the highly skilled people is now more integrated resulting in division of labour at the global level. With its large and young population—a large proportion knowing English, the language of global business—India has a huge advantage. Building on its strength, the country has taken first few faltering steps to seize the opportunity. India is now perceived to be a frontrunner in global knowledge economy. However, there are concerns that the country's antiquated system of higher education and training will put a brake to this forward move.

Underlying the first two trends is the challenge of competition. The idea of competition has been alien to higher education. Now, the higher education institutions are increasingly required to compete for students, teachers and funding. While still in its nascent stage, there is now competition from online learning and virtual universities. Finally, in the fast-moving world, an important characteristic for delivery of education is agility—the agility to define and redefine programmes to match needs.

As if these challenges were not enough by themselves, today there is a greater push for accountability from the public and the elected officials. Objective performance measures tied to funding forces higher education institutions to meet the expectations of its many stakeholders. In the field of education, the government is getting more and more entrenched in its management. Countries respond to these challenges in their own ways, yet, with the growing global interconnectedness, these responses cannot but be connected to the developments elsewhere in the world.

In the context of the challenges above, the purpose of higher education needs to be redefined. The concept of diversity, that is becoming a key characteristic of a large system of higher education, needs to be examined. And finally, growing competition and its changing nature has to be studied. With this, the nature of policy support and the manner the system is governed would also change.

Defining the 'Purpose' of Higher Education

Economies of pre-industrial societies were primitive and primarily agrarian. Education in such societies was restricted to a few; it had moral trappings, philosophical moorings and religious orientation. Consequently, it had no direct relationship with the economy. It was generally left to individual initiatives, requiring no planning by the state. Industrialisation, however, endowed education explicitly with an economic value through the forging of both direct and indirect forward and backward linkages between education and economy.

It is empirically established that as an economy moves from lower to higher stages of development, from simpler to complex forms, from agriculture to manufacturing and service-based; not only the range of goods and services produced in the economy increases and gets diversified, but the technological base of production is also upgraded. This leads to changes in occupational structure and enhancement of skill and knowledge requirements for employment. Education undergoes structural transformation along with the economy (Prakash, 1999: 213).

According to Alvin Toffler (1980), mass education became a necessity in the Second Wave (industrial) societies. Built on the factory model, mass education taught basic reading, writing and arithmetic, a bit of history and other subjects. This was the 'overt curriculum'. But beneath it lay an invisible or 'covert curriculum' that was far more basic. It consisted, and still does in most industrial nations, of three courses: one in punctuality, one in obedience, and one in rote, repetitive work. Factory labour demanded workers who showed up on time, especially the assembly line hands. It demanded workers who would take orders from a management hierarchy without questioning. Thus from the mid-19th century onwards, as the Second Wave cut across country after country, one found a relentless educational progression: children started school at a younger and younger age, the school year became longer and longer, and the number of years of compulsory schooling irresistibly increased.

The evolution of economic purposes of education was the single most important educational development of the 20th century. This affected most other changes—including the enormous expansion of formal education, battles over issues of equity and access, many curricular debates and economic competition amongst nations. That education can lead to economic, social and individual salvation has been accepted like a 'gospel' by an extraordinary range of thinkers, policymakers, reformers, most educators and much of the general public.

Though there has been some talk of the civic roles of education, but in most cases, the discussion comes back to international comparisons and the economic effects of illiteracy. Mass education has been seen as a humanising step forward. The symbolism apart, a glancing reference to the role of education in civic and intellectual development shows that it is often more rhetorical than substantive, as if to placate the few dissenters who embrace the older conceptions of education. Thus, the benefits of education are often assumed rather than demonstrated. The same is true of higher education. It is difficult to measure the value added by higher education over and beyond the student's innate abilities. According to Wolf (2004), 'just as an arms race does not lead to greater security despite much greater spending, the upward spiral in education credentialing may not yield social benefits commensurate to the expenditure.'

In the 1960s, the recognition of human capital as an agent of growth, transformed not only development economics but it also led to the resurgence of economics of education. The productivity enhancing effect of education and its differential impacts on income in accordance with differential educational endowments of workers attracted attention of policy makers and analysts (Prakash, 1999 : 217–18).

Thus, today higher education is seen to play a key role in the development of both human beings and modern societies as it enhances social, cultural and economic development. It is seen to promote active citizenship and inculcate ethical values. It serves both public and private purposes and is also responsible both for social and economic development. Social and economic roles of higher education and the public and private benefits that it accrues are given in Table 9.2. Precise measures of various contributions of higher education are not feasible. Due to the multiple roles of higher education and the difficulty in measuring their relative importance, there is a continuing debate as to which of these roles is the key role of higher education, and thus it

Perspectives

TABLE 9.2 Potential benefits from higher education

Benefits	Public	Private
Social	Nation building and development of leadership Democratic participation; increased consensus; perception that the society is based on fairness and opportunity for all citizens Social mobility Greater social cohesion and reduced crime rates Improved health Improved basic and secondary education	Improved quality of life for self and children Better decision making Improved personal status Increased educational opportunities Healthier lifestyle and higher life expectancy
Economic	Greater Productivity National and regional development Reduced reliance on government financial support Increased consumption Increased potential for transformation Increased potential for transformation from low-skill industrial to knowledge-based economy	Higher salaries Employment Higher savings Improved working conditions Personal and professional Personal and professional mobility

Source Adapted from IHEP (1998: 20).

remains an unsettled issue. However, it is quite clear that the potential benefits of higher education are not mutually exclusive and their relative importance would depend on the context of the debate.

The relative importance of social or economic goals of higher education would also depend upon the developments taking place in the larger society and economy. In countries where democracy has preceded economic liberalisation, there is a rapid expansion of democratic educational systems based on political principles (Dore, 1976). In such cases, the focus has been on arts and humanities with little relation to the skills required in the market economy. This resulted in the problem of over-education faced by many countries.

In the recent years, several studies undertaken across the world have focused on the inter-linkages between education and economic development and such linkages are well-established now. From an earlier focus mainly on primary and secondary education, there is now an emphasis on higher education as one of the most potent means of achieving sustainable development. It is realised that though primary and secondary education are important, it is the quality and the size of the higher education system that will differentiate a dynamic economy from a marginalised one. It is now accepted that without more and better higher education, developing countries will find it increasingly difficult to benefit from the global knowledge-based economy (World Bank, 2000).

It is now established that access to quality higher education is crucial in enabling an individual to benefit from economic opportunities and thereby leading to expansion in income and economic means (Dreze and Sen, 1995). Education does not only bring higher income but it also enables individuals to make rational decisions. As a result education is a determining factor not only in income generation and income distribution but in all decision making by the individuals.

Increasingly, higher education is being seen as an instrument for getting a set of skills, attitudes and values for participation as a productive agent in modern market economy based on technological progress achieved in recent times. Thus, academic institutions now function as business enterprises that lay premium on current needs and economic utility in place of academic values. The current trend in education will have major implications for how we think of schooling and the university, the ownership and transmission of knowledge and indeed the role of citizenship in modern society (Umakoshi, 2004).

Many developing countries are making massive efforts to achieve universal primary education and expand secondary education. For such countries, the role of higher education in support of overall education system has become increasingly important as they move from the universalisation of basic education to the progressive massification of secondary education and become stricter in demanding mandatory higher education qualifications for primary and secondary school teachers (World Bank, 2002: 81). Growing prosperity and rapid advances in communications and mass media has resulted in raising the aspirations of the people. Higher education enables upward social and economic mobility. Thus, access to higher education is seen as an effective means to meet raised aspirations.

For the higher education sector, whose main purpose is to train people with strong analytical skills, it is ironical that its own self-analysis is replete with homilies and platitudes rather than strong evidence. Nevertheless, the above discussion reiterates that there are both public and private benefits from investment in higher education. Thus, while there is a case for public spending on higher education, there is an equally strong case for higher education to be funded by the students and their families. This creates dilemma for policymakers on how higher education is to be funded and the manner in which growing private financing of higher education is to be viewed. This would obviously impact access and equity and would depend on socio-political realities and evolving economic policy.

Concept of 'Diversity' in Higher Education

There are two distinct models of higher education. First, there is 'Anglo-American' model that sees the higher education provision as heterogeneous. It encourages diversity, varied forms of provision and quality comparisons between them. Second, the 'Scandinavian model', that is based on the assumption that institutions are homogeneous, and therefore treats them equally and regards all programmes as equal. Higher education with large enrolment is incompatible with the second model. Thus, the Indian higher education system supports a diverse, decentralised system.

At the time of independence, with a small number of universities and colleges offering degrees in a limited range of subjects, it was possible to assume that all universities were equally good and hence it was possible fund them equally. Today there are more universities, more students and a much greater diversity of subjects. As a result, the characteristics and the costs of different degrees at different institutions vary widely, and therefore institutions need to be funded and treated differentially (Barr, 2004).

Fostering systemic diversity is a key issue in the emerging governance model for higher education systems worldwide. While on the face of it there appears to be a large institutional diversity in India, careful analysis shows that such diversity is largely in terms of the origin of these institutions and not in terms of offerings or differentiation in missions of these institutions. With most universities and colleges focused on ACS, institutional variation in the system does not reflect the social heterogeneity, economic complexity and the cultural variety of the country. There is a need for the higher education system to align itself with the social diversity and the more complex division of labour in the economy today. Thus, increased institutional diversity is to be pursued as an objective for a robust system of higher education.

Unfortunately, Indian higher education is driven by an unrealistic myth of uniformity. This originates from three legitimate concerns. First, it is commonly believed that all degrees are equal irrespective of the institution that awards them. Equality is further guaranteed by common curricula. In reality, degree is *also* a signalling device and the society, particularly the employers, needs a mechanism to evaluate relative quality of different institutions. Second, it is seen that inequality in quality of institutions is likely to create class-related inequality, with the well-off students attending better institutions, thus getting an easy access to social and economic opportunity. Thus, policies that ensure the levelling-off of the quality are often pursued. This usually brings everyone down to a lower level. And finally, the academic profession itself has a deep intellectual commitment to egalitarianism, though it has very elaborate hierarchies within itself.

Elite institutions are targeted for pursuing 'elitism' in higher education. According to Nicholas Barr (2004: 266), while social elitism, where social background influences access to the best universities, is wrong, 'intellectual elitism is both proper and desirable.' 'There is nothing wrong with intellectually elite universities. Equity objective should be a system in which the ability of the brightest students to study in the best universities is unrelated to their social backgrounds.' In the notion of system, both elitism and mass universality are reconciled through the promotion of institutional differentiation. Thus, it is desirable to pursue diversity in provision of Indian higher education as an important goal.

Different Missions

In large and diverse systems of higher education, institutions have different missions. Such missions usually evolve with time. In the past, the focus of institutions of higher learning used to be on religious and moral values. Higher education was meant only for the elite and intended to prepare just a few leaders for society's institutions. Though the first modern universities began appearing in Europe from the 12th century onwards and then migrated to the non-European world, but it was only in the 18th century after the French Revolution that universities played a larger role in industrial society (Perkin, 2006). Learning at work—either informally or in formal apprenticeship—was traditionally the way young people made transition to work; now many jobs require specialised high level training. As a result, during the 19th century, the synthesis of moral, civic and intellectual purposes of higher education has been eroded, giving way to professional goals.

In the last decades of the 19th century, universities had become pivotal institutions of new society. Agriculture and manufacturing became efficient, partly using scientific research from the universities. A larger number of people required specialised training. The concept of useful knowledge—rooted in practice and experience, and expanded through the application of scientific methods—began to spread. This necessitated some kind of formal schooling, but college degree was not mandated for any profession—not even medicine, law or engineering.

Over time, each profession created a liturgy about the importance of specialised knowledge—biology and chemistry for doctors, legal procedures and practice for lawyers, applied science for engineers—and this school-based knowledge began to be valued more than work-based knowledge. Thus began formal courses of study, degree requirements and licensing requirements for a variety of professions. Though it began with medicine, law and engineering, but soon spread to business, education, social work and nursing, which had lower status. This process continues still, reaching lower and lower in the hierarchy of occupational status (Grub and Lazerson, 2004: 62–63).

Though with rapid growth of professional education,[4] there was relative decline in liberal arts education, yet liberal arts education

421

found its own supporters. It is not only very large in many countries like India for historical reasons, but several elite institutions have a strong tradition of liberal arts, primarily focused on producing leaders of the society's institutions. Between the 19th century and the World War II, undergraduate liberal arts education became a prerequisite for specialised professional education and thus liberal arts education integrated with specialised professional training became a part of the higher education curriculum in the United States. Such an integrated curriculum continues to be the strength of US higher education, with few examples outside the United States. In all, there is a great variety of institutions of higher education that serve different purposes.

Institutional Typology

Changing purposes of higher education were served by different types of institutions, creating a highly differentiated system of higher education in most parts of the world. Though most people tend to agree to differentiation, yet the debate on higher education does not sufficiently recognise this. Analysts have identified four different functions of higher education and the institutional setting in which these are discharged. These are academic leadership, professional development function, technological training and development function and function of general higher education (Castro and Levy, 2001). This typology, though tentative, helps in explaining the actual and potential differentiation in higher education. This would also contribute to the debate over policy—from finance, to governance, to quality controls—by promoting an appreciation of the differences appropriate to different forms of higher education, since neither conceptually nor in terms of policy does one size fit all.

Academic Leadership

The function of academic leadership involves a highly prepared faculty, sophisticated original research published in rigorously reviewed, internationally recognised outlets; post-graduate education; and selective undergraduate education. These are usually the attributes identified with quality and require ample resources and substantial autonomy. Considered the most prestigious function within academia, it occurs more rarely than claimed, though many policy prescriptions treat the great bulk of higher education incorrectly as if it conformed, or should conform, to the academic leadership function.

Professional Development

This function refers mostly to the preparation of students for specific job markets requiring advanced, extensive formal education. The classic professions like law are joined today by fields like computer science. In many fields, pertinent research, often applied, exists alongside training. Like the academic leadership function, the professional development function is less common than claimed, and it is too often the proclaimed model for parts of higher education that are not well suited to it.

Professional higher education by mistake tries to mimic (whether by choice or coercive rules) standards and policies devised with academic leadership in mind, with disastrous consequences. In professional education, the marketplace is often a better guide to policy and judge of performance than are academically idealised peer review or accreditation systems.

Technological Training and Development

The technological function is newer, either previously nonexistent or found more commonly at a lower educational level or in on-the-job training. In addition to some applied research, this function is mostly about preparation, often short term, for direct insertion into the job market.

Here the need is paramount for strong ties to the job market in matters like curriculum development, choice of professors and evaluation of outcomes. Rapid responsiveness is crucial and should not be hampered by governance and rules more appropriate to other functions. It is also important that technical education not be simply poor quality professional education. In general, this form of higher education needs to be accorded greater respect and serve as one of the two main types of growing mass higher education.

General Higher Education

General higher education students who wind up working in jobs other than those directly in the studied subject matter forms the bulk of the Indian higher education system. This looks like a failure because it lays claim to academic leadership. Yet it needs to be pursued and valued. It is probably the form through which most students in large higher education systems can develop analytical skills in reading, writing and thinking that will be useful in a variety of possible jobs; and in broader roles for citizens. Where employment does not correspond to rigid plans of study, curriculum and pedagogy should be redesigned. It is for general higher education that accreditation systems may be most suitable. General higher education offers possibilities for distance education and other alternatives to traditional higher education.

Most people, particularly from the academia, would like to see the entire higher education sector fulfilling the academic leadership function. They often detest the continuous drift of higher education from academic to occupational purpose, yet they fail to realise that it is this drift that will induce more and more people to opt for higher education. If higher education were not the gateway to high-wage jobs, it would have remained confined to a small group of elite people. The reality is that the number of higher education institutions that would rightly qualify to fall in this category is very small. The bulk of Indian higher education is geared to train and develop young people for jobs either through specialised curricula or general curricula that help develop their analytical and thinking skills. Yet, all institutions mimic this tiny section of institutions that provide academic leadership. It is therefore not surprising that we are faced with many contradictions in our debate on higher education.

Changing Nature of 'Competition' in Higher Education

For most academics, concept of markets and competition in higher education is an anathema. However, unlike in business, the concept of market is used here in a very broad sense to denote the process of clearing of demand and supply. In higher education, supply–demand clearing takes place at two levels: one is the clearing of the supply of places in higher education with the demand for the same; and the second is the clearing of supply of the graduates from the higher education institutions and the demand for them from the labour markets. It is useful to make this distinction to understand the paradox of mounting skill shortages that co-exist with growing unemployment and underemployment of graduates. This has been discussed in detail in Chapter 5.

Clearing of demand and supply in higher education is unique. Here the students are both consumers and producers. There is a hierarchy of providers that do not necessarily pursue profit maximisation. Higher education markets are also subject to serious market failures arising primarily from information asymmetry and time lag. These factors are elaborated below to describe the distinctive market structure in higher education.

In higher education, the quality of education depends upon the quality of students. Students choose those institutions that admit more meritorious students, merit being a proxy for quality. Institutions improve their quality by choosing more meritorious students. The quality of institutions is often determined by the quality of students. The students buy and sell peer quality. This makes the students both consumers and producers of higher education.

Though economic rationale is predominant, not all students pursue higher education for economic reasons. They pursue it for a variety of reasons. Similarly, all higher education institutions do not necessarily look for economic returns. They may not pursue profit maximisation but strive for excellence or academic reputation. Prestige plays the part in higher education that price plays in the conventional markets. This reinforces the tendency of many institutions to direct their resources towards those activities that may be valued by many academics but not necessarily by the wider society. For this reason, one often goes wrong in assuming that the consumer (the student) and the producer (the higher education institution) would behave in a rational manner. Its consequences are not easy to factor in while designing a regulatory framework for higher education.

With peer effects and prestige playing important roles, higher education institutions are sharply hierarchical. Higher education is highly stratified at the top. Whereas there could be a large number of vacant seats in many institutions, a few institutions at the top end of the hierarchy attract many times the number of students that they can accommodate, making them very selective. High selectivity goes hand in hand with high reputation. According to Kirp (2003), prestige is a scarce commodity in higher education and the losers far outnumber the winners, with the winners taking it all. This makes branding very important in higher education.

With the price elasticity for higher education being low, reputed institutions that attract a large number of students could charge heavy tuition fees. However, they do not do so in all cases, since they pursue prestige maximisation rather than profit maximisation. Naturally, prices alone fail to balance the demand and supply. In fact, in the United States, where higher education is very expensive, prestigious institutions use their income from donations to attract high-quality students. As a trade off between their ability to charge high tuition and the necessity to attract meritorious students, the reputed institutions usually adopt high-tuition high-aid strategy.

Efficient market competition presumes that consumers have perfect information about price and quality. In the case of experience goods like academic programmes, need for credible consumer information is even more crucial.[5] Non-availability of such information results in market failure, often described as market failure due to information asymmetry. According to Dill (2004), information asymmetry in higher education can arise due to student immaturity, the provider furnishing misleading information or both the provider and students having only imperfect information about the true quality of the academic programmes.

For competition to assist in clearing demand and supply in higher education, its quality has to be somehow determined or at least there is need for signals about quality. Higher education institutions usually send out four major signals. These are fees and tuition, alumni giving and tangible goods financed by alumni giving, selectivity and the scientific reputation of professors (Franck and Schönfelder, 2000).

In the Indian context, signals other than student selectivity are weak. Even on selectivity, reliable information is difficult to get.

'Quasi-markets' in Higher Education

In increasingly diverse systems of higher education, the authority of the government, its mode of collective decision making, its use of command-and-control steering approaches, the budget mechanism and the monopoly of state-run higher education institutions are increasingly being questioned. It is feared that government interference may impede incentives for quality, efficiency and differentiation. As a consequence, new and less hierarchical relationships between the government and higher education providers have emerged and governments and administrators have started to experiment with more market-oriented steering and organisation models.

While the market may fail, there is a possibility that government may fail as well. Faced with this challenge, many governments and policymakers have ended up with quasi-markets in order to reach a compromise. In a quasi-market situation decisions on demand and supply are coordinated using 'market-like' mechanisms in which only some of the 'essential ingredients' of markets (Jongbloed, 2003) are introduced, often gradually. This was done in an attempt to simulate market behaviour among public institutions, as in the creation of internal markets. Though government regulation and financing still remain important co-ordination mechanisms, elements of competition, such as user charges, individual responsibilities and freedom of choice have been injected into the system.

The introduction of quasi-markets in higher education is a combination of three main developments. The first is the promotion of competition between higher education providers. The second is the privatisation of higher education, either by the emergence of a private higher education sector or by means of 'privatisation' of certain aspects of public institutions (Williams, 1991). This is evident in Indian case from Chapter 3. The third and final development is the promotion of financial autonomy of higher education institutions, enhancing their responsiveness and articulation to the supply and demand of factors and products. The move towards this has been clearly demonstrated in Chapter 4.

The arrival of market rhetoric in higher education in the early 1980s gave an extra boost to the arguments for private provision. The idea was that the private sector, armed with greater administrative flexibility, and driven by financial incentives, was more responsive to both niche and new markets. There is a widespread conviction that the 'market' will be more effective than state regulation in promoting diversity of higher education systems, both in terms of institutional types, of programmes and activities.

Despite market forces for higher education in India being active, the market for higher education in India is not yet fully developed. The problem of market and non-market failures gets further aggravated because of the awkward economics of higher education. As a result, the outcomes are far from perfect and in some cases disastrous. In this regard, the US experience with competition in higher education is illustrative. There is a huge demand in the US for information about higher education. This has taken the form of an increased number of accreditation committees, all of which are private. The role of the public sector is through independent bodies like the NSF, which has allowed competition among both private and public universities for grants and funds for scholarships. The greatest difference is in the degree of central control. In the US, there is a huge competition for faculty positions, in terms of both salaries and other benefits (remarks of Anne Krueger at the India Policy Forum, 2007 at New Delhi).

In that sense, the Indian system does not have any competition. Even the salaries in the private colleges are essentially determined by the government, which enforces elaborate criteria and guidelines that severely restrict most forms of competition. There are, however, some areas where competition has set in and the system appears to be working fine. There are two areas where the system seems to be working well: engineering colleges and business education. Where competition has been allowed, quality has improved, and that also explains why India has done well is some specific skill areas.

Perspectives

Rationale for Regulation

Perfect competition and efficient markets are an ideal that are difficult to achieve in real life. Perfect competition requires homogeneity of products, absence of entry and exit barriers, perfect knowledge and perfect mobility and unbiased behaviour to facilitate exchange to be guided only by the considerations of price. Violation of even one of them would render the competition imperfect. The discussion in the previous section shows that higher education follows an awkward economics. It breaches all conditions required for perfect competition. Under the circumstances, leaving the higher education system to the uncertainties of the market may lead to undesirable consequences—lack of competition, for instance, would be one of its main consequences. Several factors that impeded competition in the past are less important now.

Limited student mobility hindered competition and made the price quality ratio worse. With technological change in transport and communications, student mobility has now increased. In new models of education, with distance education and online learning growing in popularity, it is the programmes rather than students that move. This has extended the higher education market beyond national borders and led to enhanced competition in the higher education sector.

Higher education programmes are to an extent indivisible. An entry decision is a 'yes' or a 'no' decision. This implies that students are in a sense locked in to their respective institutions. Increasing flexibilities in programme structures, facilitating student mobility by easing credit transfers are to an extent addressing this problem.

Finally, educational production is characterised by economies of scale. Many programmes require expensive equipments and laboratories. This implies that large institutions have a cost advantage over small ones and there are substantial entry barriers for newcomers. New learning environment is changing this now.

From the above, it is seen that the changing structure and delivery of higher education and increasing use of technology are creating a competitive market for higher education. A total reliance on market forces alone, though, is not the most desirable option. While the market forces are increasingly used to coordinate and steer the higher education systems, yet their limitations are becoming clearer. Signals on quality are weak. Rising inequities, increasing exploitation of gullible students, deteriorating standards and skewed growth necessitate government intervention. The regulatory system therefore has to address the limitations of market forces. In an environment, where higher education is subject to ever changing cultural and structural changes, there is increasing public demand for regulation and new kinds of accountability.

Status and Prospects

Our key findings from the previous chapters tell us that skill shortages exist despite high graduate unemployment, and the value of a degree is diminishing in job markets in India even as it is simultaneously losing credibility all over the world. Higher education has also increasingly become unaffordable for students from poor economic backgrounds. At the same time, a number of the public institutions in India have proven to be non-viable and of poor standard. Such poor standards extend to academic research, and the small base of post-graduate education and research, particularly in science and engineering is a matter of concern. The technology infrastructure in India is still very poor. The lack of proper policy guidance has sent the wrong message to the prestigious foreign research universities and big corporates in India are not welcome to enter the higher education sector. The accreditation system currently in place has no consequences. Education in the basic sciences and subjects that are not market friendly has suffered in the recent years. Research in higher education institutions is at its lowest ebb. There is an inadequate and diminishing financial support for higher education from the government and from the society.

India faces the challenge of improving the quality of its higher education and enhancing access while maintaining equity. To realise the economic, personal and social aims of higher education within the limits of available resources and competing priorities, both the purposes and the nature of higher education have to be examined critically and realistically. The continuously changing relationship between higher education and the subsequent employment should be reflected both in the institutions and in individual choices. Creative ways have to be found out to do so. In this context, the Eleventh Five Year Plan has decided upon three objectives of higher education: access and expansion; equity and inclusion; quality and excellence.

It is difficult to understand Indian higher education today without understanding the massive and multifaceted private growth. It has many similarities to precedents and trends elsewhere, yet in several ways it is different.

Access and Expansion

The Indian higher education system overall is large and it is small. With 13.7 million students enrolled, India is behind only China and the United States, nearly matching all of Europe, all of Latin America and far outdistancing all of Africa. It is large in raw numbers. With more than 20,000 institutions—universities and colleges together—it easily tops the figures in any other country. Because the great majority are 'affiliated' institutions, with the colleges affiliated to about 120 public universities, the high figure depends on counting each college as an institution. The numbers are more than the rest of world taken together. The large numbers mean very small average enrolment in each institution, resulting in the higher education landscape being dotted with a large number of tiny non-viable institutions.

Higher education system is highly fragmented and organised sub-optimally. The number of universities and other degree-granting institutions is growing slowly, though at just about 400 this number is still very small. Due to the affiliating university system, there are a large number of small and non-viable colleges. There is a need for consolidation by merging and clustering of universities and colleges in order to achieve critical mass for effective intellectual exchange, benefit from synergy and sharing of infrastructure and facilities. Since the number of universities is small and there is little difference even among the universities, the system is driven to achieve uniformity disregarding the country's social diversity and increasingly complex division of labour in the Indian economy today. Thus, there is very little choice for students.

The system is now large compared to where it was in the recent past. At the time of independence in 1947, the system had only 100,000 students, in 20 universities and 500 affiliated colleges. Yet, even now the Indian system is small in that it still enrols only about 12 per cent of its age cohort. Several states have as little as half that rate, while a few have nearly 30 per cent. This leaves India not only far behind all developed countries but also even Brazil, China and Indonesia. Indian higher education's smallness is not merely a contradiction to the largeness. Rather, it indicates that Indian higher education has a huge room for growth. The growth rate was spectacular in the 1950s and 1960s, then predictably slipping later in the century. The number of institutions has more than tripled in the last quarter century and the system is still growing.

The enrolment pattern in the country is skewed in favour of arts and humanities. There is small enrolment at the post-graduate and doctoral levels. The colleges account for some nine-tenths of undergraduate and two-thirds of graduate enrolments. A majority of the colleges offer higher education only in the conventional streams, and therefore they are not able to attract enough candidates for admission while the seats in professional and technical higher education are limited in the public-funded institutions. Students now prefer market-linked professional and technical higher education in place of general ACS courses.

The elite institutes of higher education have a different culture and status in the Indian system and their numbers continue to be small. Below this tiny top, the quality falls rapidly, and the bulk of the institutions are of very low quality. Recently, the central government has decided to set up several IITs, IIMs and other premier institutions for higher professional education. Sixteen new central universities and 14 world-class universities are also proposed. This would be largest ever publicly funded expansion of the higher education sector. Yet, its impact on increasing enrolment numbers would be only marginal, since most of the growth of Indian higher education now takes place in the private sector.

In the recent years, there has been a clamour for the expansion of higher education in the context of mounting skill shortages. It is a paradox that in India skill shortages co-exist with the rising graduate unemployment and underemployment. Careful examination of the issue in Chapter 5 shows that while there may not be a problem of production of graduates in terms of absolute numbers, the problem is in the uneven quality of the graduates produced. This is getting aggravated with an increased appetite of industry in recent years with the country's rapid economic growth, investment boom and structural changes. Further, skill shortages are at the low end where graduate skills are not required or of blue collar skilled workers. People fail to distinguish between the general situation and specific, narrow, local needs. As a result, there is widespread misperception about general skill shortages and higher education expansion addressing that problem. Thus skill shortages are not general, but specific and often temporary due to recent developments. The solution may not lie in large scale expansion of higher education, but in identifying the shortages and finding context-specific solutions. The Indian system is skewed in favour of humanities and arts and almost four-fifths of the graduates it churns out have no employable skills. With rigid academic structures, there is little student choice and large heterogeneity in terms of quality.

Notwithstanding the arguments above, there is both potential for growth and the aspiration to expand higher education. There is a large aspiration gap in demand and supply of higher education. All the three foundations—the psychological, the social and the cultural—of people's behaviour that drive their aspirations are going through a major transition. Higher education expansion has to address this gap. Now that the labour market for skilled people, particularly highly skilled people, has become a global market, limitations of absorption in the domestic economy are no more relevant. Thus, higher education expansion is driven primarily by rising aspirations and social demand.

In a comparative perspective, Indian higher education has low percentage of mature students beyond 23–24 years. As the society and the economy develops, there is a large potential for growth in demand from mature students. Special opportunity for growth also lies in female enrolment. Despite huge growth from just 10 per cent of the total in 1950, the female share still lags at only 40 per cent, and predictably far worse in many specific fields. In most advanced countries enrolment of female in higher education exceeds that of males, and hence there is a good potential for growth.

The government plans to expand enrolment to reach 15 per cent GER by 2012. This would require additional capacity for 7.5 million students. For this growth, momentum has to be sustained and further accelerated over the next few years by adopting a multi-pronged strategy. While new universities and colleges could be established in the underserved areas, increasing the intake in the existing universities and colleges would be most cost-effective. Universities could set up campuses and colleges could run in double shift in order to optimise utilisation of infrastructure. In this regard, restrictions imposed by some state governments for second shift colleges need to be revisited.

While expanding capacity, priority needs to be given to professional and technical courses, where the supply–demand gap continues to be large. Capacity in courses where seats remain unfilled needs to be reviewed. A special drive may be launched for curricular changes and the introduction of additional skill-based courses. However, as preference for such courses are rapidly declining amongst students, these courses must be made compulsory for students pursuing professional and technical courses in universities and colleges. Expansion should, however, not be at the cost of quality and excellence. New universities and colleges must be well-funded and have necessary, infrastructure and facilities, teaching and non-teaching staff.

There is a need for consolidation through mergers. Giving due regard to the demography of the geographic regions in which a college is located, the optimal enrolment in a multi-disciplinary university could be around 10,000 students. Enrolment in a college could be 5,000 in the large cities and be about 2,000 in other areas. Public universities and colleges could be encouraged to start self-financing courses with oversight over the quality of such courses.

The existing affiliating system is indeed a drain on the university system as a lot of time, energy and resources of the universities are spent on the conduct of examination and other affiliation related works. While it may not be possible to do away with the affiliation system in totality in near future, processes may be initiated to gradually unburden universities from the affiliating responsibilities. Towards this end, it is suggested that the number of affiliated colleges, which presently could be as high as 400 per university, could be reduced to a maximum of 50 per university. Ideally, a university should affiliate colleges in three districts, but special exceptions will have to be made for universities affiliating colleges in remote and hill areas, where fewer colleges may have to be affiliated to a single university for reasons of difficult terrain.

Big and established colleges (say with enrolment more than 5,000) and colleges offering post-graduate courses could be given autonomous status and empowered to award degrees in their own names. Each affiliating university could set up an independent board of undergraduate studies to handle examination and curricular related work of the affiliated colleges.

Private institutions have grown rapidly over the past two decades and from the trends, it seems that it is destined to grow further. Thus, private higher education has a positive role in expanding access. Private colleges affiliated with public university offer a very interesting model for public–private partnership that brings in their relative strength. Several other countries including China are now using this model for expanding their higher education system.

Although there has been *de facto* privatisation through the entry of private colleges, the same is not true for private universities. The creation of private universities still requires either the central government or the state governments to pass authorising legislations. Arvind Pangariya, at the India Policy Forum 2007, argued that the system is far too constraining and obviously restricts competition. Additionally, he pointed out that each private college has to affiliate itself to some public university, and if that public university happens to have a terrible reputation, then the terrible reputation spills over to the college. It cannot build its own reputation.

Growth of private higher education leaves large gaps. Public higher education is required to fill in these gaps. The public higher education system has to step in the areas of post-graduate education and research and for education in liberal arts, humanities and languages. Public funding has to take of care of those who cannot afford higher education. Similarly, there are unreal expectations from foreign providers. It is time now to face realities and correct the systemic anomalies and wrong notions about private higher education—both domestic and foreign. While private education would enhance access, foreign providers could energise local providers, both by example and competition.

A contrasting perspective is provided by noting that if higher education was viewed as an industry—with new entrants, increased market share of the new entrants, and active involvement in shaping outcomes—the pessimism that dominated the session seems surprising. This is not just a problem created by the state but also by professional organisations, which place restrictions on the activities and pursuits of its members.

Recent debates on financing Indian higher education are primarily confined to increasing the funding levels. Public spending as a percentage of GDP in the country is often compared with that in the advanced countries. Estimated at 1 per cent (with almost the same contributed through private finance), the level of spending is not low. At the same time, given the differences in country systems, levels of development, size of the country and in definitions, comparisons should not be pushed too far. Relative effort expressed in terms of per student expenditure as a proportion of per capita GDP at 95 per cent is one of the highest in the world. However, in absolute terms and on per student basis, funding levels are very low.

The higher education system in India has so far adopted an inward looking approach, concerned primarily to meet the domestic demand for higher education. With the integration of the country with the rest of world and the growing trade, investment and mobility of people, there is a need for outward looking approaches in higher education. The Indian higher education sector should not only be able to meet the domestic demand but also the international demand for qualified and trained manpower.

Further, the focus in the past has been mainly on the formal system of higher education and that too the public university system. Under the changed circumstances, we need to take into account the higher education institutions, both from the public and private sectors. The reputed and established public universities provide a strong foundation for the higher education system in the country. Big and emerging private sector institutions provide the required dynamism and responds to the growing demand for professional courses. The private training sectors offering short-cycle courses meet the requirement of skills and competences required by fast-changing industry like the IT/ITES sector. The varied sets of institutions bring in their respective strengths to meet the diversified needs of the economy and the various stakeholders. A differentiated higher education system with high adaptive capacity is needed in the country today.

Equity and Inclusion

With increased enrolment, various disparities are less stark now, yet these persist. Gender disparities are decreasing, but at 4 to 6 per cent are still significant. Inter-caste disparities, with enrolment of ST candidates the lowest, SC candidates lower and OBC candidates slightly lower than others are still high. Inter-religious disparities, particularly lower participation of Muslims than others, are stark. With enrolment in rural areas one-third or one-fourth of that in urban areas, rural–urban divide is large. There is a wide inter-state variation in enrolment. The north-eastern states, Bihar, West Bengal and even Karnataka have much lower enrolment in higher education than the national average.

Inclusive growth is now central to development agenda. Opportunities for higher education are viewed as the most potent tool to address problem of such inequalities. Reform process has created several types of inequalities. There is an impression that the country's boom has mainly benefited a small section. Such people get access to high status and the best-paid jobs by ensuring that their children are admitted to high-quality institutions, which are very few in the country. Since family background operates in many ways to give an edge to children of privileged parents for entry in these institutions, thus policy of correction becomes necessary. Such policies are stridently opposed by those who stand to lose and seen to be compromising on excellence.

Mere expansion in institutions and intake capacity shall not necessarily make higher education inclusive. This will call for a careful planning and policy framework to make higher education accessible by all. For this, the problem of regional disparities has to be removed through targeted expansion of quality higher educational institutions in the deprived and underprivileged rural and remote areas. Economic barriers in accessing higher education have to be crossed by offering targeted scholarship, fellowship and subsidies to those who cannot afford higher education. An effective student loan programme should be put in place to finance higher education of those who cannot afford to pay.

In this context, higher education finance is caught in a dilemma between two seemingly conflicting views. One, the widespread belief that it is immoral to charge for education and therefore higher education should be free. Two, there is a trend towards less government spending even in the most established areas of public services and higher education is no exception. Despite political sensitiveness of the debate, there is consensus that there should not be any financial barriers to participation in higher education for the economically disadvantaged. In principle, this could be done by an all knowing central planner. In practice, the problem is too complex. A mass system in an increasingly complex world needs a funding mechanism which allows institutions to charge differential prices to different costs and missions. Central planning is no longer feasible.

With larger number of households capable of and willing to pay for higher education, there is scope to rationalise tuition fees in public institutions and raise resources. Furthermore, the growth of largely tuition-dependent private higher education that has pushed up the cost of higher education raising concerns about equity. Thus, well-funded schemes of freeships and scholarships for students from poor families are urgently required. There is a larger scope for student loan programmes, but these have to be properly designed. Public spending (particularly central expenditure) on students aid schemes for poor students needs to be substantially raised with simplified procedure for disbursement and the student loan financing to become a major source of funding. More specifically, students aid scheme in the form of deferred payment of fees on graduation and employment with risk of unemployment/underemployment transferred to the government could be initiated. The ICLs could be provided through a wide range of private and public sector lenders with a third party servicing of loans and government guarantees and attractive tax cuts against money spent on education would promote spending on education.

Perspectives

Put in place a 'social equity fund' for financing means-tested grants for students from poor background; guarantees for students' loans, putting in place income contingent loans for certain category of students so as to promote equity in access to higher education. Evolve an 'affirmative action policy' that provides equality of opportunity to students belonging to the rural areas and from poor families so that they compete with their counterparts in the cities and from more affluent background on equal footing in to complete their academic exercise without compromising on the overall competitiveness of the Indian higher education.

Some key developments in the debate on higher education finance relate to the growing role of private finance, cost recovery measures, fund allocation mechanisms to enforce accountability, role of the third stream and philanthropy in funding, the issue of efficient use of funds and thus debate on management of institutions, new funding arrangements with new and different types providers including cross border providers, distance education and e-learning, and so on, and public funding to address issues relating disparities in participation and inequity in access to higher education.

Quality and Excellence

There are substantial variations in quality across institutions of higher education. While there are a small number of high-quality institutions, bulk of them are of very low quality and sub-standard. Several factors are responsible for this. These include: infrastructure constraints, financial difficulties, inadequacies in regulatory framework, inconsequential accreditation, problem of faculty. The system is not geared to ensure accountability and attract talent. Public education needs systemic governance reforms. It needs greater competition so that students have effective choices. This competition requires opening up of this sector to all kinds of institutions.

In terms of financing, it is seen that the relative role of the government has continually declined. The expenditure per student has declined rapidly over the years. The central government's role is marginal and skewed in favour of select institutions directly under its control. Resource crunch is particularly serious with respect to the state universities and colleges. Academic expenditure in the form of books and journals, consumables for labs and teaching–learning materials is often the first casualty. The inadequacy of funds has led to inadequate infrastructure and facilities and poor maintenance thereof. This is reflected in shabby classrooms, barely equipped laboratories and poorly maintained libraries. While new universities face these problems, the older universities suffer from obsolescence and dilapidated infrastructure. The physical facilities and infrastructure in colleges, particularly those that are located in rural and remote areas are extremely poor. As a result, it is unable to steer change through public funding. Finally, public funds are mostly disbursed on net-deficit financing basis to institutions (rather than students) that promotes inefficiencies in the system.

There is the need to provide additional funds to the existing public institutions to attain minimum standards of infrastructure and facilities and to bridge the shortfall of teachers. Changes in the fund allocation mechanism to improve the efficiency and effectiveness in use of public funds by institutions, and also public funding to leverage greater investment by state governments and households is necessary. There also needs to be the provision for additional funds for competitive grants to enhance competition in higher education. Furthermore, there has to be a review and harmonisation of the existing guidelines for competitive grants in order to minimise paperwork and enhance their impact with a focus on the outcome. The public higher education system has to be better funded and move away from a model that emphasises standardisation, homogenisation and the lowest common denominator.

In the recent years, with the focus on inclusive growth and increasing the number of premier institutions (seen as fulfilling the aspirations of the powerful middle class), there is political support for financing higher education. With buoyancy in tax revenue, funding from the national government may no longer be a constraint. However, enormous disparity in funding of public institutions will continue. Increased funding may also not be put to optimum use. Such increase is also unlikely to foster institutional reforms required to improve performance. This may in effect result in an intensification of an old institutional structure.

With increasing affluence and the growing middle class, a larger section of people can afford to pay for higher education. There is already a greater reliance on tuition fees by higher education institutions rather than on government grants. A further shift in this direction is possible. In fact, this appears to be only practical option to address the financial crisis faced by the Indian higher education system. Increased contribution of households for higher education would also result in the demand for greater accountability of the institutions to the students and parents. Students and parents would demand value for money.

Of all measures, the faculty and its quality has an enduring impact of the quality of higher education. The condition of the academic profession is thus central to many issues in higher education. The number of academic staff has been seriously affected by resource crunch. There has been either an official ban on the creation of new teaching positions or an unofficial restrictive approach creating hindrance in the process of recruitment of faculty members, even against sanctioned posts. The blanket ban on creation of teaching posts and the recruitment of teaching staff needs to be removed urgently.

Existing evidence suggests that improvement in teacher quality is more likely to come from selecting and retaining better teachers rather from re-training the existing teachers. Special and urgent efforts are needed to attract and retain talent in higher education. Performance-linked incentives to teachers in higher education and allowing them to retain a part of revenue generated by them through research projects, consulting, training programme, short-term courses, management and executive development programmes would help. Since teachers are highly unionised, variable salary structure, though desirable, may not be feasible. The recent decision to relax the NET for appointment in faculty positions may have adverse effect on quality. However, there has been word about the reversal of this decision.

Rather than a centrally determined uniform pay package for teachers in higher education, there should be a differentiated pay-package structure with properly aligned incentives. This should be largely driven by the funding agencies, which would pay according to their means. Apart from attracting and retaining quality teachers, ensuring that they have the incentive to continue to give their best is important. This calls for aligning their incentives with performance on a continuing basis. There is the need to introduce some kind of tenure system and implement a pay-for-performance system. The academic profession has been devalued. It no longer attracts bright people. The teaching community is demotivated. The dynamism in the knowledge sector in India is changing the job market for the academic profession. With opportunities for career growth and consultancy available in the academic profession, bright people would get attracted to this profession.

A number of reforms which is considered as a must like application oriented teaching, introduction of the semester system, introduction of continuous internal assessment, credit based choices and interdisciplinary courses, have not been implemented across all institutions because of the paucity of faculty members. Recourse to part-time and visiting faculty teachers has been adversely affecting the quality of teaching and research. Universities and colleges that have been able to introduce reforms in the teaching–learning process are found to be doing better than those that have continued to resort to conventional methods.

Accountability mechanisms in the higher education system are in disarray. The regulatory system for higher education in India is seen as rigid, ineffective and antediluvian. It is designed for a higher education system that is largely public funded. The regulatory system fails to maintain standards despite formidable entry barriers. The private sector is seen to be indulging in deceptive practices and misrepresentation of facts. Affiliating, regulatory and accreditation system, all work together to promote uniformity and cloning and do not allow experimentation and innovation.

The higher education system has not been able to respond to the changing demands on it due the inflexibility of the public universities and the archaic affiliating college system. This inflexibility is most visible in the courses and curricula that continue to be outdated and irrelevant. There is increased central control, which has led to a homogenised, standardised framework for higher education rather than a framework wherein the different states retain the ability to cater to the needs they perceive in their particular regions (Isher Ahluwalia at the India Policy Forum, 2007). There is a need to improve ability (autonomy) of institutions and put pressure on them to perform (accountability).

Perspectives

In place of a detailed planning and control approach, not found useful in the experience of many countries, a regulatory framework that takes care of the market failures and facilitates market coordination has been advocated. It is proposed that a system to curb deceptive practices and misrepresentation of facts should be put in place. Disclosure standards for higher education institutions including transparency in accounting and 'students right to know' need to be introduced. This alone can address the problem of information asymmetry and enable students and parents to take informed decisions. Recognition, affiliation and approval system of institutions has to be reviewed to plug loopholes and restore its credibility.

It is also important to decentralise wherever possible, remove duplication, rationalise and simplify procedures. An NQA and TLSNs would ensure seamless vertical and horizontal mobility of students and go for curricula renewal on an ongoing basis. The NFQ could create a unified qualification framework for the formal and non-formal systems to internalise and create bridges with the non-formal training system. Learning resources repositories in different subject areas could be put in place to enhance learning effectiveness through coordinated efforts.

With a view to resolve the paradox of high graduate unemployment and shortage of skills co-existing together, the connection between higher education and jobs has to be made more efficient. This can best be achieved by incorporating adaptability in higher education, first by creating conditions so that curriculum and content are continuously updated as per changing needs, and second by the adjustment of admission capacities between different institutions and courses as per job market requirements. The change in the curricula and content with time can be best ensured by the TLSNs that are coordinated through an independent NQA. A mix of public and private and formal and non-formal institutions should bring their respective strengths to put together a strong and dynamic higher education and training system. For a continuous engagement of higher education institutions with industry and employers, setting up of membership-based networks for development of specific skills including generic skills could be a good idea. These networks would also compile and collate labour market intelligence and make it generally available to all for making informed decisions.

It is necessary to create a university and college admission system with national testing in various subjects at different levels to facilitate admissions on the basis of merit, and regulate fees in the private unaided institutions with a focus on transparency and gradually enlarge their discretion in deciding their own fees. The enactment of an umbrella Higher Education Act for better coordination and improved governance at the system level would redefine the roles of different bodies under changed circumstances.

It is proposed that wherever possible, both the authority and the responsibilities can be decentralised in favour of the state governments so that there is a diversity of approach in dealing with issues related to higher education depending on the context of the state. There is no need for coordination across disciplines in higher education except to have a broad qualification framework. In matters of dispute, there could be a higher education tribunal to sort out issues relating to fees and admissions.

Upon an analysis of the progress made on accreditation, it is seen that accreditation serves little purpose in India. Though there are structural defects in the accreditation system in India, the process and practice used for voluntary accreditation follow international norms. The process makes use of instruments that are comparable to the best in the world. The practice of external peer review is similar to the practice followed by most accreditation systems in other countries. However, it has a limited reach, and in the absence of any consequences for accreditation, it has been rendered meaningless. For accreditation to serve a useful purpose its structure needs to be overhauled and consequences have to be built for accreditation. It is organised at the national level. It is voluntary (though at times claimed mandatory) and cyclical. In part due to capacity constraints and largely because of inconsequential nature, its coverage has been poor. While it has definitely helped in sensitising the higher education institutions towards quality, its impact in fostering accountability has been limited. It has a weak signalling power and has limited persuasive role in prospective students' choice of an institution.

Since there is a parallel regulatory system, though weak with several loopholes, accreditation in India does not play the 'gatekeeper' role in higher education as in the case of the United States. For a large system like that of India, multiple accrediting bodies with sufficient capacity to undertake cyclical accreditation are needed. While institutional accreditation could be organised at the regional level, programme accreditation has to be conducted subject wise, involving professionals in respective fields of study. Accreditation has to have consequences and the process itself has to be aligned to the regulatory framework to avoid duplication. Professional accreditation should be based on norms for professional practice, which would require being nationally defined and consistent with global norms. The role of the UGC and the professional councils needs to be redefined under the changed circumstances.

To build up excellence in Indian higher education, academic research requires special attention. Research, more specifically the performance of academic research in the country has been poor. The quality of doctoral research is particularly bad. India lags behind its competitors both in quality and volume of academic research. There is a declining interest in science and mathematics due to the changes taking place in the job markets. As a result, the long-term competitiveness of the country may be at stake. Many scientists and planners rightly bemoan the decline and fall of science. However, there is also a positive perception about India and the enterprise and inventiveness of Indians giving us an edge in certain niche technology areas. The story of research enterprise in India is thus a story of 'hopes' and 'despair'.

Optimism is partly driven by positive perception and partly by upturn in the recent years. Research funding continues to be small, but it has increased in recent years (though not as rapidly as in China). Foreign patenting activity has not picked up, but domestic patenting has grown fast, though it continues to be dominated by patents granted to the multinational companies and foreigners. After remaining stable for many years, number of publications has shown a pronounced upturn over the past five years. The impact of research from India has also been increasing over this time. Indian talent is considered top notch, even though there is concern about the small number of PhDs graduating from Indian universities and the poor quality thereof.

There are also signs of hope in academic research. Several initiatives have been taken to address various concerns. There is good access to expensive e-journals and e-resources. Several new institutions with focus on science and engineering are coming up. Differential and higher level of funding has been recommended by a number of committees and expert groups and some of it already in place. A science and engineering research board with greater autonomy and substantially large funding is being set up. Researchers are going to be provided ownership rights of the research to make research an attractive option. There are plans to set up 14 world-class universities.

Further action is required on several fronts. Scientists in Indian universities and research laboratories should strive to create new knowledge and must work in tandem to ensure that the research findings are quickly translated into application and technology. In order to prepare and produce quality scientific manpower universities and research laboratories must collaborate in order to integrate teaching and research, and to provide application oriented teaching to students. Students in universities and colleges could be required to take up projects in scientific laboratories. Scientists in research laboratories should be involved in teaching in universities and colleges. Collaborative research programmes between universities and research laboratories need to be encouraged. Universities should become powerhouses of research and development and the industry must come forward to fund universities in their drive to take up researchers.

Indian higher education is a collection of varied types of academic institutions serving different segments of students with different purposes, funded in a variety of ways, and with quite diverse levels of quality and accomplishment. One of the main challenges is to craft policies and establish institutional structures that take this reality into account. Centralised structures like the UGC or even the proposed IRAHE are obsolete. It is important to remember that most of the advanced countries pursue differentiation as an objective—one of the recent failures of the Australian higher education system has been over-uniformity.

Diversity in higher education is, therefore, to be pursued as a policy. objective. Uniform quality standards work against this very objective. Higher education serves different purposes for different people.[6] Therefore, higher education requires diverse quality standards to meet a variety of needs of different stakeholders. This also enables individual institutions to experiment and innovate.

The need to pursue diversity as an objective does not suggest that there is no necessity for any accountability. By its very nature, academic standards cannot be maintained or improved without some kind of external checks. Trust, which was long used to ensure accountability when the number of institutions was not large, does not appear to work any longer, now that the system is large and complex. This makes regulation important. Equally important is the nature of regulation, who designs it and how it is implemented. A focus on the information disclosure along with enforced self-regulation holds greatest potential for the efficient functioning of the higher education system.

The role of the state has to be redefined. It has to be more sensitive and less intrusive than its current role, best described as one size fits all. The state could have three roles. The first role is that of providing money to higher education, without taking an active role in defining or ensuring that priorities are met (advocacy role). The second role is the steering role that focuses on policy outcomes and tries to structure the market to realise those outcomes. The third is that of the widely seen regulator state, similar to current role regulating fees and cost.

Detailed planning and a control-led approach to regulation have not been found to be very useful in higher education. This has been the experience in many countries the world over. Therefore, the present system has to be substituted by a regulatory framework that takes care of market failures and facilitates market coordination.

It is important to proactively woo the big corporate sector and prestigious foreign universities to set up research universities/campuses for post-graduate education and research in science and engineering in India, in order to raise the standards of research for long-term competitiveness of the country. One way of doing this might be the identification of prestigious foreign universities (say, 500 universities in Shanghai's list of research universities) and big corporate houses in the knowledge sector and then reaching out to them. A single point contact and a time bound approach must be adopted. The bare minimum regulatory concerns need to be addressed.

While most people believe that a big push and a wholesale change in required in Indian higher education, based on analysis, I would suggest that the interventions should be strategic rather than comprehensive and an incremental approach has to be adopted to build commitment for change. Important and urgent activities that are inexpensive and would take short time could be taken up initially. In many cases, we can learn from international experiences and avoid committing similar mistakes. Structural changes would require detailed studies and commitment.

Changing Nature of 'Policy Support' and 'Systemic Governance'

As the system of higher education grows and becomes more diverse, it faces a growing complexity of the issues. Nature of policy interventions has to change. While submitting the report of the Education Commission (1964–66), its chairman Professor D.S. Kothari noted:

> It is characteristic of a world permeated by science that in some essential ways the future shape of things is unpredictable. This emphasizes all the more the need for an educational policy that contains a built-in flexibility so that it can adjust to changing circumstances. It underscores the importance of experimentation and innovation. (Kirpal, 1994)

He pointed out:

> The single most important thing needed now is to get out of the rigidity of the present system. In a rapidly changing world of today, one thing is certain: yesterday's educational system will not meet today's, and even less so, the need of tomorrow. (Kirpal, 1994)

Perspectives

The situation is more dynamic today than it was 40 years ago, and hence this prophetic statement is equally, and perhaps more relevant today.

Higher education is embedded in the history and culture of a nation and is shaped by its contemporary realities, ideologies and vested interests. With ambiguity in defining its purpose and vagueness about its quality, debate on higher education is usually full of rhetoric. Small fixes are often made without thinking strategically about the big picture. Obviously, there is no clear and coherent long-term policy for Indian higher education. The absence of reliable data makes informed decision-making difficult. As a result either ad-hocism continues to prevail, or in the absence of even ad hoc policies, chaos is created. With limited understanding of the issues, interventions by the judiciary and analysis in the media have only added to this confusion.

An informed public policy, however, would require good data. Currently, the system of collection and compilation of statistical information on higher education is poor. The MHRD of the central government, which was earlier responsible for the higher education statistics, delegated this responsibility to the UGC in the mid-1990s. Unfortunately, the UGC failed to give the kind of importance to this activity that it deserves.

There have been no efforts to evolve data standards for higher education essential for collection and compilation of statistical information of such a complex and diverse system. The response from higher education institutions is poor. The mandate of the UGC Act and rules framed there under, namely UGC (Returns of Information by Universities) Rules, 1979, were never used to obligate the universities to furnish information. Technology is also not been used to collect information. As a result, the available statistical data on higher education are sketchy and dated.

Compared to the above, the UK has a separate and independent agency, namely the Higher Education Statistics Agency (HESA) as the central source for the collection and dissemination of statistics about higher education in the UK. The National Centre for Education Statistics (NCES) in the US collects and analyses data related to education (including higher education). In addition, the Carnegie Commission on

449

Higher Education developed a classification of colleges and universities to support its programme of research and policy analysis in 1970 in the US. This classification is regularly updated. It is widely used in the study of higher education as a way to represent institutional differences. This also helps in the design of research studies to ensure adequate representation of institutions, students, or faculty in sampled data.

In India there is absence of good, sound data, making it difficult to set policy at the central, state and institutional levels. We keep making small fixes with programmes, but do not think strategically about the bigger picture. Philip Altbach, an international education expert who has been watching the developments in Indian higher education over the last two decades, laments that the government in India and academic leaders are content to do the same old thing. He points out that higher education system in India being large and complex needs good data, careful analysis and creative ideas. Referring to China having more than two dozen high education research centres and several government agencies involved in higher education policy, he is shocked to see that there is no field of higher education research in India and only a few in India are thinking creatively about higher education (Altbach, 2005a).

Considering the background of the statistical system in higher education in India discussed above, there is an immediate need for conducting a baseline survey of higher education and training system, both in the public and the private sectors. It is ironical that whereas the All India School Education Survey is being held regularly (seventh survey in this series was conducted by NCERT in 2002–2004) and there is a greater clarity on school education in India, information on higher education is vague and out of date. Data standards and classification system need to be worked out.

A system needs to be put in place to maintain unit records of all students in the higher education system linked with a unique identification number. This unique number could be the proposed citizen's National Identity Number (NIN). Till the time NIN is introduced throughout the country, a unique number can be designed and assigned to each student. A repository of such unit records of students would be a critical information infrastructure for the country. This repository would help to track the changing enrolment and completion patterns, monitor academic performance and providing accurate aggregate institution level data for planners, academicians and researchers. This would also facilitate student-centric financial aid and education loans. With this infrastructure in place, value-added services such as online enrolment and degree verification services to check fake certifications for employers and transcript services could be started.

There is the need to put in place a system of catering to the information needs of the students and parents about institutional and course performance. Surveys on graduate destinations and course experience on a regular basis and dissemination of the findings is, therefore, important and should be taken up. It is essential to establish a network of a dozen research centres for policy research on various issues related. These could be both within the university system as well as independent research organisations.

There is a need to conduct a baseline survey of the higher education and training system, both in the public and the private sectors to enable formulation of a coherent policy at the national, provincial and institutional levels. The changing national and global circumstances require us to evolve a new paradigm in higher education. There is a need to agree on a basic framework for change. With a view to initiate changes, action is required on several fronts. In some areas, detailed analysis is required to chalk out a plan of action; in other cases, action could be initiated right away.

Conclusion

In the context of several challenges and many opportunities, this book maps the growth of Indian higher education and nature of its growth with particular focus on the dynamic and growing private higher education. It describes the existing funding arrangements and suggests ways for sustainable financing that addresses concerns of access and equity. Though higher education is not merely about jobs, yet all its current concerns, related to skill shortages, quality of graduates and country's emergence in the global knowledge, are all linked to its role in skill formation. Therefore, the growth of higher education and its connection with the labour market for graduates is in many ways its central theme.

Higher education and research are inseparable. An assessment of the role of higher education in research has been done. Measures required to improve research performance have been suggested.

A transformation of higher education sector would have a major impact on the quality of output and competitiveness of all sectors of Indian economy. This would, however, require a clear vision, the wisdom to understand and appreciate the new realities and the courage to take bold decisions. In the emerging structure of a new knowledge economy, the source of competitiveness is talent. Therefore, the countries that are able to nurture talent by pursuing progressive policies in higher education will be the winners. The choice—whether we would like to be winners—is in our hands. We can craft progressive policies, seize this opportunity and shape a bright future for the country.

◆ ◆ ◆

Epilogue

There is nothing more difficult to carry out, nor more doubtful of success, nor more dangerous to handle, than to initiate a new order of things.

— Niccolo Machiavelli

THIS book describes the higher education landscape in India, identifying gaps and needs, and based on the lessons learnt from the experiences of other countries, the book provides perspectives to shape its future. The framework in the book enables clear understanding of the complexity of the system. The book looks at Indian higher education in a holistic manner and adopts a comparative approach for analysis. While reviewing various facets of the Indian higher education, the book adopts a systems approach to achieve coherence and multi-level coordination required to address its genuine concerns on a long-term basis. Changes in higher education are related to the transformation taking place in the economy, the demography and the society. Small order behavioural changes at the micro level are connected to the changes at the macro level. These are shaping the realties of Indian society, economy and the Indian higher education.

As India is a land of oddities, puzzles and paradoxes, so is its higher education system. Indian higher education is complex, with many contradictions. Instead of coming to an understanding of this complexity by actual data and research, policy is often based on the impressions of a few people. In this book, therefore, there is a deliberate focus on data in analysis. It is hoped that good data will sieve reality from myth and allow informed decision making. However, quantification is not always possible and perceptions play an important role, thus the discussions in the book also take into account common perceptions.

Despite its weaknesses, the country's recent visibility in the knowledge sector has created a distinct brand of Indian higher education. Indian graduates, particularly from some of the prestigious institutions, are sought after globally. The Indian brand of higher education can be creatively used to the country's advantage. Such perception has helped the country to achieve success in some areas. Continuous reinforcement of this success, however, clouds many perceptions of reality and we tend to fall into the trap of 'persuasion-bias'. This bias continues to perpetuate and exacerbate certain fallacies and inconsistencies.

There are several such myths. The first myth is that while there is an irrational exuberance about India shining, many people see Indian higher education in very poor light. The fact, however, lies somewhere in between. India's large and comprehensive higher education has over time built a huge pool of qualified manpower, providing the country an edge in competition in global knowledge economy. There is now the need to build in more diversity, provide greater flexibility and widen student choice. Second, it is often believed that elite institutions like the IITs are the backbone of the Indian higher education. It needs to be understood that these institutions contribute only a tiny fraction (less than half a per cent) of the overall pool of qualified manpower, even though their strict admission procedures have set in motion a competitive process with large positive spillovers.

Three, private higher education is treated as peripheral, though it is already the most dynamic and growing sector of Indian higher education. In professional areas, private institutions constitute four-fifths of the number of institutions and enrolment. The belief that the current policy and regulatory framework does not permit private participation is wrong. Had this been the case, professional, technical and medical education would not have been dominated by private players. In fact there are several ways in which the current system provides for private participation. Affiliated colleges and institutes could either be privately run government aided colleges or the self-financing private colleges. Private universities can be set up through deemed university route or there could be private universities under separate state legislations. Despite entry barriers, private investment over the past five years has been about five times that of public investment. Unpredictable and non-transparent regulatory environment however prevents more investment and is the main cause of declining academic standards.

Epilogue

Four, it believed that private and independent accreditation would improve academic standards. While the fact is that the key to effective accreditation would be to have clear and tangible consequences for accreditation. Neither private nor independent accreditation without consequences would serve any purpose. Five, the fee levels in public institutions are believed to be ridiculously low, even though in reality, faced with financial limitations, most public institutions have raised fees substantially, at least for professional courses—with the exception of central universities and universities in Bihar and Uttar Pradesh.

Six, it is felt that the problem of skill shortages in the country can be effectively addressed by increasing enrolments in higher education. The country aspires to increase enrolments significantly to reach the levels of enrolment in advanced countries or emerging economies on a medium-term basis. Specifically, it is targeted to increase enrolment to 15 per cent (from the current 11 per cent) by 2012. This goal is desirable and even needed to meet growing demand for higher education with rising prosperity and improvements in school education. But, from the labour market point of view, current enrolment levels by and large adequate and match the country's occupational structure. Having more graduates of the same type would accentuate problem of graduate unemployment and underemployment. There is a greater need for manpower with diverse skills. The skill shortages are at the low end, where graduate skills are not required, or where the need is of blue collar skilled workers. People fail to distinguish between the general situation and specific, narrow, local needs. As a result, there is a widespread misperception about general skill shortages and higher education expansion addressing that problem.

Seven, it is believed that increased public spending would automatically result in better higher education. In term of percentage of GDP, estimated at 1 per cent (with almost the same contributed through private finance), level of spending on higher education is not low. In fact, relative effort expressed in terms of per student expenditure as a proportion of per capita GDP at 95 per cent is one of the highest in the world. However, in absolute terms and on per student basis, funding levels are very low. While the increased funding in the Eleventh Five Year Plan may help a small number of institutions under the national government, the bulk of the system under the state government would continue to face financial hardships, particularly to meet recurrent expenses. Rationalisation of the fee structure is thus important. This should however be accompanied with liberal student financial aid. This could be grants, but largely loans with income contingent repayments as increasingly used in countries around the world for student loans. This would make higher education free at the point of use. In the interest of efficiency, public funding should be performance-based to promote both equity and excellence.

Seven, it is commonly understood that the lack of academic autonomy prevents universities from changing curriculum. The fact is that all universities have total autonomy in academic matters. However, there are little or no incentives for the teaching community in the universities to keep their curriculum up-to-date. In many cases, the number of teachers in each faculty is small and their capacity is limited to be able to do so. There is a need to improve ability (autonomy) of institutions and put pressure on them to perform (accountability) including change of curriculum.

And, finally, it is seen that the existing regulatory bodies—UGC, AICTE, and so on—have failed to maintain standards. Thus, a new regulatory body is being considered. The fact however is that instead of a new regulatory body, a new way of regulating higher education that promotes both autonomy and accountability and fosters private investment is required. As the continuation of the UGC is an 'anachronism' today, so would be the setting up of the IRAHE. Such central structures to govern a complex and increasingly diversified system would serve little purpose. The entire regulatory arrangement has to be overhauled keeping in mind the increasing professionalisation of various occupations. Rather than a single agency, multiple agencies would be required, each with clearly defined role and some kind of tribunal to resolves disputes between them. Public funding arrangements have to be divorced from the new regulatory framework.

Public policy for higher education in India faces the dilemma of the legitimacy of ever-widening ends and reality of limited resources. There is not only the demand for more opportunities for higher education, but also greater diversity, not in just subject range, but in terms of institutional arrangements as well as how subjects are taught and the research is done. Equity and quality must not be seen as two independent and conflicting objectives. These should be seen as complementary. In all, the change in the higher education system requires a paradigm shift in our thinking.

A fundamental problem faced by Indian higher education is that public policy assumes that all institutions are homogeneous and therefore treats them equally and regards all programmes as equal, while large system of higher education as India has is incompatible with this model of higher education. In reality, Indian higher education is heterogeneous and need to regard this heterogeneity as proper. Policy needs encourage diversity, varied forms of provision and quality comparisons between them. Even public funding policy needs to support a diverse and decentralised system. Issues of social cohesion are of paramount importance at the school level, but in higher education, there is brutal competition. Central planning in funding of diverse system or in matching the skills of graduates with their preferences and the demands of the labour market would not serve the purpose in a very dynamic situation today. Market forces can do a better job.

Recognising the fact above, the Indian Prime Minister Dr Manmohan Singh said in his Civil Services Day Speech on 21 April 2006:

> Public policies are often not based on long-term concerns. These do not carefully weigh the trade off between seemingly contradictory goals and ignore that the markets are now the main arbitrators of resource allocation. The role of the government is to create an open environment and more demanding standards of transparency and accountability so that the markets function efficiently. The government has to strike a delicate balance between growth and an equitable and inclusive development taking into account the forces of globalization and the prevailing socio-economic realties.

The government has to play a steering role in higher education that focuses on policy outcomes and tries to structure the market to realize those outcomes are met.

Based on the arguments above, the book has several suggestions to shape the future of Indian higher education. However, without going into the nitty-gritty of each of them, an attempt has been made to define the options and solutions at a level of detail that underscores the practicality of each suggestion and more importantly provides a broad direction for change. The country has a unique opportunity to convert demographic surplus to its economic strength. This would require the creation of a competitive environment in higher education that ensures both public and private institutions develop and become more responsive and innovative. This may require radical change and comprehensive reforms. However, considering the nature of Indian polity and society, strategic intervention with an incremental approach would be the best way forward.

◆

Notes

Introduction

1. More details at may be found at http://www.ed.gov/about/bdscomm/list/ hiedfuture/index.html

Chapter 1

1. This survey on geographical diversity of students in Indian universities was done by the author in the year 2004.
2. This is based on the Association of Indian Universities (AIU) data. As per AIU 2003-04, this number was merely 7,753. However, author found this number at 12,263 for 2003-04 merging the data from 82 universities collected by the AIU with the projected data for another 83 universities collected by the UGC for 2001-02. Out of 308 universities (that existed in 2003-04), 109 universities reported no international students and 34 universities did not respond. Overall, there is a great deal of confusion on the issue of international student enrolment in India.
3. IUB was renamed as Association of Indian Universities (AIU) in 1973.
4. This is based on the fact that by 2011, India will have about 150 million people in the 18-23 age group.

Chapter 2

1. In 1829, a group of mechanics and workingmen in New York City declared, 'Next to life and liberty, we consider education the greatest blessing bestowed upon mankind.' Borrowed from the Grubb and Lazeron's book by the same name.
2. Refers to Ramamurti Committee that issued its report entitled 'Towards an Enlightened and Humane Society' and Central Advisory Board for Education (CABE) Committee.
3. Organised by the National Institute of Educational Planning and Administration (NIEPA) at New Delhi.
4. At the Foundation Day Lecture of NUEPA 'Alternative Perspectives on Higher Education in the Context of Globalization' in 2007.
5. Rahul Gandhi on 17th July 2007 (*The Indian Express*, 19 July 2007).

6. HRD Minister, Arjun Singh while addressing media persons in Bhopal on 30 March 2008 (*The Hindu*, 31 March 2008).
7. Block is a smaller administrative unit within a District. Usually, a District would have 10 to 20 blocks.
8. The government has approved an outlay of Rs 103.28 billion (60 per cent on capital costs alone) on 22 May 2008.

Chapter 3

1. At the first convocation of Visva Bharati in December 1952.
2. UGC (Establishment of and Maintenance of Standards in Private Universities) Regulations, 2003.
3. Refers to 150th Report on Demand No.58 of the Department related Parliamentary Committee on Human Resource Development.
4. Writ Petition No. 19 of 2004 brought before Supreme Court through a public interest litigation.
5. Information on this may also be found on the website of the Assam Government. Available at http://www.assamgovt.nic.in.
6. As per AP High Court in the Bharatidasan case, universities are not required to seek prior approval of the AICTE for starting professional courses, though they are expected to maintain standards as per AICTE norms.
7. Details of institutional profiles and expansion plans have been taken from the institutional websites and from the article, 'Higher Education: Let the Thousand Flowers Bloom' that appeared in *The Economic Times*, Kolkata, 6 April 2008.
8. This university has been set up by Lovely Sweet House at Jalandhar famous for its 'laddus', a traditional Indian sweet.
9. Tax evasion of Rs 267.50 million was unearthed by the IT Department in the raids at nine premises of the coaching, foreign placement agencies, and such in Delhi and Mumbai in 2007 (*The Hindu*, 15 August 2007).
10. Six of the top 10 and 3,500 of the overall 7,800 students selected through IIT-JEE 2008 were associated with numerous coaching institutions in Kota (*The Times of India*, 31 May 2008).
11. There is international experience on this. The Federal Trade Commission (FTC) in USA has Guides for Private Vocational and Distance Education Schools (on advertising, promotion and marketing).
12. Based on AICTE Advt. No. AICTE/Legal/04(01)/2007 issued in April 2007.
13. Based on AICTE Advt. No. AICTE/Legal/04(02)/2007 issued in April 2007.

Chapter 4

1. At the Round Table of the Association of Indian Universities (AIU) on Financing Higher Education in India, 4–5 June 2004, Trivandrum (unpublished).

2. The Supreme Court in India laid down dual track fee policy for professional unaided institutions in 1992. This was declared as unconstitutional in 2005 by a bigger bench of the Supreme Court in 2005.
3. This is based on survey on financing of universities by the author.
4. By the author while he was working as Coordinator (New Initiatives) at the UGC.
5. Revised model education loan scheme is available at http://www.iba.org.in/educational_loan.asp.
6. Based on personal communication with Professor Nichols Barr at the London School Economics. He has worked on design of education loan schemes for a number of countries.
7. A concept paper on National Graduate Students Repository was issued by UGC Expert Committee of which the author was member-secretary in September 2005.
8. Extract from *Higher Education in the Next Decades–Policy for the State of West Bengal*.
9. Many countries in the world (Australia, UK, Chile, and so on) have shifted to performance-based funding to get value for money from public spending on higher education.
10. The federal government supports higher education in the US primarily through student grants. These grants are available to students studying all accredited institutions—whether these institutions are public or private. This is the single most important incentive for higher education institutions in the US to get accredited.

Chapter 5

1. Many college graduates work as security guards, maids and nannies in China. Five hundred new graduates applied for six traditionally taboo positions working with the dead at a Beijing Funeral home. In a widely publicised survey released by the *China Youth Daily*, 35 per cent of the youth said that they regretted their university experience and more than half said that they nothing of use (Melvin, Sheila. 2006. 'China's College Revolution', *The Wilson Quarterly*, 10(4): 37–44).
2. The residual factor (factors other than capital and labour) is referred to as 'Total Factor Productivity' or TFP by economists.
3. Other conditions responsible for differences in economic well-being of nations may include contribution of government policies, business practices, cultural norms like tendency to work harder, or other unmeasureable or immeasurable factors.
4. Non-workers broadly constitute students not participating in paid or unpaid work, persons engaged in household chores, persons not even helping in unpaid work in family cultivation, etc., dependents—infants and elderly people, pensioners, beggars, vagrants, prostitutes, persons living on remittances and rent, and so on.
5. As per the report titled 'Some aspects of operational land holdings in India, 2002–03' based on NSS (59th round), the average land holding was merely 1.06 hectare in 2002–03 reducing from 1.34 hectare in 1991–92 and 1.67 hectare in 1981–82.

6. Figures for 2004–05 are derived from 61st Round Survey on the basis of data provided by NSSO. Employment in 1993–94 and 1999–2000 is as per the 2001 Report of the Task Force on Employment Opportunities (Planning Commission). The employment levels for the three periods derived by adjusting the NSS population to the census population.

7. Enrolment for 2004–05 is from the Annual Report (2004–05) of the University Grants Commission and the Stock for 2001 is from the 2001 Census of India; Stock (2005) and Outturn 2004–05 are estimated by the author.

8. See Grubb and Lazerson (2004). A one-year programme would typically comprise a dozen courses and students have the option to take larger number of courses in a particular field of study to major or graduate in that field.

9. Whereas education is an open-ended process leading to the development of mind and involves inputs in the cognitive and affective domains, the specific goal of training is to impart technical skills and usually involves inputs in the psychomotor domain.

10. Though there is some similarity, these are different from community colleges in the United States and Canada, where such colleges have open door admission policy, provide cheaper option and pathways for entry to regular four-year colleges.

11. Based on personal communication with Dr Xavier Alphonse, Founder-Director of ICDRDE, Chennai, the organisation that is leading community college movement in India.

12. As identified by the Task Force on Skill Development set up by the Planning Commission.

13. On 17 October 2006 *The New York Times* reported that skills gap threaten technology boom in India. Referring to severe constraint in the supply of qualified manpower, *The Financial Times*, London on 20 July 2006 sounded alarm over educational failings in India. *The Wilson Quarterly* in its autumn 2006 issue carried an article by Philip Altbach, an international education expert, bringing out that India with its tiny quality education sector cannot sustain leadership in global knowledge economy.

14. Recently a reputed columnist blamed the Ministry of Human Resources Development (HRD), Government of India for the shortage of pilots due to inadequacies of Indian higher education in her column in the *Times of India*, while another story the same day was about the glut of pilots in the country with many private pilot training institutions coming up in recent years. In any case ministry of HRD does not have any role in pilot training programmes.

15. Based on the US Secretary of Labour's Commission on Achieving Necessary Skills (or SCANS) in Grubb and Lazerson (2004: 5).

16. Bulge mix is percentage of employees in 0–3 years experience over the total population of professionals.

Notes

Chapter 6

1. The Prime Minister announced the government's intentions to raise R&D expenditure to 2 per cent of GDP in the next five years at the 94th Indian Science Congress and reiterated in the 95th Congress at Andhra University.

2. Project of UGC Research Handbook was coordinated by the author in his capacity as coordinator of new initiatives in the year 2005.

3. This covers the top 21 of the most cited out of 149 countries in all fields from the ISI Essential Science Indicators Database (Online version). In the 10-year period (January 1994–August 2004), ISI recorded about 9 million articles, notes and reviews, published in roughly 9,000 indexed journals. ISI Essential Science Indicators categorises these journals into 22 broad disciplines. Each journal is assigned to a discipline. The number of citations received by these 7 million items for the period was roughly 53 million.

4. This ranking and its methodology may be found at the SJTU website. Available on http://ed.sjtu.edu.cn/rank (last accessed on 6 July 2007).

5. This ranking and its methodology may be found at the THES website. Available on http://www.thes.co.uk/worldrankings (last accessed on 6 July 2007).

6. According to Nobel Laureate Joseph E. Stiglitz (May 2004), America may be able to maintain competitive advantage at the very top, the breakthrough research—the invention of next laser. But majority of even highly trained engineers and scientist are engaged in what is called ordinary science, the important day-to-day improvements in technology that are basis of long-term increases in productivity—it is not clear if America has long-term competitive advantage here.

7. As per Dr R A Mashelkar, a former DG, quoted in 'Public R&D Labs Face Attrition Heat', *Business Standard*, Kolkata, 7 August 2007.

8. Based on analysis of UGC data by the author.

9. Jadavpur University (Kolkata), Jawaharlal Nehru University (New Delhi), University of Hyderabad, University of Madras (Chennai), University of Pune, Bombay University, Madurai Kamraj University (Madurai), North Eastern Hill University (Shillong) and Calcutta University.

10. All 26 federal grant agencies in the United States post opportunities for competitive grants on the grant.gov website offering single source of search and apply option for all researchers (*Research Global*, February 2005: 17).

11. Refers to letter dated 26 December 2006 from Chairman, National Knowledge Commission to the Indian Prime Minister.

12. On the basis of reply furnished to Lok Sabha in response to question no. 21606 in May 2007.

13. This suggestion is based on 'Pump Priming with US Horsepower', *The Economic Times*, Kolkata, 17 September 2007.

14. The author led this initiative as coordinator, new initiatives while at the UGC in 1999.
15. United States National Security Language Initiative aims at increasing the number of US students studying languages deemed as 'critical'. These include Arabic, Azari, Bengali, Chinese, Mandarin, Farsi, Gujarati, Hindi, Korean, Marathi, Pashto, Punjabi, Russian, Pajak, Turkish, Urdu and Uzbek.
16. Professor Philip G. Altbach on research university while speaking to Fulbright New Century Scholars at Cairo in February 2006.
17. Alison Richard, Vice-chancellor, University of Cambridge, quoted in *The Economic Times* (2008f).

Chapter 7

1. Noted in respect of the United States in the Fourth Issue Paper for the Commission on the future of Higher education (Schray, 2006).
2. Entry 66 reads: 'Co-ordination and determination of standards in institutions for higher education or research and scientific and technical institutions.'
3. Entry 25 reads : 'Education, including technical education, medical education and universities, subject to the provisions of entries 63, 64, 65 and 66 of List I; vocational and technical training of labour.'
4. Decision of the UGC not to include Amity University, a private university set up by an Act of the UP Legislature in 2005, was declared illegal by the Delhi High Court and the UGC was directed to include Amity University in the list of universities on its website (*The Indian Express*, 2007g).
5. As on 16 August 2003, the UGC had specified 142 degrees.
6. Andhra University has 405 colleges, Bangalore University has 400 colleges and Osmania University has 390 colleges affiliated to them.
7. This was the finding of the survey 'Understanding of private higher education in India: A stockholder's perspective', conducted by a marketing consultancy and research company on behalf of FICCI in 2006.
8. In the face of complaints on this account, AICTE issued pubic notice No. AICTE/Legal/04(01)/2007 issued in April 2007.
9. In a non-collusive oligopoly, firms recognise their interdependence but do not collude with each other. They act in their own best interest. However each firm takes into account the output and price decisions of its competitor before making its own decisions.
10. In *J.P. Unnikrishnan and others versus State of Andhra Pradesh and others* (1993) 1 SCC 645.
11. Both tuition and development fees for merit and payment seats (not exceeding 15 per cent) for various professional programmes in private unaided institutions were to be fixed by the respective state governments.

Notes

12. *Eleven-Judge Bench in TMA Pai Foundation versus State of Karnataka,* (2002) 8 SCC 481.
13. *Five-Judge bench in Islamic Academy of Education versus State of Karnataka,* (2003) 6 SCC 697.
14. In *P.A. Inamdar versus State of Maharashtra,* (2005) SCC 537.
15. AICTE Public Notice issued vide Advt. No. AICTE/Legal/03(01)/2006-07. Available online at www.aicte.ernet.in/download/Unapproved.doc (downloaded on 15 May 2007).
16. The full text of the Bill may be found on the PRS Legislative Research website. Available at http://www.prsindia.org/docs/The_Foreign_Educational_Institutions_Bill_2007.pdf.
17. Letter from the human resources development minister to the Left, quoted in *The Indian Express* (2007b).
18. Report of the Indo-Malaysia Joint Study Group on Comprehensive Economic Partnership Agreement (June 2005).
19. In Chhattisgarh Universities case relying on its own earlier judgement in March 1995 in *Tamil Nadu and others versus Adhiyaman Educational and Research Institute.* Quoted from Supreme Court's judgement of February 2005 in the Writ Petition No. 19 of 2004.
20. Such a body is already being planned.
21. Returns of information by universities and colleges could be mandated under the UGC Act read with Right to Information Act. These rules could also define misrepresentation and deceptive practices in advertising, promotion and marketing by higher education institutions.

Chapter 8

1. Definition provided in 'Quality Assurance in UK Higher Education: A Brief Guide' published in 1998.
2. This information is based on contacts established with 177 countries by the GUNI Secretariat.
3. Detailed guidelines can be found at the OECD website. Available at http://www.oecd.org/edu/internationalisation/guidelines.
4. Details of the two-stage accreditation process may be found in Mariamma Varghese (2007).
5. Teachers in higher education are expected to attend two refresher courses before they are eligible for career advancement or promotion.
6. The AICTE adopted an objective criterion for reduction of seats. For faculty strength short up to 25 per cent, no additional intake was sanctioned; for shortage from 25 to 50 per cent, a pro rata reduction in intake was ensured and in case the shortage was more than 50 per cent, institutions were not allowed to admit any students (*The Times of India,* New Delhi, 8 June 2005).

7. For this purpose Central Civil Services (CCS) conduct rules are being amended (*The Economic Times*, 2008b).
8. This suggestion was given by the chief mentor of Infosys, Mr N.R. Narayana Murthy in the Fourth Ravi Matthai Memorial Lecture organised by the Academy of Human Resources Development at Bangalore in November 2005.

Chapter 9

1. As per Buddhadeb Bhattacharjee, the Chief Minister of West Bengal, in an interview to *The Hindustan Times* (*The Hindustan Times*, 2007).
2. *The Cambridge Encyclopedia of the English Language* has put the number of English language speaking people in India as 350 million—already the largest English speaking country in the world.
3. Very Low Income < Rs 90,000; Low Income Rs 90,000–200,000; Middle Income Rs 200,000–1 million; High Income > Rs 1 million.
4. Professional education is closely linked to growing importance of science and is distinguished from lower-level vocational education imparted in schools.
5. It could be argued that products of higher education are 'post-experience' goods, whose quality can be accurately assessed only after the education is completed. Such goods would warrant even more rigorous efforts at consumer protection.
6. The government, regulatory bodies and even courts seem to pursue uniform quality standards in higher education.

References

Agarwal, Pawan. 2005. 'Deferred Fee Option to Contain Brain Drain', *The Hindu*, New Delhi, 7 August.
——. 2006a. 'Higher Eeducation in India: The Need for Change', ICRIER Working Paper No. 180, New Delhi, June 2006. Available online at http://www.icrier. org/publication/working_papers_180.html (accessed on 30 May 2007).
——. 2006b. 'Private Tuitions: Causes And Effects', *Education World*, September.
——. 2006c. 'Higher Education Services And Trade Liberalization', in Rupa Chanda (ed.), *Trade In Services And India: Prospects And Strategies*. New Delhi: Wiley (India).
——. 2006d. 'Total Lesson from Crisis', *The Indian Express*, New Delhi, 25 July.
——. 2007a. *Private Higher Education In India: Status And Prospects*. Observatory on Border-less Higher Education (OBHE), UK, July 2007.
——. 2007b. 'Higher Education- I: from Kothari Commission to Pitroda Commission', *Economic and Political Weekly*, 42(7): 554–56.
——. 2008a. 'India in the Context of International Student Circulation', in Hans De Wit (ed.), *The Dynamics of International Student Circulation in a Global Context*, pp. 83–112. Rotterdam and Taipei: Sense Publishers.
——. 2008b. *Privatization and Internationalization of Higher Education in the Countries of South Asia: An Empirical Analysis*. Available online at http://www.saneinetwork. net/pdf/SANEI_VIII/7.pdf (downloaded on 22 April 2009).
Ahmed, Sadiq and Ashutosh Varshney. 2008. 'Battles Half Won: Political Economy of India's Growth And Economic Policy Since Independence', Working Paper No. 15, Commission on Growth and Development, The Word Bank, Washington, DC.
Association of Indian Universities (AIU). 2007. 'Student Mobility: International Students in Indian Universities', Occasional Paper 2007. New Delhi: AIU.
Aiyar, Pallavi. 2007. 'Crazy about English in China', *The Hindu* (op. ed), Kolkata, 27 June.
All India Council for Technical Education (AICTE). 1999. *Technical Education in India: 1947–97*. New Delhi: All India Council for Technical Education.
——. 2005. *AICTE Annual Report, 2004–05*. New Delhi: AICTE.
——. 2007. 'Background Paper for the National Conference on Development of Higher Education in India', 17–18 December 2007, New Delhi, India.
All India Management Association (AIMA). 2003. *Report of the High Level Strategic Group–India's New Opportunity (2020)*. New Delhi: All India Management Association (AIMA).

Altbach, Philip G. 1982. *Higher Education in the Third World: Themes and Variations.* Singapore: Maruzen Asia.

Altbach, Philip G. 1999. 'The Perils of Internationalizing Higher Education: An Asian Perspective', *International Higher Education*, 15(Spring): 4–5.

——. 2005a. 'Higher Education in India', *The Hindu*, 12 April.

——. 2005b. 'Universities: Family Style', *International Higher Education*, 39(Spring): 10–12.

——. 2006. 'The Dilemmas of Ranking', *International Higher Education*, 42: 2–3.

——. 2007a. 'Vedanta University: A Flawed Pipe Dream', *The Hindu*, ePaper, 29 August.

——. 2007b. 'The Imperial Tongue: English as the Dominating Academic Language', *International Higher Education*, 49(Fall): 2–3.

——. 2008. 'Sub-Prime Crisis in Higher Education', *International Higher Education*, 51(Spring): 2–3.

Anandakrishnan, M. 2004. 'Higher Education in Regional Development: Some Key Pointers', Indo-UK Collaboration on Higher Education—Policy Forum Workshop. 12–13 February.

——. 2006. 'Privatisation of Higher Education: Opportunities and Anomalies', paper presented at the conference *Privatisation and Commercialisation of Higher Education* organised by NIEPA, 2 May 2006. New Delhi.

Anderson, Jo Anne. 2005. *Accountability in Education.* The International Academy of Education and the International Institute for Educational Planning. Education Policy Booklet Series. Available online at http://www.worldfund.org/assets/files/LitandLinks/IIEP-Accountability.pdf (accessed on 30 July 2007).

Arimoto, A. 1997. 'Market and Higher Education in Japan', *Higher Education Policy*, 10(3/4): 199–210.

Arunachalam, S. 2004. 'On Publication Indicators', *Current Science*, 86(5): 629–32.

Autor, D. 2006. 'Computerization and the Division of Labour: How Computerization Changes What People Do', paper presented at the NBER Neemrana Conference, January 2006.

Avery, C., M. Glickman, C. Hoxby and A. Metrick. 2004. 'A Revealed Preference Ranking of U.S. Colleges and Universities', NBER Working Paper No. 10803, September.

Azad, J.L. and R. Chandra. 2002. 'Partnership of Private Sector in Financing and Management of Higher Education—An in-depth Study'. National Institute of Educational Planning and Administration, June 2002.

Banga, Rashmi. 2005. *Critical Issues in India's Service-Led Growth.* ICRIER Working Paper No. 171, October. New Delhi: Indian Council for Research on International Economic Relations (ICRIER).

Barnett, R. 1994. 'The Idea of Quality: Voicing the Educational', in G.D. Doherty (ed.), *Developing Quality Systems in Education*, pp. 68–82. London: Routledge.

Barr, Nicholas. 2004. 'Higher Education Funding', *Oxford Review of Economic Policy*, 20(2): 264–83.

Bardhan, Pranab. 1984. *The Political Economy of Development in India.* New York: Basil Blackwell.

References

Bashir, Sajitha. 2007. *Trends in International Trade in Higher Education: Implications and Options for Developing Countries*. The World Bank: Washington, DC.

Becker, G. 1964. *The Human Capital: A Theoretical and Empirical Analysis with Special Reference to Education*. New York: Columbia University Press.

Benderly, B.L. 2008. 'Feeling the Elephant', in *Science Careers*, 4 January 2008.

Berman, Eli, John Bound and Stephen Machin. 1998. 'Implications of Skill-biased Technological Change: International Evidence', *Quarterly Journal of Economics*, 113(4): 1245–80.

Bertrand, O. 1998. 'Education and Work', in Jacques Delors (ed.), *Education for the Twenty-First Century: Issues and Prospects*, pp. 157–92. Paris: UNESCO Publishing.

Béteille, André. 2005. 'Universities as Public Institutions', *Economic and Political Weekly*, 40(31): 3377–81.

Bhagwati, J. 2004. *In Defense of Globalization*. New Delhi: Oxford University Press.

Bhalla, Surjit. 2007. *Second among Equals: The Middle Class Kingdoms of India and China*. Washington D.C.: Institute of International Economics.

Bhushan, S. 2006. 'Foreign Education Providers in India: Mapping the Extent and Regulation'. Report submitted to the OBHE, March 2006.

Blaug, M. 1973. *Education and the Employment Problem in Developing Countries*. Geneva: International Labour Office.

Bray, M. 1998. 'Privatisation of Secondary Education: Issues and Policy Implications', *Education for the Twenty-First Century: Issues and Prospects*, pp. 109–113. Paris: UNESCO Publishing.

Brennan, J. 2004. 'The Social Role of the Contemporarily University: Contradictions, Boundaries and Change', in *Ten Years on: Changing Education in a Changing World*. Published by Centre of Higher Education Research and Information (CHERI). Buckingham: The Open University Press.

Büxhel, Felix, Andries de Grip and Antje Mertens. 2004. *Overeducation in Europe: Current Issues in Theory and Policy*. Cheltenham: Edward Elgar.

Central Advisory Board of Education (CABE) Committee. 2005a. *Report on Autonomy of Higher Education Institutions*. Report submitted to the Government of India, June 2005.

———. 2005b. *Report on Financing of Higher and Technical Education*. Report submitted to the Government of India, New Delhi.

Carnoy, M. 1999. 'Globalization and Education Reform: What Planners Need to Know', International Institute for Educational Planning (IIEP) Report No. 63, Paris.

Castro, Claudio de Moura and Daniel C. Levy. 2001. 'Four Functions in Higher Education', *International Higher Education*, 23(Spring): 5–6.

Chapman, B. and C. Ryan. 2003. 'The Access Implications of Income Contingent Charges for Higher Education: Lessons from Australia', Discussion paper No. 463, Australian National University, Centre for Economic Policy Research, April.

Chatterjee, Partha. 2002. *Social Science Research Capacity in South Asia*. New York: Social Science Research Council (SSRC).

469

Clausen, Christopher. 2006. 'The New Ivory Tower—The US Higher Education', *The Wilson Quarterly*, Autumn 2006, 30(4): 31–36.

Coglianese, Cary and David Lazer. 2003. 'Management-Based Regulation: Prescribing Private Management to Achieve Public Goals', *Law and Society*, 37(4): 691.

Commonwealth of Australia. 2003. 'Our Universities: Backing Australia's Future.' Available online at http://www.backingaustraliasfuture.gov.au/ (accessed on 29 April 2009).

Das, Gurcharan. 2006. 'Deeper into India's Soul', *The Times of India*, New Delhi, 11 March.

Delors, J. 1996. 'Learning the Treasure Within', report to the International Commission on Education for the Twenty-first Century. Paris: UNESCO Publishing.

DfES, 2003. *The Future of Higher Education*. Department for Education and Skills, Government of UK, January 2003. Available on http://www.dfesgov.uk/hegateway/here form.index.cfm (accessed on 10 May 2007).

Dill, David D. 2004. *Transparency and Quality in Higher Education Markets: Public Policy for Academic Quality*. Available online at http://www.unc.edu/ppaq (accessed on 10 July 2007).

Dossani, Rafiq. 2008. *India Arriving: How this Economic Powerhouse is Redefining Global Business*. New York: AMACOM-American Management Association.

Dore, R.P. 1976. *The Diploma Disease*. London: George Allen & Unwin.

Dreze, J and Amartya Sen. 1995, 'Basic Education as a Political Issue', *Journal of Educational Planning and Administration*, 9(1): 27–43.

Department of Science and Technology (DST). 2006. *Research and Development Statistics, 2004–05*. New Delhi: Ministry of Science and Technology, Government of India.

De Wit, Hans. 2007. 'Changing Dynamics in International Student Circulation: Meanings, Push and Pull Factors, Trends, and Data', in Hans de Wit and Others (eds), *The Dynamics of International Student Circulation in a Global Context*, Rotterdam, The Netherlands: Sense Publishers.

Directorate General of Employment and Training (DGET). 2006. *Employment Exchange Statistics 2006*. New Delhi: Directorate General of Employment & Training. Ministry of Labour & Employment, Government of India.

Dutta, Soumitra and Simon Caulkin. 2007. 'The World's Top Innovators', *Indian Management*, March: 71–79.

El-Khawas, E. 2001. *Accreditation in the USA: Origins, Developments and Future Prospects*. Paris: International Institute for Educational Planning (IIEP).

Frank, R. 2001. 'Higher Education: The Ultimate Winner-Take-All Market?', in M. Devlin and J. Meyerson (eds), *Forum Futures: Exploring the Future of Higher Education, 2000 Papers*. San Francisco: Jossey Bass.

Franck, Egon P. and Bruno Schönfelder. 2000. 'On the Role of Competition in Higher Education–Uses and Abuses of the Economic Metaphor', *Schmalenbach Business Review*, 52: 214–37.

Freeman, R.B. 2005. 'Does Globalization of the Scientific/Engineering Workforce Threatens US Economic Leadership', National Bureau of Economic Research (NBER), Working paper No. 11457. Cambridge, MS: NBER.

References

Gangan Prathap. 2006. 'Time to Publish: The Scientific Efficiency of Nations', *Current Science*, 91(11): 1438.

Ganguly, Ashok. 2007. 'Blue Sky for the Future', *The Telegraph*, Kolkata, 27 December.

Ganguly, Prabuddha. 2005. 'Industry-Academic Interaction in Technology Transfer and IPR: Initiatives in India', *Research Global*, 9: 18–19.

Garvin, D. (1980). *Economics of Economic Behaviour*. New York: Academic Press.

Ghose, Ajit K. 2004. 'The Employment Challenge in India', *Economic and Political Weekly*, 39(48): 5107–16.

Gibbons, Michael. 1998. *Higher Education Relevance in the 21st Century*. UNESCO World Conference on Higher Education, 5–9 October, Paris.

Government of India. 2008. Report of the High Level Group on Services Sector, New Delhi, March.

——. 2006. Report of the Working Group On Attracting and Retaining Young People to Careers in Science and Technology. Report submitted to the Govt. of India, July 2006.

——. 2005. *Economic Survey*. New Delhi: Ministry of Finance.

——. 2000. *A Policy Framework for Reforms in Education*. A report of the special subject group on 'Policy Framework for Private Investment in Education, Health and Rural Development. Prime Minister's Council on Trade and Industry. New Delhi.

Global University Network for Innovation (GUNI) Secretariat. 2007. 'Delphi Poll, 2006', in *Higher Education in the World–Accreditation for Quality Assurance: What is at Stake*. Barcelona: GUNI.

Grubb, W. Norton and Marvin Lazerson. 2004. *The Education Gospel: The Economic Power of Schooling*. Cambridge, Massachusetts: Harvard University Press.

Gupta B.M. and S.M. Dhawan. 2006. *Measures of Progress of Science in India: an Analysis of the Publication Output in Science and Technology*. New Delhi: National Institute of Science, Technology and Development Studies (NISTADS).

Gupta, Ashwini and P.K. Datta. 2005. 'Indian Innovation System—Perspective and Challenges', in *National Innovation Systems (NIS) in the Asia Pacific Region*. New York: UNESCAP.

Hahn, Ryan. 2007. *The Global State of Higher Education and the Rise of Private Finance (2007)*. Washington, DC: Global Center on Private Financing of Higher Education, Institute for Higher Education Policy (IHEP).

Hanna, Donald E. 1998. 'Higher Education in an Era of Digital Competition: Emerging Organizational Models', *Journal of Asynchronous Learning Network*, 2(1): 1–32.

Hancock, Alan. 1998. 'Contemporary Information and Communication Technologies and Education', in Jacques Delors (ed.), *Education for the Twenty-First Century: Issues and Prospects*. Paris: UNESCO Publishing.

Hansda, S.K. 2001. 'Sustainability of Services-led Growth: An Input-Output Analysis of Indian Economy', RBI Occasional Working Paper, Vol. 22, Nos. 1, 2 and 3.

Hanushek, Eric A. 2005. *Economic Outcomes and School Quality*. Paris: International Institute for Educational Planning. Paris. Education policy series 4. Available online at http://unesdoc.unesco.org/images/0014/001410/141027e.pdf

Hanushek, E.A. and S.G. Rivkin. 2004. 'How to Improve Supply of High Quality Teachers,' in D. Ravitch (ed.), *Brooking Papers On Education Policy 2004*, pp. 7–44. Washington DC: Brookings Institutional Press.

Harberger, A. 1998. 'A Vision of Growth Process', *American Economic Review*, 88(1): 1–32.

Harman, G. 2006. 'Research and Scholarship', in James J.F. Forest and Philip G. Altbach (eds), *International Handbook of Higher Education*, pp. 309–28. Dodrecht, The Netherlands: Springer.

Hauptman, A.M. 2006. 'Higher Education Finance: Trends and Issue', in James J.F. Forest and Philip G. Altbach (eds), *International Handbook of Higher Education*, pp. 83–106. Dodrecht, The Netherlands: Springer.

Henrekson, M. and N. Rosenberg. 2001. 'Designing Efficient Institutions for Science-Based Entrepreneurship: Lessons from the US and Sweden', *Journal of Technology Transfer*, 26(3): 207–31.

IHEP. 1998. *Reaping the Benefits: Defining the Public and Private Value of Going to College.* Washington, DC: IHEP.

International Labour Organization (ILO). 2007a. *Key Indicators of the Labour Market (KILM).* Geneva: ILO.

——. 2007b. *Global Employment Trend for Women.* Geneva: ILO.

Jayaram, N. 2002. 'The Fall of the Guru: The Decline of the Academic Profession in India', in Philip G. Altbach (ed.), *The Decline Of The Guru: The Academic Profession In Developing And Middle Income Countries*, pp. 207–39. Chestnut Hill, MA: Centre for International Higher Education, Boston College.

——. 2006. 'National Perspectives: India', in James J.F. Forest and Philip G. Altbach (eds), *International Handbook of Higher Education*, pp. 747–67. Dodrecht, The Netherlands: Springer.

Johnstone, Bruce D. 2005. 'Higher Educational Accessibility and Financial Viability: the Role of Student Loans'. Available online at http://www.gse.buffalo.edu/org/ (downloaded on 15 March 2008).

Jongbloed, B. 2003. 'Marketisation in Higher Education, Clark's Triangle and the Essential Ingredients of Markets', *Higher Education Quarterly*, 57(2): 110–35.

——. 2004. 'Funding Higher Education: Options, Trade-Offs and Dilemmas', Paper for Fulbright Brainstorms—New Trends in Higher Education, CHEPS, University of Twente, Netherlands.

Kapur, Devesh and Megan Crowley. 2008. *Beyond the ABCs: Higher Education and Developing Countries.* Working Paper, Number 139 (February 2008), Centre for Global Development.

Kapur, D. and P.R. Mehta. 2004. 'Indian Higher Education Reform: From Half-Baked Socialism to Half-Baked Capitalism', CID Working Paper No. 108. Available online at http://www.cid.harvard.edu/cidwp/108.htm (downloaded on 30 March 2008).

Kim, Sunwoong. 2005. Unpublished MS. 'Political Economy of Massification of Higher Education in South Korea: Public Policy Choice On Elitism Versus Accessibility and Private-Public Mix'.

References

Kinser, Kevin and Daniel C. Levy. 2006. 'For Profit Higher Education: US Tendencies, International Echoes', in James J.F. Forest and Philip G. Altbach (eds), *International Handbook of Higher Education*, 107–20. Dodrecht, The Netherlands: Springer.

Kirp, D.L. 2003. *Shakespeare, Einstein, and the Bottom Line: The Marketing of Higher Education*. Cambridge, Massachusetts: Harvard University Press.

Kirpal, Prem. 1994. 'Remembering Daulat Singh Kothari', *Defence Science Journal*, 44(3): 203–05.

Knight, Jane. (2005). Commercial Cross-border Education: Implications for Financing Higher Education. In Higher Education in the World: The Financing of Universities (pp. 113–12). GUNI Series on the Social Commitment of Universities 1. Barcelona: GUNI.

Kochhar, Kalpana, U. Kumar, R. Rajan, A. Subramanian and I. Tokatlidis. 2006. 'India's Pattern of Development: What Happened, What Follows?', IMF Working Paper WP/06/22.

Kostoff, Ronald N., Dustin Johnson, Christine A. Bowles, Sujit Bhattacharya, Alan S. Icenhour, Kimberly Nikodym, Ryan B. Barth and Simha Dodbele. 2007. 'Assessment of India's Research Literature', *Technological Forecasting and Social Change*, 74(9): 1574–1608.

Krishnadas, K.C. 2007. *R&D Going Global, Study Finds*. Available online at http://www.eetimes.eu/germany/202403119 (downloaded on 12 December 2008).

Lakhotia, S.C. 2005. 'India's Ambitions to Be a World Leader in S & T Depend Upon a Drastic Overhaul of the University System', *Current Science*, 88(11): 1731–35.

———. 2006. 'The Private Fit in the Higher Education Landscape', in James J.F. Forest and Philip G. Altbach (eds), *International Handbook of Higher Education*, pp. 281–92. Dodrecht, The Netherlands: Springer.

Lee, M.N.N. 2003. 'International Linkages in Malaysian Private Higher Education', *International Higher Education*, 30(Winter): 17–19.

Levy, D.C. 2006. 'The Private Fit in the Higher Education Landscape', in James J.F. Forest and Philip G. Altbach (eds), International Handbook of Higher Education, pp. 281–92, Dodrecht, The Netherlands: Springer.

———. 2008a. 'Commonality and distinctiveness: Indian Private Higher Education in International Perspective', in Asha Gupta, Daniel Levy and K.B. Powar (eds), *Private Higher Education: Global Trends and Indian Perspectives*. New Delhi: Shipra Publishing.

———. 2008b. 'Access Through Private Higher Education: Global Patterns and Indian Illustrations', Programme for Research on Private Higher Education (PROPHE) Working Paper Series, Working Paper No. 11, April 2008.

Ma, Wanhua. 2007. 'The Flagship University and China's Economic Reforms', in Philip G. Altbach and Jorge Balan, *Transforming Research Universities in Asia and Latin America: World Class Worldwide*. Maryland, United States: Johns Hopkins.

Madhava Menon, N.R. 2006. *Towards An Appropriate Regulatory Framework For A Sustainable Scheme Of Private Higher Education In India*. Report of the National Seminar on Privatisation and Commercialisation of Higher Education (2 May 2006). National Institute of Educational Planning and Administration, New Delhi.

Marginson, Simon. 2007. 'Global Position and Position-Taking: The Case of Australia', *Journal of Studies in International Education*, 11(1): 5–32.

Mcarthur, J. W. and J. D. Sachs. 2002. 'The Growth Competitiveness Index: Measuring Technological Advancement and the Stages of Development', in Klaus Schwab, Michael E. Porter, Jeffrey Sachs, Peter K. Corneluis and John W. McArthur (eds), *The Global Competitiveness Report 2001–2002*. New York: Oxford University Press for the World Economic Forum.

Mehta, Pratap Bhanu. 2008. 'It's Landmark', *The Indian Express*, New Delhi, 11 April.

Menand, Louis. 2007. 'The Graduates', *The New Yorker*, New York, 21 May.

Ministry of Human Resources Development (MHRD). 1992. 'Programme of Action 1992: National Policy on Education 1986'. New Delhi: Ministry of Human Resource Development (MHRD), Department of Education, Government of India.

——. 2004. *Report of the Review Committee of the IITs*. Report submitted to MHRD, GOI.

——. 2005. 'Report of the Task Force for Basic Scientific Research in Universities', report submitted to Government of India, May 2005.

——. 2006. *Annual Report*. New Delhi: MHRD, Department of Secondary and Higher Education. Government of India.

——. 2006b. *Analysis of Budgeted Expenditure on Education 2003–2004 to 2005–2006*. New Delhi: Planning and Monitoring Unit, Department of Higher Education. Ministry of Human Resource Development, Government of India.

Mazumdar, Tapas. 2007. 'Who Killed the NCTE?', *The Telegraph*, Kolkata, 1 August.

Melvin, Sheila. 2006. 'China's College Revolution', *The Wilson Quarterly*, Autumn: 37–44.

Mohrman, Kathryn, Wanhua Ma and David Baker. 2008. 'The Research University in Transition: The Emerging Global Model', *Higher Education Policy*, 21: 5–27.

Moore, R.M. 2004. 'The Rising Tide: "Branding" and the Academic Marketplace', *Change*, 36(3): 56–61.

Mitra, R.M. 2006. 'India's Potential as a Global R&D Power', in M. Karlsson (ed.), *The Internationalization of Corporate R&D*, pp. 267–306. Östersund: Swedish Institute for Growth Policy Studies (ITPS). Available online at http://www.itps.se/ (accessed on 28 November 2006).

National Institute of Educational Planning and Administration (NIEPA). 2006. Report of the National Seminar on Privatization and Commercialization of Higher Education on 2 May 2006. New Delhi: NIEPA.

National Knowledge Commission (NKC). 2006. *Report to the Nation 2006*. New Delhi: NKC, Government of India. Available online at http://www.knowledgecommission. gov.in (downloaded on 12 January 2008).

——. 2006a. 'Note on Higher Education', released on 29 November. Available online at http://www.knowledgecommission.gov.in/downloads/recommondations/ highereducationnote.pdf (downloaded on 24 April 2009).

References

National Knowledge Commission (NKC). 2006b. 'Report to the Nation 2006'. Submitted to the Prime Minister, 28 September 2006.

———. 2008. 'Report on Science and Math Education'. Letter dated 2 May 2008 from Chairman, NKC to the Prime Minister.

National Association of Software and Services Companies (NASSCOM). 2005. *The IT Industry in India: Strategic Review 2005*. New Delhi: NASSCOM.

National Sample Survey (NSS). 2003. *Report No. 490: Household Consumer Expenditure and Employment and Unemployment Situation in India*. New Delhi: National Sample Survey Organization.

National Science Foundation (NSF). 2003. The Science and Engineering Workforce: Realizing America's Potential. Available online at www.nsf.gov/nsb/documents/2003/nsb0369/nsb0369_5.pdf (accessed on 29 April 2009).

Natarajan, R. 2000. 'University-Industry Cooperation, Collaboration and Partnership'. Presented at the Presidents of World Prestigious Universities Forum on the Theme, 'Higher Education and Development of High-Tech in the 21st Century–University and Enterprises', Beijing, China.

Nath, Manoje. 2005. 'Burning the Book: Clue to Bihar's Decay is in Its Universities'. *The Times of India*, New Delhi, 21 March.

Nehru, J.L. 1989. *Letters to Chief Ministers, 1947–64*, Vol. 5. Oxford: Oxford University Press.

National Sample Survey Organisation (NSSO). 2006. *Employment and Unemployment Situation in India 2004–05, NSS 61st Round (July 2004–June 2005)*. New Delhi: National Sample Survey Organisation, Government of India.

Neave, G. and F. Vught. 1994. *Government and Higher Education Relationships across Three Continents: The Winds of Change*. Oxford: Pergamon.

Obst, Daniel. 2008. 'National Policies for International Education'. Available online at www.iienetwork.org/page/116248/ (downloaded on 24 April 2008).

OBHE. 2007. 'A Careful and Timely Vision? US-Based Georgia Institute of Technology Eyes a Branch Campus in India'. Available online at http://www.obhe.ac.uk/cgibin/news/ftarticle.pl?id=649&mode=month (accessed on 26 June 2007).

———. 2004. 'Sylvan Closes India Campus Citing Lack of Co-Operation from UGC- A Victory for Quality or Confusion?' Available online at http://www.obhe.ac.uk/cgibin/news/article.pl?id=262&mode=month (accessed on 11 June 2007).

Organisation for Economic Development and Cooperation (OECD). 2007. *OECD Employment Outlook, 2007*. Paris: OECD.

———. 2003. *Governance of Public Research: Towards Better Practices*. Paris: Organisation for Economic Development and Cooperation.

———. 2002. *Frascati Manual*. Paris: OECD.

Open Doors. 2005. 'International Students: Leading Countries of Origin'. Available online at http://opendoors.iienetwork.org (accessed on 10 March 2007).

———. 2006. 'International Students: Leading Countries of Origin'. Available online at http://opendoors.iienetwork.org (accessed on 10 March 2007).

Parikh, Kirit. 2007. 'A Fair System', *Times of India*, New Delhi, 10 February.

Parthasarathi, A. 2005. 'Fusion to Improve Higher Education', *The Hindu*, 19 October.

Perkin, Harold. 2006. 'History of Universities,' in James J.F. Forest and Philip G. Altbach (eds), *International Handbook of Higher Education*, pp. 159–206. Dodrecht, The Netherlands: Springer.

Pinto, M. 1984. *Federalism and Higher Education: The India Experience*. Bombay: Orient Longman.

Planning Commission. 1999. *Approach Paper for the Tenth Five Year Plan*. New Delhi: Planning Commission.

——. 2002. Report of Special Group on Targeting Ten Million Employment Opportunities a Year in the Tenth Five Year Plan. Planning Commission, India: New Delhi.

——. 2007. *Eleventh Five Year Plan (2007–12)*. Volume I: Inclusive Growth, New Delhi: Government of India.

——. 2007. *Eleventh Five Year Plan (2007–12)*. Volume II: Social Sector, New Delhi: Government of India.

Powar, K.B. 1999. 'The AIU at Seventy Five', *University News*, 37(12): 1–2, 22 March.

Powar, K. B. and V. Bhalla. 2006. 'Foreign Providers of Higher Education in India: Realities, Implications and Options', Position Paper 1/2006, Dr. D.Y. Patil University and Edupro Foundation, Pune, December 2006.

Polaski, Sandra. 2004. 'Job Anxiety is Real—And It's Global', Carnegie Endowment Policy brief No. 30. April. Available online at http://carnegieendowment.org/publications/

Prakash, Shri. 1999. *Educational Planning*. New Delhi: Gyan Publishing House.

Prathap, Gangan. 2006. 'Time to Publish: The Scientific Efficiency of Nations', *Current Science*, 91(11): 1438.

PricewaterhouseCoopers. 2006. 'Globalisation and Complexity: Inevitable Forces in a Changing Economy', *9th Annual Globalisation CEO Survey*, pp. 30–39. London: PricewaterhouseCoopers.

Rangarajan, C., Padma Iyer Kaul and Seema. 2007. 'Revisiting Employment and Growth', ICRA Bulletin, September 2007.

Raza, M., Y.P. Aggarwal and M. Hasan. 1985. 'Higher Education in India: An Assessment', in J V. Raghavan (ed.), *Higher Education in the Eighties*, pp. 95–173. New Delhi, India: Lancer International.

Romer, P M. 1993. 'Idea Gaps and Object Gaps in Economic Development', *Journal of Monetary Economics*, 32(3): 543–73.

Roy, Subir. 2005. *Made in India: A Study of Emerging Competitiveness*. New Delhi: Tata McGraw Hill.

Rosenzweig, Mark R. 2006. 'Global Wage Differences and International Student Flows'. Available online at www.nyu.edu/africahouse/forresearchers/africana/Mig120506Rosensweig.pdf (downloaded on 24 April 2009).

Sanyal, C.B. and M. Martin. 2006. *Financing Higher Education: International Perspectives*. Palgrave Macmillan. GUNI series on the social commitment of universities 1, 2006. Higher education in the world: the financing of universities.

Sanyal, Bikas C (ed.) 2006. *Higher Education in the World Report 2007: Accreditation for Quality Assurance: What is at Stake?* Barcelona: Palgrave Macmillan and GUNI.

References

Schray, V. 2006. *Assuring Quality in Higher Education: Key Issues and Questions for Changing Accreditation in the United States*. Available online at http://www.ed.gov/about. bdscomm/list/hiedfuture/reports/schray2.pdf/ (Accessed 5 July 2007).

Sen, Amartya. 1970. 'The Crisis in Indian Education'. Lal Bahadur Shastri Memorial Lectures, 10–11 March 1970, in S.C. Malik, *Management and Organization of Indian Universities*. Shimla: Indian Institute of Advanced Study.

Shah, Ajay. 2005. *Improving Governance Using IT System*. New Delhi: Ministry of Finance, Government of India.

Singh, Amrik. 2004. 'Challenges in Higher Education', *Economic and Political Weekly*, 39(21): 2155–58.

Singh, Manmohan. 2007. *PM's Remarks at the Full Planning Commission Meeting*. Available online at http://pmindia.nic.in/speech/content4print.asp?id=585 (downloaded on 13 September 2007).

Spence, A Michael. 1973. 'Job Market Signalling', *The Quarterly Journal of Economics*, MIT Press, 87(3): 355–74.

Spencer, Diana. 2008. 'UK: Booming Private Sector', *University World News*, 31 March 2008.

Srivastava, Ravi. 2007. 'National Knowledge Commission: Meeting Social Goals or Neo-liberal Reform?', *Economic and Political Weekly*, 42(10): 812–15.

Stella, Antony. 2002. *External Quality Assurance in Indian Higher Education: Case Study of the National Assessment and Accreditation Council (NAAC)*. Paris: International Institute for Educational Planning.

Stella, A. and A. Gnanam. 2005. 'Cross-Border Higher Education in India: False Understandings and True Overestimates', *Quality in Higher Education*, 11(2), 227–37.

Stembridge, Bob. 2007. 'Innovation in India'. Available online at http://scientific. thomsonreuters.com/m/pdfs/klnl/8418407/innovation.pdf (downloaded on 25 March 2008).

The Business Standard. 2007. 'Unapproved Institutes to Come Under AICTE Lens', *The Business Standard*, Kolkata, 3 August.

The Business Standard. 2007a. 'Where Are the Jobs', *The Business Standard*, Kolkata, 17 July.

———. 2007b. 'Georgia Tech Campus to Come Up in Andhra', *The Business Standard*, Kolkata, 6 June.

———. 2008. 'Govt to Subsidise Interest On Educational Loans', *The Business Standard*, Kolkata, 5 May.

The Economist. 2001. 'The Next Society: A Survey of the Near Future,' *The Economist*, 8246(361).

———. 2005a. 'Free Degrees to Fly', Special report on higher education, *The Economist*, London, 26 February 2005.

———. 2005b. 'Survey of Higher Education', *The Economist*, London, 10 September.

The Economic Times. 2007. 'TCS Staff Strength Touches 1 Lakh', *The Economic Times*, Kolkata, 29 July.

The Economic Times. 2007. 'Plan Panel, HRD Ministry may Lock Horns over Education Sector', *The Economic Times*, Kolkata, 25 August.

——. 2008a. 'Infy Hires 3rd Year Engg Students to Cut Costs', *The Economic Times*, Kolkata, 13 June.

——. 2008b. 'The Professor As Businessman', *The Economic Times*, Kolkata, 19 May.

——. 2008c. 'It's Official: Big Daddies of IT Hired Less in '07', *The Economic Times*, Kolkata, 21 May.

——. 2008d. 'India Plans Patents Awareness Drive', *The Economic Times*, Kolkata, 19 May.

——. 2008e. 'Higher Education: Let The Thousand Flowers Bloom', *The Economic Times*, Kolkata, 6 April.

——. 2008f. 'What Makes a World Class University,' *The Economic Times*, Kolkata, 7 January.

The Hindu. 2007a. 'India Tops in Providing Education Loans: Chidambaram', *The Hindu*, New Delhi, 9 December.

——. 2007b. 'No Private Universities in Kerala: Minister', *The Hindu*, New Delhi, 19 September.

——. 2007c. 'IT Evasion by Coaching Institutes Detected', *The Hindu*, New Delhi, 15 August.

——. 2008. 'Private Partnership in Education Welcomed', *The Hindu*, New Delhi, 31 March.

The Hindustan Times. 2007. 'I Cannot Build Socialism in One State. I Have to Follow Capitalism', *The Hindustan Times*, Kolkata, 18 July.

The Indian Express. 2007a. 'Turmoil at Oxford University as Moderniser Quits', *The Indian Express*, New Delhi, 12 September.

——. 2007b. 'Foreign Univ Bill: Arjun Addresses Left Concerns', *The Indian Express*, New Delhi, 6 August.

——. 2007c. 'Knowledge Panel Wanted Red Tape Cut, Ministry Chooses to Add Bureaucratic Layer', *The Indian Express*, New Delhi, 24 July.

——. 2007d. 'Educating Course', *The Indian Express*, New Delhi, 19 July.

——. 2007e. 'Govt Plans to be Guarantor for Student Loans', *The Indian Express*, New Delhi, 12 July 2007.

——. 2007f. 'For Best Among the Best It is IIT Bombay Again', *The Indian Express*, 11 July.

——. 2007g. 'HC to UGC: Recognise Amity University', *The Indian Express*, 5 July.

——. 2007h. 'Educating Our Universities', *The Indian Express*, New Delhi, 28 June.

——. 2007i. 'No Quota: JNU Reserves Points Instead', *The Indian Express*, The Sunday News Line, New Delhi, 23 April.

The Statesman. 2007. 'Greater Role for Varsities in Assessment Process: NAAC', *The Statesman*, Kolkata, 2 August.

The Telegraph. 2007. 'Policy Shift On Private Colleges', *The Telegraph Metro*, Kolkata, 7 June.

The Times of India. 2007a. 'Panel for Higher Education in Trouble', *The Times of India*, Kolkata, 29 August.

References

The Times of India. 2007b. 'Tax Students Taking Up Foreign Jobs: House Panel', *The Times of India,* Kolkata, 20 August.

———. 2008. 'Kota Savors Super Six in IIT Top 6', *The Times of India,* Kolkata, 31 May.

Technology Information, Forecasting and Assessment Council (TIFAC). 2006. *FDI in R&D Sector: Study for the Pattern in 1998–2003.* New Delhi: TIFAC.

Teixeira, P., B. Jong Bloed, David Dill and A. Amaral, (eds). 2004. *Markets in Higher Education: Rhetoric or Reality?* Dordrecht, Boston, London: Kluwer Academic Publishers.

Tilak, J.B.G. 2004. 'Absence of Policy and Perspective in Higher Education', *Economic and Political Weekly,* 39(21): 2159–64.

———. 2005. 'Higher Education in Trishanku', *Economic and Political Weekly.* 40(37): 4029–37.

———. 2007. 'Student Loans and Financing of Higher Education in India', *Journal of Educational Planning and Administration,* 21(3): 231–56.

Toffler, Alvin. 1980. *Third Wave.* New York: Bantam Books.

Trow, M. 1973. *Problems in the Transition of from Elite to Mass Higher Education.* Published by Carnegie Commission on Higher Education. Berkeley. California: McGraw-Hill.

University Grants Commission (UGC). 2005. *Annual Report 2004/05.* New Delhi: UGC.

University Grants Commission (UGC). 2007. Report on Development of Higher Education during Eleventh Five-Year Plan. New Delhi: UGC.

Umakoshi, Toru. 2004. 'Private Higher Education in Asia: Transitions and Development', in Philip G. Altbach and Toru Umakoshi (eds), *Asian Universities: Historical Perspectives and Contemporary Challenges,* pp. 33–52. Baltimore, Maryland: JHU Press.

United Nations Education, Scientific and Cultural Organization (UNESCO). 2006. *Global Education Digest 2006: Comparing Education Statistics Across the World.* Paris: UNESCO Institute of Statistics.

———. 2007. *Global Education Digest.* Paris: UNESCO.

Usher, Alex. 2005a. 'Statistical Overview', paper presented at the 2nd International Barcelona Conference on Higher Education, Barcelona, 1 December.

———. 2005b. 'Global Debt Patterns: An International Comparison of Student Loan Burdens and Repayment Conditions', Canadian Higher Education Report Series, Educational Policy Institute, Toronto.

———. 2006. 'Statistical Overview', in James Forest and Philip G. Altbach (eds), *International Handbook of Higher Education.* Dodrecht, The Netherlands: Springer.

Usher, A. and M. Savino. 2006. 'A World of Difference: A Global Survey of University League Tables'. Available online at www.educationalpolicy.org/pdf/World-of-Difference-200602162.pdf (downloaded on 10 January 2008).

Varghese, Mariamma. 2007. 'Large Volume Assessment of the Quality of Higher Education Institutions', *University News,* 45(01): 5–15.

Verbik, Line and Lisa Jokivirta. 2005. *National Regulatory Frameworks for Transnational Higher Education: Models and Trends.* London: Observatory on Borderless Higher Education.

Virmani, A. 2005. 'A Tri-Polar Century: USA, China and India', ICRIER Working Paper No. 160, New Delhi.

479

Visaria, P. 1998. 'Unemployment Among Youth in India, Level, Nature and Policy Implications', ILO Employment and Training Paper No. 36. New Delhi: Institute of Economic Growth.

Ware, J. 2002. *Understanding Distributed Work: The Future of Work Project.* Available online at http://www.creative-va.com/img/Understanding_Distributed_Work. pdf (downloaded on 23 February 2009).

Williams, G. 1991. 'The Many Faces of Privatization', *Higher Education Management*, 8(3): 30–57.

World Bank. 2000. *Higher Education in Developing Countries: Peril and Promise.* Washington DC: World Bank.

———. 2002. *Constructing Knowledge Societies: New Challenges for Tertiary Education.* Washington DC: World Bank.

———. 2003. 'A Policy Note on the Grant-in-Aid System in Indian Education', Report No.3, South Asia Human Development Sector, November 2003.

———. 2004. 'Measuring Trade in Services Liberalisation and its Impact on Economic Growth: An Illustration', World Bank Group Working Paper. Available online at http://www-wds.worldbank.org/external/default/WDSContentServer/IW3P/IB/2001/11/22/000094946_01090804015359/Rendered/PDF/multi0page.pdf (downloaded on 23 February 2009).

———. 2006a. *Skill Development in India: The Vocational Education and Training System.* Washington: World Bank.

———. 2006b. *India's Employment Challenge: Creating Jobs, Helping Workers.* Washington, DC: World Bank.

———. 2008. *Global Economic Prospects: Technology Diffusion in the Developing World.* Washington DC: World Bank.

World Trade Organization (WTO). 1998. 'Education Services: Background Note', by the Secretariat, World Trade Organisation. S/C/W/49, 23 September 1998.

Wolf, Alison. 2002. *Does Education Matter? Myths about Education and Economic Growth.* London: Penguin.

———. 2004. 'Education and Economic Performance: Simplistic Theories and Their Policy Consequences', in *Oxford Review of Economic Policy*, 20(2): 315–33.

Wong Wai Sum, 2005. *Safeguarding the Quality of Cross-border Education: The Role of Governments and Quality Assurance Bodeis.* Seminar on Cross-Border Education, UNESCO Bangkok Office. Available oneline at www.aparnet.org/documents/0507wong_wai_sum_quality_assuring_cbe.pdf (accessed on 29 April 2009).

◆

Index

donation(s)
for higher education, 145–47

economic planning, in India
influence of Soviet Union on, 405
economic purposes
education, of, 169
Education Loan Interest Subsidy Scheme, 157
Education skills
vs. work skills, 215–18
Electronic Multi-Media Research Centres (EMMRCs), 398
Eleventh Plan
higher education in, 42
employment
prospects of, 188–91
software and service sector, in, 187
employment exchange
registration in, 184–85
employment pattern
India, in, 177–82
employment trends
India, in, 183–86
end users
certification by, 239–40
English language
proficiency in, 223–25
among Indians, 410
enrolment, 91
disparities in (*see* Disparities, in enrolment)
higher education, in, 7, 8, 28
subject and level-wise, 9–10
of international students, in India, 11–13
overseas (*see* Overseas enrolment)
entrepreneurial activities
by higher education institution, 145
expenditure
on higher education, 161

faculty shortage
engineering institutions, in, 390
and resource crunch, 387–88
Federation of Indian Chambers of Commerce and Industry (FICCI), 323
Fees
regulation of, 326–29
Financial aid
to students, 153–55
Financial burden
of higher education, 139
Foreign providers
concerns from, 110–11
India, in, 81–86
regulation of, 333–34
formal education
role in socialisation process, 171
formal sector
India, in, 207–09
Fund for Improvement of Post-Secondary Education (FIPSE), 149

General Agreement on Trade in Services (GATS)
and higher education, 340
Georgia Tech
India, in, 84
Grant-in-aid (GIA) system, 71
grants
to students by government, 116
Gross enrolment ratio (GER), 10–11
in higher education, 56
and skill distribution, 197

Higher education
benefits from, 417
diversity in (*see* Diversity in, higher education)
purpose of, 415–16
quasi market in (*see* Quasi market, in higher education)
Higher Education Information Systems Project (HISP), 153

Index

Index

About the Author

Pawan Agarwal is a civil servant from the Indian Administrative Services. He is currently Secretary to the Government of West Bengal. He has earlier served as Director in the Indian government's Ministry of Human Resource Development, as well as Financial Advisor and Coordinator of new initiatives for India's University Grants Commission—a position in which he developed substantial expertise in higher education policy and practice, and gained a broad understanding of the issues and challenges faced by India's colleges and universities.

During the year 2005-06, he was a Fulbright New Century Scholar on Higher Education from India. He was also affiliated to the Indian Council for Research on International Economic Relations (ICRIER). In course of his affiliation, he undertook a comprehensive review of Indian higher education, which was released by ICRIER as a working paper. He was a visiting scholar under the Science and Engineering Workforce Program at the Harvard University and at the India-China-America Institute at the Emory University, Atlanta (United States). During his Fulbright visit, he gave several seminars in the United States, including those at the Harvard University, MIT, University of Michigan and the World Bank. As a part of the New Century Scholars Programme, he studied higher education in a comparative perspective with his Fulbright colleagues from over 20 countries. He has received the prestigious 2009 Endeavour Executive Award from the Australian Government. For which, he shall be a Visiting Scholar at the Centre for the Study of Higher Education at the University of Melbourne during 2009-10.

Apart from comprehensive review of Indian higher education for ICRIER, his other important studies/publications include private higher education for Observatory on Borderless Higher Education, higher education and labour markets for the World Bank. Indian higher education from Latin American perspective for Inter-American Development Bank, privatisation and internationalisation trends in South Asian countries for South Asia Network of Economic Research Institutions. His current research focuses on international student mobility, labour markets for higher science and technology professionals, and the behaviour of education services (particularly higher education) in the market place.

◆